Teaching New
Religious Movements

AAR
AMERICAN ACADEMY OF RELIGION

TEACHING RELIGIOUS STUDIES SERIES

SERIES EDITOR
Susan Henking, Hobart and William Smith Colleges

A Publication Series of

The American Academy of Religion
and
Oxford University Press

TEACHING LEVI-STRAUSS
Edited by Hans H. Penner

TEACHING ISLAM
Edited by Brannon M. Wheeler

TEACHING FREUD
Edited by Diane Jonte-Pace

TEACHING DURKHEIM
Edited by Terry F. Godlove Jr.

TEACHING AFRICAN AMERICAN RELIGIONS
Edited by Carolyn M. Jones and Theodore Louis Trost

TEACHING RELIGION AND HEALING
Edited by Linda L. Barnes and Inés Talamantez

TEACHING NEW RELIGIOUS MOVEMENTS
Edited by David G. Bromley

AMERICAN ACADEMY OF RELIGION

Teaching New Religious Movements

EDITED BY
DAVID G. BROMLEY

UNIVERSITY PRESS

2007

OXFORD
UNIVERSITY PRESS

Oxford University Press, Inc., publishes works that further
Oxford University's objective of excellence
in research, scholarship, and education.

Oxford   New York
Auckland   Cape Town   Dar es Salaam   Hong Kong   Karachi
Kuala Lumpur   Madrid   Melbourne   Mexico City   Nairobi
New Delhi   Shanghai   Taipei   Toronto

With offices in
Argentina   Austria   Brazil   Chile   Czech Republic   France   Greece
Guatemala   Hungary   Italy   Japan   Poland   Portugal   Singapore
South Korea   Switzerland   Thailand   Turkey   Ukraine   Vietnam

Copyright © 2007 by The American Academy of Religion

Published by Oxford University Press, Inc.
198 Madison Avenue, New York, New York 10016

www.oup.com

Oxford is a registered trademark of Oxford University Press

Library of Congress Cataloging-in-Publication Data
Teaching new religious movements / edited by David G. Bromley.
    p. cm. — (AAR teaching religious studies series)
Includes bibliographical references and index.
ISBN 978-0-19-517729-9
1. Cults—Study and teaching.   2. Sects—Study and teaching.
I. Bromley, David G.
BP603.T43 2007
299—dc22   2006049355

9   8   7   6   5   4   3   2   1

Printed in the United States of America
on acid-free paper

Contents

Contributors

William Sims Bainbridge earned his doctorate from Harvard University and currently works in the Division of Information and Intelligent Systems of the National Science Foundation. He is the author of eleven books, four textbook-software packages, and about two hundred shorter publications in the social science of religion, information science, and technology. He has published extensively on new religious movements, including the general textbook *The Sociology of Religious Movements* and sociological case studies of two movements: *Satan's Power* and *The Endtime Family*. His latest book, *God from the Machine*, analyzes religious cognition and conversion by means of multiagent artificial intelligence computer simulation, and he is currently completing *The Secular Abyss* on the consequences of secularization. With Rodney Stark, he wrote three books outlining a general social-scientific approach to religion: *The Future of Religion, A Theory of Religion*, and *Religion, Deviance and Social Control*. His software employed innovative techniques to teach theory and methodology: Experiments in Psychology, Sociology Laboratory, Survey Research, and Social Research Methods and Statistics. He edited *The Encyclopedia of Human–Computer Interaction* and co-edited a series of volumes concerning social implications of nanotechnology and of technological convergence.

Eileen Barker, OBE, FBA, is Professor Emeritus of Sociology with Special Reference to the Study of Religion at the London School of Economics (LSE). Her main research interests over the past thirty-five years have been cults, sects, and new religious movements, but since 1989 she has spent much of her time investigating changes in the religious situation in post-Communist countries. She has over 230 publications, which include the award-winning *The Making of a Moonie: Brain-washing or Choice?* and *New Religious Movements: A Practical Introduction*, which has been published in seven languages and is currently being translated into four more. In the late 1980s, with the support of the British government and mainstream churches, she founded INFORM, a charity based at the LSE that provides information about new religions that is as accurate, objective, and up to date as possible. She has also acted as an advisor to a number of governments and official bodies and law-enforcement agencies around the world.

David G. Bromley is Professor of Sociology and Religious Studies at Virginia Commonwealth University. His research interests include sociology of religion, social movements, deviance, and political sociology. He has written or edited over a dozen books on religious movements. His most recent books are *Defining Religion: Critical Approaches to Drawing Boundaries Between Sacred and Secular; Cults, Religion and Violence; Toward Reflexive Ethnography: Participating, Observing, Narrating;* and *The Politics of Religious Apostasy.* He is former president of the Association for the Association of Religion; founding editor of the annual series, *Religion and the Social Order,* sponsored by the Association for the Sociology of Religion; and former editor of the *Journal for the Scientific Study of Religion,* published by the Society for the Scientific Study of Religion.

Douglas E. Cowan is Assistant Professor of Religious Studies and Social Development Studies at Renison College, the University of Waterloo. Among other books, he is the author of *Cyberhenge: Modern Pagans on the Internet,* and is co-editor (with Lorne L. Dawson) of *Religion Online: Finding Faith on the Internet,* and (with Jeffrey K. Hadden) of *Religion on the Internet: Research Prospects and Promises.* He is co-general editor of *Nova Religio: The Journal of New and Emergent Religions,* and is currently writing three books: *More Than Pointy Hats: The Material Culture of Modern Paganism; Sacred Terror: Religion and Horror on the Silver Screen;* and *A Brief History of Cults and New Religions,* with David G. Bromley.

Lorne L. Dawson is Professor of Sociology and Chair of the Department of Religious Studies at the University of Waterloo in Canada. He has published many articles dealing with new religious movements, is the author of *Comprehending Cults,* and is editor of *Cults in Context* and *Cults and New Religious Movements: A Reader.* Many of his recent publications focus on theoretical analyses of the cultural significance of new religious movements, and he has taken a leading role in studying aspects of religion and the Internet, co-editing (with Douglas Cowan) the book *Religion Online.*

Eugene V. Gallagher is the Rosemary Park Professor of Religious Studies at Connecticut College, where he has taught since 1978. He is the author of *Divine Man or Magician? Celsus and Origen on Jesus, Expectation and Experience: Explaining Religious Conversion, The New Religious Movements Experience in America,* and co-author of *Why Waco? Cults and the Battle for Religious Freedom in*

America, as well as articles on religions in the ancient Mediterranean world and the contemporary United States. He was the founding Director of the Connecticut College Center for Teaching and Learning and now serves as chair of the American Academy of Religion's Committee on Teaching and Learning.

John R. Hall is Professor of Sociology at the University of California at Davis and former director of the U.C. Davis Center for History, Society, and Culture and the University of California Edinburgh Study Centre. In addition to having published a number of journal and encyclopedia articles and book chapters, he is the author of a scholarly book on religious and secular communal groups, *The Ways Out: Utopian Communal Groups in an Age of Babylon,* and has written a sociological and cultural history of Peoples Temple, *Gone From the Promised Land: Jonestown in American Cultural History.* His most recent books include *Cultures of Inquiry: From Epistemology to Discourse in Sociohistorical Research* and *Apocalypse Observed: Religious Movements, the Social Order, and Violence in North America, Europe, and Japan.* In addition, he has edited several books, including *Reworking Class;* he co-edited *Visual Worlds* with Blake Stimson and Lisa Tamiris Becker; and he co-authored *Sociology on Culture* with Mary Jo Neitz and Marshall Battani.

Massimo Introvigne is Managing Director of the Center for Studies on New Religions (CESNUR) in Torino, Italy, and is the author or editor of forty books in Italian, Spanish, English, German, and French and of more than a hundred chapters and articles in scholarly journals about the history and sociology of new religious movements. In 2001, he edited the award-winning *Enciclopedia delle religioni in Italia* (Encyclopedia of Religions in Italy). He is a lecturer at the Pontifical University of the Holy Cross in Rome, Italy.

Janet Jacobs is Professor of Sociology and Women's Studies and Sociology at the University of Colorado, Boulder. Her research focuses on women, religion, and the social psychology of identity formation. Her books include *Divine Disenchantment: Deconverting from New Religious Movements, Victimized Daughters: Incest and the Development of the Female Self,* and, most recently, *Hidden Heritage: The Legacy of the Crypto-Jews,* for which she received the 2003 Distinguished Book Award from the Society for the Scientific Study of Religion. She is the editor of *Religion, Society and Psychoanalysis* and *William James: The Struggle for Life.* Her articles have been published in *Signs: A Journal of Women in Culture and Society, The Journal for the Scientific Study of Religion,* and *The Sociology of Religion.* She is currently engaged in a study of gender and cultural memory.

J. Gordon Melton is the Director of the Institute for the Study of American Religion in Santa Barbara, California, and Research Specialist in the Department of Religious Studies at the University of California, Santa Barbara. He founded the Institute for the Study of American Religion in 1969 as a research facility focusing on the study of America's many religious groups and organizations, especially the many small and unconventional religions. He has authored more than twenty-five books, including *The Cult Experience, The Biographical Dictionary of Cult and Sect Leaders, The Encyclopedic Handbook of Cults in America, The New Age Encyclopedia,* and *The Encyclopedia of African American Religion.* His *Encyclopedia of American Religions,* now in its sixth edition, has become a standard reference book on North American religious bodies. He is senior editor of four series of books on American religions and is past president of the Communal Studies Association.

Susan J. Palmer is Professor of Religious Studies at Dawson College and an adjunct professor and part-time lecturer at Concordia University in Montreal, where she specializes in new religious movements. She is author of numerous articles as well as author/editor of several books, including *The Rajneesh Papers; The Moon Sisters, Krishna Mothers; AIDS as Apocalyptic Metaphor; Children in New Religions;* and *Millennium, Messiahs, and Mayhem.* Her most recent book is *Aliens Adored: Raël's UFO Religion.*

Sarah M. Pike is Associate Professor of Religious Studies at California State University in Chico. She received her PhD from Indiana University, Bloomington, and is the author of *Earthly Bodies, Magical Selves: Contemporary Pagans and the Search for Community* and *New Age and Neopagan Religions in America.*

James T. Richardson is Professor of Sociology and Judicial Studies at the University of Nevada, Reno. He teaches sociology of religion, sociology of law, social movements, and collective behavior, as well as social and behavior evidence class for judges in the Judicial Studies master's program. He has been conducting research in minority religions for most of his career, and has authored, co-authored, or edited nine books and about two hundred articles and book chapters. His latest book is *Regulating Religion: Case Studies from around the Globe.* Richardson is a former president of the Association for the Sociology of Religion, and has served as officer of a number of other professional organizations. He consults on legal actions involving minority religions, and has served as an expert witness in a few cases involving such groups.

Thomas Robbins received his PhD in sociology from the University of North Carolina in 1973. He is an independent sociologist of religion. He is the author of *Cults, Converts, and Charisma* and of numerous articles, essays, and reviews in social science and religious studies journals. He is co-editor of six collections of original papers including *In Gods We Trust; Millennium, Messiahs, and Mayhem;* and *Misunderstanding Cults.*

E. Burke Rochford Jr. is Professor of Sociology and Religion at Middlebury College in Vermont. He has studied the Hare Krishna movement for over thirty years. He has published numerous articles on the movement's development, in addition to his book *Hare Krishna in America.* His recent research has focused on family development and change in ISKCON's North American communities. His book *Hare Krishna Transformed* will be published in 2007.

John A. Saliba has been Professor of Religious Studies at the University of Detroit Mercy since 1987, having taught there since 1970. In the early 1990s he took part in a three-year study of new religious movements conducted for the Vatican by the International Federation of Catholic Universities. He has compiled two major bibliographies on new religious movements: *Psychiatry and the Cults* and *Social Science and the Cults*. Among his major publications are *Christian Responses to the New Age Movement: A Critical Assessment* and *Understanding New Religious Movements*.

Stuart A. Wright is Professor of Sociology and Associate Dean of Graduate Studies at Lamar University. Dr. Wright received his PhD from the University of Connecticut in 1983. He was N.I.M.H. Research Fellow and Lecturer at Yale University in 1984–85 before arriving at Lamar. He is the author of the monograph *Leaving Cults: The Dynamics of Defection* and editor of *Armageddon in Waco*. Dr. Wright worked with the congressional subcommittees in 1995 investigating the government's role in the Waco siege and standoff. He also testified in the hearings as an expert. Dr. Wright was also hired as a consultant to defense attorneys in the Oklahoma City bombing trial of Timothy McVeigh. He is completing a book manuscript on the Oklahoma City bombing based on his experience with the case.

Teaching New
Religious Movements

Teaching New Religious Movements/Learning from New Religious Movements

David G. Bromley

Throughout Western history there have been numerous periods of religious innovation. These periods and the specific groups involved in them have been studied retrospectively by humanities and social science scholars. There is also a long tradition of conservative Christian literature that condemns the heretical theologies both of other religious traditions and of sectarian movements within Christianity. It was after World War II that serious social science scholarship began on a number of sectarian religious movements, such as the Amish, Jehovah's Witnesses, and Father Divine's Peace Mission. The 1960s and 1970s witnessed the beginning of an extraordinary period of religious and secular experimentation in Western societies. If new religious movements, New Age groups, and communal/experimental communities that emerged during these decades are combined, it was an unprecedented period of innovation and experimentation. What has distinguished this period from earlier eras is that a well-developed set of theories and methods for studying emerging movements and a group of scholars possessing these skills are in place. The result has been the emergence of a new interdisciplinary area of study—new religions studies (NRS)—the focal interest of which is the study of new religious movements (NRMs).

NRS developed primarily in sociology and religious studies but also in anthropology, history, psychology, and other disciplines. The interdisciplinary nature of NRS has meant that a variety of disciplinary perspectives are reflected in studying the new groups. Among the most central issues that are being researched by NRS scholars are the movements' sociocultural wellsprings, social meanings and significance, implications for understanding macro-social processes such as secularization and globalization, growth and decline, relationships to the established social order, and affiliation and disaffiliation patterns. Because a large number of new movements appeared at the same historical moment and some became embroiled in high-profile controversies, NRS scholarship has also been influenced by these public controversies, with the result that research has been conducted on social control measures directed at NRMs, new developments in law, media coverage of NRMs, abusive and exploitive practices in NRMs, violence by and against NRMs, and allegations of brainwashing/mind control. All of these issues are touched on in one or more of the chapters in this volume.

Because NRS now approaches a half century of de facto existence, it faces the problem of defining its identity more formally. NRS, like other areas of study, is sustained through teaching and research, which are both important for the area's identity. In fact, there is now a substantial corpus of theory and research on NRMs based on the development of movements over the last several decades. By contrast, there has been little published work on how the knowledge base of NRS can be related to the teaching enterprise. This volume seeks to begin the process of defining NRMs as an area of study by focusing on teaching. The objectives of the volume are twofold: (1) to provide a review of the major findings and ongoing debates in the study of NRMs and (2) to translate the findings and debates into guidance for those interested in pursuing a more detailed investigation of the subject matter or using the subject matter for classroom presentation/discussion. The working assumptions of the volume are that a grounding in the area literature is requisite for organizing meaningful learning situations and that the volume will be most useful for teaching purposes if the substantive knowledge is linked to issues that will be engaging in learning situations. The volume is intended for use by serious students and faculty who are seeking a resource that provides comprehensive, accessible information on NRMs and a scholarly perspective on NRMs as a form of religious innovation.

The volume is organized topically around subjects that both reflect issues under study and are likely to be of interest to those engaging the area of study for the first time. Following this introductory essay, Part I provides context by examining the definitional boundaries of the area of study, varying disciplinary perspectives on NRMs, unique methodological problems encountered in the study of NRMs, and the controversies that have enveloped both scholars studying NRMs and the movements themselves. Part II contains seven chapters that examine issues central to teaching about NRMs: the larger sociocultural significance of NRMs, their distinctive mythic and ritual systems, leadership and organization, the interrelated processes of joining and leaving NRMs, the organization of gender roles in NRMs, the occurrence of corruption and abuse within NRMs, and violence by and against NRMs. Part III provides perspective on teaching as well as informational resources for teaching about NRMs. There are chapters on pedagogical issues in NRS, the Internet as a source of information about NRMs and the controversies in which they are embroiled, a description and assessment of the various research and policy organizations that disseminate information and evaluations of NRMs, and an annotated bibliography that identifies a broad range of significant published work that can be used to teach NRS effectively. Each chapter contains a concise, balanced synopsis of the current state of knowledge and ongoing debates, followed by a presentation of the implications of the knowledge and debates for teaching that particular subject matter.

Orienting Perspectives in Teaching New Religious Movements

J. Gordon Melton begins the volume with an inquiry into the question of how this emerging area of study should be delimited. What do we mean by the term "new religious movement"? Melton suggests that an adequate definition of a new religious movement should be inclusive because new groups are in fact extremely diverse; should identify the way that the new group is connected to already established religious traditions because new groups typically are not completely novel but rather draw on one or more existing religious traditions; and should not attempt to stipulate characteristics that new groups have in common beyond those associated with the organizational features that tend to be found in any new movement. While NRMs do not have any inherent characteristics in common, Melton argues, they do share as a product of their newness social and cultural marginality and, as a result, are likely to enlist few allies but are likely to generate determined opponents. The organizational features that new movements do share are of considerable importance in understanding the style and pattern of their activity. New movement organizations are likely to innovate rather than perpetuate tradition, create new contexts for traditional beliefs and practices, and are populated by converts rather than members born into the group. Another way of distinguishing NRMs from other religious groups is to contrast them with the various types of churches (the dominant form or religious organization in Western society), sects (groups that share major elements of the dominant faith tradition[s] but take exception to some beliefs and practices and adopt strict requirements that lead them in the direction of exclusivity), and ethnic religions (usually transplanted religious groups that operate within an ethnic community).

Melton suggests that an effective way to familiarize students with the diversity of religious groups around them, which compels them to begin organizing and classifying groups, is what he terms a New Religions Scavenger Hunt. This project involves mapping the presence of NRMs in one's immediate environment and producing a community directory of new religions. A variety of sources can be used to initiate the scavenger hunt: phone listings, bulletin boards in New Age bookstores, the Internet, and reference works. Descriptive information about each group is then compiled, and the result is an informative booklet that provides a comprehensive listing of the diverse religious traditions in the immediate locale. Students can also present individual reports on their research projects as a means of generating class discussion.

However new religions are defined, the study of NRMs is an interdisciplinary area of study. As a result, there are very different theoretical perspectives on these movements. While a broad range of disciplines have contributed to NRS, including sociology, psychology, religious studies, theology, history, anthropology, and women's studies, John Saliba focuses on the first four disciplines because they have been particularly consequential in the development of NRS.

As Saliba notes, both psychology and psychiatry have a long history of ambivalence toward religion, partly as a result of the strong influence of Freud in the development of those disciplines. It is not surprising, therefore, that a major segment of psychological theory and research has been uncongenial toward NRMs, and oppositional groups have frequently invoked psychological theory. The traditional psychological approach has contributed to the public and scholarly controversy surrounding NRMs. However, there is a less confrontational tradition within psychology and social psychology, as Saliba documents, that produces empirical findings much closer to those of NRM scholars working in the sociological, religious studies, anthropological, and historical traditions.

Sociological studies of NRMs have addressed a range of issues beyond the individual level of analysis, such as the sociocultural conditions that lead to the formation of NRMs, the social locations of NRM recruits, the dynamics of affiliation and disaffiliation processes, the development of NRMs as social movements and organizations, and the societal response to these movements. A major thrust of sociological theorizing has been to create typologies of NRMs in order to distinguish the diverse belief systems, organizational forms, and leadership styles they exhibit. There has been theory and research on the problematic elements of NRMs as well, such as various abusive practices, illegal activities, and violence. There is a general recognition among social scientists that NRM practices are not unproblematic simply because they operate under the cultural rubric of religion. A primary reason that sociological theorizing on NRMs has been more nonjudgmental in tone is that a substantial proportion of sociological research has involved case studies of individual NRMs, utilizing participant observation methods. For social scientists engaged in participant observation research, a primary objective is to understand the social and cultural worlds of these movements from the perspective of members.

Religious studies as a discipline focuses more on the cultural aspects of religion, in contrast to the social and organizational focus of sociology. From a religious studies perspective, NRMs are not inherently different from their more established religious counterparts. Indeed, one major task for religious studies scholars is to identify the various cultural traditions from which NRMs draw, since virtually all new religious movements draw on or are connected to some existing religious tradition. In the same way that sociologists have placed less emphasis on the cultural aspects of religion and are more interested on what NRMs reveal about social organization generally, religious studies scholars are primarily concerned with cultural issues and with what NRMs reveal about religious culture generally. Thus the effort is how to apply what is known about religion in its various forms to the existence and meaning of NRMs. Like sociologists, religious studies scholars also have developed typologies and classificatory systems, but again these are from a cultural rather than an organizational perspective. By adopting a comparative, historical approach and engaging in participant observation of groups, work in religious studies is quite comparable to and compatible with theory and research from a sociological perspective.

Scholarship from a theological perspective is quite distinct from psychology, sociology, and religious studies, as a primary focus of this work is to assess the theological systems of NRMs from an existing-faith perspective. Particularly, theological work from evangelical and fundamentalist perspectives has been extremely critical of NRMs. As a result there has been a certain affinity with psychological research despite the inherent tensions between conservative religion and secular psychology. Some of the scholarship produced by theologians is quite valuable to those working from other disciplinary perspectives, given the sophistication of theologians in interpreting the nuances of various theological positions. In addition, some more moderate theologians have concluded that it is more important to understand NRMs than to condemn them. This interpretive work is reasonably compatible with scholarship in other disciplines and it brings sophistication to the presentation of NRM religious worldviews.

Saliba offers a number of hints to those teaching courses or course segments on NRMs. New religions are not a contemporary anomaly; religious movements have occurred across history and cultures. They also typically draw on established religious traditions in some way. Bringing a historical, cross-cultural perspective to the study of NRMs and focusing equally on continuities and discontinuities with established traditions help students to contextualize these movements. It is also important to contextualize the research by including multidisciplinary perspectives, since new religions studies is an interdisciplinary field and since the disciplines each bring insights and limitations to the theory and research. Placing NRMs in appropriate cultural, historical, and tradition contexts through appropriate disciplinary lenses also helps students avoid the mistake of generalizing about NRMs. In order to place students in a position to achieve a sophisticated understanding of NRMs, it is obviously critical that they have balanced sources of information. Saliba makes a number of recommendations on sources of information that will achieve this objective. Balance requires taking on some of the difficult issues and problems that NRMs present, and not simply celebrating religious diversity. New religions are not beyond critique merely because they are religious or ostensibly idealistic. Some groups have engaged in violence and abusive, exploitive practices. Saliba offers suggestions for handling these issues as well.

In the following chapter, I consider the methodological challenges that NRS faces as an emerging area of study. There are several foundational issues. One is that there are hundreds of NRMs; only a tiny fraction of these movements have been studied at all, and an even smaller number have been studied systematically over time. Since NRS is interdisciplinary, the available studies also reflect a diverse array of theories, approaches, and methods, which makes developing complementary, cumulative knowledge problematic. At present the primary knowledge base in NRS consists of case studies based on participant observation fieldwork. The process of developing participant observation practices that are appropriate to NRM research and reporting on those practices has gradually been emerging over the last several years. Among the issues that have received attention are how to select groups for study; how to gain access to the movements; and how to initiate, conduct, and terminate the research project. The available evidence suggests that initial contacts with groups are made based on a variety of factors: serendipity, researcher interests, the movement's proximity or visibility, and controversy surrounding the group. However, groups, not researchers, determine actual access, and favorable reception by an NRM appears to depend on factors such as the group's prior experiences with researchers, any public relations implications, the movement's need for third-party assessment, and personal trust. Access is also a matter of degree, and researchers have found that access to various segments and levels of a movement may vary, with limited entree to upper-leadership levels being a particularly persistent problem. One way that some researchers have gained entry to less accessible movements is by undertaking covert research, but a broad consensus in the field has emerged that covert research is problematic on both instrumental and ethical grounds.

Once researchers have gained admittance to a movement, the question arises as to what role they will occupy. Most commonly, researchers are treated as potential converts since that is the defined role that is most readily available. However, groups may accept researchers if they perceive some tangible gain from the relationship. Experience suggests that it is relatively unpredictable whether a researcher–group relationship will prove workable and durable, as in a number of cases relationships have remained tenuous or collapsed. In the event that an ongoing researcher–movement relationship is sustained, one of the most difficult problems that researchers face is maintaining the balance between participation and observation. While there is considerable disagreement on the appropriate balance to be struck, there is a clear trend toward participating as fully as possible, with the result that a number of researchers have reported that it is a challenge to maintain personal boundaries during the research. Even if researchers do work out a viable role for themselves with respect to the movement, the controversial nature of NRMs means that research projects take place within a larger context. The movements themselves are seeking legitimation while oppositional groups and control agencies are seeking to delegitimate the movements. In the face of this ongoing tension, a number of scholars are electing to produce work that is informative to both the scholarly community and the movements themselves. In general, researchers are arguing for a research process that is transparent; understands one's own motivations through the research process; maintains a capacity for independent, critical reflection; and honors a primary loyalty to the scholarly community. It is clear that no matter how scholars resolve these various issues, there is some stigma associated with studying stigmatized groups.

The outcome of the research, of course, is the accumulation of information about a particular NRM. There are several key challenges to researchers. One is gaining greater access to upper-level leadership, since charismatic leaders are so critical in the early development of many NRMs. Another is ensuring that profiles of NRMs include the organizational diversity that characterizes many movements. A third is reflecting the membership diversity that occurs, with particular concern for including and accurately assessing the input from current members, former members, and apostates.

I have observed, as do a number of other authors in this volume, that students are likely to have strong preconceptions about NRMs but lack both independent, personal knowledge about these groups and even the most basic research skills through which questions might be answered. Therefore I recommend developing an open, inquiring perspective on NRMs, perhaps by giving students a survey that will reveal the limitations of what they think they know or discussing similarities between new and established traditions to make otherwise strange groups more familiar. The objective is to create an anomaly that will motivate students to adopt a problem-solving rather than a judgmental approach to the subject matter. Students can then be introduced to the wealth of information available on NRMs and can learn to distinguish differences in the value and perspective of alternative information sources. Having developed insight into the utility of the various sources of information available, students are better positioned to examine information on specific NRMs. Preparing profiles of groups from different sources will reveal the contrasting depictions of these groups and allow students to inquire about the perspectives and interests reflected in these various depictions. With a greater appreciation of the complexity of sorting out alternative sources of information, students can begin to grapple with the problems that researchers face in conducting research on NRMs that must make sense of the often conflicting data they encounter in conducting fieldwork. Students may then be ready for a personal or simulated encounter with an actual group. While students will not be able to engage in a complete participant observation project, they should be able to review literature, formulate hypotheses, develop a research instrument and strategy, and produce a written or oral report based on the information they are able to collect. In this way, students can develop beginning-level research skills, appreciate the complexity of the research process, and develop the knowledge necessary to evaluate ethnographies that they encounter in course assignments.

A full sociological understanding of NRMs involves more than gaining a perspective on the groups themselves; it is equally critical to apprehend the social reaction to these movements, as the societal response created the larger context for their initial development. James Richardson and Massimo Introvigne examine the societal reaction to NRMs from two established social science perspectives—countermovements and moral panics—and highlight the role of the media in shaping public perceptions of NRMs. Countermovements construct their organizational purpose from the movements they oppose, and they develop a symbiotic relationship with them. The countermovements to NRMs are generally divided into two types: the religiously based counter-cult movement, which focuses primarily on the heretical nature of NRM doctrines, and the secular wing of the anti-cult movement (ACM), which focuses on behaviors of NRMs (particularly recruitment practices and organizational structures) as the basis for their opposition. The larger ACM is composed of those personally concerned about individuals' affiliation with NRMs, who provide the membership and resource base for the countermovement, and professional experts and hostile former NRM members, who provide legitimation for the ACM cause. The ACM has gradually developed both an organization structure and an ideology, with the former becoming national and later international in scope and the latter becoming increasingly more sophisticated and medicalized.

The "moral panics" approach to NRMs is based on a social constructionist view of social problems. The argument is that moral panics constitute a special category of social problem in which the issue or group becomes the focus of exaggerated attention from a variety of interests, with the goal of mobilizing public support for social-control initiatives against the targeted "folk devils." Most commonly these interests include the media, the public, law enforcement agencies, and politicians and legislators. Applying the moral-panics perspective to the controversy surrounding NRMs, Richardson and Introvigne note that, in this case, the folk devils are the charismatic gurus who allegedly possess the capacity to brainwash their vulnerable followers.

Richardson and Introvigne observe that the media have been a predominant influence in constructing cults as a social problem. Since most individuals have never actually encountered an NRM directly, public opinion has largely been shaped through media accounts, which have been primarily hostile and negative. Research on media coverage has revealed that most journalists have relatively little direct knowledge of NRMs, have shared popular misconceptions, and have conducted little independent investigative journalism.

In providing guidance to instructors teaching about the cult controversy, Richardson and Introvigne caution that students are likely to share these popular prejudices and are probably unfamiliar with scholarly work on the subject as well as with the stigma attached to research on NRMs. They suggest that examining historical counterpart cases, such as the campaigns against Roman Catholics and Mormons, is a useful means of distancing students from their immediate sociocultural context and allowing them to see that there is a more general dynamic at work in the contemporary controversy. A parallel approach would be to use contemporary moral-panic episodes, such as the Satanism scare and drug panics, to illustrate the dynamics of such episodes. Other possibilities are in-class exercises that reveal to students how they do in fact harbor prejudices and misconceptions as a means to motivate them to examine groups and issues more dispassionately. The comparative approach that Richardson and Introvigne advocate can be extended to engaging students in reading scholarly and ACM literature in order to provide a means of assessing the different perspectives on NRMs. Finally, the authors suggest creating a fictitious group with classic cult characteristics and assigning students the task of analyzing the group from different perspectives.

Central Issues in Teaching New Religious Movements

New religions have attracted a great deal of public attention, but the simple facts are that most NRMs are extremely small, do not retain a significant proportion of those who initially join, have little impact on the larger society, and may not survive as organizational entities in the long run. Further, the prevailing position in sociology is that secularization is the predominant trend in charting the future of religion. This raises the question of how to assess the significance of NRMs both individually and collectively. Lorne Dawson takes on these issues, analyzing the various positions that social scientists have taken in trying to account for NRMs. Most broadly, he argues, the positions can be divided into two interpretive perspectives: those that regard NRMs as a social problem and those that view NRMs as indicators of larger patterns of social change.

NRMs are regarded as a social problem because they pose a challenge to the established social order. As Dawson points out, NRMs provide visible evidence of resistance to the existing social order, and the increasing regimentation of that order makes conflict with groups that propose alternatives highly likely. In terms of building support for delegitimation and containment of NRMs, opponents have focused on recruitment practices, alleged to be the product of brainwashing, and episodes of violence. Four different approaches have been taken to understanding NRMs as indicators of larger patterns of social change: NRMs as a protest against modernity, NRMs as laboratories of social experimentation, NRMs as a re-enchantment of society, and NRMs as a response to the dialectic of trust and risk in late modernity.

The protest-against-modernity approach draws on the work of Peter Berger and interprets NRMs as a reaction to the increasing deinstitutionalization of the private sphere of social life by re-sacralizing social life and creating stronger anchors for individual identities and social relationships. An alternative formulation of this position comes from Roy Wallis, who separates groups into world-affirming and world-rejecting movements, emphasizing that the movements can protest by either rejecting convention social arrangements or creating even more radical extensions of these arrangements. The social-experimentation approach draws on the work of Robbins and Bromley, who argue that the significance of NRMs derives from their attempt to resist the current system of social organization and to experiment with alternatives, whether in a traditionalist or a modernist mode. Significant areas of experimentation include sexuality and gender relations, economic and social organization, proselytization, and health and therapy. The re-enchantment approach draws on the work of Stark and Bainbridge, who have developed a cyclical theory of religiosity. According to this perspective, the contemporary pattern of secularization is a prelude to a resurgence of religiosity, albeit in perhaps a different form. The argument, then, is that religion is changing, not disappearing, and disenchantment will give way to re-enchantment.

Finally, the explanation of NRMs as a response to the dialectic of trust and risk in late modernity represents an extension by Dawson of Anthony Giddens's work. Dawson argues that new religions cannot be fully apprehended in terms of either accommodation or resistance to modernity; the situation is more complex. New religions creatively adapt to and resist modernity simultaneously and in diverse ways. The hallmark characteristics of new forms of religiosity, according to Dawson, are an emphasis on individualism, experience rather than belief, fulfilling individual needs and desires, turning inward rather than outward in search of religious truth, pragmatism on issues of religious doctrine and authority, and tolerance in relating to other religious views. Dawson turns to Giddens's theory of the causes and consequences of modernity as an explanation for the emergence of these new forms of religiosity.

In order to explore the implications of the position that he summarizes, Dawson suggests drawing on students' own experiences of modernity and how attributes of this type of social order lead individuals to search for alternatives. He also suggests drawing on the popular-culture themes in films and books such as *Star Wars, Matrix, Harry Potter,* and *Lord of the Rings,* with which students will be familiar, for evidence of contemporary forms of spirituality and enchantment. Such cultural material can serve, for example, as the basis for discussions of whether these artistic products are trivial and evidence of continuing secularization or of re-enchantment. And students can discuss the personal significance of the themes and characters as a means of connecting their everyday experiences with the larger societal forces and trends that social scientists seek to discern.

Susan Palmer and I examine the distinctive qualities of myth and ritual in NRMs. In religious studies, there are sophisticated theoretical debates on the nature and meaning of both myth and ritual. We briefly outline some of the major positions on each. To date, however, the study of NRMs has not addressed the major issues in these areas. Rather, NRM scholars have focused on conducting case studies of specific movements; myth and ritual, therefore, have been examined contextually as a way to understand the symbolic and social order within individual movements. NRM myth and ritual do have two obvious qualities that distinguish them from their counterparts in more established religious traditions: they are in the process of development and they are oppositional in nature. Otherwise, NRM myths and ritual forms are extremely diverse. We elect to examine cases that demonstrate the oppositional nature of these forms in NRMs. We also distinguish between NRMs that adopt different orientations toward the dominant social order, as world-affirming or world-rejecting movements. Finally, we consider a major emphasis in many NRM myths and rituals—that of origin/separation, charisma, and restoration/salvation. That is, NRMs often express their rejection of the dominant social order by rewriting foundational narratives concerning origin/separation, charisma, and restoration/salvation. In many world-affirming movements (such as the Raelians, Scientology, Osho), individuals are claimed to have originally possessed godlike qualities, although such qualities are thought to have originated in different ways. In these cases, individuals somehow become separated from their own true essence, and the revelations that NRMs provide offer enlightenment on true essence and origins. In many world-rejecting groups (such as Unificationism, The Family International, the Branch Davidians), the emphasis is collective. That is, humankind as a group or family was initially connected to the creator but became separated in the divine kingdom. What both world-affirming and world-rejecting movement narratives share is a reformulation of origin myths that challenges conventional understandings and offers an explanation for current human problems in terms of separation from original purpose.

Charisma myths are central to NRM identities, as these movements are closely identified with prophetic founders whose revelatory experiences and charismatic authority provide the legitimation for the movements. The leader's charismatic standing is constructed in a variety of ways: by assuming a new name or identity that has spiritual meaning, through one or more revelatory experiences that establish the charismatic leader's unique knowledge and authority, or through a succession of charismatic claims that increase the leader's authority over time.

Restoration/salvation myths create the basis for the NRMs' resolutions for the problems of humankind. Each movement identifies its own solution to human problems based on its origin/separation myths. Whether the movement is world-affirming or world-rejecting, it claims unique knowledge, based on the charismatic leader's revelations, that offers the potential for restoring humankind to its rightful place in the cosmos. In each case the movement is the product of its possession of vital knowledge, and its members enjoy special status as the impending world transformation unfolds. A key difference between world-affirming and world-rejecting movements is that, in the former, individual transformation is paramount and precedes collective transformation, while in the latter, it is the reverse.

The rituals of NRMs are, of course, complex and diverse. The key rituals are those associated with restoration/salvation, since these movements regard themselves as at a pivotal moment in history when fundamental changes are about to occur. In world-affirming movements, these rituals are intended to transform individuals by restoring the godlike qualities that they have lost; the presumption is that, as individuals assume their authentic nature, interpersonal and collective problems will diminish. In world-rejecting movements, restoration/salvation rituals involve collective effort, and individuals assure themselves restoration/salvation by playing an appropriate role within the group that will lead to collective restoration/salvation.

Susan J. Palmer and I offer four specific lessons for teaching students about ritual. The focus of our teaching suggestions is ritual, but the lessons are applicable to myth as well. We recommend a number of exercises, such as getting students to think about what distinguishes ritual from other experiences in their own lives, when ritual has and has not been meaningful to them, and where ritual observances can be found in popular culture. The second lesson involves having students create their own ritual in order to recognize the difficulties involved, and then examining the same process in which members of new religious groups have engaged. In the third lesson, we suggest a field trip through which students can engage in participant observation and can experience an NRM ritual personally, with specific guidelines for the experience. Finally, the most challenging lesson asks students to locate and analyze an NRM ritual, using one of the major interpretive frameworks available.

Stuart Wright deals with one of the most controversial issues in new religions studies: affiliation with and disaffiliation from NRMs. As Wright points out, NRMs do not initially possess a significant membership base; they grow through recruitment of new members. NRMs also emerge as movements that challenge the established social order. These two facts make it evident why NRMs typically encounter resistance from established interests and why such intense effort has been expended to discredit affiliations with them. Of course, NRM growth is a product not only of affiliations but also of retaining those who are recruited. Wright's chapter addresses both issues, which have been at the forefront of scholarship on NRMs.

Affiliation is most often studied at the individual level. As Wright points out, however, social and cultural factors influence the size of the pool of available converts from which NRMs have to recruit. A number of explanations for the availability of potential recruits during the 1960s and 1970s have been posited, such as a crisis of moral meaning, family disorganization, a decline in mediating structures, deinstitutionalization, secularization, and legal changes. Wright reviews these often overlapping explanations. The vast majority of empirical work has been case studies of specific NRMs, and there are a number of issues that have been debated with respect to this process. These include whether affiliations tend to be sudden or gradual, whether they are under the control of an autonomous actor or passive responses to group influences, and whether they are uniform or diverse in terms of motivation and the involvement process. Wright says that the evidence in general points to gradual, active-actor, diverse motivation, and process explanations. Several specific models of the affiliation process have been offered, such as those by Lofland and Stark and Levine.

The history of NRM growth suggests that understanding the process of exiting an NRM is just as important as understanding affiliation, since NRMs in general have not been very effective in retaining affiliates. The process that Wright refers to as disengagement/defection involves some combination of disillusionment (disruption of one's cognitive plausibility structure), disaffection (breaking of emotional bonds), and severance of ties to the social organization (disaffiliation). Wright reviews several studies that suggest specific factors that lead to a distancing from cognitive, emotional, and organizational ties. Beyond the motivational framework to explain defection, some scholars have employed role theory to describe this process. While exiting NRMs has been a voluntary process in the overwhelming majority of cases, external intervention and coercive extraction through "deprogramming" have been significant factors in NRM disaffiliation, a result of the popular explanation of brainwashing as the cause of NRM affiliation. Deprogramming is significant both as an indicator of NRM–societal tensions and because deprogrammed former members are more likely to be hostile toward their former movement. Deprogramming is also more likely to produce apostates, or former members who align with oppositional groups in the campaign against cults. Apostates have been particularly effective in galvanizing public sentiment and mobilizing governmental interventions against NRMs.

Wright suggests a number of exercises that instructors can implement in classroom situations to start students thinking about NRMs. One is to map NRMs locally. The mapping exercise forces students to think about what constitutes a new group, how to distinguish newer from more established groups, and what degree of change from an existing tradition is sufficient to justify referring to a group as new. The class objective can be to produce an operational definition of newness. The mapping process inevitably leads to collecting information on various groups, a process that introduces students to fieldwork and data gathering. Once NRMs have been located, it may be possible to interview converts, assuming appropriate precautions are taken; this gives students some first-hand experience with testing one or more theories on conversion as well as bringing an NRM to life. If contact is made with an NRM that has been in existence for some time, it may be possible to compare its first- and second-generation members. If fieldwork is not desirable or feasible, there are still opportunities to study the conversion process by having NRM members come to the classroom or by reading conversion accounts. These latter methods simply require that instructors provide additional contextual material on the implications of public and published presentations. A similar process can be used in studying former members, with the exception that former members often are more difficult to locate unless they have adopted an apostate role, which provides only one possible view of a group. It is highly instructive, nonetheless, to compare current and former member accounts of their experiences in order to understand how biographical experiences are socially constructed.

E. Burke Rochford examines both the distinctive organization and the leadership characteristics of NRMs. As he notes, the controversy surrounding NRMs has colored popular conceptions of both. An array of social scientists have argued that the emergence of NRMs must be understood in historical context, particularly the tumultuous events of the 1960s and 1970s. The development of NRMs as organizations is in no small measure a product of the countercultural currents of those decades, and the decline in NRM fortunes is equally strongly connected to the waning of the counterculture. In trying to place NRMs in a social science framework, Rochford reviews the traditional church, denomination, sect, and cult typologies as a prelude to discussing the challenges that NRMs pose to these categories. A number of NRM scholars have taken the position that NRMs possess unique characteristics that are associated with their newness, such as their contestive stance, their charismatic leadership and revelations, and their stigmatized status, collective organization, syncretism, first-generation membership, and selective demographic profile. These distinguishing characteristics argue for analyzing NRMs as a distinctive category rather than attempting to fit them into existing organizational typologies.

Charismatic leadership and authority are central to the NRM's organization, particularly in the formative stages. Given the volatility of charismatic leadership, one of the pervasive trends in NRMs is a gradual routinization of charisma. It is not uncommon for NRM leaders to develop strategies for resisting charisma routinization, and Rochford reviews a number of the more common methods. It is not necessarily the case that NRM leaders resist the routinization of charisma, however; they may choose other alternatives, such as abdication, lowering the charismatic claims, and encouraging a transition to more institutionalized leadership. Given the crucial role that the founders/ leader plays in the development of an NRM, his or her death is a critical juncture in a NRM's history; however, the evidence suggests that most movements navigate this period successfully. While most NRMs survive once they are organizationally established, their organizational success is quite variable. Success, of course, can be defined from a variety of perspectives, and Rochford reviews the most influential theories of movement success.

Rochford notes that students are likely to be particularly suspicious of NRM leadership and organization, subscribing to the conventional view that both are exploitive. He suggests a series of exercises that allow students to adopt an open, inquiring perspective. For instance, Rochford initially attempts to convince students to question what they think they know by asking them to state what they think, to identify the sources of that information, and then to place themselves inside an NRM. Producing a tentative attitude toward NRMs facilitates a more balanced assessment as the course proceeds. Rochford takes a similar approach toward a discussion of charisma. He offers suggestions for getting students to see charisma as a relationship rather than as a set of inherent characteristics. Once they are responsive to this perspective, it becomes easier for them to understand charismatic relationships and how individuals might become part of abusive or exploitive relationships. Understanding charisma relationally also permits students to address the questions of what might make those relationships unstable and how charismatic leaders might seek to preserve their privileged positions in the face of challenges. With regard to organization, Rochford recognizes another issue for students: identifying with an organization that limits personal freedom. He suggests asking students to consider reasons individuals might join highly structured communal groups and also to identify the characteristics of communal groups in more conventional organizations as a means of understanding participation in an NRM. As to putting these various lessons together, Rochford recommends having students create a fictitious NRM as a means of testing whether they understand the basic organizational characteristics.

Another means of providing students with a perspective on NRMs and the controversy surrounding NRMs is to encourage them to undertake their own research. Rochford recommends asking students to explore the various perspectives on a selected NRM. This means examining and comparing the information available on scholarly sites, group-maintained sites, and oppositional group sites. A variety of questions naturally arise about the sources and the meaning of conflicting information. The website project can be followed up with a term paper on NRM organization that examines a specific group. Finally, Rochford suggests visiting an NRM or having representatives in class so that students can relate to the group and its members in more human terms. He offers a range of questions to structure the student-group encounter.

Research has indicated that men's and women's experiences in NRMs vary considerably. Pike observes that there are two opposed feminist positions on NRMs: that NRMs are often abusive of women as a result of a charismatic relationship in which males typically are leaders and females are followers; alternatively, some feminists have argued that the realities are more complex and require more nuanced interpretations based on an examination of how women create meaning in specific NRM environments. Pike advocates integrating the two approaches by examining sexist and abusive practices, but at the same time being open to women's own interpretations of their involvement in specific movements. Pike divides NRM experimentation with gender roles into four types: male dominance, female dominance, partnerships, and merged gender roles. She then explores how these types are manifested in conceptions of deity; NRM leadership and organization; and sexuality, marriage, and family for both nineteenth- and twentieth-century movements.

Conceptions of deity include a monotheistic male god, a female form of deity, a divine pair, or a universal source of power that transcends gender. Although there are exceptions, movements with dominant male god conceptions are more restrictive in defining women's roles while those with goddess, dual godhead, or divinity beyond gender conceptions are more likely to afford more gender equality. With respect to leadership, the most common pattern in NRMs is males as founders or charismatic leaders and females often predominating as disciples or followers. However, there are also notable cases of NRMs with female leaders, male leaders with women surrounded by women in complementary leadership roles, and females and males with equal authority. The gender patterning of leadership also may change over time, and in some cases women have assumed leadership in movements that were initially headed by men. It is also the case that women may exert considerable influence in movements headed by men as they acquire power, either formally or informally. NRMs have also experimented with a variety of marital and sexual relationships, including celibacy, variations on traditional heterosexual marriage, plural marriages that are male dominated, and various types of free love, extra-marital, or homosexual relationships. Experimentation with sexual and marital relationships frequently is accompanied by alternative forms of family, parenting, and childrearing. While conceptions of deity, leadership forms, and marital arrangements may appear to be restrictive for women, they do not necessarily translate into restrictive practices; correspondingly, experiments that promise liberation do not necessarily fulfill their promise.

In teaching about gender roles in NRMs, Pike observes that it is important to have students' preconceptions articulated first so that the class is open to all points of view. She recommends asking students to examine gender roles in the religious traditions with which they are already familiar, and she provides a list of questions as a prelude to comparing the practices adopted by various NRMs. A second exercise is to have students read accounts by or about women's experiences in NRMs, used as a basis for class discussions or presentations. With this knowledge base, students can be asked to imagine themselves as gendered members of NRMs or to assess the meaningfulness or appropriateness of alternative gender roles. The detailed information on both nineteenth- and twentieth-century NRMs available from written and Internet sources offers the possibility of assignments that ask students to compare and contrast gender arrangements during different historical periods. Finally, Pike recommends field trips or classroom visitations that allow alternative gender arrangements to be explored in conversations with current NRM members.

Janet Jacobs briefly reviews the history of scholarship on NRMs, noting the various social and psychological perspectives that have been utilized to study NRMs through alternative theoretical and disciplinary lenses. As NRS has developed, feminists began to examine the previously overlooked implications of theologies that supported male dominance and led to the control of female behavior and sexuality. Feminist scholars thus brought to NRS a more critical perspective that incorporated the potential and reality of movements to engage in exploitive and abusive practices. Ethnographic fieldwork corroborated a persistent pattern of abuse and exploitation in some movements, which has led to a more balanced overall assessment of NRMs. Abusive practices have included the sexual abuse of children, incest, rape, battering, forced prostitution, and sexual manipulation. Jacobs observes that NRMs vary on a great many dimensions; the only characteristic that distinguishes groups on sexually abusive practices is a patriarchal, charismatic style of leadership. The specific group characteristics that are most prominent in groups that present an unusually high potential for abuse and violence include a dominant male charismatic leader, a hierarchical male leadership structure, doctrinal beliefs that privilege male superiority, strong gender norms governing behavior, and a highly paternalistic family structure. Findings by feminist scholars have not received ready acceptance by NRM scholars already beset by a range of controversies surrounding NRMs. It has taken a concerted effort by feminist scholars to have their voices heard, which makes this chapter a particularly important contribution to the volume. The message from feminist scholars is clear and correct: religious rights should not be defended at the expense of women's rights.

Jacobs draws on Frederich Engels's work, tracing the historical development of the patriarchal family and the role of the religious institutions in legitimating that power relationship. She argues that these historical forces have led to a succession of religious cultures in which women are defined as property and sexual commodities. NRMs predictably have followed this same logic as movement leaders have assumed the role of a "divine father" and exercise male entitlement privileges, sometimes in abusive and violent fashion. Jacobs reviews several theories that specify more clearly the relationship between abuse and exploitation of women in NRMs and patriarchal control.

The subjects of sexual abuse and exploitation are extremely sensitive issues, and Jacobs cautions teachers to recognize the importance of preparing students appropriately before initiating discussion or assignments in this area. There is a real potential for counterproductive results, such as creating trauma in students who have themselves been abuse victims, inadvertently playing to voyeuristic impulses, or trivializing abuse by blaming victims. It is also important for students to understand that NRMs are not unique in their abusive practices; in this fashion NRMs can function as a lens through which students can better understand a significant problem in their own social world. There is now sufficient case study material that, once students have a proper theoretical grounding, they can use to examine specific NRMs and analyze abusive patterns. Jacobs suggests The Family as a particularly informative case for exploring the relationship between paternalism and sexual violence, how women are sexually objectified, and how women's sexuality is commodified. This case also raises interesting, complex questions about what constitutes consent in highly inequalitarian situations or why women would "consent" to participate in relationships with a high potential for exploitation and abuse. The fact that abusive practices exist, of course, raises questions about what social response is appropriate. In the case of NRMs, oppositional groups have attempted forcible extractions of individuals from movements, termed deprogramming, and in the case of the Branch Davidians, federal agents assaulted the community, resulting in a tragic loss of life. The appropriate way to respond to problematic or dangerous situations has yet to be resolved, and students would gain a sense of the complexity of the issues involved by debating various policy alternatives.

Thomas Robbins and John Hall take on the complex issue of violence involving NRMs. This is an critical issue in teaching about NRMs, since allegations of violence or violent tendencies has been one of the means through which oppositional groups have sought to raise public apprehension about new movements. Robbins and Hall focus on the major cases that occurred beginning in the 1970s: the Peoples Temple murder-suicides in 1978, the Branch Davidian murder-suicides in 1993, the Solar Temple murder-suicides in 1994, the Aum Shinrikyo murders in 1995, and the Heaven's Gate collective suicides in 1997. It is judicious to exercise caution in linking NRMs to violent tendencies, since there are hundreds of new groups and very few cases of violence, most movements are not entirely new but rather are connected in some fashion to established traditions, NRMs are probably more likely to be the targets than the perpetrators of violence, even allegations of violence tend to draw intense media coverage, and cases of established religious groups being involved in violence have not been uncommon historically.

One of the central debates on the violence issue is whether violent episodes are internally or externally precipitated. Several models of violent episodes involving NRMs have been formulated. Marc Galanter is one of the few scholars focusing primarily on internal factors, such as group isolation, leader grandiosity, leader domination, and governmental mismanagement. Most others propose models that are premised on movement–societal interactions as precipitating factors. Hall, Schuyler, and Trinh distinguish between two alternative ideal-type scenarios. The "warring apocalypse of religious conflict" type is one in which there is escalating tension between a movement and its external opponents, with media and government siding with opponents. By contrast, in the "mystical apocalypse of deathly transcendence" type a "mystical" group retreats from the earthly realm. I propose a "dramatic denouement" model, suggesting that movement–societal conflicts may move through three phases: latent tension, nascent conflict, and intensified conflict. However, escalating conflict is not inevitable, as contestation, accommodation, and retreat are all options. Conflicts that do intensify may yield a moment of "dramatic denouement" in which a final reckoning is sought and that leads to either an "exodus" (collective withdrawal) or a "battle" (coercion). Robbins and Hall then examine some of the internal factors (apocalypticism, charismatic leadership, lack of institutionalization, totalistic organization, and internal conflict) and external factors (escalating conflict, deviance amplification, dualistic orientations by both movement and opponents) that are most commonly involved in the various violence models. They ultimately conclude that both internal and external factors are relevant in explaining the cases at hand, although the importance of various factors may vary from case to case.

Teaching about violence is a challenging task since violence is a sensitive topic and students are likely to have preconceptions about cults. Robbins and Hall suggest beginning by creating an open atmosphere, encouraging students to recognize the controversial nature of the topic, their own preconceptions about NRMs, and the importance of critical thinking. Once the appropriate classroom atmosphere is created, more substantive goals can be pursued: how to define violence, alternative disciplinary perspectives on violence, historical or cross-cultural case study to gain perspective on contemporary cases, evaluation of the various models that have been proposed, and exploration of whether violence is unique to NRMs or more generally related to religion. These substantive goals can be pursued through various types of classroom lectures, discussions, and exercises, as well as assigned readings and media materials.

There is a wealth of information available on the violence issue. In creating assignments, it is particularly important to teach students the difference between scholarly and nonscholarly materials, and to treat the latter as data to be analyzed. This opens up productive examination of a broad range of materials. There are major archives on a few of the major violence episodes that offer students a real opportunity to conduct their own analyses of those events using the alternative models that have been developed. Documentary films offer similar opportunities for analysis and critique. Another creative alternative is to have students act out roles in a fictional episode of potential violence so that they are able to directly confront the kinds of situational pressures that arise in the cases that have actually occurred.

Resources for Teaching New Religious Movements

In his chapter on pedagogical issues, Eugene Gallagher notes that students often enter courses on NRMs with a "hermeneutic of suspicion"; they are therefore predisposed to a pervasive cynicism about these movements that closely approximates the ideology of anti-cult activists. Students also are unlikely to have any academic background in religion. The combination of cynicism and lack of background essentially disempower students' critical, analytic skills. A key goal in teaching about NRMs is to encourage students to approach the movements from the perspective of their memberships. Gallagher alerts teachers to the existence of analogous resistance to open learning in other areas, such as multiculturalism, and concepts for analyzing learning resistance, such as stereotypes. He argues that in the face of hostile media coverage, students' predispositions, cult stereotypes, and the "methodological doubting" that characterizes the academic enterprise, teachers face a significant challenge in convincing students simply to take NRMs seriously as religions. Gallagher therefore advocates adopting the posture of "methodological believing"—an effort to accept points of view from which one is otherwise distanced as a means of discovery, connectedness, and understanding.

Even though methodological believing can be presented as play, a game in which to temporarily participate, teachers should not underestimate the challenge in trying to overcome the predisposition to doubt, particularly when contentious groups and issues are involved. If students can be helped to become aware of their own operating assumptions and understand that these assumptions have implications for whether they can truly hear voices of minorities and dissenters, then a major goal of liberal education is achieved.

Another key element of encouraging openness as students encounter the study of NRMs concerns the issue of rhetorics. Students will already be familiar with or be confronted with an array of concepts (cult, apostate, apologist, brainwashing, deprogramming) that incorporate ideological positions. Empowering students to see these rhetorics as representing specific interests, and encouraging students to discover the conditions under which these rhetorical positions are plausible to their adherents and others, offers a means of developing critical analytical skills and also of allowing students to connect with positions that they do not share. This is particularly important in a situation in which doubt is likely to reinforce positions that students already hold and which support conventional understandings. The ultimate objective is to empower students to develop the capacity to critically and receptively entertain multiple points of view and to become active learners.

The kind of active learning that Gallagher espouses, of course, has its risks and may present teachers with the possibility of performing an unfamiliar role in the teaching process. Gallagher therefore offers some specific suggestions on how to articulate goals for a course, exercises for developing critical analysis skills and methodological believing capability, films that can engage students in discussion of issues likely to emerge in the study of NRMs, and case studies that allow a course to be responsive to student interests and current events.

It is to be expected that as new, innovative religious groups have formed, they would adopt the technologies of the age. Douglas Cowan addresses the use of the World Wide Web by NRMs. He begins by drawing a distinction between religion online, using the Internet to provide information by or about religious groups, and online religion, using the Internet as an interactive site for religious activities of various types. Not surprisingly, the former is much more common than the latter. In fact, there is considerable debate over the meaning and viability of online religion. One set of characteristics that might be used to determine the existence of an online community includes interactivity, membership stability, identity stability, "netizenship" and social control, personal concern, and occurrence in a public space. A second issue is the utility of information on the Internet. The voluminous but unfiltered information available on the Internet is a critical issue with respect to NRMs, given their controversiality, and thus it is particularly important to apprehend accurately the interests represented by various sites. In general there are sites that are either supportive or critical of NRMs, research sites that seek to avoid partisanship in either direction, and discussion forums. Each type of site pursues a different agenda, and these agendas should shape the way that information provided is used. The third issue—whether the Web is an effective religious recruiting tool—has been particularly contentious with regard to NRMs, since these movements have been accused of employing "brainwashing" practices. However, the evidence gathered to date provides no support for the contention that the Internet is a successful and effective recruiting medium.

Cowan provides useful insights on the advantages and disadvantages of using the Internet in teaching about NRMs. One advantage of the Internet is that it captures much more quickly the changes that characterize the dynamic development of NRMs. There is also information on a great number of groups that have not been studied by scholars. Another useful feature of the Internet is that it offers the opportunity for access to groups that may not be geographically proximate or that may not be appropriate for site visits for a variety of reasons. It also becomes possible to engage in "virtual tours" of groups that otherwise would be accessible only through printed materials.

The information on NRMs available over the Internet is extremely diverse and variable in quality, but there are a number of sites organized by NRS scholars that offer a wealth of information that is useful for teaching purposes. Cowan identifies several of the most valuable sites. These various advantages offered by the Internet notwithstanding, it is extremely important that instructors provide guidance in the use of Internet sites and materials, since students are typically unprepared to interpret the type and quality of information they will encounter. Cowan provides some guidelines for assessing Web sites, such as determining who developed and operates the site, identifying the source of information posted there, and locating a range of sites so that a balanced, informed Internet search is conducted.

Another teaching resource may be online discussion groups of various types. These sites offer students an opportunity to experience the controversies in which some NRMs become embroiled. They also allow students to assess the extent to which online communities are actually being formed by applying the defining characteristics of an online community to these sites. Since the sources of Internet information are so diverse and vary so dramatically in perspective, Cowan suggests turning this potential problem into an asset by having students bring information from different types of sites to class so that the value of understanding alternative sources of information and the value of a balanced research process can be reinforced.

Involving students in research projects that use the Internet offers obvious advantages in teaching about NRMs. At the same time, teachers must be aware of the pitfalls involved and be sure to offer students appropriate guidance. The problems that teachers may face include plagiarism, appropriate citation of sources, use of Internet sources in place of scholarly and other resources, and ethical issues. If students are going to participate in online discussion groups, for example, they must confront problems such as appropriate self-identification and protection of others' identities during the research process. Cowan offers guidelines for ensuring that appropriate and ethical practices are followed in conducting Internet research.

One of the major problems that students confront in the study of NRMs is that there are numerous sources of available information on NRMs, and they often sharply conflict with one another. While alternative theories and debates are common to many areas of study, the degree of controversy in NRS research is particularly pronounced given the contested nature of NRMs and the fact that both movements and their opponents are making appeals in terms of ultimate values. In her chapter, Eileen Barker presents and analyzes the major sources of information on NRMs and the controversies in which they have become embroiled. While in one sense this presents teachers with a problem, from another perspective it offers a valuable opportunity to teach critical assessment skills. As Barker frames the presentation, a useful way to distinguish among the diverse sources of information about NRMs is in terms of the questions that they ask. She identifies seven important sources of information: NRMs themselves, cult-awareness groups (CAGs), counter-cult groups (CCGs), human-rights groups (HRGs), cult-defender groups (CDGs), the media, caring professions, and attorneys. Each of the set of groups is constructed as an ideal type in the Weberian tradition, with the objective being to identify the social location, constituency, and interests that lead to the specific kind of information dispensed by that category of group.

NRMs ask the question, "What is so good, exclusive, new, special, and right about the movement?" As these groups consist of NRM leaders and members, predictably their primary interest is self-promotion—persuading others that they possess ultimate truth. By contrast, CAGs ask "What do the movements do that is actually or potentially harmful to their own members, to other people and/or to society in general?" Initially formed by families of NRM converts, CAGs focus on the negative, harmful aspects of NRMs and seek means of gaining control over them. Designating NRMs as cults and their members as victims, and the process of gaining and maintaining members as brainwashing are at the core of CAG ideology. For CCGs, the question at issue is "What do the movements believe that is wrong?" These groups most often represent conservative religious traditions and aver a concern with what they define as NRM heretical doctrines rather than organization and practices. ROGs represent scholars from a variety of academic disciplines who pursue the question "What are the movements like?" ROGs seek to explore matters such as NRM beliefs, practices, organization, leadership, affiliation/disaffiliation patterns, and relationships with conventional society. The focal concern of HRGs is "In what ways are NRMs discriminated against?" HRGs are less concerned with religion than with minority status, and they seek to defend the legal/human rights of a range of minority groups and movements. In some cases NRMs have created

HRGs specifically to defend their interests, with defense of other minorities being a distinctly secondary concern. Cult-defender groups (CDGs) ask, "What is good and true about NRMs?" In most cases CDGs are connected in some fashion to NRMs and seek to promote a favorable image of a single movement or NRMs in general. The media, while not cult-watching groups, do in effect monitor NRMs by constructing the public images of the movements that are the primary source of information about NRMs for most individuals. Given the way in which news is socially constructed, their focus is "What will make a good story?" The media are most likely to reflect a CAG perspective, since the requisites of news construction most closely parallel the negative, dramatic depiction of NRMs as cults. The caring professions, most notably therapists of various persuasions, are concerned with "How can the former member be helped?" Since the primary goal of therapists is to assist clients in re-estab-lishing control over their personal lives, NRM experiences may be cast as either positive or negative experiences. Finally, attorneys address the question, "How can the court be persuaded to pronounce that the defendant is guilty (or in-nocent) of a particular offense?" Attorneys are significant to the cult-watching process because they contribute to the construction of legal outcomes that become a key part of the social environment that NRMs inhabit.

Barker suggests classroom exercises that may enhance students' capacity for recognizing, analyzing, understanding, and critically assessing the images of NRMs that they are likely to encounter in NRS. Simple exercises, such as having students describe their perceptions of ordinary classroom situations, may suffice to convince students of how varied perception is of even mundane occurrences. Building on the diverse interpretations of the same phenomena that are possible, students can be encouraged to apply this insight to the inter-pretations of NRMs. Once they have sufficient information about NRMs to work with, students might seek to apply the typology that Barker has constructed as a means of sorting out and interpreting the contrasting images of NRMs that exist. She provides a number of Web sites, representing the various types of cult-watching groups, that can be sources of information for such an exercise. Barker also suggests field visits and classroom presentations by members of NRMs and/or representatives of various types of cult-watching groups. This kind of experience is of particular value in that it provides personal contact with the sources of information students are seeking to assess. Students will then be in a position to assess these information sources directly and raise questions that will test their capacity for critical analysis. In order to develop a sympathetic understanding (*Verstehen*) of any NRMs or cult-watching groups, which is piv-otal to an overall assessment and understanding, Barker suggests some role-playing exercises in which students address the concerns of individuals in those specific social locations.

The volume concludes with an annotated bibliography compiled by Wil-liam Sims Bainbridge. Each chapter in the volume contains references on the chapter topic, and these references serve as useful guides to more detailed investigation of the specific points under consideration. Bainbridge offers a more broadly based bibliography that will be useful both to teachers and to students by reaffirming which sources are particularly helpful for teaching purposes and offering sources not included in the chapter reference lists. Bainbridge organizes the bibliography into several sections. The "major issues" section includes sources on the definition of an NRM, disciplinary perspectives on NRMs, methodological and ethical issues, meaning and significance of NRMs, organization and leadership, joining and leaving NRMs, gender roles, abuse and exploitation in NRMs, violence involving NRMs, issues in classroom teaching, and Internet resources. The section on specific movements includes references on Amana, Aum Shinrikyo, Branch Davidians, Bruderhof, Church Universal and Triumphant, Falun Gong, Krishna Consciousness, nineteenth-century communes, Oneida, pagan/Wicca groups, Peoples Temple, Process, Rosicrucianism, Scientology, Shakers, Shiloh, Spiritualism, UFO groups, Unificationism, and Zen Buddhism. While a number of these groups are discussed in the volume chapters, many are not. These additional groups offer teachers a range of other examples that can be used in classroom lectures and exercises to complement information on the most visible groups. In the section on primary materials, Bainbridge calls attention to the wealth of primary data on historical and contemporary groups available through archives, Web sites, and move-ment-sponsored publications; and he offers some guidance on accessing these sources for teaching purposes.

Engaging Students

As NRS has developed over the last several decades, an impressive corpus of theory and research has been assembled. There are detailed case studies both of a number of groups and of individual participants. There is ample knowl-edge on key issues such as the sociocultural context in which NRMs emerge, their mythic and ritual systems, leadership and authority structures, organi-zational forms and developmental processes, and affiliation and disaffiliation patterns. On each of these issues there are ongoing debates that energize future theory and research as well as student inquiry. The controversy sur-rounding some NRMs also raises questions about possible exploitation and violence among NRMs, on the one hand, and religious intolerance and societal repression, on the other hand. Scholars have been attracted to NRS because NRMs provide a window on religion in the making, reveal the interests that established institutions seek to defend, represent sometimes radical experi-ments with alternative forms of social organization, and offer insight into the adaptation of religion to late modernity. Students are likely to be drawn to the study of NRMs because they are new, often attractive to young adults, and controversial.

Teaching about NRMs and learning about NRMs pose a challenge precisely because these movements have attracted so much public notoriety. Students are likely to be fascinated by NRMs but also to harbor the popular miscon-ceptions about cults that are so widespread in North America and Europe. Virtually every contributor to this volume has identified as a major obstacle to the teaching enterprise students' resistance to treating NRMs simply as religions. The contributors offer a variety of suggestions ranging from open sharing of preconceptions to challenging prejudices and stereotyping as critical to creating an open learning environment in which differing conceptions are revealed and freely explored. Engendering receptiveness to alternative interpretations of NRMs shifts students' orientations away from preconceptions and toward curiosity and exploration; in place of pre-existing answers are questions, problems, and anomalies. Contributors recommend encouraging students to draw on their own experiences to understand how others might perceive the world in a different way, to consider historical and cross-cultural examples of similar groups that distance students from assumptions they would otherwise make, and to connect NRMs to religious traditions with which they are already familiar as a means of reducing their apparent strangeness.

Once students have adopted a more inquiring, exploratory orientation, there is a wealth of information available. NRMs, their opponents, the media, and NRS scholars offer very different interpretations of groups and events. NRS scholarship of the kind provided in this volume can serve as an intellectual anchor for a dynamic learning process. Contributors caution that it is important to offer students diverse, balanced information that neither privileges nor denigrates NRMs. It is also crucial to offer guidance on the value and use of the various sources of information. What emerges, of course, is a much more complex, nuanced view of NRMs than either the movements or their detractors would offer.

With an appropriate understanding of the information at their disposal, students are in a position to gather and interpret information on NRMs. Contributors recommend specific projects to apply the information students have assimilated, such as presentations, papers, and debates. Even more instructive projects are creating local directories of NRMs, classroom visits from current and former NRM members, virtual tours, and field trips that put students in direct touch with NRMs and their members. Finally, students can be challenged to apply what they have learned. Among the suggested assignments are creating new ritual forms, taking on the role of an NRM member, creating a fictitious group that incorporates key elements of a new religious movement, and creating conflict scenarios in which an NRM may become involved as a means of confronting the difficult decisions facing public policy makers.

What teaching about NRMs offers is an opportunity to make the study of religion come alive in a way that is particularly relevant. In the process, students can learn to question their own preconceptions, understand how minority groups and traditions meet resistance from established interests, witness how groups with ostensibly noble purposes fail and betray their own goals, become more discerning in assessing diverse sources of information, increase their capacity for critical thinking, and gain at least a preliminary sense of how to enter and appreciate an unfamiliar social and cultural milieu. For all these reasons, the study of NRMs can make a significant contribution to the ultimate goal of teaching, furthering liberal education.

PART I

Orienting Perspectives in Teaching New Religious Movements

Introducing and Defining the Concept of a New Religion

J. Gordon Melton

Just what is a "new religion"? In the middle of the twentieth century, scholars assumed that cults were small, somewhat ephemeral religious groups that were headed by a charismatic leader and that advocated decidedly different teachings from those predominating in mainstream society. As they began to turn their attention to the groups that had been called cults, scholars found a host of problems with those assumptions. For example, they learned that some groups were quite large international bodies and that some "new" religions had been around for a century or more (Nelson 1969). Scholars encountered a variety of new religions that were teaching exactly what the mainstream religious community affirmed (Tony Alamo Foundation) but still found themselves prominent on lists of cults. They also observed groups that suddenly changed their status and moved relatively quickly from being a new religion to one with social acceptance (Worldwide Church of God, Soka Gakkai) or vice versa (Branch Davidians).

There was equal ambiguity about what was meant by charismatic leadership, which led to a variety of leadership forms with the same designation. For example, *charismatic leadership* sometimes has meant simply (1) self-asserted leadership (the method used by most religious founders) as opposed to institutional appointment after having met various qualifications; (2) the demonstration of various skills and traits that make one especially attractive to the public, as demonstrated by leaders such as Billy Graham or Desmond Tutu; or (3) the distinctive or supernatural attributes that believers ascribe to an individual that allow a leader to be set apart and assigned a special new role in the cosmos. Such charismatic leaders might be regarded as an avatar, a satguru, an end-time messenger, a spiritual channel, or one of a variety of messianic titles. Examples could be multiplied for leaders of new religions who have demonstrated charisma in one of the three ways, but not the other two.

In addition to the ambiguity surrounding the concept of charisma, scholars tended to overplay the significance of charismatic leadership. Originally, it was tied to an understanding of the ephemeral nature of new religions that scholars believed would lead to a fatal trauma, splintering, and even demise upon the passing of the charismatic leader. However, observations of new religions have not substantiated that expectation. Indeed, virtually all new religions survive the death of their founding leaders to continue much as before. Also, the overemphasis on the role of charismatic founders has often been accompanied by a lack of appreciation of the genuinely religious nature of the community that a founder calls into being. Although founders play a vital and necessary role in the creation of new groups, unless people find their religious needs being met within them, the groups could not survive for long. After the first decade, the religious dynamics within groups gradually assume far more importance in heightening their vitality and continuance than the role of any leader (Miller 1991).

Defining New Religions

In moving toward a more adequate definition of a new religion, scholars have suggested several attributes that such a definition might have. Among the critical considerations are the importance of inclusiveness, the relationship of the group to older religious traditions, and the absence of common attributes beyond the characteristics associated with new movement organizations.

First, a definition should be broad enough to cover the wide spectrum of new religions, including such well-known groups as the Unification Church, the Church of Scientology, and the International Society for Krishna Consciousness, as well as older new religions like the Jehovah's Witnesses and the Theosophical Society and such divergent groups as, for example, the Sufis, the Vedanta Societies, the Healing Tao, Tenrikyo, Wicca, the Celestial Church of Christ, the Radha Soami Beas, and the Nation of Islam.

Second, it should note the relationships of the different new religions to the older religious traditions. Overwhelmingly, new religions are variations on old religions, and a considerable part of the "strangeness" of any particular new religion can be understood in light of the beliefs and practices perpetuated (or altered) from the older religion in which it is rooted. Many new religions appear unfamiliar, foreign, and out of place because they are importing a mainstream religion from another part of the world. Thus, the Hare Krishna movement is mainstream in Bengal, the San Francisco Zen Center offers a popular form of Japanese Buddhism, and the Divine Light Mission's secret practices are no secret in the northern Indian Sant Mat tradition. (Almost all of the exceptions to this general observation that new religions are variations on old religions are those several groups that self-consciously attempt to merge two traditions. Prominent examples include the Unification Church, which merges Christianity and Korean shamanism, and the French group Madarom, which attempts to synthesize Hindu and Western Esoteric traditions.)

Recognizing the roots of individual new religions contextualizes them within the massive movement of the world's religions to the West, while making clear that some grasp of the modern diffusion of the world's religions is needed to appreciate the seemingly sudden emergence of "new" religions in a Western context. While most of us are familiar with Islam, Hinduism, and Buddhism, we are less conversant with the smaller world religious traditions such as Jainism, Taoism, and Zoroastrianism. Sant Mat, which has flourished in the West, is still rarely mentioned in world religion texts, while sectarian Shintoism, usually mentioned in passing, has been a particularly important source of new religions in the United States (such as Tenrikyo and Konkokyo) with the growth of the Japanese American community since World War II.

Yet to be included in world religions texts is the other Western religious tradition, the one that never integrated into the dominant Western Christian culture. While Western scholars lavished attention on Christianity, the competing dissenting tradition that we now call Western Esotericism continued since its emergence as ancient Gnosticism. The Esoteric impulse has transmuted and persisted through a variety of minority communities until it experienced a notable revival in the sixteenth century, following the Protestant Reformation's creation of space for alternative religious expressions throughout Europe. Today's Esoteric community has emerged out of the succession of movements that began with Christian Cabala in the sixteenth century and established itself in Rosicrucianism, Speculative Freemasonry, Spiritualism, Theosophy, ceremonial magic, and most recently Wicca and the New Age movement. Not unrelated, the Christian Science/New Thought tradition also continues to produce its share of new religious organizations. The single largest block of new religions in the West is the product of Western Esotericism, a tradition now being defined in the works of, for example, Faivre (2000), Godwin (1994), Hanegraaff (1996), Judah (1967), and Melton (2003).

Third, a definition should not be premised on a presumption of shared characteristics among new religions. That is to say, as our knowledge of new religions has expanded, we have come to realize that no single characteristic or set of characteristics are shared by all new religions (that is, by all the groups that have been called cults) and that any effort to define them by such a set of characteristics admits of too many exceptions. Although many groups recruit young adults, a number find most of their new members as older adults. Most new religions appeal to a cross section of the public and are not distinctive relative to members' religious background, educational background (though a few are notable for their appeal to the better educated), and economic class. There is no evidence of the presence (above that in the general population) of any pattern of psychological or mental disorders. While many groups are led by charismatic founders, many of the more well-known new religions have already made the transition to collective institutionalized leadership (Church of Scientology, ISKCON, Church Universal and Triumphant).

Though new religions do not share common characteristics, they can be described by their marginal position in society. In general, new religions exist on the fringe of the culture and society in which they exist. As David G. Bromley has pointed out, new religions are generally those that exist in a high level of cultural alienation and simultaneously are socially distanced from influential leaders (government officials, mainstream religious leaders, the intelligencia). New religions manifest a bewildering array of beliefs and practices. They also manifest different expectations within their membership relative to deviations on matters of doctrine and the performance of spiritual practices. However, almost all new religions differ on significant points from the faith practiced within the larger religious bodies of their host culture. They assume the role of competitor with older religions. Christian new religions tend to deny important affirmations of the Christian tradition and/or advocate practices rejected by the majority in the Christian community. In the case of Asian religions, new groups differ from Christianity at almost every point. New religions follow a faith that either significantly differs from mainstream Christianity or represents a different religious community altogether. Groups also differ in their reaction to their break with the dominant religious community, some trying to accommodate (as when Asian religions incorporate positive statements about Jesus in their presentation of their faith) or emphasize the difference (by denouncing the corruption of the larger religious institutions).

Unlike the older and more established religions, new religions have few allies in the dominant social system. As minority religions, they generally do not have members in high places in even local governments, much less state and national offices. Ignorance of new religions is pervasive in scholarly circles, even in theological and religious studies departments, which rightfully concentrate on the larger, older, and more influential religions. Again, new religions, especially the larger and more controversial ones, vary in their response to their social alienation. A few—most notably the Unification Church—have attempted to integrate into the social scene and actively find allies at the highest levels of government (with marginal success). Others have made their rejection of the mainstream a major part of their presentation of themselves to prospective members, compromising that position only when faced with serious legal problems (Jehovah's Witnesses, The Family International).

Because of their cultural and social alienation, new religions have become the object of concern by a number of watchdog, cult-awareness, and Christian counter-cult groups. (See Eileen Barker's chapter in this volume for a detailed discussion of cult-awareness groups.) The former, epitomized by the International Cultic Studies Association (the American cult-awareness group that originated as the American Family Foundation) and the Association for the Defense of the Family and the Individual (Europe), have attacked the new religions primarily on social grounds (their taking young adults from the mainstream of society and family) and have attempted to mobilize government agencies, law-enforcement officials, professionals, and church groups into a coalition to suppress them. Counter-cult organizations have generally opposed the new religions on cultural grounds (their deviations and differences with Christian orthodoxy) and have carried on a significant propaganda campaign primarily aimed at keeping Christians from being lured away into error (Cowan 2003). Such watchdog groups further illustrate the fringe status of new religions.

Even as Bromley has emphasized the placement of new religions on the social scene, sociologist Eileen Barker has pointed out that, at any given moment, most new religions are in fact new organizationally (Barker 2004). Of the hundreds of new religions, most are still in their first generation and as such share a set of common attributes. Barker rightly argues that new religions generally represent innovation rather than continuation of previous tradition, that they set old traditions in a new context, and generally they have far more members who converted to the faith than grew up in it. These characteristics alone identify new religions as a distinctive group of religions that are both interesting and deserving of further scrutiny.

New religions take on additional interesting attributes as they transition to their second and third generations, become more accommodating to their host society (or not), and retain or lose their youth. New religions, as minority religions, also tend to be relatively unstable over time. They have greater difficulty holding the second generation, and even into the third and fourth generations, they must pay considerable attention to recruiting new members if they are to survive. Thus, while the social profile of new religions changes over time, the groups continue to differ from the larger mainstream religions.

Drawing upon the last generation of research and analysis of new religions, and reviewing these most recent suggestions concerning the social placement and nature of new religions, one can propose a workable definition. New religions are religious groups that exist socially and culturally on the fringe, differ significantly in belief and practice from the dominant religious institutions of the culture in which they are located, and have minimum ties to and allies within the dominant government, religious, and intellectual structures of the society in which they operate.

Types of Religious Groups

We can put some meat on the bare bones of that definition of new religions by comparing these groups with three other prominent types of religious groups found in Western society. First among these are the churches, the dominant forms of religious life as exemplified in the larger Christian denominations—the Roman Catholic Church, the Church of England, the Evangelical Church of Germany, the Southern Baptist Convention, the United Church of Canada, United Methodist Church, the Presbyterian Church (USA)—that is, those groups that are members of or could be considered for membership in organizations such as the World Council of Churches. The hundreds of Christian denominations, and the various cooperative organizations that they have founded, have defined normative religion in the West. Secular leadership in Western societies tends to be drawn from these groups, and legal codes tend to be based on the religion of these organizations.

In contrast to the Christian denominations are the sectarian groups, such as the Jehovah's Witnesses and Seventh-Day Adventists. These groups, at least formally, agree with the large denominations on the basics of religion. They profess the same faith and advocate the same practices; however, they tend to differ on issues of strictness, in that the sectarian groups allow much less deviation and demand closer attention to the performance of religious duties (from personal devotion to moral uprightness). While the denominations tend to be more inclusive, sects tend to be more exclusive. In the West, Christian groups form a continuum that ranges from small, conservative, exclusive sects to large, liberal, inclusive churches (Johnson 1963). Sects have shown a distinct tendency over time to lose many of their sectarian peculiarities and take on the attributes of dominant religious bodies.

New religions, denominations, and sects, however, by no means exhaust the prominent types of religious groups in the modern West. A fourth important type is the one herein called the *ethnic religion*—that is, a religious group defined by its operation almost entirely within a minority ethnic group that exists within the larger host society. These religions have usually been transplanted from another country to serve an immigrant community (often one continuing to use a different language), within a particular Western country. In general, such groups confine their activities to a single ethnic/linguistic group, even after the majority in the group adopts the host nation's language. Ethnic-based religious groups include the Japanese Buddhist organizations (such as the Buddhist Churches in America), Asian Hindu temples, and the many mosques serving various Middle Eastern and South Asian constituencies.

The most familiar Western ethnic religions are the associations of synagogues and rabbis (Orthodox, Conservative, Reform, Reconstructionist, Hasidic) within the Jewish community. In North America, the Jewish organizations have come closest to joining American mainstream life and show some similarity to the Eastern Orthodox community, while continuing to serve a single ethnic community, nurturing Hebrew as a second language, and perpetuating a religious life that contrasts sharply with the dominant Christian faith.

Ethnic religions (especially those with Asian traditions) differ noticeably from new religions in that they tend to refrain from one of the major conflict-provoking attributes of new religions: active proselytization in the general population. While new religions attempt to recruit members from the host culture, occasionally using high-pressure techniques akin to those of sectarian Christian bodies, ethnic religions usually do not disturb the larger society and limit their primary recruitment efforts to the relatively small ethnic community. Thus, leaders of ethnic religions can often gain access to societal influentials, not just as leaders of their constituency communities but also as local representatives of prominent religions based in other nations.

Life on the Fringe

New religions differ from these three other major types of religious communities in the West. In contrast to the denominations, they offer a religion that substantively differs from mainstream Christianity. Christian-based new religions, while continuing much that would identify them with the tradition, deviate from (or, more positively stated, propose innovation to) the tradition on essential belief and practice to the point that the majority of denominations would not recognize them as fellow believers, even though they identify themselves as Christian (metaphysical Christianity, Christian Science, Teachings of the Inner Christ, etc.).

New religions also differ from the sectarian groups. Sects have a stricter definition of essential Christianity and often emphasize a practice that has been ignored by the larger Christian community (for example, speaking in tongues, foot washing, Sabbatarianism). They make an even more critical break with the new religions, whom they see as preaching a different religion altogether. Sectarian groups are harshest on new groups in the Christian tradition that have denied what are viewed as essential beliefs (especially the doctrine of the Trinity and the correlative belief in the full divinity of Christ). Generally, the large denominations view sectarian groups as fellow Christians while having substantial differences with them on a variety of lesser issues.

Like new religions, ethnic churches differ radically from the dominant Christian churches in their belief and practices: they follow one of the dozen or so global religious traditions. Unlike sectarian groups, ethnic churches show no sign that they will change over time and become a mainstream Christian denomination; for the foreseeable future, they will remain a distinctive minority religious community. However, as the Jewish community has demonstrated, the ethnic churches offer the possibility of becoming an accepted, or at least tolerated, part of the religious establishment, especially as the churches are identified as local representatives of countries with which the host country is allied or has ongoing diplomatic relations.

New religions advocate a belief and ritual system that manifests discontinuity with the dominant religious groups in the West (by advocating a non-Christian faith or an unacceptable form of Christianity) and offer little hope of ever evolving into a Christian denomination (though that has occurred on at least one occasion, in the case of the Worldwide Church of God, which, in the 1990s, dropped a number of its more unacceptable beliefs). Also, new religions attempt to draw membership from the host culture, and in the case of non-Christian new religions, they lose their identification with the religious tradition.

That being said, most Western countries, especially in the years since World War II, have become ever more tolerant and accepting of different religious groups and have written minority religious rights into their legal codes. Most new religions live in relative peace with the surrounding culture, and most remain known to only the few specialists studying new religions. However, some new religions have found themselves in relatively tense situations with the surrounding culture. The two most important factors that heighten tension levels for new religions are violence and high-pressure proselytization. The active recruitment of new members on city streets in the 1970s, and the resulting rapid growth of a few new groups, occasioned the first public controversies about new religions; parents expressed their anger at groups that removed their sons and daughters from society and siphoned them off into unfamiliar religious structures. But as groups drop their high-pressure recruitment policies, the tension levels drop.

Since the 1960s killings associated with the Black Muslims and the Manson Family, the issue of violence has not only plagued those relatively small number of groups involved but also has been used to denounce other high-profile new religions. The incidents of violence took groups that were earlier largely unknown (Solar Temple), considered sectarian groups (Branch Davidians), or even mainstream Christian churches (Peoples Temple) into the limelight and quickly placed them on the list of dangerous cults. Involvement in various illegal actions, from smuggling to fraud to the use of illegal drugs, also quickly led to heightened tensions with law enforcement. The arrest and conviction of a group's leader using religion as a cover for illegal activity have, like violence, often led to the complete dissolution of the group (Church of Hakeem, Missionaries of the New Truth).

Besides involvement in violence or visible proselytization, advocacy of questionable beliefs and practices can also heighten a group's tension with the larger society. Groups call attention to themselves by adopting a different sexual ethic (polygamy, pedophilia, sex magick); living as separatists or communalists (or both); serving a distinctive diet (veganism, macrobiotics); or placing medical restrictions on members (no doctors, no blood transfusions). If one or more of these divisive call attention to a group, their additional attributes may also bring approbation, especially such attributes as a conservative view of the role of women in the group, the espousal of apocalyptic beliefs, a perceived foreignness, racial exclusiveness, or ultra-authoritarian leadership. It is, of course, these distinctive beliefs and practices that make these groups both interesting to students and an intriguing object of research for scholars.

The New Religions Scavenger Hunt

In presenting the subject matter of new religions to their classes, instructors will confront a spectrum of challenges, many of which grow out of the controversial nature of and contested space inhabited by those groups under consideration. Among these issues, possibly less controversial but no less contested, is the basic understanding of new religions that will define the boundaries of the class. That definition will, of course, be affected somewhat by the discipline in which the class is based and the set of questions to be discussed; however, whatever discipline is used, instructors can benefit from some focused conversations among scholars that have recently occurred, which this chapter attempts to summarize.

From my own teaching experience, I have found that students are most reluctant to tackle the definition issue and the ongoing conceptualization of the world of new religions. Narrow definitions of what constitutes a new religion tend to exclude too many exceptions, and broad definitions tend to lose meaning in vague abstractions. The path around this quandary begins by providing copious examples of new religions (as different as Wiccan covens, Hindu ashrams, Christian apocalypticists, and Muslim mystics).

At the same time, I introduce a set of terms that seem to resonate with most students—terms like *cult, weird, strange,* and other somewhat emotive words. These are used quite freely the first week of the course, and then they are gradually discussed in terms of what is being said when the words are used. Thus the negative connotations of *cult* in popular discourse are offered as rationale to abandon the term in most cases, while the branding of groups as "weird" or "strange" is noted as saying more about the speaker's cultural limitation and lack of cosmopolitanism than conveying any information about the group. Using these terms also provides an entrée into the discussion of the changes in terminology and definition that have occurred relative to new religions over the past several decades.

A class research project to map the presence of new religions in the community can be a fruitful way to communicate much information concerning new religions and how they exist and make their way in the world. I have called this mapping project the "New Religions Scavenger Hunt." The object of the project is to produce a snapshot of the new religions in the community by creating a directory of these religions and the associated service organizations as they exist at the time. I generally introduce the project at the end of the first week of class.

To explain in greater detail, after I define the term "new religion," I first raise the issue of how one might go about finding the local centers of the new religions. I begin with the Yellow Pages. Like old religions, the headquarters of new religions generally have a telephone and can be found under a variety of headings. In the lists of churches, they will be found under subheadings such as "Buddhist," "Hindu," "Interdenominational," "Nondenominational," and "Other." Students should also look under "Religious Organizations," "Synagogues," "Mosques," "Occult," and "Yoga." Thus, simply from the phone book, students can construct a core list of new religious groups in the immediate community. Since they will be looking for groups with less familiar names, various Christian sectarian and ethnic religions will also appear in the first version of the directory. This allows further discussion of the different types of religious groups while at the same time making students more aware of the pluralism that exists in their neighborhood.

Second, I supplement the phone book with the weekend newspaper. The local newspaper usually carries, on Saturday, one or more "religion" pages that include many advertisements for local religious centers. Occasionally new religions are listed, including some that do not have a phone listing and that meet in rented halls. Even for those groups listed in the phone book, the newspaper usually carries information on meeting times that is generally excluded from the Yellow Pages listing. Many cities also have free community-based weekly newspapers that can be culled for additional information.

Third, most communities now have one or more New Age bookstores that carry materials that range across the spectrum of new religions. Here students can find books from gurus, channelers, and alternative medical practitioners. More important, for purposes of this exercise, students can find bulletin boards with flyers and business cards from local leaders in the alternative religious community, brochures from local groups, and in most cities, a networking magazine that carries advertisements for different local new religions. These bookstores, and related stores that specialize in religious paraphernalia, are prime disseminating points for different religious teachings and contact points for religious seekers.

Fourth, I introduce the students to the reference sources in their school library. Primary among these references is the *Encyclopedia of American Religions*, which has entries on most of the new religions in the country, along with addresses for their national headquarters. In addition, there are book-length directories that deal in greater depth with more specialized aspects of the religious community. These directories are produced and revised frequently, and just as regularly decline in usefulness as they age.

Fifth, this discussion of print media leads directly to a discussion of the Internet and its usefulness and limitations in mapping the local community's new religions. Many of the larger new religions have Web sites that include current directories of their centers around the country; many local centers also have their own Web sites. Surfing the Internet can be a most fruitful way to locate the otherwise obscure religious groups in the community. Today, many groups use the Internet as their primary means for establishing contact (Cowan and Dawson 2003) and screening potential recruits, as well as others from the outside who inquire about the groups (Wicca and ceremonial magic groups being prime examples). The primary problem with the Internet is its growing number of obsolete sites, which, for purposes of this project, continue to carry out-of-date contact information. Many Internet sites representing new religions are amateur efforts by people who lose interest in maintaining and updating the site.

Finally, along with describing the many ways to discover new religions in the community, I introduce the spectrum of tasks required to complete the Scavenger Hunt. Possibly the most important task is finding someone (or possibly more than one) who will agree to receive the information generated and compile it into a coherent document. Initially, that person compiles the core directory from the phone book and other print media. Since almost all students have an e-mail address, distribution of the directory can be easily accomplished electronically.

After a week to think about the required tasks, each member of the class is asked to sign up for a particular job. Some will take the initial core directory and mine the Internet for information. Others will visit the local New Age bookstores to retrieve information, especially about groups that do not have Web sites. And as the directory grows, other students will begin visiting the various churches, temples, centers, ashrams, and offices to gather literature, while still others will visit those same centers to take pictures and build a photo databank. (Pictures taken with digital cameras are easily downloaded into the directory and, among other things, vividly illustrate how very different the facilities for new religions are from common church buildings.)

Knowing that the directory should be finished toward the end of the semester/quarter, a date for its completion is set and then dates for the additional tasks, especially the downloading of the pictures, are set. As part of the work, students complete a one-page information form on each of the new religions. In the classes I have taught, some students chose to work on these forms as an alternative to doing a term paper (which would concentrate on one particular group). The one-page sheet lists all of the contact information on the group (address, telephone number, e-mail address, and Web site), the name of the local leader(s), brief descriptive material concerning the center (including references to any larger organization with which it might be affiliated), and bibliographic citations.

In the process of building the directory, students add new groups and organizations somewhat indiscriminately. As the work shifts to writing descriptions of the groups, they will discover that a variety of churches with innovative ministries, sect groups, and ethnic religions have found their way onto the list. This observation presents additional opportunities to discuss whether particular groups belong on the list. In addition, I encourage including groups and individuals who offer services that represent and interact with the new religions on the list. Thus the larger New Age world of hatha yoga practitioners, doctors of alternative medicine, metaphysical bookstores, psychics, and retreat leaders are in the directory to show how they function (in much the same way as parachurch organizations support and serve the Christian churches).

I set aside time each week for class discussions and reports. In some cases, I have students give oral reports that summarize written assignments, or we might discuss the impact of a guest speaker. Part of these weekly discussions is set aside for ongoing feedback on the progress of the Scavenger Hunt. This is the time for students to mention new groups that have been found, describe obstacles to completing an assignment, and share their experiences from visiting different groups. I have found that students are eager to share stories of their encounters with members of new religions while they are still fresh in their minds. Some have anxieties about visiting groups that have been the subject of negative news reports. Others question the status of groups that seem not to meet the definition of a new religion.

In the end, the New Religions Scavenger Hunt should have resulted in a box full of literature gathered in the process of assembling the directory, the completed directory (the major work product, complete with pictures), and a set of one-page descriptions of most of the groups listed in the directory. After the class is over, I gather this material and deposit it in the university library as a most useful bit of local history. Over time, if and when the project is repeated, this material will become a baseline from which change and stability among new religions could be measured.

The Scavenger Hunt, by honoring a variety of contributions to its completion, has proved to be one of the most engaging activities in the study of new religions. Through print media, the Internet, interviews with group members, and visual images, class members begin to confront the substance of new religions and provide the context from which teachings can proceed.

Conclusion

The Scavenger Hunt puts the definition of a new religion to the test. The definition offered above was developed out of several decades of observation of new religions and many conversations with colleagues. However, it should not be taken as the final word; rather, it is the starting point as you prepare to teach and the basis for a dialogue with your students as they discover a new world of religious phenomena.

As instructors, we should take the public's ongoing encounters with local groups as an opportunity to continue our own education and expand our own view of new religions. After some four decades of observation, I am still amazed at the new phenomenon, especially when I get into the field and see what I have missed on previous visits. It is certainly the case that the fresh perspectives my students have brought to the study have become one of those creative irritants that keep the discussion of new religions an open conversation.

REFERENCES

Barker, Eileen. 2004. "What Are We Studying? A Sociological Case for Keeping the 'Nova.'" *Nova Religio: The Journal of Alternative and Emergent Religion* 8, 88–102.

Cowan Douglas. 2003. *Bearing False Witness? An Introduction to the Christian Countercult.* Westport, CT: Praeger.

Cowan, Douglas, and Lorne Dawson. 2003. *Religion Online: Finding Faith on the Internet.* New York: Routledge.

Faivre, Antoine. 2000. *Theosophy, Imagination, Tradition: Studies in Western Esotericism.* Albany: State University of New York Press.

Godwin, Joycelyn. 1994. *The Theosophical Enlightenment.* Albany: State University of New York Press.

Hanegraaff, Woulter J. 1996. *New Age Religion and Western Culture: Esotericism in the Mirror of Secular Thought.* Leiden: Brill.

Johnson, Benton. 1963. "On Church and Sect." *American Sociological Review* 28, 539–549.

Judah, J. Stillson. 1967. *History of the Metaphysical Movement in America.* Philadelphia: Westminster Press.

Melton, J. Gordon. 2003. *Encyclopedia of American Religions.* 7th ed. Detroit, MI: Thomson/Gale.

Miller, Timothy, ed. 1991. *When Prophets Die: The Post Charismatic Fate of New Religious Movements.* Albany: State University of New York Press.

Nelson, Geoffrey K. 1969. *Spiritualism and Society.* London: Routledge & Kegan Paul.

Disciplinary Perspectives on New Religious Movements: Views from the Humanities and Social Sciences

John A. Saliba

The rise of new religious movements (NRMs) has been one of the hallmarks of Western culture over the last fifty years. Scholars from different disciplines have been involved in studying and trying to explain the origin and success of NRMs in an age when religion seemed to be on the decline. The new movements have also been a source of conflict and debate, sorting scholars into four major camps: (1) those who look on them as social and/or psychological aberrations, (2) those who examine them as social or cultural organizations, (3) those who study them as genuine religious expressions, and (4) those who denounce them as false religions and/or diabolical intrusions in the search for truth. The literature on new religions or cults is voluminous and, not surprisingly, varies in quality. Teachers who include new religious movements in their syllabi are faced with the task not only of grappling with the different disciplinary approaches but also of selecting the appropriate literature and giving a fair presentation of the main issues that some of the NRMs have brought to the fore. Several disciplines—namely, psychology, sociology/anthropology, religions studies, and theology—have figured prominently in the study of new religions. It is important to bear in mind that scholars in these disciplines had well-developed theoretical and methodological approaches to religion (Connolly 1999) before they directed their research efforts to the NRMs (Saliba 2003).

The Psychology of New Religious Movements

One of the earliest interests in the new religious movements has been psychological in nature. Psychology studies the individual, especially the attitudes and characteristics that color a person's worldview and the emotions that drive him or her into action. Closely related to psychology is psychiatry, which is a specialization within medicine that focuses on the diagnosis, prevention, and treatment of mental and psychological disorders. Psychology uses several research methods, such as naturalistic observation, case studies, surveys, and both correlational and experimental research (Morris and Maisto 1998: 5) in order to understand human motivations, emotional states, and various illnesses. Under the influence of Freud, the majority of psychologists and psychiatrists have, until recently, taken a negative view of religion, considering it as a form of neurosis (Wulff 1997). New religions have often been approached within this general psychological framework. Three major questions have dominated the psychological studies on new religions: Is there a cult personality whose weaknesses attract individuals to NRMs? What is the process that leads a person to become a member? And what effects does membership have on one's mental and psychological state?

Many attempts have been made to draw a profile of the person who is likely to be attracted to and join a new religion. In general, the individual who joins a new religious movement is deemed likely to possess several of the following characteristics: deprivation, alienation, inclination to be preoccupied with religious questions, uncertainty about his or her identity, and having experienced a personal crisis (Saliba 2003: 77–90). The conclusion is that the person who joins a new religion is neither mentally nor psychologically healthy. Such a view has been incorporated in a document published by the American Psychiatric Association (Committee on Psychiatry and Religion 1992: 28), which states:

> The white middle-class, idealistic young people who form the majority in most contemporary cults are often lonely, depressed, and fearful of an uncertain future. They tend to be dependent. They have strong needs of affection. Unable to provide for their own emotional sustenance, they need external forces for a feeling of self-worth, a sense of belonging, and a reason for living. They feel resentful and are often hostile towards society at large; it has disappointed them and does not value them. The freedom as well as the demands of adulthood, eagerly awaited by many, may be overwhelming to them.

One of the notable attempts to link personality types with particular religious movements was made by Tommy and Frank Poling (1986) in their study of members of the Hare Krishna movement. These researchers observed that many factors, including early family discord and the substitution of a strong male father-substitute did not, by themselves, suffice to explain membership in ISKCON. They identified another predispositional factor that they called "sensate personality"—that is, one that "seeks happiness in tangible material aspects of life" (1986: 2). Prospective recruits to ISKCON have a strong inclination to satisfy their sense experiences and are afraid of becoming victims of sense gratification for its own sake. This inclination, coupled with the structure of ISKCON, where sense orientation is expressed so openly, particularly in its devotional practices and food preparation, enables members to validate and endorse their general orientation. At the same time, ISKCON provides an ideology and a way of life that enable members to control and/or sublimate their sensuality and pursue a higher and nobler goal. Others (e.g., Magaro, Miller, and Sesto 1984) have linked members of ISKCON and InterVarsity Christian Fellowship with a depressive personality and those of Transcendental Meditation and Divine Light Mission (Elan Vital) with catatonia.

Negative psychological evaluations of the leaders of new religious movements have also been the norm. Colin Wilson (2000), for example, surveys several religious movements throughout history and prefers to call their founders "charlatan messiahs" who are driven by the inordinate desires for sex and power. And Storr's (1996) study of gurus is equally devastating. Storr argues that while not all gurus are pathological individuals, they are likely to be narcissistic, intolerant of criticism, and incapable of friendship.

This negative psychological assessment of new religious movements and their members probably can best be seen in the study of conversion. The conversion model favored by many psychologists to explain why people join NRMs is the brainwashing theory, which argues that new recruits are lured into the movements by various deceptive techniques and then strongly indoctrinated into their respective ideologies. Relying heavily on studies of Chinese and Korean communist techniques used to change the ideology of their political prisoners, these psychologists maintain that members of new religious movements undergo a similar process. Though those individuals recruited by NRMs may have some predispositions making them vulnerable, it is the leaders of the NRMs who take advantage of this adolescent weakness and lure prospective candidates into accepting promises of a better and happier life. Once individuals join, they are practically held captive (emotionally, if not also physically) and indoctrinated, sometimes rather heavily, with the particular movement's goals and philosophical and theological assumptions. New members are sheltered and at times isolated from the rest of society. They do not freely choose their new faith but, rather, fall victims to it. Because they are constantly reinforced in their new belief system, which they never question, they are incapable of evaluating their commitment and cannot by themselves decide whether to stay or leave. The late Margaret Singer (2003: 17) was one of the most forceful and vociferous proponents of this view. She argued that although there are other factors, like family background and individual crises, that make a person more vulnerable to the new religions, "everyone is susceptible to the lure of these master manipulators." Singer described in some detail the process of brainwashing, or thought reform, during which new members' time and environments are carefully controlled while their behavior and attitudes are changed to conform to the new cultic ideology and lifestyle. Members are recruited by the use of both physiological and psychological persuasion techniques. Becoming a member of an NRM is thus not a decision taken freely by the individual but, rather, the result of clever marketing methods and skillfully orchestrated influence processes.

Not all psychologists agree with this negative view of those who join new religions and of the deleterious effects of membership. While some of the hypothesized predispositions to cult membership can be found in those who are attracted to NRMs, they also exist in many young adults who never join a new religion. It is also quite possible that membership in NRMs might create serious mental and physical problems for some of their members. Some former members have made such claims concerning long hours of meditation, a celibate and/or vegetarian lifestyle, and a high level of commitment. However, the effects of group membership cannot be judged by examining the state of only those who have left the movements. The psychological and mental conditions of current members must also be taken into consideration.

Several psychologists have, therefore, directed their efforts to the evaluation of the mental and psychological health of current NRM members by using standard testing techniques and by comparing the results with control groups made up of individuals who have never been NRM members. Among the best studies in this respect are those of Marc Galanter and his associates (Galanter 1980, 1986, 1983; Galanter, Rabkin et al. 1979) who conducted extensive studies of the Unification Church. Galanter, who prefers to call new religions "charismatic groups," concluded that the emotional states of those who joined this movement show significant improvement after conversion. He links this psychological well-being to the cohesiveness members felt with the Church. The rather small percentage of those who joined after the introductory workshops developed greater attachment to the Church's creed. Galanter found that those members who stayed and complied with the movement's unusual marital arrangements exhibited greater distress, but this was counteracted by the affiliative ties with the organization. In his study of Church dropouts, Galanter (1983) corroborated his main thesis that neurotic distress can be alleviated by membership and heightened by alienation from the group.

In addition to members of the Unification Church, Galanter's research has included a number of millennial groups and healing movements. He states:

> One might therefore conclude that members of charismatic groups
> experience a relief in neurotic stress on joining, and that maintaining
> that relief (i.e., a sense of psychological well-being) depends on the
> intensity of their relationship with the group: if they disaffiliate,
> they experience distress; if they remain close, they keep their psy-
> chological well-being. This "relief effect" serves to reinforce mem-
> ber's involvement in the group and also continually reinforces
> their acceptance of the group's beliefs by rewarding them for their
> conformity and acceptance. (1999: 9)

Other studies seem to support Galanter's view that membership in new religious movements is not, as a rule, detrimental to a person's psychological and mental state. Weiss and Comrey (1987) subjected a large sample of Hare Krishna movement devotees to a variety of psychological tests and found that there was little difference between their psychological states and that of the rest of the population. Similarly, Latkin (1990) applied several standard psychological tests to members of Rajneeshpuram and concluded that communal living was generally beneficial. Many studies on meditation (Murphy and Donovan 1988), a common practice among many new religions that stem from the East, have concluded that meditation can have beneficial effects on the physical, mental, and psychological conditions of those who practice it.

Several psychologists are also reformulating the theory of conversion as a process composed of several stages taking place over a period of time. Rambo (1993), for example, points out that there are different types of conversion, which may be either active or passive. Such an approach, he argues, provides a more realistic account of how individuals evaluate their religious commitments, abandon the religions of their upbringings, and join churches or denominations other than the ones in which they had been raised. Although formulated mainly to explore the psychology of conversion in general, Rambo's process could easily be adapted to the new religions.

Several scholars, especially sociologists, have found the theory of brainwashing wanting and have suggested that psychology alone may not provide an adequate theory of conversion to NRMs. Galanter (1999), himself a psychiatrist, seems to support this view since he examines a new religious movement as a social system and tries to explain the psychological and emotional states of individual NRM members within the framework of a community. Others have developed sociopsychological theories of conversion to explain in some detail how a person could move from a traditional belief to an alien belief system and lifestyle. One theory, the drift model of conversion, describes the new convert as going through a long period of internal change rather than experiencing a sudden transformation brought about mainly by outside factors. In this model the convert is a willing participant in the conversion process and not a victim upon whom conversion has been forced. Downton's analysis (1980) of how a convert to Elan Vital (Divine Light Mission) passes through twelve distinct changes before becoming a full member is a unique and classic application of this theory.

Other scholars, using the same sociopsychological approach, have tried to combine both models. Long and Hadden (1983) have pointed out that new members must be socialized into the movement's ideology and practice, and that this socialization process includes both the group's techniques to mold members into a community and the individual's own quest and evaluation. Lofland and Skonovd (1981) have developed a much more complex theory that unites the various conversion motifs (such as the intellectual and the experiential) with various levels of intensity. In their view, no single path to conversion describes what happens when an individual joins a new religion. Their model includes coercive persuasion (or brainwashing) as a theoretical possibility.

This approach is consistent with more recent studies of religion that have veered from the concept of conversion as an expression of pathology and from the theory that NRMs recruit members and maintain them by brainwashing or coercive persuasion. Typical of such studies is that of Hood et al. (1996: 326), who examine several psychological models of conversion and conclude that it "is readily apparent that popular interest in new religious movements and cults cannot be explained by such pseudoscientific concepts of brainwashing. The term has also been thoroughly discredited in the contexts within which it was first applied, since no powerful psychological technique to mandate beliefs and behaviors exists."

The interest in the psychological and mental health of members of NRMs, and in the process that leads them to convert to another religious group, is likely to persist in the study of religion. It is important to see the current debate in the light of the wider issue—namely, the effects of religion in general on believers in all religions, traditional or new. The advancements made in the psychological study of religion (e.g., Jonte-Pace and Jones 2001) over the last few decades, as well as the changes recently adopted by the American Psychiatric Association (Saliba 2004: 318–20), will play a key role in the much-debated question of whether and under what conditions both traditional and new religions can be a source of positive or negative influence on the health of those who dedicate themselves to a particular belief system.

The Sociology and Anthropology of New Religious Movements

Sociologists and anthropologists have played an important role in the study of the new religions. Rather than focusing on individuals and their psychological and mental states, these two disciplines turn their attention to society and/or culture. Roberts (1984: 20), for example, writes:

> The sociological perspective focuses on religious groups and institutions or the behavior of individuals within those groups, and on conflict between groups. While religious beliefs are seen as important, they are not the exclusive focus of sociologists. In fact, beliefs are viewed as one variable of religion among many and often beliefs are found to be the effect of other social behaviors rather than the cause. Sociology does not attempt to prescribe how religion ought to work. Rather it attempts to describe accurately the social underpinnings of social groups and to generalize among common patters and apparent causal correlations.

Consequently, sociological studies of NRMs have been broader in scope and in the issues covered. They have explored how new religions might come into being, how they develop and succeed, and how they become institutionalized. They have carefully investigated the recruitment processes, which were found to be much more complex than those assumed in the theory of brainwashing (Stark and Bainbridge 1985: 305–24), and the various ways in which members leave the movements they had joined (Bromley 1998). And they have examined their finances and organizational systems (Richardson 1988) and gender-role definitions (Palmer 2004; Puttick 1997). Another important issue has been the societal and legal reactions to NRM presence (Wilson and Cresswell 1999), particularly those of the anti-cult and counter-cult movements. And more recently several scholars (e.g., Bromley and Melton 2002) have paid special attention to the violent nature of a few NRMs that have at times been portrayed by opponents of the new religions as paradigms of all NRMs.

Just as psychologists have used standard psychological methods in their study of members of new religions, so sociologists and anthropologists have applied well-tested methods in their fields to study NRMs as social and cultural systems. Historical analysis, cross-cultural analysis, experimentation (limited and only in a few cases), participant observation, survey research and statistical analysis, and content analysis (Roberts 1984: 11–20) are the common tools applied to the study of religion in general and, when applicable, to new movements.

Probably because the debate about NRMs has not been restricted to academic circles but has found its way into the public sphere and the law courts, sociological writings on new religious movements have often revolved around several main issues—namely, the labels use to designate them, the types under which they may be grouped, the best methods to study them, and the various explanations of how they come into being.

Sociologists maintain that the variety among these new religions does not allow for a simple, monolithic label. Over the last century they have made use of four major terms to describe the social differences between religious groups: church, denomination, sect, and cult. The discussion in sociology about these types of religious organizations has a long history (Hadden 1999; Hunt 2003: 33–40). Originally proposed by Weber, Troeltsch, and Niebhur, and later developed by many sociologists like Yinger, Wallis, and Johnson (Swatos 1998), the terms have been helpful in the sociological analysis of Christianity in the Western world, but they are not easily applicable to the new religious groups, especially those of Eastern origin and those that are based on the occult tradition. Moreover, the word *cult*, particularly in most psychological literature and in popular writings, has been employed as a judgmental term that contributes little to the sociological understanding of a widespread phenomenon in contemporary Western culture.

While sociologists still often use the term *cult* in the sense of a relatively new small religious group that is led by a charismatic leader, they have made attempts to adopt other terms, such as "new religious movements," "alternative religions," and "fringe religions," to make an important point—namely, that these groups need to be studied like other religious movements in different historical periods and like the various groups within the major religious traditions. Using neutral terms to designate NRMs is not just an attempt by sociologists to avoid making judgments on theological and ideological matters. It also indicates a different way of conceiving the movements and studying them, a way that leads to understanding religious change and diversity and to relating both to the social or cultural conditions in which they thrive.

Various classifications, depending on the issue or area under investigation, have been employed to understand not only the origins of NRMs but also their activities and relationships to society at large and to mainstream religion. Stark and Bainbridge (1985: 26–30), for instance, create a typology to delineate the type of organizational relationship with members. They distinguish among three types of cults based on their degree of organization and the satisfaction they offer to their members. First, there are "audience cults," which are the least organized and whose members are largely mail-order customers with only occasional attendance at specially organized events. A second type is the "client cults," which refers to groups that are more organized and structured but have members who act as individuals rather than part of a community. Finally, "cult movements" are organized entities that often demand the same kind of commitment as traditional religions. And Wallis (1979, 1985) suggests that new religions can be divided into three types according to their ideological orientation toward the world: (1) "world rejecting" (examples: ISKCON, the Unification Church, and the Children of God/The Family International), (2) "world accommodating" (examples: the Charismatic Renewal, House Churches, and Subud), and (3) "world affirming" (examples: est/The Forum/Landmark Enterprises, Transcendental Meditation, and the Human Potential Movement). He points out that these different orientations have different structures and functions and that, even though they have all come into being as a reaction to societal rationalization, they offer distinctive forms of salvation.

Others scholars, like Hunt (2003), prefer to classify NRMs with reference to the religious traditions from which they stem. Thus, he distinguishes between NRMs derived from Christianity, Hinduism, and Islam and syncretistic movements. He treats as separate categories the New Age movement, neo-pagan and esoteric spiritualities, and human potential and healing movements. The New Religious Movements Home Page Web site (Hadden 2005) lists the groups (including some traditional sects) in alphabetical order, but gives the options of organizing them by their respective faith tradition or by the religious family groupings used by Melton (2003). Wallis (1979) adopts a similarly based classification by distinguishing the movements according to their derivation: (1) indigenous traditions (Jesus People and the Children of God/The Family International), (2) imported traditions (ISKCON, the Divine Light Mission/ Elan Vital) and Transcendental Meditation, and (3) psychological (Scientology, Silva Mind Control, and the Human Potential Movement). He then compares several of their features, such as their conception of God, worldview, commitment requirement, economic base, sexual morality, conversion, leadership, and social organization. Another way to classify the NRMs is by their distinctive social features. Wilson's typology (1990) of sects and his outline of their characteristics have influenced sociological studies in this respect.

Most sociologists, however, maintain that the variety of NRMs is such that it would be difficult to list a set of features that are applicable to all. The majority of NRMs definitely set clear boundaries that mark their members as the chosen elite. But not all are communally oriented and some allow for a variety of living arrangements. Some are rather doctrinaire in their teaching techniques, others are not; some have well-organized systems of proselytization, others do not. Sociological studies of individual groups show that there is a great diversity among NRMS and caution against hasty generalizations.

The third issue revolves around the method used to study NRMs, particularly that of participant observation, which encourages researchers to establish contact with members and to take part to some limited degree in their activities and lifestyles. Fieldwork is held to be an essential element in understanding new religions. Scholars who follow this approach make an effort to represent the worldview of the believers themselves. Thus, for example, Barker's (1984) study of the Unification Church dedicates a whole chapter to describe how she gathered information on the group. Besides interviews, participant observation, and questionnaires, she talked to many parents and representatives of the anti-cult movement. Her research spanned six years and included living in Unification Church centers and attending workshops intended for potential members. Such a method contrasts sharply with one that relies solely on interviewing ex-members and their relatives and that applies outside normative standards to depict the lifestyle and worldview of the group under study.

Finally, one of the major contributions of the social sciences has been the various theories that have been proposed to explain why and how new religions come into being. In sociology and anthropology, the functional theory is probably the most common. This theory maintains that NRMs come into being to satisfy practical and psychological human needs that traditional religions are not meeting and to help people cope with human problems, particularly in periods of cultural/social change. Charles Glock (1973), one of the main proponents of this view, has explained that new religions arise in response to economic, social, psychological, ethic, and philosophical deprivations. Proponents have tried to adapt functionalism to the contemporary scene by arguing that the new religions emerge from a cultural crisis and help fulfill the needs that traditional religions have not responded to effectively.

A different theoretical approach has been proposed by Stark and Bainbridge (1985: 429–56), who interpret the rise of new religious through secularization theory and argue that they are a reaction to the secularization process. They point out that secularization brings about two responses— namely, revival within the traditional religions and religious innovation that veers from established traditions. "Not only do world churches prompt new religious groups, which seek to revive faith, but secularization prompts the formation of new religious traditions. New religions constantly appear in societies" (Stark and Bainbridge 1985: 2). The rise of new religions is thus part of a cycle. Unlike some other sociologists (e.g., Wilson 1976), Stark and Bainbridge do not foresee a "religionless future." While, for Wilson, the presence of new religions confirms the inevitable process of secularization, which will eventually result in the demise of religion at least in public life, Stark and

Bainbridge argue that religion is periodically renewed in response to the secularization process. These speculations suggest that the rise of new religions is a complex phenomenon and cannot be explained by one simple theory.

Sociologists in general consider NRMS as cultural and social expressions, and this has led to conflict with both psychologists and theologians who regard the movements respectively as producers of mental illness and expressions of dangerous unorthodox beliefs and practices. Though this conflict is not open to an easy resolution, it must be acknowledged that sociological studies have become the foundation of the study of NRMs and to any effort to evaluate them from social, legal, and psychological perspectives.

Religious Studies and the New Religious Movements

The emergence of religious studies as an academic discipline is relatively recent even though the study of religion has a long history that traces to the nineteenth century and has roots in some Greek philosophers (Sharpe 1975). Known alternatively as comparative religion, the history of religion(s), or the academic study of religion, religious studies became well established in the late 1960s. Religious studies borrowed both theories and methods from several disciplines, especially philosophy and the social sciences (Capps 1995). Six areas are usually pursued in the study of religions: description, comparison and contrast, systematization, interpretation, function, and language. The discipline also takes a global perspective and makes an effort to map the world's various religious systems. Probably, the current, most comprehensive examples of this mapping is Barrett's encyclopedia (Barrett, Krian, and Johnson 2001), which is a statistical survey of all religions, country by country. The ongoing Pluralism Project (2005) at Harvard University is another example, but it is limited to non-Jewish and Christian traditions in the United States. Here, one finds lists of different religious groups and organizations within one tradition (such as Islam or Hinduism), and NRMs are included within the respective tradition from which they stem. Short profiles of some of these centers or places of worship are provided. The Pluralism Project identifies four objectives. The first is demographic. The second is the study of these religious communities and their adaptation to American culture. The third is the response of Jewish and Christian churches. The fourth is specification of the challenges and opportunities of this new pluralism. Characteristic of this approach is the phenomenological method of abstaining from judging the truth of religious claims and of presenting the various religions as much as possible from the points of views of their respective believers. One is often overwhelmed by abundant raw data and usually is provided little, if any, interpretation.

Religious studies is more descriptive than evaluative in its orientation and has led scholars to avoid prescriptive definitions of religion and to concentrate on its various aspects or dimensions. Ninian Smart (1996), one of the most articulate proponents of this approach, enumerates the following dimensions of religion: belief system, community, mythology, ritual, ethics, religious experience, and material (cultural) expressions. Further, scholars in the field (e.g., Noss 2003) are interested in the history of religions and offer outlines of the beginnings and development of the major world traditions.

Religious studies differs from the social sciences in that it focuses on various components of religion—like myth, ritual, and belief—and is not concerned with organizational matters or relationships between religion and society. Unlike psychology and sociology, it has shown little interest in discussing some of the problematic aspects of the new movements. Classifying the new religions and linking them to traditional beliefs systems has been one of its main concerns. So also has been the question of how religions change and develop. Thus, when Momen (1999: 598) discussed the reasons for studying NRMs, he typified the position of scholars in the field when he stated that these "movements have great importance because of what they tell us about religious change and the development of religions in general."

Like sociologists, scholars in the field of religious studies shun negative concepts like *cult* as judgmental and thus incompatible with phenomenological approach. Consequently, mainline religions and alternative or fringe groups are treated equally. NRMs are included regularly in surveys, particularly when the contemporary religious scene is under investigation. It is becoming increasing common to find chapters on NRMs in textbooks on world religions. Ludwig (2001), for instance, typically surveys the major world religions, but then adds a chapter on new religions, which he sees as alternatives to the mainstream and as "sacred paths." Although he admits that a handful of these, like the Peoples Temple and the Branch Davidians, are dangerous, Ludwig applies to NRMs the same working definition or description of religion as he ascribes to all religions. He looks for causes, like modern discontent and spiritual crisis, that contribute to the emergence and success of NRMs, and he explores their common features, such as apocalyptic tendencies, strong founders, and eclecticism in their teachings. He describes briefly several nineteenth-century groups (Mormonism, the Baha'i, Spiritualism, and Theosophy) and twentieth-century NRMs (Scientology, the Unification Church, neo-Paganism, and the New Age movement). The list of discussion questions he poses at the end (Ludwig 2001: 486) provides a good indication of where the interests of scholars in religious studies lie. Among the issues raised for discussion are: (1) how NRMs come into being and whether their presence is temporary or not; (2) whether those movements that stem from the East can be considered part of the Hindu or Buddhist traditions; and (3) what the similarities and differences are between the new religions.

Molloy (2005) follows a similar procedure. He eschews the word *cult*, except with reference to dangerous groups like the Peoples Temple and Aum Shinrikyo. He dedicates a whole chapter to "Alternative Paths," and includes short descriptions of several groups such as neo-Paganism, Santeria, Theosophy, Scientology, and Falun Gong. In some cases, selections from the main writings of NRMs are being included in anthologies of religious scriptures. Van Voorst (2006) adds a chapter with selections from the scriptures of the Baha'i faith, the Church of Jesus Christ of Latter-day Saints, Christian Science, and the Unification Church. By doing so he indicates that from a religious studies perspective, the basic elements, structure, origin and development, and use of all scriptures are equally open to investigation and comparison.

Most introductory books to the study of religion follow a similar approach. Kessler (2003), for instance, takes Jonestown, alongside with Tibetan Buddhism, as examples of institutionalized religion. After describing the facts that led to the eventual demise of the community in Guyana, Kessler, relying on Wessinger's work (2000) on the subject, leans toward sociological interpretations that explain the tragedy as a form of "revolutionary suicide." Livingston includes new religious movements under his treatment of religions as social groups. He uses the word *cult* to "designate those movements that appear to represent considerable estrangement from, or indifference to, the older religious traditions" (Livingston 2005: 150). He links the rise of new religions to contemporary cultural changes; the lack of vitality in the mainline churches; the quest for personal control, spontaneity, and spiritual freedom; and the therapeutic benefits they offer. He chooses Transcendental Meditation and the Unification Church as examples, the former offering "a direct, relatively easy way to self-realization," the latter providing a family-like community, which stresses spiritual values and alienates its members from the larger society.

Classification has been a major concern in religious studies. Partin (2005) describes four major types of classification of religions: normative, geographical, philosophical, and phenomenological. He points out that most scholars have ceased to categorize religions on a grand scale and, together with scholars in other fields of study, have largely abandoned the search for the origin and evolution of religion. Two common forms of typology are currently found in religious studies. One is geographical and attempts to classify religions by their country of origin. Thus phrases like "Eastern and Western Religions," "Asian Religions," "Middle Eastern Religions," and "African Religions" are frequently used. But it is recognized that such labels are far from absolute, since many religions have migrated to other countries and different forms of the same religion can be found in different countries. Geographical categorization is used more or less as a convenient way of grouping religions in some meaningful pattern. A second form of classification is based on the type of religion, like Judaism, Christianity, Hinduism, and Buddhism. While this might work quite well with the major religions, it does not seem very appropriate when it is applied to the many tribal religions and to some NRMs. Yet some classification is deemed necessary. Partin (2005: 1817) writes:

> The student of religion seeks to find or bring some system of intelligibility to the manifold expressions of religious experience, not only to make the data manageable, but also to discern common charac-

teristics by which religions and religious phenomena be grouped together and compared with or distinguished from others.

In constructing typologies of new religious movements, most scholars in religious studies rely heavily on sociology, though they are more inclined to classify them according to major religious and spiritual traditions. Both Melton (2003) and Barrett (2001) attempt a comprehensive classification; but Melton includes his typology of NRMs within the framework of all religions, while Barrett limits it to those movements of relatively recent origin. Ellwood and McGraw (2004: 438–44) adopt a somewhat eclectic typology and include such concepts as "import religions" and "hybrid religious movements." If the study of NRMs is conducted within the framework of a world religions course, Melton's scheme seems more appropriate. Barrett's and Ellwood and McGraw's classifications, however, provide a more detailed and descriptive analysis of those religious movements that have arisen in the West over the last fifty years.

Most scholars admit, however, that several typologies are possible and that no one typology is all inclusive. Thus, Melton (2003: 1131–58) adds two lists of "unclassified" churches and religious groups and Miller (1995) includes several movements that do not fit into his schema. Also, some NRMs could easily fit into more than one type because they absorb religious views from different traditions.

Many of the above authors treat new movements in the wider context of world religions and/or as part of religious development as a whole. In pursuing this objective, some scholars have concentrated their research more specifically on one or more of the new groups. These intensive studies of one particular NRM differ from both the psychological and sociological counterparts. Probably the most distinctive differences are that (1) they make no attempt to evaluate the individual's mental and psychological states or to explore the conversion process which takes place when people join a religious group; and (2) they are not concerned with the groups as social entities and hence do not deal with the relationship between religion and society and with the organizational structure that distinguishes the various groups. These scholars are more interested in the history of the group, in the religious or spiritual makeup of the people involved, and in comparisons among the various dimensions of religion. In this respect they have followed a well-recognized principle in religious studies—namely, what a scholar writes about an individual group should express as accurately as possible the point of view of the believers and not the scholar's evaluation of it.

Chryssides' book (1991) on the Unification Church is a typical example of a monograph on an NRM from the standpoint of religious studies. He adopts the participant observation method and aims at understanding the theology of the Church, without endorsing or criticizing its beliefs, and aims at giving the insider's point of view. Chryssides outlines in some detail the Unificationist theology and makes some comparisons with Christian doctrine. He then explores the Church's religious heritage and shows the influence Shamanism,

Taoism, neo-Confucianism, and Buddhism have had on Unification thought and how these interacted with the advent of Christianity in Korea. Finally, he traces the history of the Unification Church, explains its major beliefs, and gives an account of its many rituals.

Mary Farrell Bednarowski (1989) provides an excellent example of the comparative method. She chooses six rather diverse groups—namely, Mormonism, the New Age, Theosophy, Christian Science, Scientology, and the Unification Church—and compares their respective concept of God, the way they view human nature, their eschatology, and their ethical systems. Her intent is to depict these nineteenth- and twentieth-century groups as examples of a creative human capacity within the context of culture, whether they exemplify the growing pluralism or the rise of psychological explanations of human nature, and/or the impact of modern science.

By treating NRMs as part of the religious and spiritual quest of humankind throughout the ages, religious studies scholars have indirectly acknowledged the authenticity of most new religions. These scholars have stressed the importance NRMs have not only for understanding religion in general but also for isolating particular trends that might indicate the future of religion.

Christian Theology and the New Religious Movements

Unlike most other disciplines, theology starts by taking a definite stand on the truth or falsehood of religious claims and moral principles, and thus proceeds with different assumptions and goals. Thomas Rausch states that "theology is concerned with our experience of God, particularly our experience of God as a community of faith. It is an effort to understand the faith experience of a community, to bring it to expression in language and symbol" (1993: 12). The theological approach views or examines NRMs from a particular faith perspective. It consists of the reflections believers make to increase their knowledge and understanding of their own faith. Though it borrows methods from various disciplines, it asks different questions about other religious groups. It evaluates their religious character and, if they claim to be Christian, their orthodoxy. It measures their compatibility with Christianity. It sets boundaries between what is deemed orthodox and unorthodox, moral or immoral. It is, therefore, not surprising that Christian commentaries on NRMs, often accompanied by denunciations, have been abundant, even though in some circles the new religions have been brushed aside as minor movements that are bound to be transient and have little serious impact on the mainline churches.

The most common response to the NRMs has been the apologetic one, pursued largely by evangelical and fundamentalist Christians who are concerned with maintaining their belief system in a cultural environment they perceive as threatening. Hence the emphasis is to contrast the beliefs, values, and practices of individual movements with traditional Christian orthodoxy and to prove that they contradict Christian doctrine and consequently must be totally rejected. The most extreme works from this perspective have engaged in a thorough condemnation of the NRMs. Larson (1989), for instance, starts with short descriptions of the major world religions from which many NRMs take their beliefs and practices. He realizes, for instance, that belief in reincarnation and the practice of Yoga, which have become common in the West, are better understood in the context of Hinduism. However, Larson maintains that the beliefs of non-Christian religions are not only unorthodox but also are related to Satanic powers. He sometimes chooses questionable practices of other religions and presents them as the standard acceptable behavior. Thus he briefly describes a temple of rats in southern India and leaves the reader with the impression that the worship of rats is a representative and universal Hindu custom, which he ridicules and finds deplorable. Larson makes no attempt to find out what most Hindus themselves think of the custom or to explore how it came into being and what it means to the Hindus. His approach is prejudicial and misleading. Adopting Larson's logic, one could just as well describe the ritual of a Christian serpent-handling sect and present it as a routine ritual practiced in all Christian churches.

Some Christian writers have mitigated these kinds of antagonist responses with a much more neutral comparison between the belief systems of the new religions and "orthodox" Christianity. Such works are popular among many conservative Christians because of their direct and simple style and because they act as a kind of boundary-maintenance mechanism, confirming one's belief against what is often considered to be a threatening new religion. Believers can use these comparisons as apologetic answers to counteract the evangelical efforts of some of the new religions.

A representative example of this is the work of Walter Martin (1968), whose life was dedicated to expounding and refuting the teachings of sects and cults. He starts with the assumption that one particular version of Christianity is the orthodox one and that anything different must be denounced as false. His goal is to refute the new teachings from the standpoint of the evangelical interpretation of the Bible. In so doing he passes judgment not only on new religions but also on traditional ones. For example, he correctly links ISKCON and Transcendental Meditation with Hinduism and finds that they both reject several basic Christian beliefs, such as the Trinity and the role of Jesus Christ. Martin chooses diverse religious movements (such as Jehovah's Witnesses, the Unificationist Movement, and the Way International) in order to show how they all deny and are incompatible with five basic Christian doctrines: those on God, Christ, the Holy Spirit, sin, and salvation. Even though he has read some of the primary sources, Martin makes no attempt to interpret the origins of belief systems of the groups he studies or to find common ground between them and Christianity. The same procedure, though less thorough than Martin's, is followed by House (2000) who, unlike Martin, is careful to point out that in a few cases the teachings of the new movements correspond to those in orthodox Christianity.

Recent studies by evangelical theologians (Hexham, Post, and Morehead 2004; Johnson 2002) have rejected this apologetical approach as too confrontational and as lacking in understanding of the people who join NRMs. They see it as counterproductive and as bound to have little success in reconverting cult members to their original Christian background. Influenced by the sociological method, these scholars have argued that evangelicals criticize and denounce the doctrines and rituals of NRMs without ever having visited their places of worship or having had a conversation with their members. They propose that the method of fieldwork should be adopted as a requirement before any critique of the NRMs. In fact, a new approach to evangelizing techniques may have to be constructed. Hesselgrave's renunciation of the word *cult* marks a fundamental change in the way some evangelicals are examining new religions. He writes:

> The new terminology (new religions, new religious movements), however, seems preferable in at least two aspects, First, it is less odious and does not immediately assume a combative posture. Second, it encourages researchers to start earlier and dig deeper, rather than merely inquiring into modern origins and developments. (2004: 40)

Several decades before the change proposed by some evangelicals, many Christian churches had adopted a dialogical approach to world religions. Several documents both of the Second Vatican Council (Abbott 1966), particularly those dealing with non-Christians and religious freedom, and of the World Council of Churches (Samartha 1971) have advanced a new relationship with people who belong to different faith traditions. Understanding the various faith experiences by listening to members of other religions express their beliefs, the lessening of acrimonious debates between theologians, the avoidance of attacks and condemnations, and the promotion of cooperation in areas of agreement have been the goals of this approach. Several scholars (e.g., Saliba 1982, 1986) have suggested that this method should be adopted also in the way mainline Christian churches respond to the presence of the new religions. NRMs should be regarded, not as opponents on a cosmic battle ground heralding the end of the world, but rather as religious and spiritual quests that, though different from traditional religions, may provide a fruitful challenge to the churches as well as a lesson of how to cope with contemporary religious change. These scholars conclude that NRMs are not threats to the existence of the mainline churches but rather are partners in a spiritual quest.

Teaching Courses on New Religious Movements

New religious movements are often discussed in college courses in the social sciences, religious studies, and theology. Many reasons can be advanced to show that the study of NRMs is important for understanding culture and religion. College textbooks on world religions (e.g., Kessler 2003: 12–14; Molloy 2005:

22–24) contain a section outlining the reasons for studying religions, reasons that are applicable also to the study of NRMs. One of the most common rationales given is the rise of pluralism in many parts of the world, coupled with the globalization of culture. Teaching new religions also helps the student understand religious change. To young students in particular, NRMs can be presented as a challenge to explore their own beliefs and values and cope both theoretically and practically with religious pluralism.

Several basic principles might guide teachers to select representative and balanced materials for their students. First, it should be emphasized that the newness of the movements is rather relative. Historical studies have shown that the rise of NRMs is not a unique Western phenomenon peculiar to the twentieth century. Thus in anthropology, for example, the rise of such movements has long been observed in different cultures (La Barre 1971), even in those that have no literature, and also throughout the course of Western history (Saliba 2003: 45–74).

Second, it is equally important to keep in mind that many new religions stem from well-establish religious traditions and must, therefore, be seen in a larger context. Thus, for instance, many Eastern religious movements stress the practice of some form of meditation, which is deeply rooted in traditional Eastern religions. Other groups are based on Jewish, Christian, or Islamic sources, while others combine ideas from different traditions. Similarly, many occult beliefs and practices have a long history (Ellwood and Partin 1988: 30–72) and hence are not a new phenomenon, though they have experienced a revival in the last few decades. It would also be a mistake to see or present NRMs as a surprise incursion in Western culture from outside sources. The emergence and spread of NRMs in the West has been helped both by immigration and by greater contact between cultures in an age of mass communication and globalization, but there is no conspiracy to uproot the Judeo-Christian tradition.

Third, while teachers may prefer to approach NRMs from one particular disciplinary perspective, it is useful, and sometimes necessary, to expose students to a variety of studies. Thus, for example, because the methods of sociology and anthropology have been adopted by other disciplines and because social scientists have been involved in court cases that discuss psychological issues, it is difficult, and at times impossible, to avoid crossing disciplinary boundaries. Reading materials should be chosen to express the different ways in which NRMs have been studied and to present a balanced picture of the field under investigation.

Fourth, one should avoid generalizing about new religions and their members from a few isolated cases. A classical example of this is the reported recruitment practice, called "heaven deception," followed by some members of the Unification Church in the 1970s and early 1980s. Speakers at anti-cult conferences have often assumed that this is, more or less, a universal method of recruitment, when in fact it is not. Only a few scholars (e.g., Barker 1984) have made an effort to understand what the practice was, to find out the Church's policy, and to investigate how this policy was interpreted by its members. Psychological studies are especially prone to generalization because psychologists and psychiatrists usually come in contact with people who need psychological help. It is understandable that some ex-cult members are found to be suffering from various mental and emotional dysfunctions. But they are the exception rather than the rule. And whether their difficulties were present before they joined an NRM or whether their membership induced, aggravated, or assuaged the condition is to be proved and not assumed. There are several surveys (Lilliston and Shepherd 1999; Saliba 2004) on the psychology study of NRMs that provide a more comprehensive and balanced view of the many psychological studies on NRMs.

Fifth, it is necessary to aim at presenting an objective picture of the movements under study. One can avoid an ethnocentric perspective by adopting an attitude of cultural relativism and by suspending or bracketing one's judgment. To do this one must (1) choose the best instructional resources (journals, textbooks, references works, and Internet sites), such as the introductions to the study of religion of Kessler (2003) and Livingston (2005) and the Web pages of Hadden (2005), CESNUR (Center for the Study of New Religions 2005), and the Ontario Consultants on Religious Tolerance (2005)—some materials, like those of the International Cultic Studies Association, formerly known as the American Family Foundation (2005), which assumes the brainwashing theory, should be used with care; (2) evaluate carefully reports found in the popular media; and (3) rely on first-hand contact with members of the movements.

In theology courses it is legitimate to make theological evaluations from one particular perspective. To counteract religious ethnocentrism, one can point out that to those who do not profess the Christian faith, some Christian beliefs may appear to be equally strange. Many Christians believe in the so-called rapture. This is an end-time event, when born-again Christians will be caught up in the air and meet Christ in the sky. Christ, it is held, will come unexpectedly, and those who have been saved will simply abandon whatever they are doing and rise up to the sky and vanish. At some point after the rapture, Christ will begin a thousand-year reign. Based on one possible interpretation of a few New Testament passages (Thessalonians 4:13–18; Mark 13:26–27; and Revelation 11:11–12), this belief has been recently made more widespread by the publication of the "Left Behind" novels (e.g., LaHaye and Jenkins 1995) that promote such apocalyptic and millenarian views. What one must bear in mind is that people sincerely hold on to belief systems, like those by UFO groups (cf. e.g., Aetherius Society [2005] and Unarius Academy of Science [2005]), which others judge to be ridiculous. Simply rejecting, downplaying, or attacking their beliefs does not lead to understanding, much less to solving, problems and defusing conflicts.

Another way to adhere to the principles of objectivity and justice is to bring out not only the differences but also the similarities between the beliefs and practices of NRMs and those of the mainline churches. One can, for instance, also draw attention to those areas where the NRMs are in fact "orthodox," as House (2000) has done, even though his approach is largely doctrinal and from one specific Christian denominational perspective. One of the major issues in theology is religious pluralism, which has been highlighted by the presence of NRMs and which cannot be dismissed simply by labeling other groups "unorthodox." Paul Knitter (2002) has done an excellent job in reviewing and evaluating four major theologies of religion. Though he does not apply them to the new religions, they could easily be used as a basis for understanding them, as well as for formulating a Christian response to them. In theology courses, evaluations of what the new religions teach and practice are necessary; but they can be done without maligning NRMs and their members and without assuming that the emergence of NRMs is a diabolical plot against Christianity or a herald of the imminent end of the world.

Evaluating New Religious Movements

The presence of NRMs in contemporary Western culture has certainly raised both social and legal problems. There is some foundation to designations like "deadly cults" (Snow 2003) "killer cults" (Lane 1997), or "suicide cults" (Chryssides 1999: 33–76). Groups like the Peoples Temple, Aum Shinrikyo, the Solar Temple, and Heaven's Gate are rare examples where murder and suicide were justified. Several scholars have attempted to draw up criteria for evaluating NRMs. Lewis (2001: 53–56) has listed five "early warning signs," such as a leader's inclination to dictate the lifestyle of the members, which mark those groups that should be considered a threat to society. Corbett (2000: 317–18) provides ten "warning signals" among which she includes exclusivism and isolationism and the presence of leaders who do not follow the moral standards they impose on members. She observes that such marks are not found in all groups and that some of them are present in traditional religions and secular organizations. Wessinger (2000: 276–81) lists thirteen features, including a strong sense of persecution and aggressiveness toward outsiders, found in some "catastrophic millennial groups" that are cause for concern. It is important to stress that violence is not a universal trait of NRMs. When studying violent cults, it is recommended that one place them in the larger context of religion and violence. Recent studies (Ellens 2004) have shown that even the great religions have often promoted, directly or indirectly, violence and hence religious violence is a much larger problem than violence among a few NRMs.

The aim of teaching a course on NRMs should not be solely to give students information about current religious affairs, but also to help them reflect on and understand complex phenomena that in some way or other could have an impact on their lives. NRMs may be a sign of the vibrancy of religion in the twenty-first century and, even though most of these groups might not survive or might remain marginal groups, they are having an impact on both society and traditional religions. They are also symptomatic of some of the problems inherent in all belief systems. NRMs not only encourage people to reflect on their belief systems. They also urge them to develop ways of coping with pluralism in an age of globalism and of discerning some of the major cultural and religious trends in Western culture.

REFERENCES

Abbott, Walter M., ed. 1966. *The Documents of Vatican II.* London: Chapman.

Aetherius Society. 2005. "Dr. George King, Our Founder." Available at www .aetherius.org/NewFiles/Dr_George_King.html. Accessed February 15, 2004.

American Family Foundation. 2005. "Cult-101. Resources about Psychological Manipulation, Cult Groups, Sects, and New Religious Movements." Available at http://csj.org/infoserv_cult101/cult101.htm. Accessed February 15, 2005.

Barker, Eileen. 1984. *The Making of a Moonie: Brainwashing or Choice?* Oxford: Basil Blackwell.

Barrett, David B., George T. Krian, and Todd M. Johnson. 2001. *World Christian Encyclopedia: A Comprehensive Survey of Churches and Religions in the Modern World.* 2nd ed. 2 vols. New York: Oxford University Press.

Barrett, David V. 2001. *The New Believers: Sects, "Cults" & Alternative Religions: A World Survey and Sourcebook.* London: Cassell.

Bednarowski, Mary Farrell. 1989. *New Religions: The Theological Imagination of America.* Bloomington: Indiana University Press.

Bromley, David G., ed. 1998. *The Politics of Apostasy: The Role of Apostates in the Transformation of Religious Movements.* Westport, CT: Praeger.

Bromley, David G., and J. Gordon Melton, eds. 2002. *Cults, Violence, and Religion.* New York: Cambridge University Press.

Capps, Walter. 1995. *Religious Studies: The Making of a Discipline.* Minneapolis: Fortune Press.

Center for the Study of New Religions [CESNUR]. 2005. Available at www.cesnur.org/ default.htm. Accessed January 26, 2005.

Chryssides, George D. 1991. *The Advent of Sun Myung Moon: The Origins, Beliefs and Practices of the Unification Church.* New York: St. Martin's.

———. 1999. *Exploring New Religions.* London: Cassell.

Committee on Psychiatry and Religion. 1992. *Leaders and Followers: A Psychiatric Perspective on Religious Cults.* Washington, DC: American Psychiatric Association.

Connolly, Peter, ed. 1999. *Approaches to the Study of Religion.* London: Cassell.

Corbett, Julia Mitchell. 2000. *Religion in America.* 2nd ed. Upper Saddle River, NJ: Prentice-Hall.

Downton, James. 1980. "An Evolutionary Theory of Spiritual Conversion and Commitment: The Case of the Divine Light Mission." *Journal for the Scientific Study of Religion* 19, 392–93.

Ellens, J. Harold, ed. 2004. *The Destructive Power of Religion.* 4 vols. Westport, CT: Praeger.

Ellwood, Robert S., and Barbara A. McGraw. 2002. *Many Peoples, Many Faiths: Women and Men in the World Religions.* 7th ed. Upper Saddle River, NJ: Prentice-Hall.

Ellwood, Robert, and Harry B. Partin. 1988. *Religious and Spiritual Groups in Modern America.* Englewood Cliffs, NJ: Prentice-Hall.

Galanter, Marc. 1980. "Psychological Induction into the Large-Group: Finding from a Modern Religious Sect." *American Journal of Psychiatry* 137, 1574–79.

————. 1983. "Unification Church ('Moonies') Dropouts: Psychological Readjustment after Leaving a Charismatic Religious Group." *American Journal of Psychiatry* 140, 984–89.

————. 1986. " 'Moonies' Get Married: A Psychiatric Follow-Up Study of a Charismatic Religious Sect." *American Journal of Psychiatry* 143, 1245–49.

————. 1999. *Cults: Faith, Healing, and Coercion.* 2nd ed. New York: Oxford University Press.

Galanter, Marc, Richard Rabkin, Judith Rabkin, and Alexander Deutsch. 1979. "The 'Moonies': A Psychological Study of Conversion and Membership in a Contemporary Religious Sect." *American Journal of Psychiatry* 136, 165–70.

Glock, Charles Y. 1973. "The Role of Deprivation in the Origin and Evolution of Religious Groups." In *Religion in Sociological Perspective,* ed. Charles Y. Glock, 207–20. Belmont, CA: Wadsworth.

Hadden, Jeffrey K. 1999. "Cult Group Controversies: Conceptualizing 'Cult' and 'Sect. '" Available at http://religiousmovements.lib.virginia.edu/cultsect/cultsect.htm. Accessed February 15, 2005.

————. 2005. "The Religious Movements Homepage Project." Available at http://religiousmovements.lib.virginia.edu. Accessed February 15, 2005.

Hesselgrave, David J. 2004. "Traditional Religions, New Religions, and the Communication of the Christian Faith." In *Encountering New Religious Movements: A Holistic Evangelical Approach,* ed. Irving Hexham, Stephen Post, and John W. Morehead II, 137–56. Grand Rapids, MI: Kregel Publications.

Hexham, Irving, Stephen Post, and John W. Morehead II, eds. 2004. *Encountering New Religious Movements: A Holistic Evangelical Approach.* Grand Rapids, MI: Kregel Publications.

Hood, Ralph, Bernard Spilka, Bruce Hundberger, and Richard Gorsuch. 1996. *The Psychology of Religion: An Empirical Approach.* 2nd ed. Englewood Cliffs, NJ: Prentice-Hall.

House, H. Wayne. 2000. *Charts of Cults, Sects, and Religious Movements.* Grand Rapids, MI: Zondervan.

Hunt, Stephen J. 2003. *Alternative Religions: A Sociological Introduction.* Burlington, VT: Ashgate.

Johnson, Phillip. 2002. "Apologetics, Mission, and New Religious Movements." *Sacred Tribes: Journal of Christian Missions to New Religious Movements,* 1.1. Available at www.sacredtribes.com/issue1/. Accessed January 10, 2004.

Jonte-Pace, Diane, and William B. Jones, eds. 2001. *Religion and Psychology: Mapping the Terrain. Contemporary Dialogue, Future Prospects.* London: Routledge.

Kessler, Gary E. 2003. *Studying Religion: An Introduction through Cases.* Boston: McGraw-Hill.

Knitter, Paul F. 2002. *Introducing Theologies of Religions.* Maryknoll, NY: Orbis.

La Barre, Weston. 1971. "Materials for the History of Studies of Crisis Cults: A Bibliographic Essay." *Current Anthropology* 12, 3–27.

LaHaye, Tim F., and Jerry B. Jenkins. 1995. *Left Behind: A Novel of the Earth's Last Days* (Left Behind Series, no. 1). Wheaton, IL: Tyndale House.

Lane, Brian. 1997. *Killer Cults: Murderous Messiahs and Their Fanatical Followers.* London: Headline.

Larson, Bob. 1989. *Larson's Book on Cults.* Rev. ed. Wheaton, IL: Tyndale House.

Latkin, Carl A. 1990. "The Self-Concept of Rajneeshpuram Commune Members." *Journal for the Scientific Study of Religion* 29, 91–98.

Lewis, James R., ed., 2001. *Odd Gods: New Religions and the Cult Controversy.* Amherst, NY: Prometheus Books.

Lilliston, Lawrence, and Gary Shepherd. 1999. "New Religious Movements and Mental Health." In *New Religious Movements: Challenge and Response,* ed. Bryan Wilson and Jamie Cresswell, 123–40. London: Routledge.

Livingston, James C. 2005. *Anatomy of the Sacred: An Introduction to Religion.* 5th ed. Upper Saddle River, NJ: Prentice-Hall.

Lofland, John, and Norman Skonovd. 1981. "Conversion Motifs." *Journal for the Scientific Study of Religion* 20, 373–85.

Long, John, and Jeffrey Hadden. 1983. "Religious Conversion and the Concept of Socialization: Integrating the Brainwashing and Drift Models." *Journal for the Scientific Study of Religion* 22, 1–14.

Ludwig, Theodore M. 2001. *The Sacred Paths: Understanding the Religions of the World.* 3rd ed. Upper Saddle River, NJ: Prentice-Hall.

Magaro, Peter B., Ivan W. Miller, and Thomas Sesto. 1984. "Personality Style in Post-Traditional Religious Organizations." *Psychology: A Journal of Human Behavior* 21, 10–14.

Martin, Walter R. 1968. *The Kingdom of the Cults.* 4th ed. Minneapolis: Bethany House.

Melton, J. Gordon. 2003. *Encyclopedia of American Religions.* 7th ed. Detroit: Gale.

Miller, Timothy, ed. 1995. *America's Alternative Religions.* Albany: State University of New York Press.

Molloy, Michael. 2005. *Experiencing the World's Religions: Tradition, Challenge, and Change.* 3rd ed. Mountain View, CA: Mayfield Publishing.

Momen, Moojan. 1999. *The Phenomenon of Religion: A Thematic Approach.* Oxford: One World.

Morris, Charles G., and Albert A. Maisto. 1998. *Psychology: An Introduction.* Upper Saddle River, NJ: Prentice-Hall.

Murphy, Michael, and Steven Donovan. 1988. *The Physical and Psychological Effects on Meditation.* San Raphael, CA: Esalen Institute.

Noss, Davis S. 2003. *A History of the World's Religions.* Upper Saddle River, NJ: Prentice-Hall.

Ontario Consultants on Religious Tolerance. 2005. "Academic Study of New Religious Movements (a.k.a. Cults)." Available at www.religioustolerance.org/nurel.htm/. Accessed January 25, 2005.

Palmer, Susan. 2004. "Women in New Religious Movements." In *The Oxford Handbook of New Religious Movements,* ed. James R. Lewis, 378–85. New York: Oxford University Press.

Partin, Harry B. 2005. "Classification of Religions." In *The Encyclopedia of Religion,* ed. Lindsay Jones, vol. 3: 1817–1822. Detroit: Thompson/Gale.

Pluralism Project. 2005. Available at www.fas.harvard.edu/~pluralism/. Accessed March 10, 2004.

Poling, Tommy, and Frank Poling. 1986. *The Hare Krishna Character Type.* Lewiston, NY: Edwin Mellen Press.

Puttick, Elizabeth. 1997. *Women in New Religions: In Search of Community, Sexuality, and Spiritual Power.* New York: St. Martin's.

Rambo, Lewis. 1993. *Understanding Religious Conversion.* New Haven, CT: Yale University Press.

Rausch, Thomas P. 1993. *The College Student's Introduction to Theology.* Collegeville, MN: The Liturgical Press.

Richardson, James T., ed. 1988. *Money and Power in the New Religions*. Lewiston, NY: Edwin Mellen Press.

Roberts, Keith A. 1984. *Religion in Sociological Perspective*. Homewood, IL: Dorsey Press.

Saliba, John A. 1982. "The Christian Church and the New Religious Movements: Towards Theological Understanding." *Theological Studies* 43, 468–85.

———. 1986. "Learning from the New Religious Movements." *Thought* 61, 225–40.

———. 2003. *Understanding New Religious Movements*. 2nd ed. Walnut Creek, CA: Altamira Press.

———. 2004. "Psychology and the New Religious Movements." In *The Oxford Handbook of New Religious Movements*, ed. James R. Lewis, 317–32. New York: Oxford University Press.

Samartha, S. J., ed. 1971. *Living Faiths and the Ecumenical Movement*. Geneva: World Council of Churches.

Sharpe, Eric J. 1975. *Comparative Religion: A History*. New York: Charles Scribner's Sons.

Singer, Margaret Thaler. 2003. *Cults in Our Midst: The Continuing Fight against Their Hidden Menace*. Rev. ed. San Francisco: Jossey-Bass.

Smart, Ninian. 1996. *Dimensions of the Sacred: Anatomy of the World's Beliefs*. Berkeley: University of California Press.

Snow, Robert L. 2003. *Deadly Cults: The Crimes of True Believers*. Westport, CT: Praeger.

Stark, Rodney, and William Sims Bainbridge. 1985. *The Future of Religion: Secularization, Revival, and Cult Formation*. Berkeley: University of California Press.

Storr, Anthony. 1996. *Feet of Clay: Saints, Sinners, and Madmen: A Study of Gurus*. New York: Free Press.

Swatos, William H. 1998. "Church-Sect Typology." *Encyclopedia of Religion and Society*, ed. William H. Swatos, 90–93. Walnut Creek, CA: Alternative Press.

Unarius Academy of Science. 2005. Available at www.unarius.org/. Accessed February 28, 2004.

Van Voorst, Robert E. 2006. *Anthology of World Scriptures*. 4th ed. Belmont, CA: Wadsworth.

Wallis, Roy. 1979. "The Elementary Forms of Religious Life." *Annual Review of the Social Studies of Religion* 3, 191–211.

———. 1985. "The Sociology of New Religious Movements." *Social Studies Review* 1, 3–7.

Weiss, Arnold, and Andrew Comrey. 1987. "Personality and Mental Health of Hare Krishnas Compared with Psychiatric Outpatients and 'Normals.'" *Personality and Individual Differences* 8, 721–30.

Wessinger, Catherine. 2000. *How the Millennium Comes Violently: From Jonestown to Heaven's Gate*. New York: Seven Bridges Press.

Wilson, Bryan. 1976. *Contemporary Transformations of Religion*. London: Oxford University Press.

———. 1990. *The Social Dimensions of Sectarianism: Sects and Religious Movements in Contemporary Society*. Oxford: Clarendon Press.

Wilson, Bryan, and Jamie Cresswell, eds. 1999. *New Religious Movements: Challenge and Response*. London: Routledge.

Wilson, Colin. 2000. *The Devil's Party: A History of Charlatan Messiahs*. London: Virgin Publishing.

Wulff, David M. *Psychology of Religion: Classic and Contemporary*. 2nd ed. New York: John Wiley.

Methodological Issues in the Study of New Religious Movements

David G. Bromley

New religions studies (NRS) has gradually emerged as an interdisciplinary area of study since 1970 (Barker 2004; Bromley 2004; Melton 2004; Robbins 2000). While there were earlier studies of religious movements and sectarian groups, over the last several decades a cohort of scholars from a variety of disciplines has developed a primary research interest in new religious movements (NRMs). Developing NRS poses scholars with a variety of challenges. One is the number and diversity of rapidly changing movements. There are at least hundreds of NRMs from a diverse array of religious traditions. In addition, there are a like number of New Age groups, many of which are quasi-religious in nature, as well as communal and intentional communities, some of which have a religious orientation. The simple fact is that relatively little is known about most of these groups, and only a handful have received anything approaching even a single, systematic study. As is the case for social movements in general, NRMs typically change rapidly; descriptions of them therefore quickly become dated. There are only a few movements for which there has been a series of studies reflecting successive stages of development. At this point in time, therefore, NRS is based primarily on snapshot studies of a small sample of NRMs at specific points in their developmental histories.

New religions studies also faces the challenge of being an interdisciplinary area of study. It draws primarily on religious studies and sociology and to a lesser extent on anthropology, history, psychology, and economics. NRS is based on these various disciplines but is unique in certain respects. Religious studies has traditionally emphasized cultural traditions of world religions rather than emerging traditions. Sociology has a long history of studying social movements, but primarily secular movements. Neither discipline has focused on movements and traditions that are contested and regarded as deviant by their host societies. NRS employs fieldwork methods that resemble those used in anthropology, but the groups being studied are modern in nature and mostly located in Western societies. This disciplinary diversity means that scholars work from a variety of perspectives, which brings a theoretical richness to the research process but also complicates the task of assembling a coherent corpus of knowledge. There is a comparable challenge with respect to research methods. While there have been several calls for setting a formal research agenda for the area (Balch 1985; Barker 1982; Richardson, Balch, and Melton 1993; Pitchford, Bader, and Stark 2001), the reality remains a series of studies that have been conducted from a variety of disciplinary perspectives, with differing objectives, and utilizing different methodological procedures. Nonetheless, there is some convergence in basic perspectives and methodological approaches.

Scholars working in new religions studies have generally adopted an interpretive approach to the study of NRMs, with an emphasis on describing their historical lineages, primary mythic and ritual elements, organizational development, and sociocultural significance. For both religious studies and sociology, this agenda has involved working from an emic rather than an etic perspective, which means understanding the uniqueness of each specific movement and drawing out the meaning of NRMs for members by eliciting their interpretations of their beliefs and practices. This orientation, in turn, has led to intense interest in the affiliation process, which is the most researched topic in NRS by a wide margin, and to case studies of individual NRMs. The primary method by which research has been conducted by NRS scholars, therefore, has been fieldwork utilizing participant observation techniques.

At present the foundation of NRS is the series of studies of individual NRMs. Since NRS did not exist when research began, most of the scholars for whom this is now a primary specialization had no fieldwork experience and often little background in religion. They came from a variety of disciplines and substantive specialty areas and often began work on NRMs serendipitously (e.g., Coleman 2002; Palmer 2001b; Bromley and Shupe 1979a). As a result, each researcher encountered the problems of fieldwork de novo and usually without the benefit of exchanges with other scholars conducting similar research projects. In many cases, researchers did not even incorporate the full range of their research experiences in their scholarly reports because those experiences did not fit the traditional textbook depictions of the research process (Bromley and Carter 2001a). It has been only in the last several years that there has been more open, formal dialogue on the research process in which the subtleties and complexities of fieldwork have been discussed, as researchers have discovered that problems they thought to be unique were in fact relatively common. There have been some sessions devoted to such matters at professional meetings and, more recently, a series of books that begins to explore these issues (Nordstrum and Robben 1995; Bromley and Carter 2001b; Spickard, Landes, and McGuire 2002; Blain, Ezzy, and Harvey 2004).

In this chapter I review some of the major issues in participant observation fieldwork on NRMs by identifying some patterns in work to date, issues for which there seems to be emerging consensus, and matters that are a source of continuing debate. These include how groups are selected for study; how access to movements is negotiated; and how a research project is initiated, conducted, and ended.

Group Selection

Since NRS is being created primarily on the basis of the cumulation of field-work research projects, the selection of groups is an important factor in determining the stock of knowledge. It is a daunting fact that there now are well over two thousand religious groups in the United States, a significant proportion are NRMs, and the number of NRMs continues to grow. Yet there are multiple studies of only a handful of these groups, and most NRMs have never been studied. Most groups are small and remain relatively unknown. This raises the question of which groups among the myriad NRMs have been selected for study?

Research textbook discussions of theoretical-problem and research-site selection usually presume an established field of study, in which a researcher is in a position to engage in background reading and then select a research site based on the theoretical problem to be studied. However, ethnographic reports on NRMs make it clear that NRS scholars initially selected movements for study as they became aware of them. In many cases, the initial contact with a movement was influenced by factors such as the pre-existing interests of researchers, geographic proximity of the movement, public visibility of the movement, a controversy in which the group was involved, or simply serendipity. Examples of these diverse influences abound. Nancy Tosh (2001) attributes her selection of a Wicca group directly to her personal encounter with Wicca when she was entering graduate school, but the Wiccan philosophy also resonated with magical systems of thought from her childhood. Similarly, Benjamin Zablocki (2001) attributes mystical experiences during his childhood as influencing his attraction to groups with charismatic leaders. Christel Manning (2001) traces her interest in conservative religious groups, both Christian and Jewish, partly to her personal rebellion against patriarchal religion as a teenager. Richard Ofshe (Mitchell and Ofshe 1980) first encountered Synanon 1972 when he visited a facility with a friend who had been asked by the group to provide technical assistance in setting up a sewage treatment system and subsequently received permission to study the group. David Bromley and Anson Shupe (1979a) initiated research on the Unificationist movement when a recruitment team arrived near their university, and the team leader began approaching faculty members to assist the group in gaining recognition as a campus organization. A departmental colleague passed a publicly distributed flyer from The Family International to James Chancellor (2000), who then initially met Family members when, out of curiosity, he attended a public meeting.

Group selection has also been driven to a significant degree by the controversy surrounding those movements, and particularly such issues as cult/brainwashing debate (see the Richardson and Introvigne chapter in this volume) or alleged violent tendencies. There are a number of studies of the Family Federation for World Peace (originally the Unification Church), The Family International (originally the Children of God), and the International Society for Krishna Consciousness (Hare Krishna) beginning in the early 1970s, precisely because these movements were recruiting new members aggressively and were alleged to be employing brainwashing practices. NRMs linked to violence have also received disproportionate attention (see the Robbins and Hall chapter in this volume). One striking example is Heaven's Gate, a tiny UFO group that was studied early in its history but then disappeared from public view for a number of years. The group regained public visibility only when it engaged in its collective suicide and since has been the object of considerable study and commentary (Balch and Taylor 2002; Lalich 2001).

There are several implications of how NRMs have been selected as research sites both for individual research projects and for the development of NRS. It is clear that a variety of individual motivations are involved in researchers' group selections, but it is less clear what the implications of these individual motivations are for research projects. They may not be determinative of the outcome of the research process, but they are at least significant for the initial stance the researcher takes toward the group. The initial approach in turn influences the way access is negotiated, the nature of researcher–group relationships, and the personal impact of the research process on the researcher. Personal motivations may be particularly relevant where the researchers are either current or former members of movements with loyalties or animosities toward those movements.

More systematic discussion is needed on how initial orientation to research projects play out through the research process. The sample of movements studied to date also overrepresents those movements that have been involved in public controversy. Conversion and violence issues have assumed prominence in NRS largely because of the controversy surrounding NRMs. It may be the case that recruitment and movement development patterns are influenced by involvement in conflicts. It appears that there is a growing recognition among NRM scholars that it will be significant for the evolution of NRS to better understand the implications of the sample of groups on which NRS currently is based, to broaden the range of groups being studied, and to identify key theoretical issues that will enhance the study of NRMs as emerging religious traditions.

Gaining Access

If the group/site selection decision is under the control of researchers, actual access to that group/site is under the control of the movement, assuming that researchers openly identify themselves. One might well begin by questioning why a movement would grant access to a researcher at all. From a movement's perspective, to have a scholar present in a group might well be regarded as an unnecessary distraction that would offer little benefit to the movement and would raise the specter of a host of unanticipated consequences, such as public venting of internal disputes or unwanted revelations of insider information. Particularly in the initial wave of research on NRMs, researchers were engaged in their first study of an NRM and NRMs were engaged in their first encounter with social scientists. Neither side was prepared for the encounter. As the number of ethnographic reports has grown, the variety of response patterns to researchers' requests for access has become clearer. It is also evident that both social scientists and NRMs are becoming more sophisticated in negotiating access.

Not all movements have been receptive to researchers. Indeed, it has not been uncommon for movements to exclude researchers who announce themselves or to limit access. The Church of Scientology has significantly limited scholars' access; the movement has provided tours of facilities and closely monitored visits by scholars, but there is no body of scholarship on Scientology that compares with the extensive work conducted on Unificationism, The Family International, Hare Krishna, and neo-paganism. Amway, which a number of scholars have treated as a quasi-religious movement, is a privately owned corporation and has consistently denied scholars access to its gatherings (Bromley 1998b). Susan Palmer (2001a), who has studied a number of NRMs, reports having been summarily rebuffed by the Black Hebrews, Druids, and Free Daist Communion and having encountered resistance from E. J. Gold and the Rajneesh. Access may also vary for the same movement at different times. In her work on the Rajneesh, Marion Goldman (2001) gained access to the movement because she followed several other social scientists who had built good working relationships with the movement. However, her access became extremely constricted as the movement moved into a state of factionalism and hostility with the surrounding community. She retained access to the movement premises, but her ability to elicit information from informants continuously decreased.

Where movements do grant access to researchers, there often are various motivations at work, usually that prior experiences with researchers have yielded what movement leaders regarded as "positive experiences," the movement regards the researcher as a future convert or public relations ally, or the movement is in a highly contested situation in which scholars' accounts are perceived as preferable to reports by opponents or the media. However, in those various circumstances, a certain amount of trust is often essential, and the personal characteristics of the researcher then may be a significant factor. In Miguel Leatham's (2001) research on Nueva Jerusalén, for example, his own conservative religious background was a significant factor in his acceptance by the movement. Similarly, one reason that members of The Family International trusted James Chancellor (2001) with sensitive information was that he shared their Christian commitments. Chancellor reports praying with Family members, which created a sense of common spiritual values. In her research on three different religious groups, Christel Manning (2001) found that being a woman established a common bond and basis for mutual identification with women informants in those movements, even though she did not share their social and religious conservatism. Other factors that might be important in gaining access include age, ethnicity, and sexual orientation (Wilcox 2002).

Of course, access is more complicated than simple entry into a group. Even where access is permitted, the type and extent of access have varied considerably. Larger movements typically have a variety of organizations and locations, and access to one does not necessarily ensure access to others. Since movements often are beset by factions, this is a key issue if researchers are attempting to describe entire movements or present their findings as representative. For example, Shupe and I (1980) gained access to a Unificationist mobile fund-raising team, but access to the movement's administrative center required further negotiation. The Unificationist Seminary proved even more elusive, as seminary leaders were unimpressed by the researchers' prior written work, which they regarded as "unhelpful." Access was finally arranged through a dissident faculty member, and seminary leaders never did meet with the researchers. During this period, the East and West Coast branches of the movement also were at odds, and access to the West Coast branch had to be negotiated independently. In some cases, researchers have gained sufficient trust from influential figures in a movement that they obtain at least initial acceptance in other parts of the movement. Burke Rochford (2001) was able to obtain a letter of introduction from a respected guru that facilitated his access to Hare Krishna temples across the United States. Similarly, James Chancellor (2000, 2001) received permission from Family International leaders to visit any Family home anywhere in the world. This kind of access obviously provides researchers with much more representative samples and allows greater generalization about movement characteristics and activities. Eileen Barker attended several Unificationist conferences before being asked to conduct research on the movement in England. It required two years of negotiation before she was able to obtain an agreement to gain the right to control the selection of interviewees for her study. The result, however, was that she was able to independently survey virtually all Unificationists in England at that time (Barker 1984: 13–15).

The importance of access raises the question of how to proceed when it is anticipated that access will be denied or it has been denied. This question has produced a debate over overt versus covert participant observation. It has been rather common for journalists to engage in covert research as a means of adding drama to their stories, and it was relatively common for social scientists as well during the early phases of NRM research (Palmer 2001b: 133). Some methods textbooks have advocated covert research methods for studying various types of "extremist groups," including NRMs (Del Balso and Lewis 1997). Certainly the best known case was Festinger, Riecken, and Schachter's study of a small millennial group, *When Prophecy Fails* (1956), in which the use of four covert researchers who feigned psychic experiences had a dramatic effect on the very small group and possibly on the research findings the researchers reported. Both Roy Wallis's study of Scientology, *The Road to Total Freedom* (1977), and David van Zandt's *Living in the Children of God* (1991) began as covert research projects. Wallis participated for two days in a Scientology course before withdrawing from the course in order to avoid lying about the basis of his involvement (1977: 7). By contrast, van Zandt lived in a Family commune for an extended period before revealing his identity to the group. The outcomes in these two cases are interesting. Scientologists ultimately concluded that Wallis's treatment of their movement was offensive and demanded and received the right to publish a rejoinder by a social scientist practitioner as an appendix in his book. Van Zandt (1991: 186) reports that members of The Family were bemused by his identity revelation given how active he had been in the movement and how demanding daily life was. They decided that his continued research on the group would probably be a benefit to the movement, as the accounts he was likely to produce would be more favorable than the hostile press coverage they were receiving at the time. These various cases suggest that, beyond the ethical issues involved, covert research has unpredictable consequences for a research project once the researcher's actual intentions are revealed.

Covert research has become increasingly controversial on ethical grounds, and most professional associations and scholars have argued that the practice is unwarranted in most cases, usually counterproductive, and unethical in most circumstances (Erickson 1967; Richardson 1991a, 1991b; Zablocki and Robbins 2002: 13). Stone (1978) has noted that covert research may lead researchers to focus on more negative aspects of the group in order to justify their deception. It is also clear that deception places greater stress on researcher, particularly to the extent that the group accepts the researcher in good faith; creates continuing tension about how and when the identity subterfuge can be terminated; and poses an additional moral quandary when research results are reported. Covert research has become increasingly rare as the advent of Institutional Review Boards (IRBs) has all but eliminated such research by university faculty.

Conducting the Research Project

Once researchers have gained access to a movement, they confront a variety of management problems. Among the most common issues NRM researchers have encountered are identifying and maintaining a mutually acceptable role, defining the balance to be struck in the participant-observer role, managing internal and external pressures, and assessing the utility of divergent sources of information.

Developing a Viable Role

One of the first issues that NRM researchers confront is how they will define themselves and what definition the group will accept (Davis 1986; Pettigrew

1981). Even if NRM scholars seek to present a researcher identity, probably the most common response from movements has been to treat the researcher as a potential convert, since that is the role occupied by almost all nonmembers and it is the role for which the group has prepared. Numerous researchers report that they were placed in that category, and this identity creates potential instability in the future. Richardson, Stewart, and Simmonds (1978) report that the group regarded them as potential converts who had been sent by God, and in fact members competed to see who could convert them first. When the group later concluded that conversion was unlikely, it appears that members decided that the researchers' presence served a still undefined higher purpose that would ultimately be revealed to them and they were encouraged by the fact that some converts had found the group through the researchers' writings. For their part, the researchers responded by openly acknowledging differences in religious beliefs and emphasizing that their presence in the group was for research purposes; their strategy worked in this case and they were able to maintain a long-term relationship (see also Gordon 1978). Burke Rochford (2001) participated in religious rituals, worked in a Krishna school (gurukula), and adopted elements of the movement's lifestyle. In this fashion he developed a relatively stable role as a fringe member who was regarded as not having quite made a full commitment.

While in some cases researchers and groups have reached some type of mutual accommodation, in other cases relationships have unraveled. Dick Anthony declined to discuss his religious beliefs while studying a Jesus Freaks group, but this led to increased pressure to disclose and ultimately to his withdrawal from the situation (Robbins, Anthony and Curtis 1973). Miguel Leatham (2001) was accepted into the Nueva Jerusalén community, a millenarian movement in Mexico founded on a Marian apparition, as both a "pilgrim" and a researcher. However, over time tensions increased as the group discovered his disinclination to make a commitment to the group, despite Leatham's best efforts to avoid situations in which his lack of commitment would be apparent. Ultimately his relationship with the community began to deteriorate. In the case of John Lofland's participant observation of the Unificationist movement, the group nominally accepted his self-presentation as a researcher but continued to treat him as a potential convert. Ultimately the group tired of his continued reluctance to make a commitment, and he was asked to leave (1966: 270–75).

The available evidence suggests that groups do accept the researcher role when they anticipate some advantage from that role. Otherwise, as Susan Palmer comments, the word *sociologist* "denotes a boring, depressingly secular, time-wasting, spiritually contaminated nerd" (2001a: 107). One common form of advantage is favorable publicity or protection from unfavorable publicity. In Miguel Leatham's (2001) research project, the leaders of Nueva Jerusalén expected that Leatham would act as a spokesperson for the group when tension with the larger society intensified. His unwillingness to do so was one of the factors that increased their disenchantment with his continued presence in the group. Nancy Tosh (2001) was a member of Wicca at the same time as she was researching the group. The group apparently presumed that as a member she would not reveal unflattering information about the group in her writings. The group was mistaken, however, and Tosh became the target of group hostility for her disloyal conduct. Susan Palmer also reports being rather routinely presented with requests, by groups she was studying, for assistance with problems they were facing with regard to the media, governmental agencies, or the courts (Palmer 2001a: 104–5).

However careful researchers are in trying to maintain working relationships with the movements under study, there are events that they cannot anticipate or control. For example, in his work on the Hare Krishna, Burke Rochford encountered the movement at a time when its rigid insider–outsider distinction was weakening. Rochford (2001) was able to occupy the role of a fringe member of the group, a position that would not have been available at an earlier time. By contrast, Marion Goldman (2001) began studying the Rajneesh at a time when the movement was becoming more isolated. The result was that members were assigned to spy on her activities, access to the group became more difficult, and members were reluctant to converse with her. James Chancellor (2000, 2001) was given almost unlimited access to Family members and records largely because the group had experienced a succession of raids on its homes because of child-abuse allegations. Even though The Family International prevailed in most of those cases, the leaders made a conscious decision to try to put the past behind them by having an outsider document its history, beliefs, and practices. Although Family leaders were not entirely satisfied with the resulting scholarly product, it clearly was preferable to the hostile treatment the movement had been receiving in the press and from anti-cult organizations.

Balancing Participation and Observation

The extent of identification with groups in which scholars are conducting participant observation has long been an issue in the social sciences. Positivistic social science has traditionally privileged observation over participation, and involvement that calls into question the ultimate locus of researcher loyalty has been termed "going native." In this tradition the scientist is presumed to be a neutral observer and must maintain distance from the research subject. There is also a moral dimension to this tradition. In the usual case of a dominant tradition studying an alternative or native tradition, the agent of the observing culture is presumed to possess an "objective" knowledge that is superior to the alternative or native tradition's self-understandings. Spickard (2002: 238) comments on this common feature of anthropological and sociological ethnography:

> In a sense, such anthropological and sociological ethnographies are just two different ways of presenting "the Other." Anthropological "Others" have traditionally live in far-off places and been seen either as restless natives or as exotic relics that need preserving. So we

control them or protect them, keeping them at arm's length because they are not "Us." Sociological "Others," on the contrary, are potential friends and neighbors. We get to know them in order to change them—to make them copies of ourselves.

As Carter and I (2001a: 4–5) describe this privileging of the observer role: "The appropriate structuring of the role is given in its semantic construction with 'observer' as the anchoring noun and 'participant' as the modifier." Howard Becker's classic article titled "Whose Side Are We On?" (1967) symbolized the growing recognition that research was itself a social and political process that inherently involved alliances of various kinds.

In NRS, as in other areas of the humanities and social sciences, there has been a pronounced theoretical and methodological shift toward participating as fully as possible in order to directly experience the logic of beliefs and actions from the perspective of the actors. In *The Vulnerable Observer*, Ruth Behar (1996: 5) cites Clifford Geertz in commenting that "You don't exactly penetrate another culture, as the masculinist image would have it. You put yourself in its way and it bodies forth and enmeshes you." Scholars have conceptualized being open to influence and even personal transformation in various ways. Kenneth Liberman (2001) argues that it is impossible to gain significant insight about a group if researchers do not take the groups they are studying seriously, and taking them seriously means being open to being transformed by them. He argues for retaining a critical capacity while also being open to transformation by striving for "clarity," by which he means "the capacity to think both within and outside whatever philosophical routines I am employing, without being made a prisoner of my own analytic routines." Daniel Capper (2003) takes a similar approach in describing "scientific empathy," which takes the form of "evenly hovering attention." Benjamin Zablocki (2001) has advocated what he terms "maximum feasible immersion," which means immersing oneself in the group as fully as possible and remaining open to the possibility of conversion. Similarly, Kurt Wolff (1964: 237–45) endorses "surrendering" to the group. He terms his approach "cognitive love," which connotes complete involvement and requires suspension of pre-existing beliefs so that observation is not selective, treating everything that occurs in the group as pertinent rather than importing an external agenda, identifying with the group rather than a subject matter, and taking the risk of being hurt through involvement rather than engaging in self-protective actions. For him, not to proceed in this way means that "I am not fully man who is studying, and it is not fully man I am studying" (1964: 245).

Given the social and cultural distance between researchers and groups in many cases, it might be thought that the primary problem for researchers is rising to a sufficient level of involvement. However, a number of researchers report that maintaining one's distance is at least an equal problem, precisely because alternative traditions can be personally compelling. Palmer (2001b) reports that several of her graduate-student peers affiliated with the groups that they had been sent to study. Zablocki (2001: 229) also reports that two of his graduate students converted to the movements they were studying and that he himself came to the "brink" of conversion on several occasions. Such reports are not uncommon (see also van Zandt 1991). While some scholars clearly have been deeply influenced by the traditions they have studied (Liberman 2001; Rochford 2001), most have consciously sought to maintain some degree of distance from the groups during the research process. One of the most common solutions is to identify some space where the researcher can retreat to regain an observer perspective. Richardson, Stewart, and Simmonds (1978) worked as a team, maintained a "base camp" where they could meet each day and mutually reflect on their own reactions to ongoing events, and used the team to maintain solidarity amid constant group efforts to convert them. Lalich (2001: 136) recommends that researchers make sure they have ample time alone, away from group influence, and maintain regular contact with outsiders as a reality check. Zablocki (2001) has recommended using research teams so that the variety of researcher responses to the research situation can be discussed.

Of course, rather than be influenced by groups being studied, the opposite can happen as well when researchers inadvertently influence the behavior of members. Eileen Barker (1984: 24–25) notes that in one incident following what she regarded as simply a description of the Divine Principle as part of participating in a workshop, another participant announced that she now fully accepted Reverend Moon as the Messiah. In another incident, after hearing Barker provide an accurate account of the movement, a member reported that she recognized that her continuing ambivalence about the movement and her decision to leave the movement were justified. Richardson, Stewart, and Simmonds (1978) received over fifty letters from individuals requesting more information about the group after they published an article (since the group was referred to by a pseudonym), and the group actually gained converts as a result.

In most cases where researchers have been able to negotiate a stable participant-observation role, they are able to complete their projects and exit the research situation relatively uneventfully. However, because the researcher–group relationship can be unstable and groups may change unexpectedly, research relationships may be terminated abruptly by the researcher or the movement. Miguel Leatham (2001) reported becoming increasingly disillusioned with the leadership of Nueva Jerusalén after discovering exploitive practices, encountering increasing resistance as he began interviewing dissident members, and facing growing tension over his unwillingness to convert or serve as a public spokesperson for the group. Leatham ultimately suspected that his fieldnotes were about to be confiscated and left the community at night on foot in order to preserve his research materials. Susan Palmer was suddenly denied further access to the Raelian movement after granting a media interview that movement leadership defined as unflattering, although she subsequently reestablished a more amicable relationship with the movement.

Managing Internal and External Pressures

NRS scholars have discovered that successfully navigating the research role means contending with critical scrutiny and pressure from both NRMs and opponents and control agencies. Researchers therefore often find themselves in a complex political matrix that adds a level of complexity to fieldwork. On one side, many NRMs are seeking public legitimation and therefore may engage in any number of strategies (beyond attempting to convert researchers) designed to create a favorable public image for outsiders, including scholars studying the movements (Horowitz 1978, 1983; Lalich 2001; Muster 1997). Such influence attempts include limiting the access of scholars to members who are loyal to the movement, limiting the topics of discussion during interviews or the kind of organizational records to which researchers will be allowed access, staging events or tours to which outsiders are invited that present the movement in the most favorable way, hiring public relations firms or training members as public relations representatives to create a favorable image of the movement, and allowing access to movement leadership only under highly controlled public occasions.

In a few cases where researchers have produced findings unacceptable to NRMs, movements have attempted to influence the publication of those findings in various ways. Burke Rochford engaged in a protracted discussion with Hare Krishna members prior to publication of his book *Hare Krishna in America* (1985). Julius Rubin was refused permission to study the Bruderhof, and its leadership orchestrated a campaign to prevent publication of his book *The Other Side of Joy* (2000). As previously noted, Roy Wallis agreed to publish an appendix to his book in which his interpretations of the movement were challenged. James Beckford was sued by the Unificationist movement over an article published in *Psychology Today* and agreed to issue a public apology as part of the settlement. While such contentious relationships are not commonplace and each involves a complex sequence of events, these cases indicate the difficulties of carrying out the participant-observation role. None of these tactics is unique to NRMs, of course, but they complicate the task of researchers attempting to achieve an insider understanding of NRMs. Since in most cases researchers continue to regard themselves and are regarded by group members as outsiders, the task of generating rapport and trust while maintaining distance is a diplomatic challenge.

At the same time, NRS scholars confront organized oppositional movements and an array of institutional gatekeepers who are pursuing various social control agendas and who regard NRMs as disreputable, disruptive, or even dangerous. NRS scholars have been sharply criticized by NRM opponents as apologists or advocates who fail to maintain a sufficiently critical stance toward these movements (Horowitz 1978; Kent and Krebs 1998a, 1998b; Beit Hallahmi 2001). In response to such criticism, NRS scholars have articulated two goals for research on NRMs. One is providing interpretations of NRMs that meet the standard of good scholarship, which means interpretations that are informative to both the movements and the scholarly community, as opposed to being either empowering or disempowering to either movements or their opponents. As Harvey (2004: 247) puts the matter in the context of studying paganism: "If what I write is recognizable to Pagans as a reasonably accurate reflection on their religion and to scholars as an interesting contribution to critical reflection seeking understanding of religiosity, then my work is scholarly." The other goal is dispelling cultural myths about NRMs that are based on stereotyping of diverse groups. As Roy Wallis (1977: 218) commented about the role of social science researchers:

> Saying [what is so about society] may sometimes conflict with what perfectly virtuous and respectable persons believe to be so, and may sometimes accord with what persons and agencies who are not generally viewed as virtuous and respectable claim to be so. This does not make them spokespersons or apologists. It makes them responsible social scientists and citizens.

NRS scholars thus face the problem of "walking a tightrope" (Shupe and Bromley 1980) between movements and control agents and opponents, with each side monitoring scholars' activities and accounts for evidence of disloyalty. For NRS scholars engaged in participant observation fieldwork, the result seems to be that their participation is rarely as committed and uncritical as NRM insiders would prefer and observation is rarely perceived as sufficiently detached and critical to satisfy opponents and control agents.

In some cases, the controversy surrounding NRMs has transcended academic debate and has involved NRS scholars in dealing directly with various institutional gatekeepers. For example, NRS scholars have served as expert witnesses in litigation involving NRMs, conducted sponsored research for NRMs, served as consultants to police agencies in cases of potential or actual violence involving NRMs, or acted as civil libertarian activists in cases of legislation that would impact religious groups. There often are compelling professional and civic motives for using academic expertise in these other social forums, such as attempting to prevent or counter expert testimony that does not accurately represent the consensus, preventing violence, or opposing legislation that would reduce religious freedom. The problem with playing these various roles is that they often involve contested situations in which scholarly knowledge is placed in the service of achieving political ends. Scholars find themselves operating in forums where political victories rather than understanding are the objective and where scholars are obliged to reduce the complexity of their findings to accommodate an adversarial setting. At the present time, the appropriateness of involvement in these various roles is being actively debated.

While there is no working consensus on these issues, there appear to be some emerging principles that can be applied to specific situations. There is general agreement that the research process should be transparent and that researchers should fully disclose details of the research process as well as agreements negotiated in conjunction with the research process. Second, there is a growing awareness that maintaining clarity and insight concerning personal motives, organizational purposes, and costs/risks attending lines of action selected in conjunction with research or activist roles is critical. Third, the importance of maintaining a capacity for independent critical reflection throughout the research process—the capacity to simultaneously be in and not in a situation—is understood. Finally, researchers acknowledge the primacy of the scholarly role and scholarly community—that the foremost responsibility of NRS scholars is to bring back to the community insight and perspective that enhance the understanding of religion as a social and cultural form.

Irrespective of the resolutions that NRS scholars make to these political problems, there is a virtually inevitable stigma attending the study of marginal groups (Adams 1998; Ferrell and Hamm 1998). Numerous researchers studying diverse types of marginal groups have concluded that the stigma attached to the group also becomes associated with them. Ferrell and Hamm (1998: 4) note that researchers who study marginal groups "push at the very boundaries of professionally acceptable scholarly inquiry. They risk having their research denigrated on grounds of bias, subjectivity, over-involvement, and 'overrapport.'" By contrast, scholars studying mainline religious groups rarely face this problem. As Neitz (2002: 42) has put it,

> I have naively wondered why it is that other scholars wonder if I am a witch, or a Charismatic Catholic, and question the legitimacy of my work, while for the prominent white, male scholars in my field to research Protestants does not compromise them in any way. No one questions their legitimacy in speaking for "their" people, nor their authority to do so.

Gathering and Assessing Information

There are a number of problems in determining what sources of information to use and how to make sense of the information received from those sources. Several key categories have become increasingly important in NRS fieldwork: leaders and followers; members, former members and apostates; and various factions or divisions within movements.

Even in the least differentiated movements there is, in most cases, a key distinction between leaders and followers. However, it has been particularly difficult for NRM researchers to gain meaningful access to upper-echelon leaders. Research on NRMs has been based almost exclusively on contacts with rank-and-file members and mid-level leaders. As in many other kinds of organizations, top-level leaders are protected by organizational lieutenants against unwanted intrusions. In the case of NRMs, it is extremely common for the founder-leaders of movements to withdraw from most contact with members in order to preserve their charismatic qualities. For example, in the case of The Family International, Moses David Berg secluded himself only a few years after founding the movement and never again had contact with followers except through his prophetic writings and occasional personal correspondence. In addition, mid-level leaders gain power by having privileged access to top leadership and therefore often attempt to mediate any access. Robert Balch and Langdon (1998: 200) point out that the circle of leaders around Love Israel in the Love Family were successful in disguising Love Israel's extravagant lifestyle and debilitating drug use, which virtually bankrupted the group, despite the fact that the group was quite small and lived communally. In the case of Aum Shinrikyo, it appears that very few movement members were aware of the leadership's involvement in the murder of dissidents or of plans to carry out the sarin gas attacks on the Tokyo subway system. In both of these cases, social scientists offered public defenses of the groups, only later to learn of inner-circle conspiracies (Balch and Langdon 1998: 200; Beit-Hallahmi 2001: 35–36).

The result is that much of the theorizing about leadership is based on leaders' pronouncements, historical documents, retrospective interpretations based on organizational changes, or former members' and apostates' accounts. Since movements can change rapidly and such changes are likely to be initiated by leadership, lack of access to leadership leaves scholars without the capacity to anticipate or interpret changes in movements. This problem was dramatized by the unraveling of leadership in the Peoples Temple and the secret conspiring within the leadership of Aum Shinrikyo, both of which resulted in episodes of violence. NRS scholars are acutely aware that more systematic information on how leadership is exercised and decisions are made within leadership ranks will be significant in advancing the field.

Many NRMs are a complex web of international organizations that sometimes are associated with different nations. During the formative years of NRMs, these various organizational and national units often are held together by loyalties to the movement's founder-leader. However, it is relatively common for movements to have factions that coexist in an uneasy alliance with one another. One of the more challenging tasks for researchers is to gain access to these various factions and provide an analysis and description of the movement as a whole. For example, The Family International has basic units (homes) around the world, but homes in various nations have differed in their compliance with movement policy. As a result, acceptance of specific policies, such as the "Flirty Fishing" practice that became a source of controversy for the movement, has differed considerably (Melton 1994). In this instance, James Chancellor (2000) was able to visit homes of members of The Family International in a number of countries and thereby gain a sense of the complexity and diversity of the movement as a whole. By contrast, the Unificationist movement has major organizational centers in South Korea, Japan, and the United States, all of which have had uneasy relationships with one another. While there has been extensive study of Unificationism in the West (Bromley and Shupe 1979b; Barker 1984; Lofland 1966), overall perspective on the movement is limited because there is very little information about the movement in Asia. The importance of factions in understanding movements was highlighted by Burke Rochford's research (2001) on Hare Krishna. In that movement there was serious disagreement between liberal and conservative wings over how to handle revelations of child abuse in movement schools. Liberals wanted to publicly disclose the abuses and institute reforms while conservatives were concerned that public exposure would sully the reputation of Prabupada, the revered movement founder. During his research, Rochford gained valuable insight into movement politics but also paid a price by writing about the abuses and incurring the disfavor of one of the factions. The emerging body of movement case studies has increased NRS scholars' recognition that research on movements' internal political dynamics is critical to understanding movement development.

Because NRMs both gain and lose members, there are two obvious sources of information on movements at the individual level: members and former members. In addition, because some NRMs have been involved in conflicts internally and externally, there are former members with grievances against their movements who have allied with oppositional groups, or apostates (Bromley 1998a). It is important in gathering data to distinguish among current members, former members, and apostate members. Committed current members are usually likely to provide favorable accounts of movements. However, research on conversion indicates that in fact members have varying degrees and types of loyalty to the movements they have joined, some current members are in the process of leavetaking, and some members have reason to reveal insider information for their own purposes (Barker 1984: 21). Useful information may be available from former members, as most are not hostile to their movements, some have more information about the actual workings of the movements than less experienced current members, and former members have a perspective on their movements by virtue of having been both insider and outsider (Wright 1987). Lalich (2001: 140) comments that use of former member information may be vital: "Especially taking into account the level at which a person functioned while in the group, a former-member informant who was in leadership or had other kinds of access to privileged locations or information is a valued source of information." For these reasons the accounts provided to researchers by members and former members are both useful, and researchers who have utilized reports from both sources have found each to be reliable for their purposes (Zablocki 1996; Balch and Langdon 1998). Apostates are influenced in a significant way by their alliance with oppositional groups, are much more likely to seek public attention than either current or former members, and are much more likely to offer "atrocity story" accounts of NRMs (Bromley 1998a). Anti-cult groups have relied heavily on hostile former members and apostates as a key element in their oppositional strategy. They are therefore likely to be less useful as a sole or primary source of information. However, apostates may be an important source of information of certain kinds, such as internal movement factions and conflicts or insider activities that neither members nor former members are disposed to reveal.

Most researchers have concluded that the most appropriate approach is what is termed "triangulation," or drawing on the full range of information so that an informed assessment of the research issues can be made (Balch and Langdon 1998; Carter 1998; Richardson 1991b; Zablocki 1996). The decision to use a variety of sources of information, however, is likely to raise tensions, as movements typically attempt to undermine the credibility of hostile former members and oppositional groups question the credibility of loyal current members. In their simultaneous study of Unificationism and the anti-cult movement, Shupe and I (1979a) initially had relatively uncontested access to both the movement and opponents, as each saw advantages to being studied by social scientists. However, as it became apparent to each group that the researchers were talking with their opponents, tensions escalated. Ultimately the research relationship with the anti-cult movement disintegrated when it became evident to movement leaders that the researchers would not accept their brainwashing explanation for NRM affiliations.

Exiting and the Aftermath of the Research Project

While there is an extensive literature on accessing and sustaining working relationships with NRMs, there has been relatively little discussion of exiting a research project. Snow (1980) has offered criteria for determining when a research project is reaching a point of conclusion, some of which relate to theory and data and others of which concern factors external to the project itself. With respect to the former, criteria include taken-for-grantedness (the research process no longer proves interesting or problematic; rather, events are assuming a taken-for-granted quality), theoretical saturation (no data are being gathered that contribute to a theoretical understanding of the group or process under study), and heightened confidence (the researcher is confident that the theoretical framework is validated by findings). With respect to the latter, resource depletion, time constraints, and project completion pressure may result in the researcher's exiting the field.

Beyond the reasons that Snow offers, it appears that one common reason that NRM researchers terminate projects is that they were unable to sustain a role that was mutually acceptable (Lofland 1966; Palmer 2001a). As already noted, some researchers have been expelled or have lost meaningful access. For example, Susan Palmer (2001a, 2001b) lost access to the Raelians after remarks that she made to journalists were regarded as critical of the movement, and Shupe and I (1980) lost access to the anti-cult groups when we refused to accept parental claims that NRM members were brainwashed. In other cases the research role became sufficiently tenuous that the researcher concluded that research materials might be confiscated. For example, Miguel Leatham (2001) ultimately ended up packing his belongings and walking out of the remote village in the dead of night to be sure the fruits of his labors would not be lost. Similarly, Marybeth Ayella (1990: 570–71) discovered that her fieldnotes mysteriously disappeared one evening after she declined to participate in a group event and there was clearly escalating tension over her resistance to conversion. To date scholars have reported little about how they continued research projects once participant opportunities were terminated. There is also virtually no literature on "revisits" and their implications (Burawoy 2003).

Terminating a research project and exiting a research site are sometimes much more complex processes than researchers anticipate. Liberman (2001), Tosh (2001), and Snow (1980) all reported sufficient connectedness to the groups they were studying (traditional Buddhist, Wiccan, and Nichiren Shoshu, respectively) that they experienced personal distress at separating from the group and considerable difficulty in reorienting to an academic environment. Even for cases in which the research project has been formally concluded, the implications of the project may continue in unexpected ways. For example, researchers have sometimes been involved in extended litigation growing out of their research, as Rochford's (2001) experience in reporting on child abuse in the Hare Krishna movement illustrates. Researchers also report being so personally affected by the research process that their perspective on the group and on all future research is profoundly influenced. Perhaps most striking was Goldman's (2001) experience in returning to Rajneeshpuram, discovering the extent to which her behavior had been secretly monitored, and recognizing retrospectively the fear that she had lived under daily during her fieldwork.

Methods in the Classroom

Teaching about NRMs is a challenging undertaking because NRM myths, rituals, organization, and leadership are likely to seem strange to students; students are likely to generalize about NRMs. Some of the movements have been involved in public controversies, and students are likely to approach the subject matter with relatively strong preconceptions and relatively little knowledge. While NRS has been developed to a significant extent on the basis of participant observation fieldwork, the preceding sections of this chapter underscore the complexity of this process and the difficulties that even experienced researchers face in successfully completing a project. Given that students are likely to have strong preconceptions about cults but are unlikely to have either knowledge of fieldwork methods or any fieldwork experience, it makes sense to create as much background and perspective for students as possible before encouraging them to engage in direct contact with NRMs. Perspective can be created successively by developing receptivity and a problem-solving approach, understanding the available sources of information and their utility, working with various sources of information and gaining an understanding of the interests they represent; collecting and analyzing readily available information on selected groups; and only finally engaging in a direct encounter with one or more NRMs.

Based on this logic, the first step in teaching this subject matter is to establish an inquisitive rather than an inquisitional orientation (Eugene Gallagher and Thomas Robbins and John Hall offer specific suggestions on this issue in other chapters in this volume). In addition to the advice that Robbins and Hall and Gallagher provide, explaining the various postures that scholars assume in studying NRMs may be one way to encourage students to maintain openness in approaching the subject matter. One simple exercise that may push students to confront their predispositions is a simple in-class survey (which could easily be extended to out-of-class individuals) that asks students to list some groups that are examples of "cults" and enumerate the characteristics of groups that they regard as cults. Then they can be asked to identify the sources of their information, which are most likely to be media or Web site accounts, and to report what they independently know about the beliefs, rituals, leadership, membership, and organization of these NRMs. Through this kind of exercise students are likely to recognize that they have little actual knowledge about these groups or their members and that their presumptions are based largely on media accounts. Another means of connecting students to NRMs is to point out their relationship to established traditions with which students may be familiar as well as their novelty and innovativeness. Simultaneously, some of the avowed values and objectives of specific groups can be discussed (world unification, peace, gender equality, living a religious life, racial unity, individual self-fulfillment, rejection of materialism) along with the material documenting the hostile response many groups have received. The objective is to create an anomaly (groups that are both familiar and strange, have values with which students can identify but are stigmatized) that students can be encouraged to resolve through further study.

If students are willing to adopt an inquisitive posture and a problem-solving perspective, then the next step is to guide them toward the abundant sources of information on NRMs. One possibility is to assign students to discover any NRMs that are in their immediate locale; they may well be surprised to discover the number and diversity of religious groups of which they were unaware (Melton discusses this type of assignment). The existence of NRMs in their environment may increase students' perception of the relevance of studying NRMs and the potential for gathering information about them. The key in encouraging students to begin gathering information on NRMs is to provide guidance in determining the meaning and utility of different sources of information. As several contributors in this volume point out, there are numerous sources of information on NRMs: the movements themselves, oppositional groups, media reports, and scholarly sources. Information from these various sources may take the form of published materials, Web sites, or videos. Students will be empowered by guidance in the use of these various information sources (Eileen Barker provides valuable perspective on this issue); the sharp contrasts in perspective that they will encounter, along with balanced interpretation of the perspectives from which the information is constructed, may increase their motivation for further inquiry. It is critical to teach students the value of "triangulation," or the use of multiple sources of information, in conducting a research project. These multiple sources of information will be particularly valuable to students in resolving the anomalies that they encounter as they come to understand the interests and perspectives represented in each information source.

Once students have a solid grasp of the types of information available on NRMs and a context for understanding the utility of the various information sources, they are in a better position to begin exploring specific NRMs. Groups may be selected on the basis of proximity, class interest, or information availability; choosing groups for which there is already an abundance of information offers obvious advantages in maximizing course time. With one or more groups selected, students can begin building alternative profiles of those groups based on different information sources. The categories of analysis can parallel other chapters in this volume (myth, ritual, leadership, organization/ development, affiliation/disaffiliation). The information compiled can then be analyzed in terms of the interests and objectives represented in the information sources. One reasonable exercise is to assign students different information sources (movement, opponents, media, scholarly, current/former/apostate members) and encourage the class to adopt a problem-solving perspective on assessing the diverse sources of information. This assignment can easily be formatted in terms of discussion, papers, presentations, or debates. A complementary assignment that may increase student's perspective on the contemporary controversy over NRMs is to engage in the same exercise using nineteenth-century groups as the examples. There is a particularly rich literature on the history of Mormonism and Catholicism that exemplifies many of the same issues that arise in the study of contemporary NRMs. It is also possible to engage in cross-cultural comparisons on the same basis; the emergence and controversy surrounding the Falun Gong in China is a well-documented case.

After students have gained sufficient background on the study of NRMs, they can begin to learn about the various problems that participant observation fieldwork entails. Some of the major challenges in fieldwork that are discussed in the first section of this chapter can now be explained more meaningfully. The distinctive orientation of the scholar engaged in participant observation will also be clearer to students. One informative exercise to clarify the difference between approaches to NRMs is to ask students to contrast the orientation of NRM scholars and those of advocate, opponent, or journalistic interpreter. With a background understanding of the fieldwork process, it is more feasible for students to engage in a direct encounter with NRMs and their members. While it is unlikely that they will be able to experience the full fieldwork experience, they may well be able to engage in some of the steps sufficiently to gain an appreciation of the process. Students can select a group, even if some of the choices are hypothetical, as a means of developing a legitimation of conducting the research process. They should be able to read the background literature on groups available in their locale and formulate some issues they wish to investigate or develop a specific hypothesis to be tested. Based on the experiences of NRS researchers, they can formulate a strategy for approaching the group, prepare a list of questions to be pursued in meetings with movement members, develop categories of analysis (e.g., myth, ritual, organization, leadership) and specific issues to be explored (e.g., gender relations, childrearing, spiritual experiences, conversion experiences, status of the movement founder), and negotiate the terms of access to the movement. One or more fieldwork visits can be used to collect information. The student report or presentation constitutes an exercise in adopting and defending a specific stance in portraying the group.

If NRMs are not available or accessible, it may be possible to simulate a fieldwork project. In this event, students could engage in the same process of group selection, background reading, and issue or hypothesis construction. If previously researched groups are selected, it may be possible to report on the experiences in approaching the group and negotiating a research role. Since many movements maintain extensive Web sites, it may be possible to take a virtual tour and collect information on the same categories and issues. In place of interviews with current and former members, accounts may be available from documentary films, scholarly books and articles, Web sites, or media interviews. While this type of project may lack some of the appeal of a direct encounter with an NRM, it is more realistic in some other respects. Students can learn to apply the problem formulation, information gathering, and critical analysis skills in the much more commonplace situation of needing to understand a group or set of events without the benefit of being able to conduct fieldwork.

As a final step in the research process, it is instructive to ask students to compare the findings of the class projects with their initial self-reports about the characteristics of cults and to assess what they have learned about gathering, assessing information sources, and understanding ways of life that differ from their own. If students have increased their capacity for understanding their own preconceptions, critical analysis, empathetic understanding, and participation in diverse sociocultural environments, the teaching experience will have been a success.

REFERENCES

Adams, Rebecca. 1998. "Inciting Sociological Thought by Studying the Deadhead Community: Engaging Publics in Dialogue." *Social Forces* 77, 1–25.

Ayella, Marybeth. 1990. "They Must Be Crazy: Some of the Difficulties in Researching 'Cults.'" *American Behavioral Scientist* 33, 562–77.

Balch, Robert. 1985. "What's Wrong with the Study of New Religions and What Can We Do about It?" In *Scientific Research and New Religions: Divergent Perspectives*, ed. Brock Kilbourne, 24–39. San Francisco: American Association for the Advancement of Science.

Balch, Robert, and Stephen Langdon. 1998. "How the Problem of Malfeasance Gets Overlooked in Studies of New Religions: An Examination of the AWARE Study of the Church Universal and Triumphant." In *Wolves within the Fold*, ed. Anson Shupe, 191–211. New Brunswick, NJ: Rutgers University Press.

Balch, Robert, and David Taylor. 2002. "Making Sense of the Heaven's Gate Suicides." In *Cults, Religion, and Violence*, ed. David G. Bromley and J. Gordon Melton, 209–28. Cambridge, UK: Cambridge University Press.

Barker, Eileen. 1982. "From Sects to Society: A Methodological Programme." In *New Religious Movements: A Perspective for Understanding Society*, ed. Eileen Barker, 3–15. New York: Edwin Mellen.

————. 1984. *The Making of a Moonie: Choice or Brainwashing?* Oxford: Basil Black-well.

————. 2004. "What Are We Studying? A Sociological Case for Keeping the 'Nova.'" *Nova Religio* 8, 88–102.

Becker, Howard. 1967. "Whose Side Are We On?" *Social Problems* 14, 239–47.

Behar, Ruth. 1996. *The Vulnerable Observer.* Boston: Beacon Press.

Beit-Hallahmi, Benjamin. 2001. "'O Truant Muse': Collaborationism and Research Integrity." In *Misunderstanding Cults: Searching for Objectivity in a Controversial Field*, ed. Benjamin Zablocki and Thomas Robbins, 35–70. Toronto: University of Toronto Press.

Blain, Jenny, Douglas Ezzy, and Graham Harvey, eds. 2004. *Researching Paganisms.* Walnut Creek, CA: Alta Mira Press.

Bromley, David G. 1998a. "The Social Construction of Contested Exit Roles: Defectors, Whistleblowers, and Apostates." In *The Politics of Religious Apostasy*, ed. David G. Bromley, 19–48. Westport, CT: Praeger, 1998.

————. 1998b. "Transformative Movements and Quasi-Religious Corporations: The Case of Amway." In *Sacred Companies: Organizational Aspects of Religion and Religious Aspects of Organizations*, ed. N. J. Demerath, III, Peter Dobkin Hall, Terry Schmitt, Rhys H. Williams, 349–63. New York: Oxford University Press.

————. 2005. "Whither New Religions Studies: Defining and Shaping a New Area of Study." *Nova Religio* 8, 83–97.

Bromley, David G., and Lewis F. Carter. 2001a. "Re-envisioning Field Research and Ethnographic Narrative." In *Toward Reflexive Ethnography: Participating, Observing, Narrating*, ed. David G. Bromley and Lewis F. Carter, 1–36. Oxford: Elsevier Science.

————, eds. 2001b. *Toward Reflexive Ethnography: Participating, Observing, Narrating.* Oxford: Elsevier Science.

Bromley, David G., and Anson Shupe. 1979a. "Evolving Foci in Participant Observation: Research as an Emergent Process." In *Fieldwork Experience: Qualitative Approaches to Social Research*, ed. William Shaffir, Alan Turowitz, and Robert Stebbins, 191–203. New York: St. Martin's.

————. 1979b. *"Moonies" in America: Cult, Church, and Crusade.* Beverly Hills, CA: Sage.

Burawoy, Michael. 2003. "Revisits: An Outline of a Theory of Reflexive Ethnography." *American Sociological Review* 68, 645–79.

Capper, Daniel. 2003. "Scientific Empathy, American Buddhism, and the Ethnography of Religion." *Culture and Religion* 4, 233–53.

Carter, Lewis. 1998. "Carriers of Tales: On Assessing Credibility of Apostate and Other Outsider Accounts of Religious Practices." In *The Politics of Religious Apostasy*, ed. David G. Bromley, 221–38. Westport, CT: Praeger.

Chancellor, James. 2000. *Life in The Family: An Oral History of the Children of God.* Syracuse, NY: Syracuse University Press.

————. 2001. "The Family and the Truth." In *Toward Reflexive Ethnography: Participating, Observing, Narrating*, ed. David G. Bromley and Lewis Carter, 37–51. Oxford: Elsevier Science.

Coleman, Simon. 2002. "But Are They Really Christian? Contesting Knowledge and Identity In and Out of the Field." In *Personal Knowledge and Beyond: Reshaping the Ethnography of Religion*, ed. James Spickard, J. Shawn Landres, and Meredith McGuire, 75–87. New York: New York University Press.

Davis, Dona. 1986. "Changing Self-Image: Studying Menopausal Women in a Newfoundland Fishing Village." In *Self, Sex, and Gender in Cross Cultural Fieldwork*, ed. Tony Whitehead and Ana Lamy, 240–62. Urbana: University of Illinois Press.

Del Balso, Michael, and Alan Lewis. 1997. *First Steps: A Guide to Social Research.* Toronto: Nelson.

Erikson, Kai. 1967. "A Comment on Disguised Observation in Sociology." *Social Problems* 14, 367–73.

Ferrell, Jeff, and Mark Hamm, eds. 1998. *Ethnography at the Edge.* Boston: Northeastern University Press.

Festinger, Leon, Henry Riecken, and Stanley Schachter. 1956. *When Prophecy Fails.* New York: Harper Torchbooks.

Goldman, Marion. 2001. "The Ethnographer as Holy Clown: Fieldwork, Disregard, and Danger." In *Toward Reflexive Ethnography: Participating, Observing, Narrating*, ed. David G. Bromley and Lewis Carter, 53–76. Oxford: Elsevier Science.

Gordon, David. 1978. "Getting Close by Staying Distant: Field Work on Conversion-Oriented Groups." Paper presented at the annual meeting of the American Sociological Association, New York.

Harvey, Graham. 2004. "Pagan Studies of the Study of Paganisms? A Case Study in the Study of Religions." In *Researching Paganisms*, ed. Jenny Blain, Douglas Ezzy, and Graham Harvey, 241–56. Walnut Creek, CA: Alta Mira Press.

Horowitz, Irving, ed. 1978. *Science, Sin, and Scholarship: The Politics of Reverend Moon and the Unification Church.* Cambridge, MA: MIT Press.

———. 1983. "Universal Standards Not Uniform Beliefs: Further Reflections on Scientific Method and Religious Sponsors." *Sociological Analysis* 44, 179–82.

Kent, Stephen, and Theresa Krebs. 1998a. "Academic Compromise in the Social Scientific Study of Alternative Religions." *Nova Religio* 2, 44–54.

———. 1998b. "When Scholars Know Sin: Alternative Religions and Their Academic Supporters." *Skeptic* 6, 36–44.

Lalich, Janja. 2001. "Pitfalls in the Sociological Study of Cults." In *Misunderstanding Cults: Searching for Objectivity in a Controversial Field*, ed. Benjamin Zablocki and Thomas Robbins, 123–55. Toronto: University of Toronto Press.

———. 2004. *Bounded Choice: True Believers and Charismatic Commitments.* Berkeley: University of California Press.

Leatham, Miguel. 2001. "Ambiguous Self-Identity and Conflict in Ethnological Fieldwork on a Mexican Millenarian Colony." In *Toward Reflexive Ethnography: Participating, Observing, Narrating*, ed. David G. Bromley and Lewis Carter, 77–92. Oxford: Elsevier Science.

Liberman, Kenneth. 2001. "Ethnographic Practice and the Critical Spirit." In *Toward Reflexive Ethnography: Participating, Observing, Narrating*, ed. David G. Bromley and Lewis Carter, 93–116. Oxford: Elsevier Science.

Lofland, John. 1966. *Doomsday Cult.* Englewood Cliffs, NJ: Prentice-Hall.

Manning, Christel. 2001. "Conversations among Women: Gender as a Bridge between Religious and Ideological Cultures." In *Toward Reflexive Ethnography: Participating, Observing, Narrating*, ed. David G. Bromley and Lewis Carter, 117–32. Oxford: Elsevier Science.

Melton, J. Gordon. 1994. "Sexuality and the Maturation of The Family." In *Sex, Slander, and Salvation: Investigation of The Family/Children of God*, ed. James Lewis and J. Gordon Melton, 71–96. Stanford, CA: Center for Academic Publication.

————. 2004. "Toward a Definition of 'New Religion'." *Nova Religio* 8, 73–87.

Mitchell, Dave, and Richard Ofshe. 1980. *The Light on Synanon*. New York: Seaview Books.

Muster, Nori. 1997. *Betrayal of the Spirit*. Urbana: University of Illinois Press.

Neitz, Mary Jo. 2002. "Walking between the Worlds: Permeable Boundaries, Ambiguous Identities." In *Personal Knowledge and Beyond: Reshaping the Ethnography of Religion*, ed. James Spickard, J. Shawn Landres, and Meredith McGuire, 33–46. New York: New York University Press.

Nordstrom, Carolyn, and Antonius Robben. 1995. *Fieldwork under Fire*. Berkeley: University of California Press.

Palmer, Susan. 2001a. "Caught Up in the Cult Wars: Confessions of a Canadian Researcher." In *Misunderstanding Cults: Searching for Objectivity in a Controversial Field*, ed. Benjamin Zablocki and Thomas Robbins, 99–122. Toronto: University of Toronto Press.

————. 2001b. "Spiritual Etiquette or Research Ethics? An Innocent Ethnographer in the Cult Wars." In *Toward Reflexive Ethnography: Participating, Observing, Narrating*, ed. David G. Bromley and Lewis Carter, 133–56. Oxford: Elsevier Science.

Pettigrew, Joyce. 1981. "Reminiscences of Fieldwork among the Sikhs." In *Doing Feminist Research*, ed. Helen Roberts, 62–82. London: Routledge and Kegan Paul.

Pitchford, Susan, Christopher Bader, and Rodney Stark. 2001. "Doing Field Studies of Religious Movements: An Agenda." *Journal for the Scientific Study of Religion* 40, 379–92.

Richardson, James. 1991a. "Reflexivity and Objectivity in the Study of Controversial New Religions." *Religion* 21, 305–18.

————. 1991b. "Experiencing Research on New Religions and Cults: Practical and Ethical Considerations." In *Experiencing Fieldwork: An Inside View of Qualitative Research*, ed. William Shaffir and Robert Stebbins, 62–71. Newbury Park, CA: Sage.

Richardson, James, Robert Balch, and J. Gordon Melton. 1993. "Problems of Research and Data in the Study of New Religions." In *The Handbook on Cults and Sects in America*, ed. David G. Bromley and Jeffrey K. Hadden, 213–29. Greenwich, CT: JAI Press.

Richardson, James, Michael Stewart, and Roberta Simmonds. 1978. "Researching a Fundamentalist Commune." In *Understanding the New Religions*, ed. Jacob Needleman and George Baker, 235–51. New York: Seabury.

Robbins, Thomas. 2000. "Quo Vadis the Scientific Study of New Religious Movements." *Journal for the Scientific Study of Religion* 39, 515–24.

Robbins, Thomas, Dick Anthony, and Richard Curtis. 1973. "The Limits of Symbolic Realism: Problems of Empathetic Field Observation in a Sectarian Context." *Journal for the Scientific Study of Religion* 12, 259–72.

Rochford, E. Burke, Jr. 1985. *Hare Krishna in America*. New Brunswick, NJ: Rutgers University Press.

————. 2001. "Accounting for Child Abuse in the Hare Krishna: Ethnographic Dilemmas and Reflections." In *Toward Reflexive Ethnography: Participating, Observing, Narrating*, ed. David G. Bromley and Lewis Carter, 157–80. Oxford: Elsevier Science.

Rubin, Julius. 2000. *The Other Side of Joy: Religious Melancholy among the Bruderhof*. New York: Oxford University Press.

————. 2001. "Contested Narratives: A Case Study of the Conflict between a New Religious Movement and Its Critics." In *Misunderstanding Cults: Searching for*

Objectivity in a Controversial Field, ed. Benjamin Zablocki and Thomas Robbins, 452–77. Toronto: University of Toronto Press.

Shupe, Anson, and David G. Bromley. 1980. "Walking a Tightrope: Dilemmas of Participant Observation of Groups in Conflict." *Qualitative Sociology* 2, 3–21.

Snow, David. 1980. "The Disengagement Process: A Neglected Problem in Participant Observation Research." *Qualitative Sociology* 3, 100–122.

Spickard, James. 2002. "On the Epistemology of Post-Colonial Ethnography." In *Personal Knowledge and Beyond: Reshaping the Ethnography of Religion*, ed. James Spickard, J. Shawn Landres, and Meredith McGuire, 237–25. New York: New York University Press.

Spickard, James, J. Shawn Landres, and Meredith McGuire, eds. 2002. *Personal Knowledge and Beyond: Reshaping the Ethnography of Religion*. New York: New York University Press.

Stone, Donald. 1978. "On Knowing How We Know about the New Religions." In *Understanding the New Religions*, ed. Jacob Needleman and George Baker, 141–52. New York: Crossroad Books.

Tosh, Nancy. 2001. "Mirror Images: Wicca from the Inside Out and the Outside In." In *Toward Reflexive Ethnography: Participating, Observing, Narrating*, ed. David G. Bromley and Lewis Carter, 181–96. Oxford: Elsevier Science.

van Zandt, David. 1991. *Living in the Children of God*. Princeton: Princeton University Press.

Wallis, Roy. 1977. *The Road to Total Freedom*. New York: Columbia University Press.

Wilcox, Melissa. 2002. "Dancing on the Fence: Researching Lesbian, Gay, Bisexual, and Transgender Christians. In *Personal Knowledge and Beyond: Reshaping the Ethnography of Religion*, ed. James Spickard, J. Shawn Landres, and Meredith McGuire, 47–62. New York: New York University Press.

Wolff, Kurt. 1964. "Surrender and Community Study: The Study of Loma." In *Reflections on Community Studies*, ed. Arthur Vidich, Joseph Bensman, and Maurice Stein, 233–63. New York: John Wiley.

Wright, Stuart. 1987. *Leaving Cults: The Dynamics of Defection*. Washington, DC: Society for the Scientific Study of Religion.

Zablocki, Benjamin. 1996. "Reliability and Validity of Apostate Accounts in the Study of Religious Communities." Paper presented at the annual meeting of the Association for the Sociology of Religion, New York.

———. 2001. Vulnerability and Objectivity in the Participant Observation of the Sacred. In *Toward Reflexive Ethnography: Participating, Observing, Narrating*, ed. David G. Bromley and Lewis Carter, 223–45. Oxford: Elsevier Science.

Zablocki, Benjamin, and Thomas Robbins, eds. 2001. *Misunderstanding Cults: Searching for Objectivity in a Controversial Field*. Toronto: University of Toronto Press.

New Religious Movements, Countermovements, Moral Panics, and the Media

James T. Richardson and Massimo Introvigne

The modern phenomenon of new religious movements (NRMs) originated in the late 1960s and early 1970s mainly in the United States, but then spread to other parts of the world, including especially Western Europe. NRMs have generated considerable interest and concern among members of the general public as well as among societal leaders since their inception. Why these movements developed at this time in modern Western societies has been the subject of much speculation and research (Anthony and Robbins 1982; Bellah 1976; Tipton 1982; Wuthnow 1976).

NRMs were first greeted in the U.S. context as a welcome respite from the throes of anti–Vietnam War demonstrations and other civil disturbances and social movements. However, concern developed rapidly as word spread of many young people's getting involved with "high-demand" NRMs that were encouraging or even requiring major changes in lifestyle and career plans. While the number of young people joining NRMs was never large in proportional terms, the numbers were large enough to attract the attention of public officials and the media. Some parents of those joining the groups were particularly concerned about their offspring giving up career plans for a life devoted to the strange teachings of a little known religious figure. Particularly noteworthy was the social origin of most recruits, who tended to be from relatively well-educated and affluent backgrounds. Why significant numbers of the best educated and most affluent generation in American history turned to various new forms of religion became a major question for many, as the societies affected by NRMs grappled with the meaning of this unexpected development of interest in religion among some of its youth.

Parents, siblings, and friends of many NRM recruits occupied social locations within American society that facilitated drawing attention to the issues
raised by the development of NRMs. When parents became concerned at
news that their son or daughter had dropped out of college to join one of the
new NRM groups, they were socially well connected enough to garner attention from media and societal leaders to their perceived problem. Contacts
with the media and political leaders followed, with predictable effects. The concerns of parents resonated with the values of those in positions of societal
leadership, in part because of their similar social origins. Indeed, there are
anecdotes of children of societal leaders joining the NRMs, a development that
made real the grounds for the reactions expressed by some parents of NRM
participants.

As concern grew over NRMs, intense social responses to NRMs occurred
in the form of a countermovement, a hostile public reaction, and scathing media coverage. Given the forcefulness of the responses to NRMs, it is impossible to understand their organizational development without incorporating the
societal reactions to them. These responses offer clear illustrations of some
important concepts from the studies of social movements, deviance, and the
mass media. This chapter will focus on the concept of the *countermovement*,
from the social movements literature, and on the idea of *moral panic*, from
deviance studies, as key ways to understand the societal reactions to NRMs. We
will also examine the crucial role played by the media in countermovements and
moral panics.

Countermovements

Many social movements provoke countermovements led by those opposed to
the values and actions of the initial movement. NRMs are no exception to this
general rule. Indeed, NRMs rather quickly found themselves collectively and
individually doing battle with various organizations whose purpose was to
oppose specific NRMs or NRMs in general. These organizations, referred to
collectively as the anti-cult movement (ACM), were based on the assumption
that the majority of NRMs were destructive to individuals, families, and even
societies. The broad movement opposing NRMs, which has been referred to
as an "international social movement industry" (Shupe and Bromley 1994a:
viii), has been studied by a few scholars (e.g., Shupe and Bromley 1980,
1994a), but not nearly as much as have the various movements that led to the
rise of the ACM. Shupe, Bromley, and Darnell (2004: 185) note that countermovements such as the ACM derive their "organization purpose from the
existence of other movements." This symbiotic relationship is the most important aspect of an explanation of countermovements such as the ACM.

As Massimo Introvigne (1993, 1995) notes, the ACM can usefully be sub-
divided into two components that are significantly different in their approach
to NRMs. Introvigne refers to one major branch of the ACM as the counter-
cult movement (CCM), by which he means an ideologically oriented

countermovement that focuses on the *content* of the beliefs of NRMs. CCM groups, which are mainly made up of evangelical Protestant ministers and laypeople, are concerned about NRMs' drawing young people away from the "true faith" of evangelical Christianity. CCM participants assert that NRMs represent false religions and that their heresy is grounds for opposing them. Indeed, the strength of opposition from CCMs is sometimes formidable, deriving as it does from a tendency for CCM participants to define NRMs as false religions and even evil (see Cowan 2003). Introvigne (1995) observes that it is problematic for CCM groups to promote "brainwashing"-based interpretations of participation in NRMs, given that CCM groups are themselves often members of conversionist-oriented religious groups, which are also subject to charges of brainwashing. However, this problem has sometimes been overcome, as CCM and secular ACM participants work together for the common cause of opposing NRMs. (See Shterin and Richardson 2002 for one example of such cooperation in a major legal case in Russia.)

The other branch of the ACM represents itself as secular in its focus; it is concerned with the actions taken by NRMs to recruit and maintain participants, instead of group doctrines. Participants in this branch are often nonreligious secular humanists or members of the mental health profession (or both), although there is a smattering of other professionals, such as ministers and rabbis, as well as members of the legal profession. The focus on *behaviors* is used as a justification by the secular branch of the ACM for actions taken to suppress participation in NRMs. The claim is that the behaviors used by NRMs to recruit and keep members are misleading at best and coercive at worst. "Deed, not creeds" is the motto of this branch of the ACM, a mantra used as a rationale for social-control efforts. The underpinning for this justification is the "action versus belief" distinction that permeates legal considerations in the United States, where efforts are being made to suppress groups claiming to be religious.

The organizational structure and ideological posture of both types of ACM groups are worthy of examination. There are several types of participants in ACM groups, including those who have a relative or friend involved in an NRM, those who claim that their professional expertise can assist with removing or counseling those in NRMs, and those former members of NRMs who have chosen to participate in an ACM group. There is sometimes an overlap in categories, especially the latter two, as a number of "deprogrammers" and "exit counselors" (terms made part of the lexicon by the ACM) are former members of NRMs themselves (i.e., Hassan 1988). There is also a significant difference in the type of professional involved in the two segments of the ACM, with mental health professionals and lawyers dominating the more secular ACM organizations while pastors, usually of more evangelical orientation, have leadership roles in CCM groups.

Each of the three major categories of participants in ACM groups plays an important role in the group. The first group (those concerned about a friend or family member in an NRM) furnishes the resources necessary for ACM groups to function, as well as the primary reason for the groups to exist. The second category (professional experts) furnishes legitimation for the group by allowing the members' professional credentials to be used in furtherance of the particular cause of the ACM group. Also, the professionals help develop and promote an ideological position used to warrant the interventions called for by the group. The latter category (former NRM members), although representing a minuscule percentage of former NRM members, also helps with legitimation and ideological justification by claiming first-hand experience with the "evil cult" from whence they somehow escaped (often through being deprogrammed themselves (see Bromley 1998; Lewis 1986).

As Shupe and Bromley (1994b) note, there has been considerable organizational evolution of the ACMs over the decades of their existence. Originally ACM groups were local or at best regional informal groupings of people, mostly parents of NRM members. However, eventually some national organizations coalesced out of these early efforts, and more professional leadership was attracted. The ACM organizations that survived became more professional in their orientation and more sophisticated in their tactics (Shupe and Bromley 1994b: 9–24). Although hampered in the United States by lack of direct governmental support (unlike similar groups that developed in Europe; see Richardson and Introvigne 2001), these self-help groups have managed to impact popular perceptions and even public policy toward NRMs.

Development of a sound ideological basis for interventions has been crucial to the success of ACM groups as they have evolved. Given the tradition of a First Amendment guarantee of religious freedom in the United States, coupled with the fact that most participants in NRMs are of legal age, considerable effort has been required to develop a rationale that justifies the existence of ACM groups, as well as their efforts to exert control over NRM groups and individual members. The ideological basis that was promoted made use of the brainwashing metaphor derived from the Korean War experience of a few POWs staying in Korea after the war, as well as the experience referred to as "thought reform" by Robert Lifton in his study of resocialization techniques used after the communist takeover in China (Lifton 1963).

The brainwashing idea was then popularized by coverage of the Patty Hearst trial (Fort 1979; Richardson and Kilbourne 1983) and became available as a culturally acceptable explanation of why otherwise intelligent and well-educated young people would participate in strange religions. Although the brainwashing concept had little basis in scientific fact (Anthony 1990; Anthony and Robbins 2004; Richardson 1993a), it became a ready social weapon to use against unpopular NRMs (Bromley and Richardson 1983; Richardson 1991). Efforts to employ the brainwashing metaphor against NRMs, especially in legal cases, were initially quite successful (Richardson 1995). However, eventually the lack of a scientific basis for use of the term in such a voluntaristic context, as is usually the case with NRMs, was demonstrated to the courts, and usage of the term declined (Anthony and Robbins 1995; Richardson 1993a). As Shupe and Bromley (1994b: 9–24) and Anthony (1990) and Anthony and Robbins (2004) noted, ACM experts became more sophisticated over time in their claims about the process of recruitment and retention in NRMs, and they shifted the jargon from simple brainwashing to other mental health and medical terms that seemed more substantial and defensible. Terms such as *post-traumatic stress syndrome* and *dissociative states* came to be used as explanatory devices, as efforts were continued to define participation as a mental health problem instead of a religious choice made by legal adults (Richardson 1993b).

Thus participation in NRMs became "medicalized" (Richardson and Stewart 2004), which helped the ACM groups avoid First Amendment issues in attacking NRMs in the United States. This "medical" approach was also used by ACM groups in other countries (Anthony and Robbins 2004; Richardson 1996), and it became the dominant method of exerting control over NRMs during the last few decades. In the European context, the term *mental manipulation* was the equivalent of the term *brainwashing* in the United States, and was an approach promoted especially by European ACM groups and even some governments such as in France and Belgium (Duvert 2004; Fautré 2004; Richardson and Introvigne 2001).

The key elements of the ACM countermovement, therefore, include its ideology (the argument that brainwashing or mind control reduces the capacity of NRM affiliates to make autonomous, voluntaristic choices), countermovement organizations (that served to mobilize troubled family members, petition governmental officials, and enlist support from the media to influence public opinion); rituals through which NRM affiliates can be separated from groups (the deprogramming ritual designed to pressure individuals to renounce their affiliations), and apostates (former NRM members who affiliate with the ACM and offer personal testimony to cultic manipulation).

Moral Panics about New Religious Movements

One way to view the organizational goals of ACM groups is as attempting to promote "moral panics" about NRMs. The term *moral panic* first appeared in print in the 1970s, most notably in a book by Stanley Cohen (1972) entitled *Folk Devils and Moral Panics*, which offered an explanation for the exaggerated response to hooliganism by "mods and rockers" in England in the early 1960s. Cohen was struck by the "fundamentally inappropriate" reaction to relatively minor events involving some juvenile vandalism that occurred in one small seaside resort in England.

The term moral panic has become prominent in the sociology of deviance, as demonstrated by the well-received volume by Eric Goode and Nachman Ben-Yehuda (1994) entitled *Moral Panics: The Social Construction of Deviance*. As a part of their analysis, Goode and Ben-Yehuda present descriptions of major actors in the development of moral panics. Included are (1) the press, (2) the public, (3) law enforcement, (4) politicians and legislators, (5) action groups, and (6) "folk devils." They also discuss the application of the "disaster analogy" to the idea of moral panics, a term which refers to the tendency to refer to the object of a developing moral panic in terms reminiscent of a natural disaster, such as a flood or earthquake.

A number of studies of deviance have made use of the concept of moral panic or related terms over the past few decades as a part of the "constructionist" perspective taken from deviance studies (Jenkins 1992, 1998; Richardson, Best, and Bromley 1991). Surprisingly, the important volume by Goode and Ben-Yehuda (1994), while discussing many historical examples of moral panics involving religion, does not deal with the moral panic that developed concerning NRMs, except for references to "atrocity tales" circulated about the Unificationist movement (Bromley, Shupe, and Ventimiglia 1979). However, Introvigne (1999a, 2000) has examined the social reaction to NRMs in terms of a moral-panic episode.

The term moral panic refers to situations in which something that has been defined as a social problem becomes the focus of exaggerated attention from media, politicians and other opinion leaders, law enforcement, and action groups. The thrust of the focused effort is to garner public support to take action against the perceived problem. Social problems are themselves socially constructed, as has been shown by numerous studies. For example, Kitsuse (1962) discusses the lack of relationship between objective reality and activities that come to be designated as social problems. The negative definition of NRMs that developed soon after NRMs began attracting public attention in American society is a good example of this process of social construction and political negotiation.

Defining something as a social problem constitutes one level of concern for the populace and government officials, and this occurred early in the response to NRMs. However, to move beyond this designation into the realm of a moral panic represents a significant escalation of concern about a given social problem. Such a change usually means that some organizational effort has been successful at redefining the social problem at issue. In the case of NRMs, it is clear that the efforts of some ACM "action groups," which Goode and Ben-Yehuda (1994: 28) refer to as "moral entrepreneurs" (using the term from Becker 1963: 147–63), have been crucial. Especially the influence of ACM groups on the mass media has contributed greatly to the moral panic that developed over NRMs during the latter part of the last century.

A moral panic could be construed as resulting from the "overconstruction" of a social problem, whereby misleading and even false information is developed and disseminated by those promoting the moral panic. This promotional activity raises concern, and even fear, among the public that is greatly disproportionate to the actual threat to society. The issue becomes prevalence, not existence, and the overall effort is to exploit a few occurrences to convince the public and government officials that such occurrences are much more frequent and dangerous than they actually are.

"Folk statistics" demonstrating the alleged threat are treated as accurate and are spread by whatever means is available, usually including and especially the mass media. An example of such a folk statistic discussed by Goode and Ben-Yehuda (1994: 57) is the widely disseminated claim that 50,000 children were being murdered every year in America by Satanists. This same claim also was found in research in Australia and New Zealand, where it played a key role in the social construction of the "Satanism scare" in that part of the world (Richardson 1997b). Analogous "statistics" have been bandied about by ACM groups concerning how many people have been involved in NRMs; however, as Shupe and Bromley have noted (1994b: 15), the total number of participants in communal NRMs—the ones engendering greatest concern—was never more than 25,000 at any one time in the United States. But the amount of air time and column inches given to the alleged cult problem led many to conclude that the numbers (and the threat) were much greater than was actually the case.

Moral panics also always involve the development of "folk devils." As Goode and Ben-Yehuda (1994: 28) note, "A folk devil is the personification of evil." They go on to state,

> All moral panics, by their very nature, identify, denounce, and attempt to root out folk devils. . . . Folk devils are *deviants*; they are engaged in wrong-doing; their actions are harmful to society; they are selfish and evil; they must be stopped, their actions neutralized. (29)

The ACM developed both a generalized folk devil and some specific ones over the years in their efforts to oppose NRMs. The generalized version of an NRM folk devil is the mysterious guru with all-powerful psychological techniques for hypnotizing or brainwashing those who come within his grasp. Something of a Pied Piper myth developed concerning leaders of NRMs: America's youth were considered by some ACM leaders to be defenseless against the wiles of these all-powerful gurus. There was some specific focus on a few NRM leaders, such as David Berg, who founded the The Family International (originally the Children of God), and especially the Reverend Sun Myung Moon, founder of the Unificationist Church (UC). Public opinion data from two decades ago suggest that Reverend Moon may have been the most hated and feared person in America at that time—this in spite of the fact that Unificationist membership was relatively small and that few people had actually ever met a member of the UC (Bromley and Breschel 1992; Richardson 1992). Given his oriental origins and the way in which Unificationist actions (such as mass weddings) drew public attention to the movement, Moon served as a proto-typical folk devil and was an important target person for the ACM.

An example of a moral panic that reveals how NRMs can become implicated in seemingly unrelated events occurred in Italy in 2004. A heavy-metal rock band, The Beasts of Satan, was found to be responsible for three or more murders that were committed in ways that suggested Satanic ritual elements were involved. Both secular ACM and CCM groups in Italy immediately exploited this development, claiming that the group was part of an international Satanic conspiracy involving as many as 500,000 people in Italy and that this incident was an example of the evils brought on by cults. Given the paucity of real ex-members of virtually nonexistent Satanic groups in Italy, the mass media, especially talk shows on radio and television, made use of other former cult (NRM) members, some of whom were quite willing to say that their former cult was "just as bad" as Satanism. This joining of Satanism and NRMs contributed at the time to the development of a relatively short-lived moral panic in Italy.

Sects and cults (the popular, negative, way of referring to NRMs) have often been seen as quintessential targets of moral panics. They are politically weak, usually unpopular because of their strange-appearing beliefs and practices, and are perceived as disruptive of the normal life of ordinary families, given their tendency to recruit the youth of the society. Jenkins states,

> Sects perform a convenient integrative function by providing a
> common enemy, a "dangerous outsider" against which the main-
> stream can unite and reassert its standards and beliefs. Depending on
> the legal and cultural environment of a given society, the tension
> between sects and the mainstream community might result in active
> persecution or it can take the form of ostracism and negative stereo-
> typing. (1996: 158)

Media and New Religious Movements

It is no accident that Goode and Ben-Yehuda (1994) give primacy to the press in their discussion of the various key "actors in the drama of moral panics." They discuss press coverage of the mods and rockers episode in England as involving "exaggerated attention, exaggerated events, distortion, and stereotyping." They discuss "over-reporting" of events and the use of language to make the episodes seem more serious than they were (1994: 24–25). They note the stereotypic pattern of reporting and state,

> The press ... put together a composite picture, containing a number
> of central elements. It was almost as if a new story could be written
> simply by stitching these elements together. There was very little
> interest in what actually happened; what counted was how closely a
> news account conformed to a stereotype. (25–26)

In short, one indication that a moral panic is taking place is the stereotypical fashion in which the subject is treated in the press.

ACM groups of both types make heavy use of the media. Indeed, arguably the mass media are the most important resource available to the ACM industry. The media also make use of ACM groups and are often willing to publish articles or produce television and radio programs that promote implicitly or explicitly the views of the broader ACM. This occurs in part because of a confluence of values between ACM leadership and those directing the media. (See Richardson 1996 for examples of this sharing of common values, and Beckford 1985 for an analysis of other factors influencing NRM coverage by the media.)

When NRMs first appeared on the media scene, little research was done about the role played by the media in the anti-cult scare. There was an initial assumption that NRMs were widespread, which would explain why so many people had opinions and some knowledge of them. However, when scholarly research revealed that there were relatively few NRMs and most were small, there was a question about why such strong negative opinions were so widespread among both elites and the general public (Bromley and Breschel 1992; Richardson 1992). This question led to a focus on the function of the media in disseminating information about NRMs. One notable Gallup Poll demonstrated this large role: over 90 percent of people interviewed had negative feelings about Reverend Moon and his followers, but only 2 percent admitted to ever having seen a member of the UC! Somehow people were forming opinions without direct experience, and the media seemed the most likely candidate responsible for "informing" the public.

Eventually some serious research was done on media coverage of NRMs to test the assumptions being made about the impact the media had on perceptions concerning NRMs. There have been several major studies of media treatments of NRMs, including in the United States (van Driel and Richardson 1988a, 1988b), Europe, and the United Kingdom (Beckford 1985; Beckford and Coles 1988; Richardson 1997a; Selway 1992). There have also been focused studies dealing with related major events, such as the conflagration at Waco in 1993 (Richardson 1995; Shupe and Hadden 1995).

Much of this research was based on content analysis of print media coverage in an effort to find out what some media outlets were reporting about NRMs and what the tone was of the coverage. This approach was first used by van Driel and Richardson (1988a), and then also applied in Australia (Selway 1992) and the United Kingdom (Beckford and Coles 1988). Results of the research have been remarkably consistent. Although the amount of media coverage has varied somewhat, and journalists have become somewhat more discerning in their coverage over time, the overwhelming finding has been extreme negativity in coverage of NRMs. This negativity has been demonstrated by the choice of language (cult versus new religion, for instance, and a strong tendency to use terms like brainwashing to describe recruitment practices) and by the selection of "experts" quoted in the stories (that is, ACM spokespersons dominated, with scholars of religion left out). In-depth reporting seldom occurred; instead, a "stream of controversies" (Beckford 1985) approach was used, with the media feeding on these controversies for material rather than journalists conducting serious investigative reporting.

This research did not explain the negativity of media coverage, which was the focus of a subsequent study on the attitudes of journalists who wrote stories about NRMs (Richardson and van Driel 1997). All journalists who had written stories in the earlier content-analysis research of van Driel and Richardson were sent questionnaires in an attempt to assess their attitudes toward NRMs and their knowledge of them. The mailing list of the Religious Writers Association was also purchased, which included about three hundred members, and they were also sent the questionnaire. Response rates were low but the responses were revealing. Journalists who responded knew very little about the scholarly research on NRMs, and they were prone to regard the groups as deviant entities in need of control. They were likely to accept the brainwashing/mind control explanations for why people participate in NRMs. Indeed, some respondents even indicated being willing to serve as moral entrepreneurs—something that Beckford (1985) had also noted in his earlier research in the U.K., in which he found that some journalists even referred people who had contacted them to ACM organizations.

These findings about journalists' stories about NRMs are revealing, as they demonstrate that reporters may be disposed to participate in campaigns to develop moral panics about NRMs. Most journalists producing stories on NRMs possess little knowledge of the groups about which they are writing, and they share the values of the dominant culture, which are at odds with the values espoused by most NRMs. Thus most journalists (and perhaps, by extension, editors and publishers) seem quite willing to jump on the ACM bandwagon and defend the normative values of the society of which they are a part. Few journalists seem cognizant of issues concerning religious freedom; instead, they seem willing to participate in developing moral panics about NRMs, not only in the United States but in other countries as well. Thus representatives of the media in effect play a key role in the efforts of countermovements to promote concern and even moral panic about NRMs.

Suggestions for Classroom Interactions

In assessing how to teach students about ACMs and CCMs in a way that is both insightful and reasonably balanced, it is important to remember that college students are by no means immune to misconceptions about popular culture. On many unfamiliar subjects, students—like other members of society—rely on media accounts, fiction, and popular culture. Even graduate students of religion, who might be expected to be more knowledgeable, are likely to reveal popular misconceptions, such as that all NRMs members are brainwashed, all cults are dangerous, and Satanists engage in child sacrifice. These preconceptions must be taken into account with any assignments designed to help students understand NRMs and the controversies surrounding them. The suggestions that follow are premised on the assumption that students have been familiarized with a countermovement and/or moral framework for interpretive activity.

It is also important to apprise students of the role that NRM scholars have played in the public controversy over cults. Some prominent academic scholars of NRMs have been personally involved in the "cult wars." (See Introvigne 2001; Richardson 1998 for discussion by this chapter's authors about their personal involvement in the cult wars.) They have debunked folk theories about cults and sometimes have been accused by ACMs or CCMs of being "cult apologists." Some ACM Web sites maintain lists of academics singled out as "cult apologists," where students may perhaps find their teachers or the authors of their textbooks. It is therefore useful to discuss with students how studying NRMs, the ACMs, and the CCM has involved NRM scholars as both researchers and participants in the controversies surrounding NRMs. (See David Bromley's chapter in this volume for an extended discussion of methodological issues in the study of NRMs.)

Both the countermovement and moral panic perspectives are informative on this point, as each perspective offers an explanation for why academic researchers are likely to become targets of the countermovement or moral crusade. Moral panic theory is a valuable interpretive tool because it maintains that moral panics are usually based on actual problems and dangers that have been amplified rather than invented by moral entrepreneurs within movements such as the ACM and CCM. The allegations of these movements therefore should not be dismissed, but rather the nature, form, and process of problem construction by oppositional groups can be explained and interpreted in ways that this volume suggests. In its focus on alliance building, countermovement theory is useful in interpreting the way that the confluence of values between ACM representatives and societal leaders has helped the ACM and CCM influence the media, politicians, and general public.

Teaching about countermovements, moral panics, and the media offers a unique opportunity to show the social response to NRMs. A variety of assignments and exercises can be used to demonstrate the predictability of the occurrence and the forms that current social opposition to NRMs take, how public perceptions of NRMs are distorted, the dynamics of moral-panic episodes, and the nature of subversion claims that emerge. Assignments can include both written and oral presentations and exercises that allow students to creatively implement the perspective they have gained from their reading.

It may be useful to establish that the contemporary crusades against cults and sects are by no means new or unique. If students can understand how intense societal tensions can produce new movements and simultaneously the social reactions to these new movements, they will be oriented toward interpreting the sociocultural conditions under which these movements and societal reactions occur. Creating a cognitive distance by examining historical cases can be very helpful in this regard, and there is substantial literature on nineteenth-century anti-Mormonism and anti-Catholicism (Billington 1962; Davis 1960; Higham 1955; Miller 1983) for this purpose. Instructors can provide baseline information on historical anti-cult campaigns and ask students to compare these with contemporary anti-cultism. Alternatively, students can read both historical and contemporary sources and conduct the comparison via oral or written reports. The allegations of mind control and social subversion made against Mormons and Catholics (Arrington 1968; Bunker and Bitton 1975; Davis 1960) are strikingly similar to allegations made today against contemporary groups (Bromley, Shupe, and Ventimiglia 1979; Lewis 2003: 155–213; Richardson and Kilbourne 1983). Apostate accounts, a major source of these allegations, can also be employed for comparisons of historical and contemporary groups (Bromley 1988a, 1988b). There are numerous apostate accounts available for comparing nineteenth-century Catholicism, some of which have been reprinted (Johnson 1998; Monk 1836/1977), and Mormonism (Givens 1997; Launius and Thatcher 1994; Miller 1983), particularly with contemporary Unificationism (Edwards 1979; Elkins 1980; Swatland and Swatland 1982; Underwood and Underwood 1979). The way these important figures in countermovements and moral panics have been created and used to heighten a sense of public danger is central to understanding the intensity of societal reactions to NRMs. These figures are particularly instructive because, in some cases, their biographies have been almost completely fabricated and because they have had an impact significantly disproportionate to their numbers or influence within their respective groups (Bromley 1998; Johnson 1998). At the same time, it is important not to conflate countermovement-sponsored apostates with other former movement members or to a priori discredit all former-member accounts. (See Stuart Wright's chapter in this volume for perspective on the processes of joining and exiting NRMs that characterizes most participants' experiences, as well as Richardson, van der Lans, and Derks 1986.) Former members have in a number of cases provided valuable insights into the internal dynamics of movements (Hong 1998; Muster 1997; Williams 1998) and are an important component of the methodological strategy for basing assessments on a strategy of triangulation (Carter 1998; Richardson, Balch, and Melton 1993).

Another way of demonstrating the existence and impact of counter-movement activity and moral panics is through simple class exercises. For example, Pfeifer (1992) conducted a quasi-experiment in which students were provided with a brief paragraph describing an intensive socialization experience. The socialization experience was attributed to one of three groups: Unificationist recruits, marines in boot camp, or monastic novitiates. Based on this simple description, respondents were asked to assess the psychological characteristics of the putative affiliates. Not surprisingly, negative personal characteristics were most often attributed to Unificationists, despite the fact that respondents had virtually no personal knowledge of Unificationism and had never met a Unificationist. This exercise could easily be replicated in a classroom situation, using a currently high-profile NRM, or students could conduct the experiment with a sample of acquaintances.

An even simpler exercise is to ask class participants themselves to estimate the membership size, or solicit estimates from a sample of acquaintances, of better known, controversial NRMs for which membership estimates are reasonably reliable. Countermovement activity and moral panics almost always result in significantly inflated estimates of the size for groups perceived as dangerous. The first author of this chapter demonstrated this tendency when teaching a class of judges in the summer of 1986. During a course on social and behavioral sciences and the law, he was asked to talk about his research on NRMs. He did this by first asking the class of a dozen judges from around the country how many members of the Unificationist movement they thought were in the country. Estimates ranged from 300,000 to 1.5 million. The judges were astounded to be told that there had never been more than 10,000 Unificationists in the United States at any one time and that current membership was probably less than 3,000.

Either of these exercises leads naturally to a discussion of where individuals obtain information about NRMs, how distorted information is generated and circulated, what groups have an interest in generating discrediting or threatening information about NRMs, and why corrective processes fail to operate during periods of heightened tensions. The dynamics of moral panics can be documented by comparing various instances of panic episodes. The comparison process will reveal the common elements described by Goode and Ben-Yehuda (1994). A variety of contemporary panic episodes are readily available for comparison purposes, such as drugs (Reinarman and Levine 1997) and child endangerment (Best 1990; Jenkins 1998). A rich compilation of theory and research has been produced on the outbreak of fears of Satanic cults. This episode is particularly useful because it is contemporary and there are readily available sources that can be used to compare the claims of the countersubversion movement (Kahaner 1988; Raschke 1990; Terry 1987) with social scientific analyses of the moral panic episode (Ellis 2000; Richardson, Best, and Bromley 1991; Victor 1993). There are also direct comparisons of the anti-cult and anti-Satanic episodes (Bromley 1994; Bromley and Cutchin 1999) and apostate accounts by individuals claiming to have been members of Satanic groups (Smith and Pazder 1980; Stratford 1988), along with critical analyses of their claims (Hernstein and Trott 1993; Mulhern 1991). An excellent, easily accessible video resource on moral panics about Satanic cults that captures the qualities of moral panics and contains cult stereotypes is the award-winning 1995 television movie *Indictment: The McMartin Trial*. The McMartin case was one of the most sensational Satanic cult cases, in which daycare center operators were accused of committing multiple instances of sexual abuse and homicide, an indictment largely based on the testimony of young children whose accounts were the product of social worker investigatory techniques (Mulhern 1991; Nathan 1991).

The cult controversy offers an intriguing opportunity to examine the subversion claims generated by the anti-cult movement against the critique of those claims by NRM scholars. Students have an opportunity to read and analyze work by anti-cult proponents, such as leading ACM representative Margaret Singer (1979, 1995) and CCM figure Walter Martin. Singer's *Cults in Our Midst* (1995) and Martin's *The Kingdom of the Cults* (1977) are classic works in their respective genres. These treatments of NRMs can be compared with a variety of works by NRM scholars that conceptualize the groups under study as new religious movements rather than cults, offer ethnographic descriptions designed to provide insight into members' perspectives rather than evaluative claims about dangerous and destructive groups, and link affiliation with NRMs through socialization rather than brainwashing models. A variety of texts that interpret NRMs from this perspective are available for comparison with anti-cult claims (Bainbridge 1997; Chryssides 1999;

Dawson 1998, 2003; Hunt 2003). Timothy Miller's volume, *America's Alternative Religions* (1995), illustrates NRM scholars' descriptions of a range of NRMs. Direct analyses of the ACM (Shupe and Bromley 1980) and the CCM (Cowan 2003) are also available. A single source that encompasses the debates over cults, and brainwashing in particular, is Zablocki and Robbins's *Misunderstanding Cults* (2001).

A comparable view of the debates can be gained through an examination of Web sites. A good example of an ACM-oriented Web site is one maintained by Rick Ross (www.rickross.com), while Anton Hein's Web site exemplifies a CCM viewpoint (www.apologeticsindex.org). Comparable institutionally supported Web sites include those of the International Cultic Study Association (www.csj.org) and the Christian Research Institute (www.equip.org). More academically oriented Web sites include the New Religious Movements Homepage (http://religiousmovements.lib.virginia.edu) and the Center for the Study of New Religions Web site (www.cesnur.org). Using either published works or Web sites, students can prepare summations of anti-cult claims and NRM scholars' critiques of those claims.

Students can gain perspective on the policy implications of the cult controversy by analyzing the 1986 Report of the Task Force on Deceptive and Indirect Techniques of Persuasion and Control (DIMPAC), available at www.cesnur.org/testi/DIMPAC.htm. The DIMPAC report was submitted to the American Psychological Association (APA) by a commission chaired by Margaret Singer; it summarizes the rationale offered for the position of the ACMs in the late 1980s. (The report ultimately was not accepted by the APA.) Students can then use the reviews prepared by APA official reviewers Benjamin Beit-Hallahmi (a scholar who is himself close to the ACMs) and Jeffrey D. Fisher (available at www.cesnur.org/testi/APA.htm) to identify the basis on which anti-cult claims have been critiqued.

All of the exercises described above draw on scholarly, media, or countermovement sources. An alternative exercise that enlists student creativity is to create a fictional description of a cult. As an example, the information provided to students would be as follows: A famous movie star, Heidi Bulla, has converted to a religious group known as the Holy Fourthinity, of which little is known. It is known that the group numbers at most a few hundred, that most members are in their late teens to early twenties, that members live communally, and that the group discourages all contact with family members and former acquaintances. However, the only available information on the group is contained in two documents:

1. A pamphlet produced by the movement that describes the revolutionary discovery of its founder, Brother Four. According to the pamphlet, the traditional Christian doctrine of the Trinity is based on historical errors, faulty interpretations, and the fact that the Christian churches have ignored a key Gnostic document known as the Gospel of Fire. This document has not been referred to by any historian and reportedly was lost in the second century c.e.; it has

now been revealed by Jesus Christ to Brother Four. The core of the revelation is that there is a fourth person of the Trinity—the Spirit of Fire—and that this Spirit must be honored in order to gain enlightenment and salvation. The Spirit of Fire requests from his followers worship through certain secret rites during which they light a fire and ceremonially dance around it to signify their spiritual rebirth.

2. A memorandum sent to the news media by a former member, Charity Candid, claiming that Brother Four has brainwashed her and that the Fire ceremony is an intense ritual that extends over many hours during which members are placed in a trancelike state by the ritualized singing and dancing. These rituals presage advanced, secret rituals that allegedly involve members engaging in sexual relationships with Brother Four. Both the movement and other former members have vehemently denied Ms. Candid's charges, responding that Candid was a disgruntled member whose sexual advances were rejected by Brother Four. As a result of the claims and counter-claims, journalists have pressed the group and its opponents for information, and undercover investigative reports are being prepared.

The exercise involves, in the first stage, building on the information provided here and preparing both the movement's pamphlet describing its beliefs, organization, and ritual practices and the text of Charity Candid's memorandum containing an exposé of the group as a dangerous cult. In the second stage, students are divided into three groups, asked to write respectively a short article for an anti-cult magazine, for an evangelical counter-cult magazine, and for a scholarly Web site describing the movement. All groups will use as primary material the pamphlet they have prepared and Ms. Candid's memorandum. The article for the anti-cult magazine should apply the anti-cult model to the Holy Fourthinity. The counter-cult article, while including (as most counter-cult material now does) elements of the anti-cult model, should discuss the Spirit of Fire doctrine as heretical. These articles may be organized as papers or class presentations.

If this exercise is successful, a more advanced exercise can have students stage a court trial in which former members are suing the group and its leaders for fraud and for the tort of "intentional affliction of emotional distress" resulting from the intense group rituals and high social control. The group's defense is that the former members were adults who made a voluntary choice and now regret that choice. The trial pits the cult and NRM models against one another, and reveals in a more dramatic fashion the complexity of sorting out and assessing competing claims in a contested situation. In the aftermath of the trial, students can be asked to reflect on the larger implications for religious freedom, depending on the outcome of the trial.

The larger objective of these exercises is to develop critical thinking and analysis skills in the context of a conflict that has now spanned several decades. By thinking through the intense controversy encompassing NRMs, students become more adept at understanding the social and cultural forces that shape events around them as well as their personal lives. From this perspective, a sophisticated understanding of the NRM controversy can serve as a template for examining a range of other ongoing conflicts and controversies in the public arena.

REFERENCES

Anthony, Dick. 1990. "Religious Movements and Brainwashing Litigation: Evaluating Key Testimony." In *In Gods We Trust*, 2nd ed., ed. Thomas Robbins and Dick Anthony, 295–344. New Brunswick, NJ: Transaction.

Anthony, Dick, and Thomas Robbins. 1982. "Contemporary Religious Ferment and Moral Ambiguity." In *New Religious Movements: A Perspective for Understanding Society*, ed. Eileen Barker, 243–63. New York: Edwin Mellen Press.

———. 1995. "Negligence, Coercion and the Protection of Religious Belief." *Journal of Church and State* 37, 509–36.

———. 2004. "Pseudoscience versus Minority Religions: An Evaluation of the Brainwashing Theories of Jean-Marie Abgrall." In *Regulating Religions: Case Studies from around the Globe*, ed. James Richardson, 151–78. New York: Kluwer.

Arrington, Leonard, and John Haupt.1968. "Intolerable Zion: The Image of Mormonism in Nineteenth-Century American Literature." *Western Humanities Review* 22, 243–60.

Bainbridge, William Sims. 1997. *The Sociology of Religious Movements*. New York: Routledge.

Beadle, John Hanson. 1877. "The Mormon Theocracy." *Scribner's Monthly* 14 (July), 391–401.

Becker, Howard. 1963. *Outsiders: Studies in the Sociology of Deviance*. New York: Free Press.

Beckford, James A. 1985. *Cult Controversies: The Societal Response to New Religious Movements*. London: Tavistock.

Beckford, James, and M. Coles. 1988. "British and American Responses to New Religious Movements." *Bulletin of the John Rylands University Library of Manchester* 70, 209–24.

Bellah, Robert. 1976. "New Religious Consciousness and the Crisis of Modernity." In *The New Religious Consciousness*, ed. Charles Glock and Robert Bellah, 333–52. Berkeley: University of California Press.

Best, Joel. 1990. *Threatened Children: Rhetoric and Concern about Child-Victims*. Chicago: University of Chicago Press.

Billington, Ray Allen. 1962. *The Origins of Nativism in the United States, 1800–1844*. New York: Arno Press.

Bromley, David G. 1988a. "Deprogramming as a Mode of Exit from New Religious Movements: The Case of the Unificationist Movement." In *Falling From the Faith*, ed. David G. Bromley, 166–84. Newbury Park, CA: Sage.

———, ed. 1988b. *Falling from the Faith: Causes and Consequences of Religious Apostasy*. Newbury Park, CA: Sage.

———. 1994. "The Social Construction of Subversion: A Comparison of Anti-Religious and Anti-Satanic Cult Narratives." In *Anti-Cult Movements in Cross-Cultural Perspectives*, ed. Anson Shupe and David G. Bromley, 49–76. New York: Garland.

———, ed. 1998. *The Politics of Religious Apostasy: The Role of Apostates in the Transformation of Religious Movements*. Westport, CT: Praeger.

Bromley, David G., and Edward F. Breschel. 1992. "General Population and Institutional Elite Perceptions of Cults: Evidence from National Survey Data." *Behavioral Sciences and the Law* 10, 39–52.

Bromley, David G., and Diana Gay Cutchin. 1999. "The Social Construction of Subversive Evil: The Contemporary Anti-Cult and Anti-Satanism Movements." In *Waves of Protest.* ed. Jo Freeman, 195–220. Lanham, MD: Rowman and Littlefield.

Bromley, David G., and James T. Richardson, eds. 1983. *The Brainwashing/Deprogramming Controversy: Historical, Sociological, Psychological and Legal Perspectives.* New York: Edwin Mellen Press.

Bromley, David G., Shupe, Anson D., and Joseph C. Ventimiglia. 1979. "Atrocity Tales, the Unification Church, and the Social Construction of Evil." *Journal of Communication* 29, 42–53.

Bunker, Gary, and David Bitton. 1975. "Mesmerism and Mormonism." *BYU Studies* 15, 146–70.

Carter, Lewis. 1998. "Carriers of Tales: On Assessing Credibility of Apostate and Other Outsider Accounts of Religious Practices." In *The Politics of Religious Apostasy,* ed. David G. Bromley, 221–38. Westport, CT: Praeger.

Chryssides, George. 1999. *Exploring New Religions.* London: Cassell.

Cohen, Stanley. 1972. *Folk Devils and Moral Panics: The Creation of the Mods and Rockers.* Oxford: Blackwell.

Cowan, Douglas. 2003. *Bearing False Witness? An Introduction to the Christian Countercult.* Westport, CT: Praeger.

Crook, Stephen, Jan Pakulski, and Malcolm Waters. 1992. *Postmodernization: Change in Advanced Society.* London: Sage.

Davis, David Brion. 1960. "Some Themes of Counter-Subversion: An Analysis of Anti-Masonic, Anti-Catholic, and Anti-Mormon Literature." *The Mississippi Valley Historical Review* 47, 205–24.

Dawson, Lorne. 1998. *Comprehending Cults: The Sociology of New Religious Movements.* Toronto: Oxford University Press.

———, ed. 2003. *Cults and New Religious Movements: A Reader.* Oxford: Blackwell.

Duvert, Cyril. 2004. "Anti-Cultism in the French Parliament: Desperate Last Stand or an Opportune Leap Forward? A Critical Analysis of the 12 June 2001 Act." In *Regulating Religion,* ed. James T. Richardson, 41–52. New York: Kluwer.

Edwards, Christopher. 1979. *Crazy for God.* Englewood Cliffs, NJ: Prentice-Hall.

Elkins, Chris. 1980. *Heavenly Deception.* Wheaton, IL: Tyndale House.

Ellis, Bill. 2000. *Raising the Devil: Satanism, New Religions, and the Media.* Lexington: University Press of Kentucky.

Fautré, Willy. 2004. "Belgium's Anti-Sect Policy." In *Regulating Religion,* ed. James Richardson, 113–26. New York: Kluwer.

Fort, Joel. 1979. "What is Brainwashing and Who Says So?" In *Scientific Research and New Religions: Divergent Perspectives,* ed. Brock Kilbourne, 57–63. San Francisco: American Association for the Advancement of Science.

Givens, Terryl L. 1997. *The Viper on the Hearth: Mormons, Myths, and the Construction of Heresy.* New York: Oxford University Press.

Goode, Erich, and Nachman Ben-Yehuda. 1994. *Moral Panics.* Oxford: Blackwell.

Greil, Arthur L. 1996. "Sacred Claims: The 'Cult Controversy' as a Struggle over the Right to the Religious Label." In *The Issue of Authenticity in the Study of Religion,* ed. David G. Bromley and Lewis F. Carter, 47–63. Greenwich, CT: JAI Press.

Hassan, Steven. 1988. *Combating Cult Mind Control.* Rochester, VT: Park Street Press.

Hernstein, Mike, and Jon Trott. 1993. *Selling Satan: The Tragic History of Mike Warnke.* Chicago: Cornerstone Press.

Higham, John. 1955. *Strangers in the Land: Patterns of American Nativism, 1860–1925.* New Brunswick, NJ: Rutgers University Press.

Hong, Nansook. 1998. *In the Shadow of the Moons: My Life in Reverend Sun Myung Moon's Family.* Boston: Little, Brown.

Hunt, Stephen. 2003. *Alternative Religions: A Sociological Introduction.* Burlington, VT: Ashgate.

Introvigne, Massimo. 1993. "Strange Bedfellows or Future Enemies?" *Update & Dialog* 3, 13–22.

———. 1995. "The Secular Anti-Cult and the Religious Counter-Cult Movement: Strange Bedfellows or Future Enemies?" In *New Religions and the New Europe,* ed. Eric Towler, 32–54. Aarhus, Denmark: Aarhus University Press.

———. 1997. *Enquête sur le Satanisme. Satanistes et Antisatanistes du XVIIe Siècle à Nos Jours.* Paris: Dervy.

———. 1998. "New Religious Movements and the Law: A Comparison between Two Different Legal Systems (The United States and Italy)." In *New Religions and New Religiosity,* ed. Eileen Barker and Margit Warburg, 276–91. Aarhus, Denmark: Aarhus University Press.

———. 1999a. "Religion as Claim: Social and Legal Controversies." In *The Pragmatics of Defining Religion: Contexts, Concepts and Contests,* ed. Jan G. Platvoet and Arie L. Molendijk, 41–72. Leiden: Brill.

———. 1999b. "Defectors, Ordinary Leave-takers, and Apostates: A Quantitative Study of Former Members of New Acropolis in France." *Nova Religio* 3, 83–99.

———. 2000. "Moral Panics and Anti-Cult Terrorism in Western Europe." *Terrorism and Political Violence* 12, 47–59.

———. 2001. "Blacklisting or Greenlisting? A European Perspective on the New Cult Wars." *Nova Religio* 2, 16–23.

Jacobs, Janet. 1989. *Divine Disenchantment: Deconverting from New Religions.* Bloomington: Indiana University Press.

Jenkins, Philip. 1992. *Intimate Enemies: Moral Panics in Contemporary Great Britain.* Hawthorne, NY: Aldine de Gruyter.

———. 1994. *Using Murder: The Social Construction of Serial Homicide.* Hawthorne, NY: Aldine de Gruyter.

———. 1996. *Pedophiles and Priests: Anatomy of a Contemporary Crisis.* New York: Oxford University Press.

———. 1998. *Moral Panics: Changing Concepts of the Child Molester in Modern America.* New Haven: Yale University Press.

Johnson, Daniel C. 1998. "Apostates Who Never Were: The Social Construction of Absque Facto Apostate Narratives." In *The Politics of Religious Apostasy,* ed. David G. Bromley, 115–38. Westport, CT: Praeger.

Kahaner, Larry. 1988. *Cults That Kill: Probing the Underworld of Occult Crime.* New York: Warner Books.

Kitsuse, John. 1962. "Societal Reactions to Deviant Behavior: Problems of Theory and Method." *Social Problems* 9, 247–57.

Launius, Roger, and Linda Thatcher, eds. 1994. *Differing Visions: Dissenters in Mormon History.* Urbana: University of Illinois Press.

Lewis, James R. 1986. "Reconstructing the 'Cult' Experience." *Sociological Analysis* 47, 151–59.

————. 1989. "Apostates and the Legitimation of Repression: Some Historical and Empirical Perspectives on the Cult Controversy." *Sociological Analysis* 49, 386–96.

————. 2003. *Legitimating New Religions*. New Brunswick, NJ: Rutgers University Press.

Lifton, Robert J. 1963. *Thought Reform and the Psychology of Totalism*. New York: Norton.

Martin, Walter. 1977. *The Kingdom of the Cults: An Analysis of the Major Cult Systems in the Present Christian Era*. Minneapolis: Bethany Fellowship.

Melton, J. Gordon, and Martin Baumann, eds. 2002. *Religions of the World: A Comprehensive Encyclopedia of Beliefs and Practices*. Santa Barbara, CA: ABC/CLIO.

Miller, Donald. 1983. "Deprogramming in Historical Perspective." In *The Brainwashing/Deprogramming Controversy*, ed. David Bromley and James Richardson, 15–28. New York: Edwin Mellen Press.

Miller, Timothy. 1995. *America's Alternative Religions*. Albany: State University of New York Press.

Monk, Maria. 1836/1977. *Awful Disclosures of the Hotel Dieu Nunnery*. New York: Arno Press.

Mulhern, Sherrill. 1991. "Satanism and Psychotherapy: A Rumor in Search of an Inquisition." In *The Satanism Scare*, ed. James Richardson, Joel Best, and David Bromley, 145–74. Hawthorne, NY: Aldine de Gruyter.

Muster, Nori. 1997. *Betrayal of the Spirit: My Life behind the Headlines of the Hare Krishna Movement*. Urbana: University of Illinois Press.

Nathan, Debbie. 1991. "Satanism and Child Molestation: Constructing the Ritual Abuse Scare." In *The Satanism Scare*, ed. James Richardson, Joel Best, and David Bromley, 75–94. Hawthorne, NY: Aldine de Gruyter.

Peretti, Frank E. 1991. *This Present Darkness*. Wheaton, IL: Crossway Books.

Pfeifer, Jeffrey. 1992. "The Psychological Framing of Cults: Schematic Representations and Cult Evaluations." *Journal of Applied Social Psychology* 22, 531–44.

Poggi, Gianfranco. 1990. *The State*. Cambridge, UK: Polity Press.

Pratt, Thomas D. 1991. "The Need to Dialogue: A Review of the Debate on Signs, Wonders, Miracles, and Spiritual Warfare in the Literature of the Third Wave Movement." *Pneuma: The Journal of the Society of Pentecostal Studies* 13, 7–32.

Raschke, Carl. 1990. *Painted Black*. San Francisco: Harper & Row.

Reinarman, Carl, and Harry Levine. 1997. *Crack in America: Demon Drugs and Social Justice*. Berkeley: University of California Press.

Richardson, James T. 1991. "Cult/Brainwashing Cases and the Freedom of Religion." *Journal of Church and State* 33, 55–74.

————. 1992. "Public Opinion and the Tax Evasion of Reverend Moon." *Behavioral Sciences and the Law* 10, 53–63.

————. 1993a. "Definitions of Cult: From Sociological-Technical to Popular-Negative." *Review of Religious Research* 34, 348–56.

————. 1993b. "Mental Health of Cult Consumers: Legal and Scientific Controversy." In *Religion and Mental Health*, ed. John Schumaker, 233–44. New York: Oxford University Press.

————. 1993c. "A Social Psychological Critique of 'Brainwashing' Claims about Recruitment to New Religions." In *The Handbook on Cults and Sects in America, Part B*, ed. David G. Bromley and Jeffrey K. Hadden, 75–97. Greenwich, CT: JAI Press.

————. 1995. "Manufacturing Consent about Koresh: A Structural Analysis of the Role of the Media in the Waco Tragedy." In *Armageddon in Waco: Critical Perspectives on the Branch Davidian Conflict,* ed. Stuart Wright, 153–76. Chicago: University of Chicago Press.

————. 1996. "'Brainwashing' Claims and Minority Religions Outside the United States: Cultural Diffusion of a Questionable Concept in the Legal Arena." *Brigham Young University Law Review* 1996, 873–904.

————. 1997a. "Journalistic Bias toward New Religious Movements in Australia." *Journal of Contemporary Religion* 11, 289–302.

————. 1997b. "The Social Construction of Satanism: Understanding an International Social Problem." *Australian Journal of Social Issues* 32, 61–86.

————. 1998. "The Accidental Expert." *Nova Religio* 2, 31–43.

Richardson, James T., and Brock Kilbourne. 1983. "Classical and Contemporary Brainwashing Models: A Comparison and Critique." In *The Brainwashing/ Deprogramming Controversy: Historical, Sociological, Psychological, and Legal Perspectives,* ed. David G. Bromley and James T. Richardson, 29–45. New York: Edwin Mellen Press.

Richardson, James T., Robert Balch, and J. Gordon Melton. 1993. "Problems of Research and Data in the Study of New Religions." In *The Handbook on Cults and Sects in America,* Part B, ed. David G. Bromley and Jeffrey K. Hadden, 213–29. Greenwich, CT: JAI Press.

Richardson, James T., Joel Best, and David G. Bromley, eds. 1991. *The Satanism Scare.* Hawthorne, NY: Aldine de Gruyter.

Richardson, James T., and Massimo Introvigne. 2001. "'Brainwashing' Theories in European Parliamentary and Administrative Reports on 'Cults' and 'Sects.'" *Journal for the Scientific Study of Religion* 40, 143–68.

Richardson, James T., and Mary Stewart. 2004. "Medicalization and Regulation of Deviant Religions: An Application of Conrad and Schneider's Model." In *Regulating Religion,* ed. James T. Richardson, 507–34. New York: Kluwer.

Richardson, James T., Jan van der Lans, and Frans Derks. 1986. "Leaving and Labeling: Voluntary and Coerced Disaffiliation from Religious Social Movements." In *Research in Social Movements, Conflicts, and Change.* ed. Kurt Lang and Gladys Lang, 97–126. Greenwich, CT: JAI Press.

Richardson, James T., and Barend van Driel. 1997. "Journalists' Attitudes toward New Religious Movements." *Review of Religious Research* 39, 116–36.

Selway, Deborah 1992. "Religion in the Mainstream Press: The Challenge of the Future." *Australian Religious Studies Review* 5, 18–24.

Shterin, Marat, and James Richardson. 2002. "The *Yakunin vs. Dworkin* Trial and the Emerging Religious Pluralism in Russia." *Religion in Eastern Europe* 22, 1–38.

Shupe, Anson D., and David G. Bromley. 1980. *The New Vigilantes: Deprogrammers, Anti-Cultists, and the New Religions.* Beverly Hills, CA: Sage.

————, eds. 1994a. *Anti-Cult Movements in Cross-Cultural Perspective.* New York: Garland.

————. 1994b. "The Modern North American Anti-Cult Movement 1971–91: A Twenty Year Retrospective." In *Anti-Cult Movements in Cross-Cultural Perspective,* ed. Anson Shupe and David Bromley, 3–32. New York: Garland.

Shupe, Anson, David Bromley, and Susan Darnell. 2004. "The North American Anti-Cult Movement: Vicissitudes of Success and Failure." In *The Oxford Handbook of New Religious Movements,* ed. James R. Lewis, 184–205. New York: Oxford University Press.

Shupe, Anson D., and Susan E. Darnell. 2000. "CAN, We Hardly Knew Ye: Sex, Drugs, Deprogrammers' Kickbacks, and Corporate Crime in the (Old) Cult Awareness Network." Paper presented at the annual meeting of CESNUR, Stockholm, Sweden, July 2000. Available at www.cesnur.org/2001/CAN.htm.

———. 2003. "The Attempted Transformation of a Deviant Occupation into a Therapy: Deprogramming Seeks a New Identity." Paper presented at the annual meeting of the Society for the Scientific Study of Religion, Norfolk, VA, October 2003. Available at www.cesnur.org/2003/shupe_darnell.htm.

Shupe, Anson, and Jeffrey K. Hadden. 1995. "Cops, News Copy, and Public Opinion: Legitimacy and the Social Construction of Evil in Waco." In *Armageddon in Waco*, ed. Stuart Wright, 177–202. Chicago: University of Chicago Press.

Singer, Margaret. 1979. "Coming Out of the Cults." *Psychology Today*, January, 72–82.

———. 1995. *Cults in Our Midst: The Hidden Menace in Our Everyday Lives*. San Francisco: Jossey-Bass.

Smith, Michelle, and Lawrence Pazder. 1980. *Michelle Remembers*. New York: Congdon and Lattes.

Solomon, Trudy. 1982. "Integrating the Moonie Experience: A Survey of Ex-Members of the Unification Church." In *In Gods We Trust: New Patterns of Religious Pluralism in America*, ed. Thomas Robbins and Dick Anthony, 275–94. New Brunswick, NJ: Rutgers University Press.

Stratford, Lauren. 1988. *Satan's Underground: The Extraordinary Story of One Woman's Escape*. Eugene, OR: Harvest House.

Swatland, Susan, and Anne Swatland. 1982. *Escape from the Moonies*. London: New English Library.

Terry, Maury. 1987. *The Ultimate Evil: An Investigation into America's Most Dangerous Satanic Cult*. Garden City, NY: Doubleday.

Tipton, Steven. 1982. *Getting Saved from the Sixties*. Berkeley: University of California Press.

Underwood, Barbara, and Betty Underwood. 1979. *Hostage to Heaven*. New York: Clarkson N. Potter.

van Driel, Barend, and James Richardson. 1988a. "Categorization of New Religious Movements in American Print Media." *Sociological Analysis* 49, 171–83.

———. 1988b. "Print Media Coverage of New Religious Movements: A Longitudinal Study." *Journal of Communication* 38, 37–61.

van Driel, Barend, and Jan van Belzen. 1990. "The Downfall of Rajneeshpuram in the Print Media." *Journal for the Scientific Study of Religion* 29, 76–90.

Victor, Jeffrey. 1993. *Satanic Panic: The Creation of a Contemporary Legend*. Chicago: Open Court.

Wangerin, Ruth. 1993. *The Children of God*. Westport, CT: Bergin and Garvey.

Ward, Maria [pseudonym]. 1855. *Female Life among the Mormons*. London: Routledge.

Williams, Miriam. 1998. *Heaven's Harlots: My Fifteen Years in a Sex Cult*. New York: Eagle Brook.

Wuthnow, Robert. 1976. "The New Religions in Social Context." In *The New Religious Consciousness*, ed. Charles Glock and Robert Bellah, 267–93. Berkeley: University of California Press.

Zablocki, Benjamin D., and Thomas Robbins, eds. 2001. *Misunderstanding Cults: Searching for Objectivity in a Controversial Field*. Toronto: University of Toronto Press.

PART II

Central Issues in Teaching New Religious Movements

The Meaning and Significance of New Religious Movements

Lorne L. Dawson

Every study written about new religious movements (NRMs) implicitly assumes their significance. But the subject is rarely addressed explicitly and systematically. In an immediate sense, the study of specific groups, phenomena, or situations is justified by our simple need to know more about the groups (e.g., the Church of Scientology), phenomena (e.g., who joins NRMs and why), or situations in question (e.g., the murder-suicide of members of the Solar Temple). In a less immediate sense, however, all of this research assumes that the very existence and proliferation of new religions in contemporary society is itself somehow significant. The implication is that the study of these groups is relevant to our understanding of other issues or processes. The reasoning involves placing the phenomenon of NRMs in larger contexts. In looking at the last thirty years of research on NRMs, it appears that the search for the significance of the NRMs can be divided largely into two rather opposed interpretive contexts: (1) seeing NRMs as a social problem; and (2) seeing NRMs as responses to, and hence indicators of, broader patterns of social change. In this chapter I will briefly discuss the first context, which in many respects is addressed already by other chapters in this book, and then concentrate on elaborating how a handful of sociologists of religion have sought to frame the second and more ambitious context of significance.

Statistically, the presence of new religions in modern Western societies remains marginal. Though many thousands of such religions may exist at any one time, their memberships, with few exceptions, remain inordinately small. Most NRMs have little direct impact on the lives of the citizens of the nations in which they operate. Yet sociologists of religion have been fascinated with the study of these groups. There are many reasons for this attention, but I would argue that it is driven by a common, if implicit, assumption that these small religions bear a cultural significance out of proportion to their statistical presence. This assumption is rooted in an abiding curiosity about the fate of religion in the modern world.

The changes associated with the onset of modernity are thought to have rendered the kinds of intense religious commitments associated with new religious movements obsolete and suspect. The traditional religious orders of the Catholic Church, for example, are experiencing sharp declines in their membership. But as fewer and fewer individuals find the rewards and sacrifices of becoming a priest, monk, or nun appealing, others are choosing to take on the often stiff personal demands and high social costs of becoming devotees of exotic new religions. The individuals converting to these religions tend to come, moreover, from the more privileged sectors of society. They are disproportionately young, well educated, and from the middle to upper classes. As such they represent the segment of society most exposed to the cultural trappings and material benefits of modern secular society.

Why is this happening, and what does it tell us about the future of religion? That is the fundamental question implicitly undergirding the strong interest in NRMs. Is the creation and proliferation of NRMs an anomaly or does it suggest that our common suppositions about the character of modernity need to be revised? If so, in what ways and with what consequences? The very existence of NRMs represents a potential challenge to conventional conceptions of modern society, and their ultimate significance lies in figuring out if this is indeed the case and how.

There have been many ways of approaching this issue, with varying degrees of cogency. There is much definitional and conceptual ambiguity in the discussions, with regard to both the nature of religion and the nature of modernity. But most of the analyses offered tend to focus, as Thomas Robbins (1988a: 60) observes, on "some acute and distinctively modern dislocation which is said to be producing some mode of alienation, anomie or deprivation to which [people] are responding by searching for new structures of meaning and community."

Here I will examine four interpretive frameworks that tend to offer progressively more complex and optimistic understandings of the significance of NRMs as responses to the social conditions of modernity. The first perspective links NRMs to "protests against modernity." The second perspective examines NRMs as "forums for modern social experimentation." The third perspective identifies NRMs with "the reenchantment of the world." The fourth perspective interprets NRMs as manifestations of the "dialectic of trust and risk" in late modernity.

These perspectives are far from exclusive and many of the issues, inferences, and ideas overlap. By associating the appeal of NRMs with different kinds of responses to different aspects of modern life, scholars are suggesting that the significance of NRMs can be found, and hence the ultimate rationale for studying them, in their role as barometers of broader processes of social change that impact everyone in society. But the interpretive frameworks offered are speculative, and the significance attributed to NRMs is always relative to certain audiences and their agendas.

Having dedicated most of the chapter to summarizing the key points of these interpretations of the significance of NRMs, in the last section I will address the pedagogical task of getting students to think about the issues raised and their relevance.

Seeing New Religious Movements as a Social Problem

The study of NRMs became a topic of significance in the academic study of religion, and for the wider public as well, as a result of the controversies set off by the "cult scare" (Bromley and Shupe 1981) of the late 1970s and early 1980s. The sudden emergence of several prominent new religions in the United States (e.g., the Children of God, Transcendental Meditation, the Unification Church, the International Society for Krishna Consciousness, the Rajneesh movement), combined with the tragic mass suicide of 914 members of the Peoples Temple in 1978, set off a strong backlash against the new "cults" in America. As negative media attention mounted and the parents of young converts, along with other secular and religious opponents, began to organize the anti-cult movement, scholars of religion were drawn into the public disputes about NRMs. Many felt a moral obligation to speak out against the misinformation they believed was being conveyed to the public by the anti-cult movement. Systematic research was undertaken to substantiate or refute the anecdotal evidence used to bolster the case against the cults. As the legal disputes involving NRMs multiplied (Richardson 1995), they appeared to pose a threat to the principle of religious liberty enshrined in the First Amendment of the U.S. Constitution. It was becoming increasingly apparent that the supposedly fraudulent and harmful activities of many of the new religions could not be differentiated meaningfully from the beliefs and practices of many more conventional forms of religion (Young and Griffiths 1992). The civil rights of all religious minorities were in jeopardy.

For those concerned with the allegedly deviant behavior of many members of NRMs, the significance of these groups was bound up with the attempt to raise public awareness of the "social problem" they posed. NRMs are significant because they posed a new threat to the well-being of the public. For the majority of scholars working in the field, the significance of NRMs is bound up with debunking this supposed threat. NRMs are significant because the controversy over their nature has compelled us to clarify the protections that a democratic society should extend to its religious minorities, especially in an age of increasing secularism.

In practice, two issues lay at the heart of this struggle: (1) the accusation that NRMs "brainwash" their followers (Anthony and Robbins 1992; Richardson 1993; Singer 1995); and (2) the fear that all NRMs pose a threat to public safety because some NRMs have been violent (Bromley and Melton 2002; Dawson 1998a: 128–57). The ill-defined notion of brainwashing was used to rationalize away the success of the NRMs and to justify their suppression. In response scholars sought to gain a more empirically reliable grasp of just who was joining these groups, how, and why (see Dawson 1998a: 72–127). The results of these efforts refuted the claims of brainwashing. Public concern was also piqued by the incidents of mass suicide and murder that afflicted a handful of NRMs in the 1990s (the Branch Davidians, the Solar Temple, Aum Shinrikyo, and Heaven's Gate). Through detailed case studies and comparative analyses scholars are developing a better understanding of the nature and origins of this violence. This remains a live issue, however, and hence an ongoing source of significance for the study of NRMs. For most scholars, the violence of a few groups under special circumstances will not support the presumption that other NRMs are likely to become violent. These kinds of incidents of mass violence appear to be the exception and not the norm.

In a broader sense, both the debate over brainwashing and the concern with violence are manifestations of a more general source of significance: they reflect doubts about the place of religion in a late modern context. The numerous legal disputes involving charges of brainwashing against cults have been prompted by a perceived violation of the norms of everyday life in modern societies. These societies highly value freedom and individual choice, yet not when it is exercised in a manner that defies expectations about what is "normal." Young people are to pursue education and prepare for jobs, not dedicate their lives to the study of esoteric religious texts, meditation, or the saving of souls. As James Beckford argues (2001), the intolerance and skepticism directed at NRMs are largely the result of "skirmishes along a shifting frontier" of points of conflict between the new religions and "various non-religious conditions imposed by state authorities." Legally, new religions today often get in trouble because they fail to conform to established expectations about taxation, military service, public health and medicine, education, child care, land use, and financial resources. Deviation from the standards set in each of these realms is taken to be evidence of fraud or subversive intent. Yet the appeal of all new religions stems from a certain discontent with the existing order of things. Almost by definition, new religions are dedicated to changing our lives and our societies. To that end new religions tend to defy the conventions of society, offering alternative ways of treating illness, eating, dressing, educating children, finding mates, making love, making a living, and serving the interests of humanity. Conflict with the authorities is almost assured as societies become increasingly subject to elaborate systems of regulation demanding conformity with modern, rationalized, capitalistic, and largely secular expectations.

New Religious Movements as Indicators of Broader Patterns of Social Change

The second interpretive context for grasping the significance of NRMs has been developed in a number of competing yet convergent ways. Let us examine briefly four of the most conspicuous approaches.

New Religious Movements and the Protest against Modernity

It is widely assumed today that when people turn to religion they are seeking a measure of protection from the anomic and alienating effects of modern life. Radical religious commitments in particular, like those associated with joining many NRMs, are presumed to reflect a desire to turn back the clock, to recreate within the movement and society itself the normative clarity and close social relations that are identified, rightly or wrongly, with a bygone era. In an early attempt to delineate the significance of NRMs, the sociologist James Davison Hunter (1981) tried to give some substance to this hunch by calling on Peter Berger's influential sociological theories of religion and modernity (Berger 1967; Berger, Berger, and Kellner 1974). Simplifying his complex argument, Hunter identifies NRMs with a "protest against modernity." At the heart of his argument is Berger's notion of the "deinstitutionalization" of the private sphere. This process of deinstitutionalization is the social psychological wellspring of contemporary new religious life (this summary is drawn from Dawson 2004: 77–80).

Modernity, and the demise of the traditional social order, is commonly identified with the increased institutionalization of society. Massive bureaucracies are the order of the day in the "public" sphere of modern social life, in the realms of business, government, the law, education, health care, and even religion (e.g., the Catholic Church and other large Protestant denominations). Paradoxically, however, in the private sphere of life, the most emotionally significant aspects of people's lives are being deinstitutionalized. In the name of increased personal autonomy, patterns of courtship, marriage, child-rearing, sexuality, gender roles and relations, consumption, vocation, and spirituality have all become matters of choice. But for many people the choices are becoming bewildering. Anomie and uncertainty are the by-products of the new liberty unleashed, especially when in all other regards peoples' lives are becoming ever more impersonal and subject to the dictates of a strictly formal and functional rationality. The large bureaucracies are indifferent to our idiosyncrasies, and we are being reduced increasingly to interchangeable and expendable units of labor and consumption. This is the plight of modern life: people must increasingly fashion their own identity, in the face of an indifferent society, through a series of private choices. But the identities created are inherently unstable and more a source of anxiety than comfort because we seem to be confronted with an ongoing plurality of not easily understood choices.

New religions "resacralize" daily life by anchoring private activities and identities, and to some extent even public ones, in institutions conceived once again as reflections of the natural, cosmic, or divine order. Marriage, for example, is less likely to be followed by divorce if it is understood again as a religious and eternal commitment and not merely a personal act. Ambiguity and uncertainty are reduced and meaning increased by this "demodernizing" process, which accounts for the appeal of these new and relatively radical religious commitments.

In Hunter's analysis there is little sense that the processes of modernization can be reversed, so the religious protest against modernity is ultimately futile. The sole significance of the emergence of NRMs is that they are "a sign that in some sectors of modern society, the strains of modernity have reached the limits of human tolerance, and are thus symbolic, at both the collective and social psychological levels, of the desire for relief and assuagement" (1981: 7). But actual relief from these hardships, it is implied, must come from elsewhere. NRMs are significant only as *symptoms* of a broader social malaise (see also Bellah 1976; Tipton 1982).

But for Roy Wallis, NRMs may *"either* react against, *or* celebrate, major features of [modern] society" (1982: 216; emphasis in the original). In his view there are at least two types of cults: world-rejecting and world-affirming (see Wallis 1984 as well). His description of world-rejecting NRMs bears a marked resemblance to Hunter's characterization of demodernizing religious movements. But others join world-affirming NRMs that promise to unlock their hidden human potential, offering training in esoteric techniques for relieving anxiety, increasing self-esteem and confidence, improving their health, transforming their cognitive skills, and sometimes even acquiring wealth (e.g., Scientology, est, Silva Mind Control, Rajneesh/Osho, Vajradhatu/Shambhala, Soka Gakkai, and dozens of other quasi-religious humanistic psycho-therapies). These groups infuse a spiritual dimension of meaning into the busy lives of people with firm or growing attachments to the modern industrial world (Wallis 1982: 228). Their beliefs and practices work to rationalize, justify, and further motivate the continued pursuit of achievement and material success, while offering compensations for the stresses of this life and mechanisms for coping with the guilt stimulated by indulging in the pleasures of this world or accepting its inequalities (see Dawson 2001).

In the end, though, the significance of world-rejecting and world-affirming NRMs remains much the same. They have arisen in response to certain social, psychological, and spiritual deficiencies felt by a segment of the population, and as such are indicative of certain structural strains and deficiencies in the dominant social system and culture.

New Religious Movements as "Laboratories for Social Experimentation"

Inverting the focus, Thomas Robbins and David Bromley (1992, 1993) have more optimistically sought to identify the significance of NRMs with the intrinsic contributions they make to society. This does not entail assessing the merits of what NRMs have done or being concerned with the success or failure of specific groups. The significance of NRMs as a whole, as a type of social phenomenon, depends less on the specific doctrinal or organizational innovations they introduce than on their status as a forum for social experimentation in the modern world. NRMs have become social laboratories, in other words, where people can experiment with new forms of social relations in a dominant social order that is becoming ever more bureaucratized, specialized, regulated, and preoccupied with credentials (Robbins and Bromley 1992: 3–5; 1993: 210). The experiments in question need not entail a protest against modernity per se. Rather, Robbins and Bromley (1993: 214) observe, the experimentation may involve either a traditionalist or a modernist orientation. In fact, they can encompass both elements simultaneously, being traditionalist in some regards (e.g., sexual relations) and modernist in others (e.g., in their use of new technologies; see Dawson 1998b: 147). More specifically, they suggest that NRMs are involved in noteworthy experimentation with alternative patterns of sexuality and gender relations, economic and social organization, proselytization and persuasion, and healing and therapy.

In this regard contemporary NRMs may simply be the cutting edge, they argue, of what is happening to religion in general. As Beckford (1989) has noted, religion is presently better conceptualized "as a cultural resource" rather than a "social institution" (171). Religion has been partly freed "from its points of anchorage in communities and natural groupings," which has "turned it into a resource which may be invested with highly diverse meanings and used for a variety of purposes." As a kind of "free-floating cultural resource, religion is increasingly available as a supportive setting and legitimation for innovation and experimentation in diverse areas" (Robbins and Bromley 1993: 210).

With regard to issues of gender and sexuality, for example, Robbins and Bromley note that many scholars have drawn a link between the unorthodox beliefs and practices of many NRMs, in the past and the present, and a "recurrent dissatisfaction with traditional patriarchal modes in theology and social organization" (Robbins and Bromley 1993: 210). This dissatisfaction has been aggravated in recent years by the "erosion of norms regulating gender roles and sexual intimacy" resulting from the de-institutionalization of the private sphere (Robbins and Bromley 1992: 6). In the face of the consequent moral ambiguity, NRMs have tended to offer people clarity by fostering either a return to "extreme patriarchy" (e.g., Krishna Consciousness, the Happy-Healthy-Holy movement, the Unification Church, and dozens of Christian splinter groups) or an alternative "antipatriarchy" (e.g., Theosophy, the Church Universal and Triumphant, the neo-pagan/Wiccan movement, particularly the feminist forms of Goddess worship, the Rajneesh/Osho movement, and many aspects of the New Age movement). The latter option elevates the divine feminine to a new and superior status in spiritual affairs and places women in positions of leadership in religious rites and organizations (see Aidala 1985 and Palmer 1994; their views are summarized in Dawson 1998a: 94–101).

On the economic front, NRMs have experimented with new ways of mobilizing resources that transcend the traditional congregational model. Among contemporary NRMs, Robbins and Bromley surmise (1993: 211), "noteworthy patterns of innovation reflect responses to trends toward international corporate organization, welfare capitalism, a consumer-based economy with the accompanying significance of 'leisure,' and the development of hybrid organizations that occupy niches between traditional institutional forms." The examples they have in mind range from the international corporate empire forged in support of the Unification Church to the private social welfare organizations run by the Peoples Temple, the religious theme parks created by Jim Baker and other televangelists, the tourism encouraged by the opulent New Vrindaban temple built by the Hare Krishnas in West Virginia, and the many products and services marketed by NRMs like the Church of Scientology and the Church Universal and Triumphant. To this list we might add the universities established in the United States by Vajradhatu/Shambhala, Transcendental Meditation, and Soka Gakkai. Many NRMs have purposefully blurred the lines between the realms of religion, business, education, therapy, and social welfare services to secure a material and hence perhaps a spiritual advantage (see Richardson 1988).

In these areas and the others noted, NRMs have often been the progenitors of real changes in the wider society. But their significance lies more fundamentally in their social function as forums for a vital degree of quasi-legitimate social experimentation in a pluralistic society. In addition, however, Robbins and Bromley invoke a link between the experimental character of so much new religious life and the broader tensions in modern society. They suggest that the rise of contemporary NRMs is associated with the sociocultural shift from premodern "covenantal" relations to modern "contractual" relations. They define this contrast as follows:

> Contractual social relations are those in which individuals coordinate their behavior through pledging themselves to specific reciprocal activity without pledging to one another's well-being. Covenantal social relations are those in which individuals coordinate their behavior by pledging themselves to one another's well-being without pledging specific reciprocal activity. (Robbins and Bromley 1992: 5, citing Bromley and Busching 1988: 16)

In the modern world, contractualism has gained the upper hand at the clear expense of traditional covenantal social relations. But Robbins and Bromley do not simply tie NRMs to a reaction against this new contractualism (i.e., another kind of protest against modernity). Rather, they more complexly suggest that NRMs are a reaction to the social psychological problems stemming from "the tensions between contractual and convenantal forms of social relations" (1992: 4). These tensions are "exacerbated by the expansion of contractualism." But ultimately they are rooted in the fact that the "contractual and covenantal spheres remain integrally related to one another." The tensions are "generated by the simultaneous combination of the incompatibility and the integrality of the two social forms" (1992: 5). NRMs are, in a sense, experiments in how best to combine these antithetical yet inescapable elements of social life. It remains unclear in their work, however, just how this is the case.

New Religious Movements and the Reenchantment of the World

More expansively, many sociologists of religion have interpreted the emergence and proliferation of contemporary NRMs as evidence of the revival of religious life in the face of the supposed triumph of secularization (e.g., Mol 1976; Robbins 1988b). Max Weber (1946: 282) aptly captured the consequences of the progressive secularization of the world with the phrase "the disenchantment of the world" (*die Entzauverung der Welt*). Some scholars have sought to provide a more optimistic reading of the significance of NRMs by taking up the theme of religious revival, speaking in terms of the "reenchantment" of the world. The most comprehensive recent statement of this view is provided by the British religious studies scholar Christopher Partridge (2004).

Partridge makes no attempt to deny the reality of secularization in most modern Western societies. Clearly, organized religion in its traditional forms is in retreat—more so in Western Europe, Great Britain, Canada, and Australia than in the United States. But across the Western world, levels of church membership and religious participation are in steady decline. This is undoubtedly the result of the usual set of interrelated social processes identified by sociologists: the rationalization of society, increasing institutional differentiation, growing religious and cultural pluralism, and the privatization of religion. Traditional religion has not fared well in a culture of heightened individualism and consumerism. Like many other contemporary sociologists of religion, however, he denies that this seeming loss of faith is a linear, inevitable, or irreversible process. Rather, there is sufficient evidence of a countervailing process of "sacralization" that is transforming the face of religion in response to the perennial spiritual needs of people. Religion is changing, not disappearing.

In saying this, Partridge is casting his lot with the alternative theory of secularization advanced by Rodney Stark and William Sims Bainbridge (1985). This theory stems in turn from their more optimistic theory of religion, in a modern context or otherwise. The basic premises of this theory are as follows. The first premise is that religions are about the operation of the supernatural in people's lives. Many social involvements may become quite all-consuming for individuals and hence play a religious-like role in their lives. But it is the reference to the supernatural that truly distinguishes a religious phenomenon. The second premise is the simple utilitarian principle that most of human behavior, including religious behavior, is governed by the pursuit of what we perceive to be rewards and by the avoidance of what we perceive to be costs. The third premise is that the rewards most highly prized by people are usually scarce and that the rewards at the heart of the religious quest seem to be the things least readily available, like true peace of mind or life after death. The fourth premise is that in the absence of these most-valued real rewards, people are inclined to create, exchange, and accept what Stark and William Bainbridge call "compensators." In daily life, we often appease people for incurring some sacrifice today by promising some appropriate reward in the future. In many cases the promised rewards are quite specific. But religions deal in the most general of compensators: ultimate relief from suffering, immortality for the virtuous, and knowledge of the meaning of life. These compensations require belief in the operation of a supernatural agency or force in this world.

Religions, then, are organizations that provide general compensators based on belief in the supernatural, and Stark and Bainbridge think that if we keep this simple truth in mind, there can be little doubt that religions will persist—under the conditions of modernity or otherwise. With this perspective in mind, they argue that the process of secularization should be conceived as a recurring and cyclical phenomenon. Secularization is not a uniquely modern development that entails the eventual demise of religion. Rather, it should be understood in terms of the periodic collapse of support for certain dominant forms of religion as they become complacent and overly accommodated to nonreligious features of the societies in which they developed. Secularization should not be confused with the loss of all need for supernatural compensators, but should be associated with the failure of established religions to provide sufficiently vivid and consistent supernatural compensators. As such, secularization is an intrinsic and limiting feature of all religious economies, guaranteeing the periodic renewal of religious institutions. In Partridge's words (2004: 46): "Disenchantment is the precursor to reenchantment."

Partridge offers several different kinds of fragmentary evidence in support of this thesis, which can only be briefly indicated here. First, he calls attention to the mounting survey data from Britain and Europe (and much the same can be said for Canada) of what Grace Davie (1994) calls "believing without belonging." While the vast majority of people in these societies no longer formally practice their religion with regularity, surveys reveal an abiding interest in basic religious and spiritual concerns, continued belief in God, life after death and other aspects of religion, and stronger than anticipated levels of participation in private modes of religious expression (e.g., prayer). Second, he notes the surge in occult and New Age books sales over the last thirty years and the general tolerance of "the occult" that this indicates. Third, he notes the inroads of Eastern and New Age healing practices into conventional medicine. Fourth, he discusses the growing spiritualization of the ecological movement, and use of the results of the scientific investigation of complex natural systems to restore a sense of reverence and awe to our dealings with nature. Fifth, he cites various kinds of survey data: revealing that more and more people are willing to call themselves "spiritual," if not religious; that many people can be shown to hold religious beliefs though they are unwilling to call themselves either religious or spiritual; that while belief in traditional Christian conceptions of heaven and hell are in sharp decline, belief in reincarnation is rising. In general, Partridge argues (2004: 51) that we are witnessing a narrowing of the gap between what is seen as religiously deviant and what is viewed as respectable. "It is not simply that there is a lack of consensus about what is deviant, but rather that beliefs once considered deviant are now acceptable, even respectable."

Lastly, Partridge dwells on the significance of certain developments in contemporary popular culture, discussing the attention given to such themes as UFOs and alien abductions, magic and paganism, vampirism, and the fight between supernatural forces of evil and good in general. He calls attention to the spiritual and religious themes of such TV shows as *The X-Files*; movies like *The Craft*, *Star Wars*, *The Matrix*, or *The Lord of the Rings*; books like the Harry Potter series; and dozens of video and computer games. "My point," he says,

> is simply that, whatever is intended by the producers of popular culture, there is little doubt that people are developing religious and metaphysical ideas by reflecting on themes explored in literature, film, and video games—which in turn, reflect popular reenchant-ment.... It is not insignificant that producers of popular culture are increasingly interested in alternative religious and occult themes. (2004: 53)

Other observers have their doubts, dismissing many of these popular expressions of spirituality as evidence of the trivialization of religion and the triumph of secularization (Bruce 2002; Wilson 1976). Partridge asserts otherwise, citing his own dealings with contemporary pagans and New Agers, and some others seem to agree (e.g., Porter and McLaren 1999; Stout and Buddenbaum 2001). In the end, he asserts: "New forms of religion/spirituality in which the tensions between the sacred and the secular, the spiritual and the rational, the divine and the mundane, the body and the soul are greatly reduced have taken root in the West" (Partridge 2004: 59–60).

Partridge's analysis falls short, however, of explaining why this re-enchantment is happening. Is it sufficient to cite the perennial need for spiritual compensators posited by Stark and Bainbridge? Our next approach seeks a more comprehensive answer.

New Religious Movements and the Dialectic of Trust and Risk in Late Modernity

I (1998b, 2004, 2005) have argued that most of the perspectives discussed so far fail to explain adequately the significance of NRMs because they remain wedded to the overly simplistic dictates of the theory of secularization. In casting NRMs as some kind of reaction to the "realities" of modernity, many sociologists of religion have tended to limit their understanding of NRMs to the two options delineated by Peter Berger in his seminal analysis of the place of religion in a pluralistic and advanced capitalist society:

> [NRMs] can either accommodate themselves to the situation, play the pluralistic game of religious free enterprise, and come to terms as best they can with the plausibility problem by modifying their product in accordance with consumer demands. Or they can refuse to accommodate themselves, entrench themselves behind whatever

socio-religious structures they can maintain or construct, and continue to profess the old objectivities as much as possible as if nothing had happened. (1967: 153)

Following the first accommodative option is thought to result in a diminution of the inherent "religiousness" of the phenomena under study, leading scholars to call into question their long-term ability to compete with more secular alternatives. Accommodation is associated, in other words, with the continued "internal secularization" of religious life, as delineated by Berger (1967) and others (e.g., Bruce 2002; Luckmann 1967). Following the second separatist option results in the permanent marginalization of NRMs, preventing their development into the kind of mass movements that could exercise any real influence on society. Either way the significance of contemporary NRMs is reduced dramatically, relative to past religious developments.

The situation is more complex as studies of specific contemporary NRMs reveal. Groups like the Unification Church, the New Age and the Wiccan movements, and the Pentecostalist/Charismatic movement all blend modern, anti-modern, sometimes even postmodern elements, so they defy easy classification using these categories. They involve elements of both creative adaptation to aspects of modernity and resistance to it. Building on insights from a variety of sources, I argue that there are signs of a deeper structural continuity in the features of such disparate NRMs that demonstrate their affinity with a broader shift in the religious sensibilities of modern people. The significance of NRMs rests with coming to appreciate this affinity. Many NRMs are at the leading edge of changes in the character of the religious preferences of people—changes that presumably are happening in response to even more fundamental changes in the conditions of modern life.

Dawson identifies the new religious orientation with six preferences (2004: 92; see 1998b: 138–44):

Most briefly, contemporary religious life is "marked by a pronounced ... individualism," and an "emphasis ... on experience and faith rather than doctrine and belief." The individualism in question entails putting a priority on both the needs and desires of the individual and turning inward to find the source of spiritual sustenance. This increased individualism and experiential orientation has resulted in the adoption of "a more pragmatic attitude to questions of religious authority and practice," and a remarkably more tolerant, even relativistic and syncretistic, approach to other religious worldviews and systems.

Lastly, it is accompanied by a preference for greater organizational openness in religious groups and institutions. ... This means, as Yves Lambert (1999) and I have stressed in parallel yet different ways, that the new forms of religiosity favoured in modernity tend to be this-worldly and parascientific in character (e.g., Scientology, the

New Age movement, and Eastern meditational/therapeutic groups like Vajradhatur/Shambhala, Rajneesh/Osho Foundation, or Soka Gakkai). (Dawson 1998b: 138–39)

In the literature discussing these and other similar changes in religious orientation, it remains unclear, however, just why these new sensibilities are developing. What are the broader social changes underlying these developments? Dawson has turned to Anthony Giddens's influential analysis of the consequences of modernity for some insight into this question (Giddens 1990, 1991). Giddens's account is more comprehensive and multifaceted than Berger's discussion of deinstitutionalization or Robbins and Bromley's clash of covenantal and contractual forms of social relations. It also provides a more complex explanation for the presumed persistence of a demand for religious innovations.

Simplifying matters, Giddens's argument can be broken into three parts: his diagnosis of the social-structural conditions of modernity; his analysis of the social-psychological consequences of these conditions; and his conception of the different possible responses (social, cultural, and political) to these consequences (for a fuller yet still synoptic analysis, see Dawson 2004 or 2005).

In Giddens's view, modernity is marked by three primary structural changes—changes that have permanently altered the social environment in which religions must operate: (1) the "disembedding" of social life in conjunction with a reliance on "abstract expert systems"; (2) the "institutionalization of reflexivity"; and (3) the process of globalization. These changes are dialectically interrelated, yet analytically distinguishable.

The modern development and spread of chronological time, methods of rapid and mass transportation and communication, monetary systems, and expert systems of all kinds—ranging from meteorology to surgery to computer science—have lifted people out of the more immediate frames of reference that have traditionally shaped their lives and identities. Life has become increasingly detached from the cycles of nature, the dictates of geography, and the customs and features of local social contexts. This disembedding of social life has been facilitated by the universalization of reflexivity through the progressive rationalization of all social practices. Everything we do is subject to an ongoing critique based on the continuous feedback of a commitment to reason that is oriented to the principled justification of our beliefs and actions in the light of incoming knowledge, not past customary patterns of action. In the full development of our culture, the rule of a radicalized reason has called the certainties of science itself into question (e.g., postmodernist thought). But in the mundane world, science and the expert systems associated with it have penetrated all aspects of our existence, rendering daily life an exercise in perpetual self-reflection, based on the latest findings of sociologists, psychologists, medical experts, and others. All of this is happening, of course, within a globalizing context in which events and developments in distance places are, in a complex way, impacting the conditions under which we live as well as our attitudes. Economic upheavals in one part of the globe are reshaping overnight the prospects of others thousands of miles away, just as watching the news every evening embroils thousands of people, intellectually and emotionally, in tragedies and triumphs happening half a world away.

Giddens envisions the social-psychological consequences of living under these conditions in terms of a dialectic of "trust and risk" (building on Beck 1992). At the heart of the modern global social order is trust in the abstract systems of expertise that make our world work. It is these systems that guarantee there is order—a social and technological order that transcends and coordinates the complex relations between the local and the global, individuals and social systems, nature and humanity. This trust is imperative, yet paradoxically it is perpetually imperiled by the very institutionalized reflexivity that warrants its existence. What is more, the modern societal need for trust happens in a new collective environment of risk unlike anything experienced by past societies.

The risk profile of modernity has a number of unique features. First, we are subject to risks that have been globalized, in terms of both the intensity of the risks (e.g., nuclear holocaust or planetary ecological disasters) and the expanding number of contingent events that can affect almost everyone on the planet. Second, we are subject to risks stemming from our interventions into nature, plus the "institutionalized risk environments" we have developed, like investment markets. Third, our perception of the risks has been altered in at least three ways: (1) there is an ever wider awareness of the risks to which humanity is subject, (2) there is less confidence that the risks can be averted by supernatural or magical means, and (3) people are increasingly aware of the limitations of expert systems to cope with the risks, even those they created (Dawson 2004: 84–85).

In the face of these stark realities, Giddens argues that people have sought compensation in the intense cultivation of personal relationships and in a heightened sense of subjective identity. Friendships, romantic partnerships, and parent-child relationships have taken on a magnified importance as forums for the continued cultivation of the ontological security first imparted to all of us (normally) in the earliest years of family life. In a globalizing, risk-riddled world, people have turned inward to a "reflexive project of identity construction" to create the necessary sense of meaning in their lives. Self-actualization has become the new norm of maturation and success. But identity construction requires the cooperation of others; it is the product of social interaction. As we become disembedded from the traditional collective contexts of identity formation, attention has turned to the cultivation of a new ideal—what Giddens calls "the pure relationship." Life is becoming a series of such relationships, characterized by an unprecedented ethic of "mutual self-disclosure." These idealized relationships have become the natural forums for the creation of the self-narratives that are used to impart a sense of purpose to our lives.

But in the end, Giddens worries, we may be asking too much of our intimate relationships, and some people have trouble finding such relationships at all. The reiterated promise of the exaggerated mythology of romantic love that suffuses our society is subject to episodic failures that can bring on "fateful moments" when the harsh realities rush in upon us, shattering the trust that is central to our continued and willing participation in the given social order.

In the face of the ceaseless anxiety that constitutes so much of late modern life, Giddens recognizes that many people will still seek refuge in the order provided by a religious worldview. On whole, religion is still closely associated, Giddens asserts, with the provision of trust. Religions tend to "remoralize" life, providing the reassurance required to make important commitments when only partial information and understanding are available. New religions in particular try to creatively reassert the greater transcendent, even supernatural, significance of our most personal acts, providing a safer forum for both identity experimentation and the quest for pure relationships. In some more reactionary cases they also provide a new kind of collective and traditionalist context to guide the social processes of identity formation and protection. Of course in the contemporary globalizing context, the many different religions on offer tend to relativize the claims of all. But the elective fit between the socially structured needs of many people in late modern societies and certain religious choices would seem to be sufficient to assure the survival of numerous religious subcultures.

At present, however, we lack the research to "connect the dots": to establish a correlation between people's experience of these features of modernity and their behavior, especially their religious choices. Dawson's theory is plausible but still totally speculative.

Teaching about the Significance of New Religious Movements

On the one hand, the significance of NRMs is a difficult topic to address in the classroom. The issues involved are quite sweeping in scope and the theories rather abstract. On the other hand, the theories highlight problematic features of modern life that are experienced, presumably, by many of students. To the extent that students recognize the plausibility of the identified flaws in modernity, they can develop a more empathetic understanding of why these groups exist.

To this end, instructors need to make notions like the de-institutionalization of the private sphere or the anxieties born of living in a risk-riddled society more specific and real. This will, of course, test the limits of these theories as well. Students can often identify with the ideas in broad outline and translate the suppositions into concrete examples from their own lives or that of their friends and family. But they soon note a problem. The conditions addressed by these theories may afflict everyone, to varying degrees, yet few people choose to join a NRM or even to actively espouse an alternative spiritual worldview. Clearly we need to know more about how the problems discussed are actually manifested in society, if at all, and the nature of people's responses. We need to explore the

factors that may condition the relative susceptibility of people to these deficiencies and their openness to a religious response, particularly an alternative
religious response. At present we lack the information required to close this
explanatory gap. But it remains fruitful for students to contemplate the possibilities.

It may be advantageous in raising the awareness and potential empathy of
students to begin with some fairly obvious evidence of the reenchantment of
the West through a discussion of the religious, spiritual, and mythological
iconography and themes of such emblematic manifestations of contemporary
popular culture as the *Star Wars*, *The Matrix*, *Harry Potter*, and *The Lord of the
Rings* films (and books). Simply identifying the themes in one or two of these
films can lead into a discussion of the role they may play in the tremendous
popularity of these cultural productions. Is the success of these films linked to
their mystical and supernatural elements? How is this the case? And if so,
what does it say about the demand for "supernatural compensators," to use
Stark's language, in late modern society?

Students could be asked to form groups to view and report on different
films, or everyone could watch the same movie at home or in class. Or groups
could be asked to analyze different aspects of a film or films that are raised in
an initial discussion and report back to the class or write a brief essay. There
are many options. The rather open-ended character of the assignment need
not matter since it is an exercise in consciousness raising. In an entertaining
way it engages the students in an act of "thick description," to use Geertz's
(1973) evocative description of cultural anthropology.

The storyline of *The Lord of the Rings*, for example, is replete with magical,
mystical, and downright supernatural figures and feats, cast against the backdrop of an epic struggle between the forces of good and evil. It is a tale of
sorcerers, demons, curses, and strange creatures, all focused on a superhuman
quest that will determine the fate of the world. It is a quest in which everything depends on the paradoxical perseverance of an innocent, childlike, and
reluctant hero. These are the stock elements of much of the mythological and
religious literature of the world, as are the very human subcurrents of trust,
faith, love, temptation, betrayal, fall from grace, and redemption that are
reiterated throughout the three films of *The Lord of the Rings*.

To illustrate my point, let us briefly consider some of the features of just
one of the central figures of the story, Gandalf the wizard. He is the gentle and
reassuring father figure, the sage, and he is at the heart of almost all that
happens. By repeated allusion, it is clear that he is aligned with some greater
but undisclosed wisdom and power. He is in part a magician, saving the day
through spells and supernatural feats, but he is also a prophet, darkly raising
the alarm of impending doom and intent on calling forth and uniting the
forces of resistance. He alone at first understands the peculiar logic of sending
the small and inconsequential hobbit, Frodo, to defeat the great evil force
Sauron and his vast armies of disgusting orcs. He is instrumental in forging
the fellowship of the ring that is to accompany Frodo—a diverse group of
unusual beings, mixing the innocent and outcasts. Gandalf leads the small

band through many dangers, including a magical battle with another wizard, Saruman of Isengard, who has betrayed him and seeks to serve Sauron. At the mid-point of the story, as a result of his fight with the Balrog, a monster made of fire, Gandalf is dragged into the underworld, making a dangerous journey reminiscent of the spiritual feats of shamans throughout the ages. Supernaturally he returns from certain death, transformed. "Gandalf the grey" has become "Gandalf the white." He is purified by a mysterious encounter with some greater knowledge and imbued with new and even greater powers. With his new vision of the world, he alone never loses faith in Frodo and the eventual triumph of good over evil.

Yet nearing the end of the third and final film, *The Return of the King*, in one of the most explicitly religious moments of the story, he provides a glimpse of what he has learned and perhaps how all their struggles are secondary to a greater reality. Trapped in dire circumstances, Gandalf pauses to comfort and reassure the terrified hobbit Pippin (and perhaps himself) by sharing a vision of the afterlife. The scene is set: as dawn breaks on the second day of battle, the glorious white city of Minas Tirith lies largely in ruins. Orcs and trolls are hammering at the sixth and last gate protecting the inner city. As the wood of the gate begins to splinter and soldiers rush to reinforce it, the following brief dialogue occurs (with instructions from the script):

PIPPIN (QUIET)   I didn't think it would end this way...
[Gandalf looks at the small hobbit a beat.]

GANDALF (GENTLY)   End? No, the journey doesn't end here.
[Pippin looks up at Gandalf, questioningly.]

GANDALF   Death is just another path, one that we all must take.
[Gandalf looks down to see Pippin looking up at him with fear in his eyes.]

GANDALF (REMEMBERING)   The grey rain curtain of this world rolls back and all turns to silver glass... [to himself] and then you see it...
[Gandalf breaks off, lost in reverie.]

PIPPIN   What, Gandalf? See what?

GANDALF   White   shores... And beyond... A far green country under a swift sunrise.
[Pippin stares up at the old wizard's face, softened, quiet and full of peace]

PIPPIN (QUIET)   Well, that isn't so bad.

GANDALF (GENTLY)   No... No, it isn't.

In the surfeit of confusion and violence of the battle, the moment stands out in its quiet and poetic poignancy.

The religious or spiritual content of each of *The Lord of the Rings* films mentioned is rich, and calling attention to them should raise the question of their relevance in students' minds. Why have they resonated with so many in our supposedly secular age? Have the students' views of the world been influenced by their exposure to these films? Have their expectations changed? Students may acknowledge the links to deeper currents in their psyches, born of their childhood immersion in fantasy, and this issue could become another topic to explore in relation to new religious activities. In other words, these movies can be used to explore the reenchantment thesis and to inquire if this kind of commodification of the spiritual and occult is evidence of the triviali-zation or the persistence—perhaps even magnification—of religious needs in our society.

Such a free-ranging discussion, done in small groups or with the whole class, provides a convenient forum to further investigate the nature of our shared spiritual aspirations (as postulated by Stark and others) and how they may or may not be related to a mounting sense of anxiety caused by a growing aware-ness of the risks around us. In this regard students might simply be asked to itemize the risks that they think are impinging on their lives, introducing in the process, perhaps, their own dealings with the deinstitutionalization of the private sphere, the clash of contractual and covenantal obligations. Clearly the role and function of identity construction projects and pure relationships are addressed by these popular films as well. At the core of each is a strong emphasis on the agonizing introspection and reflexivity of the heroes, and the nature and need for strong friendships—"pure relationships" characterized by self-sacrificing love and loyalty in the name of a greater good. It might be argued that such themes are part of their ideology, projecting the norms of contemporary society onto a universal stage through the fictionalized worlds and histories they propagate.

The discussion options are almost endless, and aspects of the four the-ories can be freely integrated. At this stage staying true to the details of each theory is less important than fostering an awareness of the broader interpre-tive contexts for interpreting the significance of NRMs. The theories, after all, are speculative. In the process students will learn something about the her-meneutical character of the relationship between their observations and the theories, and how NRMs can function as "objects to think with" about im-portant issues in their lives and societies.

NOTE

The quotation from the film *The Lord of the Rings: The Return of the King* is from page 509 of the movie script. See www.allmoviescripts.com/movie-scripts/509.

REFERENCES

Aidala, Angela. 1985. "Social Change, Gender Roles, and New Religious Movements." *Sociological Analysis* 46, 287–314.
Anthony, Dick, and Thomas Robbins. 1992. "Law, Social Science, and the 'Brain-washing' Exception to the First Amendment." *Behavioral Sciences and the Law* 10, 5–27.
Beck, Ulrich. 1992. *Risk Society: Towards a New Modernity*. London: Sage.
Beckford, James. 1989. *Religion and Advanced Industrial Society*. London: Unwin Hyman.

————. 2001. "The Continuum between 'Cults' and 'Normal' Religion." In *Chercheurs de Dieux dans l'espace Public*, ed. Pauline Cote, 11–20. Ottawa: University of Ottawa Press.

Bellah, Robert. 1976. "New Religious Consciousness and the Crisis of Modernity." In *The New Religious Consciousness*, ed. Charles Glock and Robert Bellah, 333–52. Berkeley: University of California Press.

Berger, Peter L. 1967. *The Sacred Canopy*. Garden City, NY: Doubleday.

Berger, Peter L., Brigitte Berger, and Hansfried Kellner. 1974. *The Homeless Mind: Modernization and Consciousness*. New York: Vintage Books.

Bromley, David G., and Bruce C. Busching. 1988. "Understanding the Structure of Contractual and Convenantal Social Relations: Implications for the Sociology of Religion." *Sociological Analysis* 49 (Suppl.), 15–32.

Bromley, David G., and J. Gordon Melton, eds. 2002. *Cults, Religions and Violence*. Cambridge, UK: Cambridge University Press.

Bromley, David G., and Anson Shupe Jr. 1981. *Strange Gods: The Great American Cult Scare*. Boston: Beacon Press.

Bruce, Steve. 2002. *God Is Dead: Secularization in the West*. Oxford: Blackwell.

Davie, Grace. 1994. *Religion in Britain Since 1945: Believing without Belonging*. Oxford: Blackwell.

Dawson, Lorne L. 1998a. *Comprehending Cults: The Sociology of New Religious Movements*. Toronto: Oxford University Press.

————. 1998b. "Anti-Modernism, Modernism, and Postmodernism: Struggling with the Cultural Significance of New Religious Movements." *Sociology of Religion* 59, 131–56.

————. 2001. "The Cultural Significance of New Religious Movements: The Case of Soka Gakkai." *Sociology of Religion* 63, 337–64.

————. 2004. "The Sociocultural Significance of Modern New Religious Movements." In *The Oxford Handbook of New Religious Movements*, ed. James R. Lewis, 68–98. New York: Oxford University Press.

————. 2005. "Privatization, Globalization and Religious Innovation: Giddens' Theory of Modernity and the Refutation of Secularization Theory." In *Religion and Social Theory*, ed. James A. Beckford and John Walliss, 105–19. London: Ashgate.

Geertz, Clifford. 1973. "Thick Description: Toward an Interpretive Theory of Culture." In *The Interpretation of Cultures*, ed. Clifford Geertz, 3–30. New York: Basic Books.

Giddens, Anthony. 1990. *The Consequences of Modernity*. Cambridge, UK: Polity Press.

————. 1991. *Modernity and Self Identity: Self and Society in the Late Modern Age*. Cambridge, UK: Polity Press.

Hunter, James Davison. 1981. "The New Religions: Demodernization and the Protest against Modernity." In *The Social Impact of the New Religious Movements*, ed. Bryan Wilson, 1–19. New York: The Rose of Sharon Press.

Lambert, Yves. 1999. "Secularization or New Religious Paradigms?" *Sociology of Religion* 60, 303–33.

Luckmann, Thomas. 1967. *The Invisible Religion*. New York: Macmillan.

Mol, Hans J. 1976. *Identity and the Sacred*. New York: Free Press.

Palmer, Susan J. 1994. *Moon Sisters, Krishna Mothers, Rajneesh Lovers: Women's Roles in New Religions*. Syracuse, NY: Syracuse University Press.

Partridge, Christopher. 2004. "Alternative Spiritualities, New Religions, and the Reenchantment of the West." In *The Oxford Handbook of New Religious Movements*, ed. James R. Lewis, 39–67. New York: Oxford University Press.

Porter, Jennifer E., and Darcee L. McLaren, eds. 1999. *"Star Trek" and Sacred Ground: Explorations of "Star Trek," Religion, and American Culture*. Albany: State University of New York Press.

Richardson, James T., ed. 1988. *Money and Power in New Religions*. Lewiston, NY: Edwin Mellen Press.

———. 1993. "A Social Psychological Critique of 'Brainwashing' Claims about Recruitment to New Religions." In *The Handbook on Cults and Sects in America*, Part B, ed. David G. Bromley and Jeffrey K. Hadden, 75–97. Greenwich, CT: JAI Press.

———. 1995. "Legal Status of Minority Religions in the United States." *Social Compass* 42, 249–64.

Robbins, Thomas. 1988a. *Cults, Converts and Charisma*. London: Sage.

———. 1988b. "The Transformative Impact of the Study of New Religious Movements on the Study of Religion." *Journal for the Scientific Study of Religion* 27, 12–31.

Robbins, Thomas, and David G. Bromley. 1992. "Social Experimentation and the Significance of American New Religions: A Focused Review Essay." In *Research in the Social Scientific Study of Religion*, Vol. 4, ed. Monty Lynn and David Moberg, 1–28. Greenwich, CT: JAI Press.

———. 1993. "What Have We Learned about New Religions? New Religious Movements as Experiments." *Religious Studies Review* 19, 209–16.

Singer, Margaret T. 1995. *Cults in Our Midst: The Hidden Menace in Our Everyday Lives*. San Francisco: Jossey-Bass.

Stark, Rodney, and William Sims Bainbridge. 1985. *The Future of Religion*. Berkeley: University of California Press.

Stout, Daniel, and Judith M. Buddenbaum. 2001. *Religion and Popular Culture: Studies on the Interaction of Worldviews*. Ames: Iowa University Press.

Tipton, Steven M. 1982. *Getting Saved from the Sixties*. Berkeley: University of California Press.

Wallis, Roy. 1982. "The New Religions as Social Indicators." In *New Religious Movements: A Perspective for Understanding Society*, ed. Eileen Barker, 216–31. New York: Edwin Mellen Press.

———. 1984. *The Elementary Forms of New Religious Life*. London: Routledge and Kegan Paul.

Weber, Max. 1946. "The Social Psychology of the World Religions." In *From Max Weber*, ed. Hans H. Gerth and C. Wright Mills, 267–301. New York: Oxford University Press.

Wilson, Bryan R. 1976. *The Contemporary Transformation of Religion*. Oxford: Clarendon.

Young, John L., and Ezra E. H. Griffiths. 1992. "A Critical Evaluation of Coercive Persuasion as Used in the Assessment of Cults." *Behavioral Sciences and the Law* 10, 89–101.

Deliberate Heresies: New Religious Myths and Rituals as Critiques

Susan J. Palmer and David G. Bromley

In the emerging area of new religions studies (NRS), there has been very little systematic discussion of myth and ritual in the new religious movements (NRM) that adopts any of the various theoretical traditions, with the notable exception of work by Bird (1978) and Westley (1983a). Rather, at the heart of NRS is a growing body of case studies of individual NRMs through which NRS scholars are mapping the range of myth and ritual practices and attempting to identify distinctive characteristics of NRM myth and ritual.

For a number of reasons, there is considerably more scholarship on NRM myths than on rituals. Doctrines and beliefs are generally more accessible through written materials and do not have to be gathered through participant observation. Oppositional groups, both religious and secular, have used NRM myths to demonstrate the heretical or absurd quality of the movements. Finally, since NRMs are virtually never completely novel but draw on existing religious traditions in various ways, religious studies scholars in particular have been interested in connecting NRM doctrinal systems to established religious traditions. By contrast, identifying ritual practices is more problematic. In new groups, formal rituals often develop slowly and are not as easily identified early in a movement's development. It is also true, particularly in communally organized movements that separate themselves from conventional society, that much of group life is ritualistic in nature, making it difficult to distinguish ritual from other types of behavior. Finally, NRM rituals have tended to be dismissed as contrived both because they challenge conventional understandings and because their newness makes them appear contrived.

The two most prominent characteristics of NRM myths and rituals are that they are in the process of being born and they are oppositional in nature. NRM myths express an oppositional stance toward the myths legitimating the institutions of the larger society—churches, state, nuclear family, government, science—or social conventions governing other types of social relationships, such as race and gender. A survey of case studies reveals that the mythmakers in new religions (usually the charismatic leaders) are deliberately and self-consciously heretical. In short, NRMs and their charismatic leaders pose a challenge to the status quo. The original myth imparted by the charismatic leader also typically undergoes surprising revisions over time, often in response to or at least in synchronicity with, changes of circumstances, censure, or pressure. Because NRM myths are in the process of being constructed and undergo frequent change, they seem to outsiders to have an artificial, carefully crafted, self-consciously concocted, expedient quality about them. They appear to be unlike the myths found in tribal societies or established religious traditions, whose origin is hidden in the mists of time or in the mystery of inadequately documented exotic or ancient cultures whose sacred narratives must be accepted by contemporary scholars as a "given" that just "happened."

This chapter will survey the research on myth and ritual conducted by NRS scholars. The mythic and ritual worlds of a range of NRMs will be described. To assist the teaching of a course in new religions studies, we have provided guidelines for teaching myth and ritual as well as offered specific lesson plans. However, before focusing on these elementary forms of new religious life, it is useful to examine the various traditional disciplinary approaches to the study of myth and ritual in mature, more conventional religious traditions.

Alternative Approaches to Myth and Ritual

There is a wealth of theory on myth and ritual in the disciplines of anthropology and religious studies; indeed, myth and ritual have become subfields in their own right. The word *myth* derives from *mythos* in ancient Greek, which simply means "story." As opposed to popular usage, in which *myth* has a negative connotation and is used to dismiss a story or claim as being false, in the context of religious studies, *myth* generically refers to a sacred story or narrative about supernatural beings (Ellwood 1973: 78). However, there are a number of alternative interpretive approaches to understanding myth. Kessler (2003: 90–92) identifies six different theoretical perspectives on myth: the rationalist, the symbolist, the functionalist, the structuralist, the phenomenological, and the myth-ritual connection. Rationalist theory views myth as a proto-scientific effort by primitive people to explain natural phenomena. Symbolic theories of myth assume that myths have hidden psychological meanings that can be decoded (Eliade 1963; Jung 1938). Functionalist interpretations of myth argue that myths operate to provide societies with meaning, identity, and a sense of social cohesion and contribute to the psychological well-being, survival skills, and socialization process of individuals. Structuralist theory approaches myths as cognitive structures, like a grammar or syntax, that allow people to resolve paradoxes in their lives and integrate their experiences of the world into a meaningful pattern, often by relating a story that begins with binary oppositions (Levi-Strauss 2000). Phenomenological theory takes the position that myths are repositories of authentic spiritual knowledge from the perspective of a culture and should be taken seriously as emic narrations of sacred histories and manifestations of a hidden sacred cosmos. Finally, the myth and ritual theory insists that these two essential components of religion are integrally related—that ritual is a reenactment of myth, just as a play is the performance of a script.

The word *ritual* derives from the Latin *ritus*. Rituals clearly are complex social forms, and the study of ritual has become a distinct area of study. The ritual studies group was established for the study of ritual at the 1977 meeting of the American Academy of Religion, with the objective of combining the normative interests of theology, the descriptive objectives of the history and phenomenology of religion, and the analytical concerns of anthropology. Definitions of ritual vary in scope. While Wuthnow defines ritual loosely as "an expressive dramatic aspect of all behavior," most scholars define the term more narrowly as "a formal liturgical act" (Bird 1978: 109). One finds conflicting approaches to the problem of defining ritual, and these differences reflect the disciplinary approach, whether anthropological, psychological, or phenomenological.

Edmund Leach conceptualizes ritual very broadly in terms of any sets of behavior that are culturally defined and communicated. For some phenomenologists and historians of religion, rituals are conscious and voluntary attempts to encounter the "numinous" (Rudolph Otto) or the "sacred" (Mircea Eliade). Anthropologist Evans Wentz focuses on the explicitly religious meanings of ritual and on the impact of its emotional force. Others, like Clifford Geertz and Victor Turner, emphasize the sociological function of ritual—how symbolic actions unify individuals into one community—but they also acknowledge the psychological power of ritual in encapsulating a people's worldview. Emile Durkheim as a sociologist, argues that societies generate myths and symbols in order to mirror themselves. For Durkheim, the idea of the sacred is essentially a social idea. Thus, a society's deepest values and social structure is reflected in its cosmology and accompanying ceremonies. Clifford Geertz argues that the convergence of symbols effected in rituals enables us to see how a people consider their religion encapsulated in specific performances whereby they can educate themselves and visitors in the essence of the abstract totality of their religious culture.

Cults and the Chasm between Disciplines

There appears to be a "great divide" between the sociological school and the psychoanalytical school of ritual studies. Whereas psychologists tend to focus on the individual's experience of religion, sociologists and anthropologists analyze religion as a social institution—as a collective enterprise. For example, Sigmund Freud (1938) represents the psychoanalytical approach and treats ritual as a collective version of the personal neurosis that he labeled "obsessive compulsion." Thus, for Freud, God is the father. By contrast, for Durkheim, God is society. Ritual is considered "normal" healthy behavior by sociologists, but is diagnosed as a symptom of abnormal, pathological states by psychologists and psychoanalysts. Psychoanalytical approaches tend to lean toward reductionism and assume that rituals are the product of neurotic compulsions; thus, a "ritual" is any irrational, symbolic or stereotyped behavior, in contrast to pragmatic, instrumental behavior that is rationally linked to empirical goals. Psychoanalytic theory treats nonrational or formalized symbolic behavior as "ritual"—that is, distinct from pragmatic ends-directed behavior linked to empirical goals.

This great divide between two disciplines becomes even wider when it is the symbolic actions of unconventional religions that are being studied. Whereas a sociologist may analyze cult rituals within the same theoretical framework used to interpret aboriginal rites or Catholic folk religion, an anti-cult psychologist is more likely to explain new meditation practices as techniques of "mind control." In a similar vein, initiation rituals are perceived as a pathological surrender to the cult leader's megalomaniacal agenda (see Saliba 1993 and this volume).

Types of New Religious Movements

For presentation purposes, it is also useful to distinguish among types of NRMs. Following Wallis (1979, 1984, 1985), NRMs are divided into world-affirming and world-rejecting movements. The former, such as est, Scientology, Osho, Raelians, and New Age groups, affirm the norms and values of conventional society and invite adherents to realize their untapped individual potential without distancing themselves from their everyday lives. The latter, such as The Family International, Unificationism, Krishna Consciousness, and the Branch Davidians, demand that adherents separate from a society that is condemned as corrupt and doomed to ultimate destruction. Wallis also identifies a third type, world-accommodating movements, which adopt a neutral stance toward society. His third type is not considered in this chapter. It is interesting to note that Frederick Bird (1978) posits an entirely compatible typology of NRMs. However, Bird classifies movements according to their system of ethics, whereas Wallis bases his typology on the movements' stances toward society.

The Mythic Worlds of New Religious Movements

A survey of NRM myths reveals a diverse array of worldviews. Consistent with their oppositional stance, NRMs typically rewrite the script describing the origin and ultimate destiny of humankind and the universe. These scripts include myths of origin and separation, which chronicle the original, ultimate purpose of creation and the separation from the essence of creation; myths that lay out the requisite path to restoration or salvation to the original, intended state; and charisma myths that establish and legitimate claims to sacred authority.

Origin/Separation Myths

Origin/separation myths are a primary basis for the radically alternative worldview of an NRM group. New religious creation myths challenge prevailing worldviews and turn upside down conventional notions of "what is." These may be original myths accessed through the charismatic founder's revelations or heretical interpretations of myths from traditional religions. Origin/separation myths are particularly important because they communicate original intent and ultimate purpose, and they offer an explanation for the current trials and tribulations faced by humanity. These problems are attributed to a separation from the original state or purpose of creation, analogous to the "Fall of Man" in Christianity. The myths then offer some means of restoration to humankind's original state, which may involve the destruction of the present social order. Revised or alternative origin/separation myths thus issue a direct challenge to bedrock assumptions and premises of the established social order.

New Age religions, which typically are world-affirming, challenge the materialism of contemporary culture through creation myths that convey a radical Gnostic view of reality in which the material world is an illusion or the creation of the world was a divine error or a malicious joke perpetrated by demiurge or rebellious son of God. Many UFO groups produce myths that subvert the Creation myth in Genesis by substituting aliens for God, and at the same time challenge a scientific worldview by blurring the line between science and magic.

According to the Raelians, for example, the biblical myth is in error (Palmer 1994, 2004). Humankind was created by an advanced, extraterrestrial race, the Elohim (those who come from the sky). The Elohim have developed the capacity to create life from DNA. They selected Earth as an experimental laboratory where they initially created plants and animals before creating humans. Humans in all religious traditions have misunderstood their origins, as reflected in the biblical creation myth and other origin myths. The implications are profound. Since humans were created by advanced but mortal entities, humans are not spiritual beings. After creating humankind, the Elohim left humans to progress at their own pace. However, since humans were unable to understand the true source of their creation, they misinterpreted their origins as reflected in the biblical creation myth (as well as the origin myths in other religious traditions).

The Ramtha School of Enlightenment, founded by J. Z. Knight, who channels the entity Ramtha, is based on a creation myth remarkably similar to that of the second-century Gnostic philosopher Valentinus (Melton 1998). Ramtha also draws on the paraphysics of David Boehm, *advaita* Hinduism, medieval alchemy, and legends of Lost Atlantis. According to Ramtha's teachings, in the beginning there was infinity of Thought, which is the equivalent of God. God assumed a unique form when Thought contemplated Thought. A foundational principle of existence is that the contemplation of thought inherently expands thought. One critical manifestation of this principle was that the contemplation of Thought expanded into Light. Humanity came into being as "particums" of Light, with each particum becoming an individual being and a god, an individual representation of the Mind of God. The particums of Light in turn contemplated the idea of Light into matter, which produced the physical universe. The light beings also created all of the forms of life that inhabit Earth. The light beings decided to assume material form, becoming god-men who then evolved over time. Each individual, therefore, is a human manifestation of God, which allows the eternal expansion of Thought.

Initially, light beings lived in their material bodies as immortal entities. As physical beings, however, the light beings began to lose touch with their divinity and experience limitations, confining them to material existence. While beings were able to reproduce their own embodied experience, they continued to become more limited and lost touch with their own divinity. Traditional forms of religion have been one of the main forces in suppressing beings' understanding of their divine nature by teaching that God and humanity are separate, when in fact they are one.

Scientology begins from the Buddhist premise that everything that is emanates from Pure Thought, and introduces immortal, omniscient, omnipotent beings called Thetans who decide to create as a game for their amusement the material universe (Bromley and Bracey 1998). In the beginning, Thetans were gods of their own universes. However, when Thetans decided to take on a series of physical bodies to experience the pleasures of material existence, through cycles of reincarnation they began losing touch with their true nature. This process occurred as a result of traumatic experiences that happened in the current and past lives of the now material beings. Traumatic experiences cause the analytic mind—which is a conscious, completely rational mechanism capable of dealing directly with experienced reality—to shut down and the reactive mind to take over and protect the analytic mind. These traumatic experiences are then recorded and stored as "engrams" (negative electrical charges) in the reactive mind. Over the course of one's lifetimes, engrams continue to accumulate, preventing the analytic mind from functioning effectively, diminishing individuals' capacity to relate to others and suppressing individuals' comprehension of their true nature.

In the Rajneesh/Osho movement, Bhagwan Shree Rajneesh developed a complex set of ideas that defies simple summary because Rajneesh believed in the priority of experience over ideas and that the world embodies inconsistency and a dynamic interrelationship of opposites (Carter 1990; Goldman 1999; Palmer 1994). Nonetheless, there are some core themes in his teachings. Rajneesh taught that all humans are innately divine—Buddhas who possess the capacity for enlightenment. However, humans do not understand who they truly are. The source of the problem is the mind, which is a mechanism for survival. In the process of developing survival strategies by using their minds, humans stop expressing their true essence and their authentic selfhood. The result is that humans live an instrumental, reactive existence, suppressing their genuine feelings as part of this survival strategy. Humans have become trapped in repressive, corrupt institutions of their own making.

Rajneesh was caustic toward a broad range of conventional institutions and relationships. One major challenge in Rajneesh mythology was traditional gender roles. In *A New Vision of Women's Liberation* (1987), Rajneesh offers his disciples a light-hearted parody of the Jewish legend of Lilith. Rajneesh's Lilith is strong, rebellious, and incompatible with Adam; by contrast, Eve is reduced to a state of slavery through monogamy. Rajneesh takes this opportunity to oppose orthodox theology and conventional sex roles, calling the Trinity "a gay men's club" and marriage "the coffin of love." In addition, humans live in an environment threatened by nuclear destruction, an AIDS pandemic, and overpopulation. In fact, Rajneesh anticipated that AIDS would produce a cataclysm of unprecedented proportions; two-thirds of humanity would perish, with only his disciples surviving unscathed.

In world-rejecting movements, there is greater emphasis on separation from a corrupt world. These movements are likely to mount a challenge to a broad range of social institutions and social relationships. Unificationism accepts the Bible as true, but regards it as a cryptogram containing truths that were uninterpretable before the divine revelations received by Sun Myung Moon (Barker 1984; Bromley and Shupe 1979). These revelations, contained in *The Divine Principle* as well as speeches and writings by Moon, constitute a new understanding of biblical truths that are a direct challenge to traditional Christian doctrine on a number of counts. Basic to Unificationist theology is a rendering of human history as consisting of three stages: Creation, Fall, and Restoration. Unificationism challenges traditional Christian doctrine that Creation emerged out of nothingness by asserting that Creation was a reflection of God's innate character. Creation was the product of God's desire and capacity for love. God's plan for Adam and Eve was that they would first perfect themselves, taking on God's perfect nature, and then enter into a unified, loving relationship with God. Subsequently they would mature spiritually, create a God-centered family, and produce sinless children. Humankind would occupy a place higher than the angels, and God would grant humans dominion over all of creation. God's original plan for humanity was subverted by the archangel Lucifer, who became jealous at the special status accorded to humans. Lucifer spiritually seduced Eve, who then entered into an illicit sexual relationship with Adam. This illicit relationship and misdirected love, which upset God's plan for his human creations, constituted the Fall of Humankind. As a result, all future human generations traced their lineage to Satan rather than to God.

Unificationism also teaches that there was a second Fall when Cain committed fratricide against his brother Abel. This division within humanity was reflected at a societal level, most notably in the modern era in the international division between aetheistic communism (Cain forces) and God-fearing democracy (Abel forces). In Unification thought, it is the separation of humans from God and the divisions among humankind that are responsible for the diverse array of political, economic, racial, familial, and interpersonal problems plaguing humanity.

Both The Family International (Bainbridge 2002; Chancellor 2000) and the Branch Davidians (Wright 1995) focused more on the extent of the Fall of Man than on rewriting the origin myth. Family doctrine is rooted in traditional Christianity and accepts much of conventional Christian belief with respect to Creation and Fall, although the theology does contain distinctive, controversial interpretations and innovations, notably the Law of Love that justifies antinomian behavior, particularly in the area of sexual mores. The Family's controversial "ministry" of Flirty Fishing was based on this heretical version of Christian love. These doctrinal innovations were contained in messages that Berg reports having received through dreams, channeled spirits, and revelations from God.

The Family challenged traditional theological understandings most directly with respect to the Fall of Man. Family theology teaches that all mainstream churches are complicit in accepting a material, corrupt, ungodly existence. Berg referred to America as the "Whore of Babylon" described in the book of Revelations. He further announced that God had rejected the established church, which he referred to derisively as "churchianity." The Family International regarded itself as the faithful remnant that would continue to follow God's word until imminent Endtime events would vindicate and reward their faithfulness.

The Branch Davidians initially accepted many of the central teachings of Seventh-Day Adventism, but departed from traditional Christian theology on a number of points as the group constituted a schismatic offshoot of a sectarian movement. The Bible was supplemented, and in certain respects supplanted, by revelations of the living prophet. The Davidians also regarded themselves as a remnant church—one that would operate as a bridge between the current, corrupted social order and the imminent new order under the guidance of a living prophet. They expected the return of Christ and the inauguration of the millennium within their lifetimes.

Charisma Myths

Charismatic leaders typically are at the center of NRM mythmaking, although the myth construction project is interactive, as it is also shaped in a dynamic fashion by the responses and cues provided by the audience-followers (Forsthoefel and Humes 2005). Because charisma emerges through leaders' prophetic actions, charisma myths in new religions are alive, in the process of being forged around the living prophet or messianic leader. New religious leaders are at once the narrators and the chief protagonists in the stories they fashion; they are the creators of their own mythopoaeic narration. Charisma myths serve to create new charismatic figures that challenge the secular or religious authority of established leaders, saints, and heroes. These myths are a call to the followers for loyalty to the prophet and service to the prophet's dream and mission, which challenge conventional sources of religious authority. Among the most common patterns in charisma myths are one or more revelatory moments through which the charismatic personas of leaders and their supernatural gifts are established, and an escalation of their charismatic claims. These revelations and elevated charismatic claims are institutionalized through movement-sponsored histories and biographies and through charismatic performances that demonstrate the leaders' special status and abilities.

One way that NRM leaders establish their charismatic status is by adopting new identities, which distance them from their mundane pasts and signify special spiritual status. Among the world-affirming movements, Raël, the leader of the Raelians, was born Claude Vorilhon in 1946. He had been a race car driver and became known as Raël to his followers after allegedly encountering space aliens in 1973. J. Z. Knight, who had been a wife and mother prior to becoming a channel, did not adopt a new name personally but did create a shared identity with Ramtha, the entity whom she began channeling in 1977. Osho was born Rajneesh Chandra Mohan in 1931 and worked as a professor for a number of years before beginning a spiritual career as Acharya Rajneesh in 1966. The founder of est was born as Jack Rosenberg and worked in a variety of menial sales-related jobs before closing the door on his previous life, moving across the country, changing his name to Werner Erhard, and founding est. Among the world-rejecting movements, the founder of Unificationism was born Yong Myung Moon to a farm family in present-day North Korea in 1920, pursued a degree in electrical engineering, and later adopted the name Sun Myung Moon (Shining Sun and Moon) after an intense spiritual experience. Moses David Berg was born David Brant Berg in 1919 to a family of evangelical missionaries. He worked as a minister and an independent evangelist before later assuming the names Moses David after establishing the Children of God. Vernon Howell was born in Texas in 1959 and had a series of largely menial jobs before entering the Branch Davidian community, where he later assumed leadership of the group and proclaimed himself to be David Koresh.

Myths of charisma often describe the archetypal hero's magical journey, or his or her visitation by a supernatural entity. Among the world-affirming movements, Raël, a French contactee who blossomed into the messianic prophet-founder of the International Raelian movement, writes of his encounter in 1973 with an extraterrestrial who endowed him with the mission of prophet. Raël reports that he was selected by the Elohim in part because he was from France, a nation open to innovative ideas, and in part because his parents represented two major religious traditions, Catholicism and Judaism. He was informed that he is the last of forty prophets who are each the product of mixed earthly and Elohim parentage. In a later book, Raël describes being taken aboard a space ship and flown to the planet of the Elohim. There he had the privilege of meeting his half-brothers, Jesus and Buddha, on the alien's planet. His selection as a prophet by the Elohim, and his revelation that humankind had been created from DNA by the Elohim and placed on earth, was the basis of Raël's charismatic status among his followers.

J. Z. Knight, the famous West Coast channeler, describes in her biography how in early 1977 she beheld the 8,000-year-old warrior Ramtha standing like a pillar of purple light in her kitchen. Ramtha was from Lemuria, part of the lost continent of Atlantis, and had lived on Earth some 35,000 years ago. Standing before J. Z. Knight, Ramtha, the Enlightened One, informed her that she was greatly loved, that she would be a source of enlightenment to the world, and that he would help her over the "ditch" of fear and limitation. Knight's charisma is rooted in her selection as a channeler for Ramtha during moments of possession, when Ramtha takes over her body and speaks through her mouth.

Osho claimed to have almost attained enlightenment seven hundred years earlier, in a previous life. However, he was killed three days before he would have reached that state. In his current life, Osho claims to have first experienced enlightenment at the age of fourteen, but achieved complete enlightenment seven years later. Osho reported that he sat down under a tree and waited for enlightenment to occur. He experienced intense blissfulness that he recounted as a total death of his former self and a rebirth. It was not, however, until years later that he began his spiritual career and revealed his earlier experiences.

World-rejecting movements tend to generate similar myths. The prophetic myths of Mother Ann Lee, the eighteenth-century prophet and founder of the Shakers, and twentieth-century Reverend Sun Myung Moon show remarkable parallels. Both beheld a vision of the Fall in which Adam and Eve disobeyed God through a sexual act. Both claimed to be the Second Coming and included a feminine aspect of God in their messianic role: Ann Lee was messiah as woman, to balance the God in man Jesus, and Moon together with Mrs. Moon are the androgynous godhead incarnate.

David Koresh began his charismatic career with the Branch Davidians by winning organizational control of the small movement. Initially his teachings were consistent with the group's schismatic Seventh-Day Adventist doctrines. He asserted charismatic authority by linking his personal biography to a biblically defined spiritual lineage. Koresh changed his name from Vernon Howell to David Koresh. By taking the name David, Koresh asserted a direct link to the biblical King David, from whom it was expected the new messiah would be descended. *Koresh* is Hebrew for "Cyrus," name of the Persian king who defeated the Babylonians before the birth of Jesus. In this way, David Koresh announced himself as a messianic figure with a divinely ordained mission. He taught that his messianic role is crucial to human salvation because Christ had died only for those who lived prior to his crucifixion; Koresh's mission was necessary to permit the salvation of all subsequent generations.

In all three cases, these leaders continued to have various types of prophetic revelations that confirmed and solidified their charismatic authority. In contrast to Christ, who was sinless and therefore embodied an impossible standard for inherently sinful humans to achieve, Koresh was a "sinful messiah." By personally experiencing sin like all other humans, Koresh asserted, he could judge sinners more fairly. Koresh taught that human sinfulness does not prevent humans from attaining salvation.

It is quite common for charismatic leaders to begin their careers with limited charismatic authority and then assume greater authority over time. This growth in charismatic authority sometimes is responsive to followers who legitimate their own commitments on the basis of the leader's charisma and sometimes represents the leader's own quest for greater authority. Raël, for example, began his charismatic career as a contactee who wrote a book and set up a ufology club. Next he asserted his role as the Last Prophet and created a religion with strict guidelines and firm boundaries. Then he revealed his true identity as the son of an extraterrestrial named Yahweh, who chose Raël's mother (a fifteen-year-old girl from a farm near Vichy) for her "virgin DNA," and the half brother of Jesus and Buddha. Osho adopted the title Acharya (an enlightened teacher) in 1966 and then the title Bhagwan (Blessed One or Self Realized, who is the pure essence of the Divine) in 1971.

Moses David Berg began his charismatic career in The Family in 1967, ministering to countercultural youth in Huntington Beach, California. Initially he was known as Uncle Dave, and he preached an anti-establishment message to youthful followers. Members soon began taking on biblical names, and Uncle Dave became Moses. By 1971 Berg had declared himself God's Prophet for the Endtime, with absolute spiritual authority within the movement. David Koresh's initial relationship with the Branch Davidians was as a handyman on the property. He subsequently became a favorite of the group leader, Lois Roden, who ultimately anointed him as her successor. However, he weathered several internal power struggles before gaining control over the group. Once in control, Koresh had a series of prophetic revelations. He taught that Christ had died only for those who lived prior to his crucifixion. Koresh thus established his messianic mission by asserting his authority to grant salvation of all subsequent generations.

Another example of a charismatic career is Gilbert Bourdin, the founder of the Holy City of Mandarom. Bourdin was a yoga teacher from Martinique who came to France as a student and was initiated into *advaita* yoga by Swami Sivananda in 1961. After a meditation retreat in the French Alps, his enlightened state was recognized by Swami Yogesh Warananda, and he became an Acharya. In 1969 he became Swami Hamsananda, wrote books on yoga, and established an ashram in the mountains of Provence near Castellane. In 1990 he assumed the messianic title of Hamsah Manarah and called press conference to announce the advent of the "Cosmoplanetary Messiah," an event that ushered in the Golden Age. Journalists were invited to attend a long coronation ceremony in which Bourdin received a series of crowns representing the world's great religions, culminating with the crown of the Cosmoplanetary Messiah that signified the unity of all faiths at the onset of the Golden Age.

In some cases, movements form around more specific mythic themes, such as race or gender, when stereotypes that have led to racial/gender oppression, enslavement, and persecution through history. In the case of race, for example, the Nation of Islam's myth of Yacoub recasts St. John of Revelations as an evil black scientist who bred the first soulless white men as a perverse experiment in his laboratory that necessitated the slaughter of thousands of black babies.

The Nuwaubians' prophet-founder, Dr. Malachi York, relates sagas of extra-terrestrial invasions that explain our planet's racial diversity in his book, *The Paleman* (1990). Hideous reptilians are the ancestors of white-skinned people, whereas black people are descended from the Annaqi, beautiful dark-skinned extraterrestrials with woolly hair and benign qualities. The curse of Ham came about because Noah's son Ham beheld his father drunk and naked, and he was beset with homosexual desires. As a consequence, all his children were born with pale skin, the symptom of leprosy.

Restoration/Salvation

According to the Raelians, humankind has now reached a sufficiently advanced state that it is capable of understanding its origin and ready to meet the Elohim. Humanity is therefore now living in the Age of Apocalypse and is presented with the opportunity to develop an interplanetary consciousness and enter the Golden Age or, alternatively, to embark on self-destruction. The Raelians seek to lead humankind toward salvation individually and collectively. On an individual level, the Elohim have retained a cell from the body of each human ever born and thus possess each person's unique DNA. Based on the quality of an individual's earthly existence, he or she may or may not be recreated from his or her DNA sample. Those who are recreated will have the right to an eternal existence on the Elohim's planet. On the collective level, the Raelians seek to establish an embassy in Israel where the Elohim can meet with representatives of all the world's governments. The Raelians propose a world government that will be run by a geniocracy, the most intelligent humans, and will operate on the principle of humanitarianism.

From a Rajneeshee standpoint, humans are already divine; they simply need to become and reflect that truth. In order to achieve enlightenment, individuals go through four stages in their search for the truth: (1) the deep-sleep stage, in which individuals simply accept dogmatic truths; (2) the searching stage, in which the multitude of answers results in confusion for the searcher; (3) the awakening stage, when the individuals accept an enlightened master who guides them in finding their true identity; and (4) the final, enlightenment stage, when the mind disappears and individuals connect with the center of their own being. Rajneesh's objective is to create the "new man," an authentic human who would be loving, honest, and trusting, one who would combine spirituality with a zest for living. Surrendering to Rajneesh and becoming a sannyasin create the basis for ultimate enlightenment.

Since Scientology doctrine teaches that each individual is actually an immortal Thetan, the primary goal for Scientology is understanding how to recapture that lost essence and return to the individual's "native state." In their native state, individuals are "at cause" in dealing with events and relationships in their everyday lives, rather than reacting to the effects of past traumas. According to Scientology, the problem that all humans face is that memories of traumatic experiences in their present or past lives are stored in the one component of their mind (the "reactive" mind) as electrical charges (engrams).

The number of engrams continues to increase, and they inhibit the individual's ability to use the rational, adaptive mind (the "analytic" mind) to relate rationally to the environment and other people. Since individuals cannot assess reality accurately or relate meaningfully to others as a result of an accumulation of engrams, constant mistrust, misunderstanding, and conflict are the result. The path to restoration of the true personal essence, therefore, is to be found in "clearing" the engrams from the reactive mind. Restoring one's true identity as a Thetan is a progressive process involving the capacity to respond to an ascending hierarchy of needs. A significant step in achieving freedom is attaining a state of "clear," which signifies that engrams have been cleared from the reactive mind. At the highest level of these "dynamics," individuals become Operating Thetans, capable of transcending all material limitations and of uniting with the universe as spiritual entities with godlike qualities. At this level, individuals are able to transcend death; as incorporeal entities, they simply locate another body to inhabit. Only Scientology has developed an understanding of how to accomplish this goal. The vision is of a world of empowered beings who are capable of expressing their true essence and relating meaningfully with others.

In The Family International, the expectation is that a thoroughly corrupted world will collapse, most likely within the members' lifetimes. From their perspective, The Family constitutes the faithful remnant who must remain separated from the corrupted world and will be spared annihilation during the reign of the Antichrist. When the Antichrist is destroyed, Family members will be raptured and live forever in the Kingdom of Heaven. During the millennium, The Family's former oppressors will receive their just punishment and The Family will be rewarded with a central role in world governance, since members truly understand the meaning of a godly government. In the meantime, the focus of Family members is on saving souls, as members may be able to hasten the onset of the Endtime as well as enhance their spiritual status through their missionary activities.

In Unificationist theology, humankind's current problems have resulted from a primordial separation from God's original plan and purpose. Through history, God has offered humanity the opportunity for restoration when sufficient "indemnity" for sinfulness has been paid. The most recent historical opportunity occurred when God sent his son, Jesus, to complete the restoration process. It was the Divine Plan that Jesus would marry and have children, thereby re-establishing a God-centered lineage; however, Jesus was crucified before completing his mission. Another messianic figure is therefore required; Unificationists believe Reverend Moon to be that figure. What is necessary for human restoration is personal unification with the messiah as well as returning all of the major institutions to God's purpose.

David Koresh taught his disciples that a central problem facing humanity is that Jesus was able to ensure salvation only for those who were born until the time of his death. A new messianic figure was therefore required to offer salvation to those born over the subsequent millennia. This spiritual mission was increasingly urgent, as the world had already entered the period of tribulation preceding the Apocalypse. Koresh and his followers saw as their mission to convert followers and prepare the way for the impending Apocalypse and establishment of the Kingdom of God. The Davidians regarded themselves as a spiritual elite (the "wavesheaf") who would ascend into heaven and assume ruling positions during the millennium. They also were involved in opening the Seven Seals, referred to in the Book of Revelations, as a prelude to the end of the world.

The Ritual Worlds of New Religious Movements

All of the NRMs under consideration here anticipate a major transformation of the world as it currently exists. The logic of how the impending change will occur varies. In world-affirming movements, the presumption is that individual change will be followed by collective change; when a sufficient number of individuals have adopted the new way, the old order will simply crumble or be transformed. In world-rejecting movements, the logic is the reverse; collective change will lead to individual change. Rejection of conventional society and the formation of a separate, exemplary group are therefore necessary to create an environment that will nurture new individuals. In both types of movements, the rituals are primarily directed toward achieving salvation/restoration, however that is conceptualized, under the aegis of the charismatic leader.

Salvation/Restoration Rituals

The central ritual among the Raelians is the "transmission ceremony" (Palmer 2004). Raël first performed this ritual in April 1976 on the Roc Plat (flat rock) of a volcanic mountain in France with forty disciples. It is now performed four times annually. Raël (or one of his representatives) dips his hands in a bowl of water and holds the initiate's head while both concentrate on establishing a telepathic link with the Elohim. For Raelians, the "baptism" is understood as a formal recognition of the Elohim, humankind's Creators, and they believe that the initiates' DNA codes are registered by the Elohim, who hover above in invisible UFOs. This ritual holds the key to immortality for Raelians in good standing through the promise of cloning to those who prove themselves worthy through their lives. As a further step, Raelians are asked to contract with a mortician to have one square centimeter of "frontal bone" removed at the end of their earthly existence. This bone fragment is then stored for collection by the Elohim to facilitate the cloning process. At the time Raelians are undergoing the transmission of the cellular plan, they must also sign a "Letter of Apostasy" renouncing their infant baptisms and send it to the church in which they were baptized.

The Raelians also participate monthly in a meditation ritual that involves sensory and sexual experimentation and imagining that one is on the planet of the Elohim and in telepathic communication with them. The ultimate objective is to achieve a sense of complete oneness with the universe, which the

Raelians describe as a "cosmic orgasm." The transmission ceremony nicely illustrates the contestive nature of NRM rituals. Raël claims that Jesus was fathered by an alien who chose a woman with pure "virgin" DNA and performed these transmissions in his time, but they had been subsequently misunderstood and applied erroneously to infant baptisms in the Catholic Church.

In the quest to create the "new man," Rajneesh taught disciples to dissolve apparent contradictions in life experience and understand them to be complementaries. The way that this transformation is to be effected is through meditation, which is understood not as a ritual practice but as a state of awareness that can be continuously realized. Daily life at Rajneeshpuram was organized around meditation that had as its goal both transforming individuals and creating a utopian community. At the individual level, there are an array of meditation practices that reflect Rajneesh's objective of synthesizing all traditions (with courses based on Tantra, astrology, past lives, massage, Tao, Zen, and many others) in a quest to realize one's true Buddha-nature.

Among the most central meditative practices is dynamic meditation. This ritual has involved four of five phases at different times, each lasting for ten minutes: breathing extremely rapidly through one's nose; jumping, dancing, screaming to release energy and painful emotions that have been stored up and to achieve catharsis; jumping up and down while shouting the Sufi mantra (Hoo, Hoo, Hoo); achieving deep relaxation by laying motionless on the floor; and celebration of one's Buddha-nature by dancing and relaxation. Another key ritual is the mystic rose, which involves one week of laughing for three hours each day, a second week of crying for three hours daily, and a third week of sitting in silence for three hours every day. At the collective level, the material and spiritual were accomplished by a twelve-hour daily work schedule known as "work as worship." Worship is understood as living in a fashion that transforms activity into creativity. This concept emphasized the meditative state in which work was accomplished, and involved ritualistic behaviors such as slow motions, frequent hugging, deep breathing, and wearing plastic gloves to avoid the AIDS apocalypse predicted by Nostradamus. Thus, even the necessary labor of cleaning toilets became a meditation ritual, imbued with symbolic meaning. The result was the building of a new community, Rajneeshpuram, perhaps the largest and the fastest-growing utopian commune in American history.

In Scientology, the central problem to be resolved is to eliminate the debilitating engrams that have accumulated in the reactive mind during one's present and past lives. The primary ritual form is auditing. Everyone begins the auditing process as a "pre-clear." A trained auditor engages the practitioner in a command/question-response exchange in order to locate engrams. The auditor is assisted by an E-meter (electropsychometer), a skin galvanometer that transmits a minute electrical charge through the body. Obstructions to the flow of energy are registered on the meter and identified as engrams. When the practitioner relives the traumatic experience that created the engram, the engram is neutralized and the experience is re-filed in the memory bank of the analytic mind as a normal, historical experience. As engrams are cleared, practitioners become increasingly more capable of relating to experiences directly rather than through the distorting filter of the reactive mind.

The Family International understands itself to be the faithful remnant that can facilitate the imminent Endtime and will survive the attending apocalpytic events. Therefore, the central ritual in The Family International is witnessing— spreading a message of salvation through faith in Jesus. This ritual activity prepares the way for Christ's return, offers salvation to those who will accept it, recruits new members for God's Endtime Army, and enhances the spiritual status of the recruiters. Witnessing has taken different forms through Family history. One of the most common forms has been simply approaching strangers in public places and offering them salvation by requesting that they join in a short salvationist prayer asking for forgiveness for their sins and acknowledging Jesus as their Savior. At other times, Family members have distributed literature ("litnessing") containing messages from Moses David Berg. The most controversial form of witnessing was the practice of Flirty Fishing ("FFing"). From a Family perspective, Jesus' prime directive is to love one another, and the ultimate goal of Family activity is to save souls. It therefore followed that in the extraordinary times leading up to the Endtime, it was legitimate to meet the physical needs of unsaved individuals if that was required to bring them to Christ. Those Family members engaging in FFing regarded this practice (sexual relations with outsiders) as a supreme sacrifice that demonstrated Christ's love in a way that was meaningful to the other person.

In Unificationism, the central problem of human existence is separation from divine purpose, symbolized by the connection of humanity to a Satanic rather than a godly lineage. As a result, the primary rituals in Unificationism have to with restoration of humanity to godly dominion. A number of aspects of Unificationist life are ritualized and directed to this purpose. Recruitment is understood theologically to constitute transferring individuals from the Satanic to the godly domain, and fundraising involves an analogous transfer of economic resources. The foundational ritual, however, is the Blessing ceremony. It is through this ritual that the problem of misdirected love that caused the Fall of Man is addressed. The ceremony is preceded by a period of celibacy through which the future marriage partners demonstrate their capacity to resist the irresponsibility of Adam and Eve and their willingness to develop a capacity for spiritual love before engaging in physical love. The Blessing itself is a lengthy, five-step ceremony. At the heart of the ritual is the Holy Wine ceremony, which results in Restoration of the partners. During the ceremony, Rev. Moon passes a chalice of wine to the bride, who sips wine from the chalice before passing it to the groom. In passing the wine to the bride, Rev. Moon is giving "true love" from "True Father," freeing the couple from Satanic lineage and linking the couple to the messianic lineage. The passing of the empty chalice from the groom to the bride to Rev. Moon completes the ritual and symbolizes a reversal of the process that led to the Fall. The new married couple is now restored to a sinless state and children born to the couple will be spiritually perfect.

The Branch Davidians were very much involved in preparation for Armageddon. David Koresh taught his disciples that the period preceding the Second Coming of Christ (tribulation) had already begun, and that divine rule would follow the cleansing of the earth. Under Koresh's leadership, the Davidians were involved in opening the Seven Seals, which are described in the New Testament Book of Revelations as a prelude to the end of the world. A major ritual of the Davidians were long Bible study sessions held on a regular basis as the group sought to discern the events that would lead to the end of the world. Koresh was involved in preparing a text on the revelations he had received with respect to the Seven Seals at the time that the FBI conducted its armed assault on the Mount Carmel community.

The other major Davidian ritual also was related to creating the Kingdom of God on Earth. In Koresh's role as a messianic figure, he sought to establish a new lineage of children that would lead to the erection of the House of David. The children born through the House of David would constitute a new lineage for humankind and would ultimately rule the world. The creation of this new lineage was carried out by Koresh's selecting wives and young girls from among his followers for ritual impregnation.

Teaching New Religious Rituals in the Classroom

Ritual can be a boring or an exciting topic for a class on religion, depending on how it is approached. Ritual is physical, practical, something done, sensual and nonverbal; it is only dull if presented as an abstract idea. Try to engage students by warning them that they are about to enter a once forbidden terrain—the comparative, value-free study of sacred rituals. You can assure them that rituals continue to be a baffling mystery—one of the most ancient and puzzling types of human behavior. Researching the ritual life of new religions is a potentially rewarding enterprise because the data are new, fresh, and waiting to be collected. Students therefore could make a valuable contribution to the field. Once students are motivated and ready to go to meeting, it is a good time to introduce them to research methodology and the issue of research ethics.

In the following paragraphs, four lesson plans are presented designed to get students actively involved in trying to figure out what rituals are, why people participate in them, what function they serve—all in the context of a course on new religious movements. These four lessons can be taught as increments or as complete lessons.

Lesson One: Defining and Identifying Ritual

Ask students a week in advance to prepare for this class by bringing in a definition of *ritual* and being prepared to read out their definitions. After hearing several definitions, ask the students to summarize the information and write down the defining characteristics of a ritual. Next, tell the students to find a partner to share a conversation about their own experiences of a ritual that they have either observed or participated in. Ask them to also talk about how the ritual affected them and then invite them to share their exchanges with the group. Some students may report feeling "warm and cozy" during Hanukkah or Christmas rituals; others report feeling "uncomfortable," "bored," or "trying not to laugh." These exchanges lead naturally to a discussion of anti-ritualism in modern life and about "empty rituals." It is also interesting to ask students how they feel about participating in family and traditional religious rituals, and whether they have participated in rituals of other faiths. You might also talk about rituals forbidden to outsiders, such as the Catholic Mass or the Muslim hadj.

Another way to build perspective on ritual is to introduce students to studies of informal, aesthetic, or popular rituals. For example, explain the notion of interaction ritual and Sir Julian Huxley's observation of the stylized aggressive and mating behavior of animals. You can also explain Robert Bocock's (1974) concept of "aesthetic rituals," of secular forms of ritual in modern life found in art galleries, sports stadiums, and rock concerts.

It is possible to draw on examples from popular culture. For sports rituals, one example is the female boxer in *Million Dollar Baby,* whose trainer has her wear a green silk robe with Celtic symbols while the audience chants in Gaelic *"mogeesh!"* as she enters the ring. The movie *Braveheart* contains a battle scene in which Mel Gibson creates a ritual just before the battle to give his men courage. A similar scene appears in *Alexander*, in which Brad Pitt creates an initiation ritual for his disgruntled soldiers. Romantic movies often contain scenes in which lovers invent a ritual to express their love, as when Ingrid Bergman and Humphrey Bogart in *Casablanca* listen to the song "As Time Goes By." (Usually students intervene at this point with many examples and start to argue about the relative merits of films; you have to be firm to keep the discussion short and on track.) Passages from John Cage's *A Year from Monday* show how ritual is akin to art. There are also examples from John Cage concerts: preparing pianos with paper and thumb tacks, listening to plumbing, or inviting the audience to participate in rapping chairs and the walls with chopsticks.

To use music as an example, ask students to bring in a DVD of their favorite music group—R&B, heavy metal, hip-hop, or reggae—that features ritualistic behavior. Each student is to identify the ritualistic gestures and the symbolism in the props, space, or costume. Ask for interpretations of the imagery and symbols. Ask whether by participating in the artists' concerts by clapping, cheering, or dancing, listeners get brainwashed into becoming avid fans.

Another approach is to explain Freud's critique of ritual as personal neurosis and obsessive compulsion. Ask students for personal examples of what they would consider pathological private ritualizing. For example, tell the story, "While cycling with a friend through a park in autumn, she suddenly stopped, picked up a shiny red leaf and ate it! When questioned, she said it was her way to celebrate the end of the summer." This story will generate a discussion of whether a private ritual or a first-time ritual qualifies as a real ritual. It is useful to cite Frederick Bird's (1978, 1979) definition of rituals as a "stylized, repeated, stereotyped, intrinsically valued, authoritatively designated act."

Lesson Two: Creating a Ritual in the Classroom

Separate students into teams and tell each group to take twenty minutes to plan, set up the space, and enact a five-minute ritual in front of the class. The rest of the class can participate if invited. When they have completed the ritual, the ritual actors must be available for questions. Then they have to interpret/ explain the meaning of their ritual. This exercise is quite theatrical, usually fun and entertaining for the students, and quite socially rewarding. It also creates a sense of how difficult it is for prophets to create a new ritual and give it an aura of authenticity.

After they have created the rituals, have students apply the lessons learned by studying NRM rituals through listing to videocassettes and reading texts. The availability of this material will vary by time and place, media coverage, or access to the NRMs themselves. Use whatever materials are accessible. For example, you can show a video of Raël baptizing his followers in a river, explain the myth on which it is based, and ask students to discuss with a partner how it is similar to and how it departs from Catholic baptism. Students can read the Raelian movement's official account of the first time this ritual was performed by reading their church history, *Les Pionniers*. Another possibility is to show a video (*The Way of the Heart*) of Rajneesh in one of his ninety-four Rolls-Royces, handing out "birthday" presents to his red-garbed disciples to commemorate the day they were initiated as neo-sannyas, and discuss the scene as an example of Kanter's (1972) transcendence mechanism. A news clip of the "Moonie" mass marriage is a nice example of a traditional ritual that has been appropriated and reinterpreted. Students are shocked by the idea that Unificationists marry in celibacy and will not consummate their marriage sexually for several more years. It helps to explain that this ritual is more akin to baptism than to a wedding and that it is also an initiation into a fully committed relationship as a devotee of Reverend Moon. The mass marriage is thus a good example of how rituals can span several categories.

Lesson Three: Researching New Religious Movement Rituals

It may be possible to go on a field trip during which students can observe and participate in NRM rituals. If so, ask them to prepare for the trip by reading about the group and its beliefs. This is a good chance to educate students in research ethics (see Bromley's chapter in this volume). It is useful to discuss with the students the notion of maintaining a balance between performing as insiders and watching as outsiders. In this context, it is possible to raise the issue of covert research. There are many examples of media investigations using this approach, such as the *Journal de Montreal's* undercover investigation of the Raelians and the undercover investigators from ABC's *Dateline* who planned an exposé on the Aquarian Concepts in Sedona, Arizona. One way to broach these issues is to show students a consent form and talk about informed consent and confidentiality as an ethical issue.

If there is going to be a field trip, it is important to discuss how to be a participant observer. Give examples that illustrate a "when in Rome" politeness when visiting an NRM and that show respect for NRM culture, such as dancing in a powwow celebrating the aboriginals of Canada or taking off one's shoes upon entering a Hare Krishna temple and chanting along with the *mahamantra*. It is also important to provide illustrations that demonstrate limits. For example, a colleague who was researching the Aryan Nations at Hayden Lake, Idaho, agreed to participate in their march on the central stage with burning crosses. Then, at one point, the marchers stopped and raised their right hands in the "*Heil*, Hitler!" salute. The colleague could not bring himself to do this and experienced a moment of acute paranoia because the march was being filmed. Other examples might include Sufi chanting during which the females wear headscarves or olive green in a room full of red-garbed *sannyasins*. Ask students if they would feel comfortable bowing to a cult leader or to the Pope or Dalai Lama (and ask what is the difference), and if they would participate in grace before The Family's meal in spite of being an atheist.

In preparing students for a field trip to a new religious movement, it is useful to provide a specific assignment for guidance and focus. Here is a sample assignment that involves three stages:

1. Describe the ritual from two perspectives, objectively and subjectively, under the subheadings "value-free description" and "self-reflexive analysis."
2. Draw a diagram of the organization and its use of sacred space: ritual objects, furnishings, the ritual actor's costume, and trajectory.
3. Interview a member on the meaning and purpose of the ritual.

After completing this assignment, students must conclude with an interpretation of the ritual. This would include a summary of the myth to which the ritual action refers and a speculative discussion about the possible psychological or social effects of the ritual action upon its practitioners. In addition, they must try to address the following six questions:

1. Does it contain borrowed appropriated elements from other religions?
2. Does it imply a rejection or criticism of any mainstream religion?
3. Does it refer to the myth/myths of the group?
4. Does it refer to an event on the life of the founder?
5. Does it refer to a sacred text?
6. Does it establish the charismatic identity of the group and/or its founder?

Lesson Four: Interpreting and Analyzing a Ritual

The final lesson asks students to study a ritual from a new religion, either in real life or captured on film, to consult the relevant group literature, and then to choose one appropriate interpretive framework for making sense of the ritual. For initiation rituals, they would observe and describe a NRM initiation, then analyze it from an anthropological perspective; as a tri-partite rite of passage, referring to the van Gennep (1960) model of the separation/liminal/reagregation phases of the rite of passage; and to Victor Turner's (1969) theory in *The Ritual Process*. Alternatively, they may analyze the initiation ritual from a Weberian sociological perspective as a charisma-building mechanism. For a healing or purification ritual, they could describe the body-spirit relationship implied in the ritual and the notion of pollution, referring to the theories of Mary Douglas (1966) or Frances Westley (1983b), and attempt a psychological interpretation of how it "works." For a meditation ritual, they could refer to the psychological model of brainwashing or mind control, using Margaret Singer's "DDD" model (Singer and Lalich 1995), and present an argument for how meditating in a cult leads to dependency, loss of choice, and impaired rational thought. An alternative framework is to interpret the ritual in sociological terms as an example of the commitment mechanism of "communion," as described by Kanter (1972).

Conclusion

New religions studies is a significant area of learning to the extent that it informs the study of religion more generally (Bell 1996, 1997; Grimes 1995a, 1995b). NRMs offer the opportunity to witness religion in the making. Case studies of NRMs based on ethnographic fieldwork provide a rich source of data on both myth and ritual for religion scholars and for students. The drama that is at the heart of compelling myths and rituals is on prominent display in NRMs. New religions offer a unique opportunity to observe the interactive development of myth and ritual, as they tend to be developed simultaneously. Further, as movements develop, there typically is a process of routinization, which can also be directly observed for NRMs. To the extent that students can observe the invention of myth and ritual, they have an extraordinary opportunity to witness and understand how religious meaning and forms are socially constructed.

ACKNOWLEDGMENT

The authors would like to thank Professor Bird of Concordia University in Montreal, Quebec, for contributing valuable ideas to this chapter and for his early important work in the area of new religious rituals.

REFERENCES

Bainbridge, William Sims. 2002. *The Endtime Family*. Albany: State University of New York Press.
Barker, Eileen. 1984. *The Making of a Moonie*. New York: Basil Blackwell.
Bell, Catherine. 1996. "Constructing Ritual." In *Readings in Ritual Studies*, ed. Ronald L. Grimes, 21–33. Upper Saddle River, NJ: Prentice-Hall.

————. 1997. *Ritual: Perspectives and Dimensions.* New York: Oxford University Press.

Bellah, Robert. 1964. "Religious Evolution." *American Sociological Review* 29, 358–74.

Bird, Frederick. 1978. "Charisma and Ritual in New Religious Movements." In *Understanding the New Religions*, ed. Jacob Needleman and George Baker, 173–89. New York: Seabury.

————. 1979. "The Pursuit of Innocence: New Religious Movements and Moral Accountability." *Sociological Analysis* 40, 335–46.

Bocock, Robert. 1974. *Ritual in Industrial Society: A Sociological Analysis of Ritualism in Modern England.* London: Allen & Unwin.

Bromley, David, and Mitchell Bracey. 1998. "Religion as Therapy, Therapy as Religion: The Church of Scientology as a Quasi-Religious Therapy." In *Sects, Cults, and Spiritual Communities: A Sociological Analysis*, ed. William Zellner and Marc Petrowsky, 141–56. Westport, CT: Praeger.

Bromley, David G., and Anson D. Shupe Jr. 1979. *"Moonies" in America.* Beverly Hills, CA: Sage.

Carter, Lewis. 1990. *Charisma and Control in Rajneeshpuram: The Role of Shared Values in the Creation of a Community.* Cambridge, UK: Cambridge University Press.

Chancellor, James D. 2000. *Life in The Family.* Syracuse, NY: Syracuse University Press.

Collins, Peter J. 1996. "Plaining: The Social and Cognitive Practice of Symbolization in the Religious Society of Friends (Quakers)." *Journal of Contemporary Religion* 2, 277–88.

Conway, Flo, and Jim Siegleman. 1978. *Snapping: America's Epidemic of Sudden Personality Change.* Philadelphia: J. B. Lippincott.

————. 1982. "Information Disease: Have Cults Created a New Mental Illness?" *Science Digest*, January, 87–92.

Cox, Harvey. 1977. *Turning East: The Promise and Peril of the New Orientalism.* New York: Simon & Schuster.

Crocker, Christopher. 1973. "Ritual and the Development of Social Structure: Liminality and Inversion." In *The Roots of Ritual*, ed. James Shaughnessy, 47–86. Grand Rapids, MI: William B. Eerdmans.

Douglas, Mary. 1966. *Purity and Danger.* New York: Praeger.

DuPertuis, Lucy. 1986. "How to Recognize Charisma: The Case of Darshan in Radhasoami and the Divine Light Mission." *Sociological Analysis* 47, 111–24.

Durkheim, Emile. 1912/1965. *The Elementary Forms of the Religious Life.* Trans. Joseph Ward Swain. New York: Free Press.

Eldershaw, Lynn. 2004. *Collective Identity and the Post-Charismatic Fate of Shambala International.* Ph.D. Dissertation. Ontario, Canada: University of Waterloo.

Eliade, Mircea. 1963. *Patterns in Comparative Religion.* New York: New American Library.

Ellwood, Robert S. 1973. *Religious and Spiritual Groups in Modern America.* Englewood Cliffs, NJ.: Prentice-Hall.

Forsthoefel, Thomas, and Cynthia Ann Humes, eds. 2005. *Gurus in America.* Albany: State University of New York Press.

Fraser, James. 1890. *The Golden Bough: A Study in Comparative Religion.* 2 vols. London: Macmillan.

Freud, Sigmund. 1938. *Totem and Tabu.* Hammondsworth, UK: Penguin.

Geertz, Clifford. 1973. *Interpretation of Cultures.* New York: Basic Books.

Goldman, Marion. 1999. *Passionate Journeys: Why Successful Women Joined a Cult.* Ann Arbor: University of Michigan Press.

Grace, James H. 1984. *Sex and Marriage in the Unification Church.* Lewiston, NY: Edwin Mellen Press.

Grimes, Ronald L. 1995a. *Beginnings in Ritual Studies,* rev. ed. Los Angeles: University of Southern California Press.

———. 1995b. *Ritual Criticism: Case Studies in its Practice, Essays on its Theory.* Los Angeles: University of Southern California Press.

Hargrove, Barabara. 1989. *The Sociology of Religion.* Arlington Heights, IL: Harlan Davidson.

Johnson, Gregory. 1976. "The Hare Krishna in San Francisco." In *The New Religious Consciousness,* ed. Charles Glock and Robert Bellah, 31–51. Berkeley: University of California Press.

Jung, Carl. 1938. *Psychology and Religion.* New Haven: Yale University Press.

Kanter, Rosabeth Moss. 1972. *Commitment and Community: Communes and Utopias in Sociological Perspective.* Cambridge, MA: Harvard University Press.

Kessler, Gary. 2003. *Studying Religion: An Introduction through Cases.* New York: McGraw-Hill.

Levine, Saul. 1984. *Radical Departures: Desperate Detours to Growing Up.* Toronto: Harcourt, Brace, Jovanovich.

Levi-Strauss, Claude. 2000. *Structural Anthropology.* New York: Basic Books.

Melton, J. Gordon. 1998. *Finding Enlightenment through Ramtha: The Ramtha School of Enlightenment.* Hillsboro, OR: Beyond Words.

Melton, J. Gordon, and Roger L. Moore. 1982. *The Cult Experience: Responding to the New Religious Pluralism.* New York: Pilgrim.

Otto, Rudolf. 1950. *The Idea of the Holy.* London: Oxford University Press.

Palmer, Susan. 1994. *Moon Sisters, Krishna Mothers, Rajneesh Lovers: Women's Roles in New Religions.* Syracuse, NY: Syracuse University Press.

———. 2004. *Aliens Adored: Raël's UFO Religion.* New Brunswick, NJ: Rutgers University Press.

Platvoet, Jan, and Karel van der Toorn. 1995. *Pluralism and Identity: Studies in Ritual Behaviour.* Leyden, UK: Brill.

Prince, Raymond. 1974. "Cocoon Work: An Interpretation of the Concern of Contemporary Youth with the Mystical." In *Religious Movements in Contemporary America,* ed. Irving I. Zaretsky and Mark P. Leone, 255–74. Princeton, NJ: Princeton University Press.

Rajneesh, Bhagwan Shree. 1987. *A New Vision of Women's Liberation.* Poona, India: Rebel Press.

Saliba, John. 1993. "The New Religions and Mental Health." In *The Handbook on Cults and Sects in America,* Part B, ed. David G. Bromley and Jeffrey K. Hadden, 99–116. Greenwich, CT: JAI Press.

Sayyid al Imam Issa al Haadi al Mahdi. (Dwight York). 1990. *The Paleman.* Monticello, NY: The Original Tents of Kedar.

Shaughnessy, James D., ed. 1973. *The Roots of Ritual.* Grand Rapids, MI: William B. Eerdmans.

Singer, Margaret, with Janja Lalich. 1995. *Cults in Our Midst: The Hidden Menace in Our Everyday Lives.* San Francisco: Jossey-Bass.

Turner, Victor. 1967. *The Forest of Symbols: Aspects of Ndembu Ritual.* Ithaca, NY: Cornell University Press.

———. 1969. *The Ritual Process.* Chicago: Aldine.

Tyler, Edward B. 1873. *Primitive Culture,* 2nd ed. 2 vols. London: John Murray.

van Gennep, Arnold. 1960. *The Rites of Passage.* London: Routledge and Kegan Paul.

Wallace, Anthony. 1966. *Religion: An Anthropological View.* New York: Random House.
Wallis, Roy. 1979. "The Elementary Forms of Religious Life." *The Annual Review of the Social Studies of Religion* 3, 191–211.
————. 1984. *The Elementary Forms of New Religious Life.* London: Routledge and Kegan Paul.
————. 1985. "The Sociology of New Religious Movements." *Social Studies Review* 1, 3–7.
Weber, Max. 1947. *The Theory of Social and Economic Organization.* Glencoe, IL: Free Press.
Westley, Frances. 1983a. *The Complex Forms of the New Religious Life: A Durkheimian View of New Religions.* Chico, CA: Scholar's Press.
————. 1983b. "Ritual as Psychic Bridge Builder: Narcissism, Healing and the Human Potential Movements." *Journal of Psychoanalytic Anthropology* 6, 80–82.
Wright, Stuart A., ed. 1995. *Armageddon in Waco.* Chicago: University of Chicago Press.
Wuthnow, Robert. 1976. *The Consciousness Reformation.* Berkeley: University of California Press.

Social Building Blocks
of New Religious Movements:
Organization and Leadership

E. Burke Rochford Jr.

Cults and new religions historically have been controversial. The late 1960s and 1970s brought about the most recent period of religious ferment and upheaval, beginning initially in the United States and ultimately spreading worldwide (Glock and Bellah 1976). At the center of the controversy were cult leaders depicted as "charlatans and madmen" (Bromley and Shupe 1981). As these leaders came into the public spotlight, so too did the organizations and communities that grew up around them. Critics argued that they were manifest expressions of greedy and ultimately destructive leaders. Radical in orientation and lifestyle, these organizations were widely condemned for endangering the lives of devoted adherents (Clark et al. 1981; Enroth 1977). In time, these and other concerns were extended to the children born into the groups (Richardson 1999).

This chapter considers a number of questions and issues central to leadership and organization within new religions. New religions represent distinctive types of organizations to the extent that they challenge the dominant social order in an effort to promote societal change and transformation. In this sense, they are both religious organizations and social movements (Lofland and Richardson 1985: 180). As religious movements, the question arises as to how they are led, organize for action, develop, and ultimately survive, given the inevitable resistance they face. Four key issues have come forward: (1) the social and historical context in which new religions emerged in the United States before spreading worldwide; (2) the distinctiveness of new religions and how they relate to other religious collectivities and organizations; (3) the role of charismatic leadership in the emergence and development of new religions; and, (4) the factors that influence the success, failure, and overall development of new religious organizations. The chapter concludes with a series of suggestions related to the teaching of leadership and organization in new religious movements (NRMs).

Social Protest, the Counterculture, and the Emergence of New Religions

Although new religions have emerged consistently across time (Finke and Stark 1992: 240), there is general agreement that they tend to swell numerically during periods of social dislocation and societal change. The 1960s and 1970s represent only the most recent outbreak of new religions during a period of social turbulence (Foster 1991). But troubled times historically come and go and with them so do the fortunes of new religious groups. While some scholars have emphasized cultural crisis and breakdown as the context that gave rise to the sixties' new religions, others have given greater weight to individual searching and the quest to overcome moral ambiguity and uncertainty.

The United States during the late 1960s and early 1970s was a time of war, social protest, and the emergence of social movements, political, psychological, and religious. As Robert Bellah argues, this was a period when the "horrors of modern history" led to "mass disaffection from the common understandings of American culture and society" and to an erosion of the legitimacy of American institutions (1976: 333). Initially many of America's youth sought to end the Vietnam War through political activism. In time, calls for broader changes emerged as youth embraced "the revolution" as a means of restructuring social and political power (Gitlin 1980; Klatch 1999). Not surprisingly, activists seeking such radical change fell short in their dreams for a more equal and just America. Thus the euphoria of the revolution gave way to despair, as burnt-out political activists became frustrated and disillusioned (Kent 2001; Klatch 1999). Many drifted into the counterculture and the world of mind-expanding drugs. Psychedelic drugs such as LSD became part of a mystical quest that promised the possibility of personal transformation, if not societal change. Extensive drug use has been noted for the early followers of the Jesus movement (Richardson, Stewart, and Simmonds 1979: 179–80), the International Society for Krishna Consciousness (ISKCON; Judah 1974: 127–37; Rochford 1985: 66–68), Zen Buddhism (Seager 1999: 43; Tipton 1982: 121–24), and a variety of other new religions and personal growth movements (Kent 2001; Tipton 1982; Wuthnow 1976: 280). Part of the attraction of new religions for some countercultural youth was the possibility to "stay high forever" (Johnson 1976: 36) through religious practice, in place of the temporary transcendence gained from drug-induced highs. These groups also afforded countercultural youth the concrete possibility of creating functioning utopian communities as alternatives to the conventional society.

The emergence of new religions can be seen as one response to the political and cultural crises that existed in the United States during the 1960s and 1970s. Indeed, a "crisis of meaning" and "moral crisis" perspective has been advanced by Bellah (1976) and his student, Steven Tipton, in his monograph *Getting Saved from the Sixties* (1982). Conversion to new religions fundamentally represented an effort by sixties youth "to make moral sense of their lives" (Tipton 1982: 185) in a society where moral boundaries were indistinct and fluctuating (Anthony and Robbins 1982). Taking a somewhat different view, Stephen Kent shows how growing frustration and despair about the perceived failure of "the revolution" provided "the key to the rapid transformation of slogan chanters of the late 1960s into the mantra chanters of the early 1970s" (2001: 36). A "crisis of *means*," rather than of meaning, led some activists to refocus their discontent away from political and structural change toward individual transformation. Thus the goal of revolutionary change remained, but now change was to be accomplished through conversion to mystical forms of religion. As one Hare Krishna devotee and former member of the Students for a Democratic Society (SDS) commented, "I realized that Krishna Consciousness could bring about the revolution, something SDS couldn't do" (personal interview, 1977; see Kent 2001 and Judah 1974 for similar statements).

As the sixties counterculture began to fade by the mid-1970s, the well-established new religions lost the constituency that fueled their growth in North America and in portions of Western Europe. As a result, they began to experience declines in recruitment and in overall levels of membership (Dawson 1998: 51; Wallis 1984: 87). To combat numerical decline, most sought new constituencies employing alternative methods of proselytizing and, in some cases, offered more diverse spiritual alternatives (Bainbridge and Jackson 1981; Rochford 1987; Wallis 1984: 87–88). The Children of God (now The Family International), for example, shifted its outreach efforts away from "hippies" and "dropouts" and toward more established middle-class "up and outs," using sex as a recruitment tool (Chancellor 2000: 7). While fueling controversy inside and outside the movement, it produced few new members (Chancellor 2000: 16). By contrast, ISKCON had considerable success in its efforts to build a congregation of Indian immigrants in North America, after it experienced a downturn in recruitment beginning in 1973 (Rochford 1985: 270–71, 278). In 2004, about half of ISKCON's North American membership comprised Indian congregational members (on the integration of Indian immigrants into ISKCON in North America, see Zaidman 2000). New religious groups also opened new recruitment fields as they expanded into Europe, Asia, South America, and other parts of the world, becoming transnational organizations.

Traditional Typologies of Religious Organizations

Cults, together with sects, denominations, and churches, represent the varied religious collectivities and organizations identified by sociologists of religion. Unfortunately no working consensus exists among scholars about the precise meaning of these concepts (Dawson 1998: 29). In part this is because religious organizations are often "mixed types," encompassing attributes that represent more than one form of religious organization (Iannaccone 1988: 242). At a deeper conceptual level, some investigators of new religions have questioned the usefulness of traditional typologies, arguing that they often distort rather than illuminate the unique character of new religions as movements and organizations. This latter issue will be considered in the next section.

Beginning with Ernest Troeltsch (1931), a basic distinction has been made between two types of religious organizations: sects and churches. *Sects* reject or are at least indifferent toward the values and norms of the larger society and are considered deviant (Rochford 1985: 216; Wallis 1976; Wilson 1991: 46–47). Other characteristics commonly associated with sects include exclusivity in their commitment demands, identification as an elect or spiritual elite, diffusion of the religious role into all spheres of life, and an emphasis on perfection through direct fellowship among members (McGuire 1997: 143; Rochford 1985: 216; Wallis 1976: 16). *Churches*, and denominational forms of religion by contrast, embrace the values and normative expectations of the dominant social order and are publicly defined as "respectable" (Rochford 1985: 216–17; Stark and Bainbridge 1985: 21). A denomination differs from a church only in that the latter dominates society (McGuire 1997: 144; Stark and Bainbridge 1985: 23).

The sect and church represent endpoints of a continuum defined by differing degrees of tension with the sociocultural environments in which they operate (Johnson 1963). Indeed, many scholars posit rejection of the social environment as the foundational feature of sects (Iannaccone 1988: 244). This normally encompasses a rejection of the legitimacy and authority of both the dominant religious traditions and the larger secular society (Wilson 1991: 46–47). Embracing this idea, Finke and Stark (1992: 41) define sects as "religious bodies in a relatively high state of tension with their environments." Wilson (1987: 31), however, argues critically that degrees of "tension" may be discernable only retrospectively and thus the concept approaches tautology. The concept of tension also presupposes a degree of interaction between sects and the societies in which they operate if ideological, strategic, and lifestyle differences are to result in expressions of public hostility and heightened tension (Rochford 1987; Wilson 1991).

Yet most groups remain largely unknown and obscure to the public, despite their deviant beliefs and factional posture (Barker 2004; Rochford 1987). Generally these latter groups reject aggressive forms of public proselytizing and fundraising, thereby largely escaping public scrutiny. Still other sectarian movements invite little public concern because they represent what Wallis (1984) refers to as "world-affirming" (e.g., Transcendental Meditation) or "world-accommodating" movements (e.g., Charismatic Renewal). Because these latter groups do not present a direct challenge to society, they are more likely to be viewed as acceptable, if not always entirely respectable. (See Rochford 1987: 112–14 for a typology of new religions and their relations to society.)

Within the sociology of religion, sects are distinguished from cults along a number of dimensions. Unlike sects, whose origins often derive from schisms from established faiths, cultic groups emerge as a result of cultural innovation or cultural importation (Stark and Bainbridge 1985: 25). Cults are a form of social organization that describes popular and unofficial religion (McGuire 1997: 144), and thus represent fundamental breaks from religious tradition (Robbins 1988: 152). Like sects, cults may also exist in a heightened state of tension with the surrounding culture (Richardson 1978; Stark and Bainbridge 1985: 26; Wallis 1976: 13), although their pluralistic stance makes them more likely to be defined as "peculiar" rather than "threatening" (Turner and Killian 1987: 257). In contrast to sects, cultic groups typically lack clear distinctions between insiders and outsiders, are loosely organized, are tolerant of other religious paths, are individualistic in orientation, are without specific sources of authority, and often are transitory (Richardson 1978; Wallis 1975: 40–41, 1976: 14). Moreover, their boundaries are ill-defined and their belief systems remain in flux (Nelson 1968). As these qualities suggest, cults normally are unable to mobilize the *collective* commitment and loyalty of followers—requirements for forging a religious organization (Wallis 1976: 15). Although Stark and Bainbridge (1985: 29) identify cult movements as full-fledged religious organizations, Swatos (1981: 19) argues that cults achieving such levels of organization are better defined as sects.

The Distinctiveness of New Religions

Recent scholarship on new religions has challenged the empirical and conceptual adequacy of church–sect typologies. Some of the analytic insights of the church–sect model have been retained, but others have been questioned and even rejected. Bromley (2005), for example, argues that new religious movements "are not fully interpretable within the church-denomination-sect-cult paradigm." At issue is whether or not the study of new religions constitutes an area of inquiry requiring its own conceptual tools and frameworks (Bromley 2005). Such a question has led some scholars to search for what distinguishes new religions as unique religious phenomena (Barker 2004; Bromley 2005; Melton 2004). Barker (2004), for example, suggests that new religions hold significant characteristics in common, *and that this can be traced to their newness.* Some of the distinctive characteristics thus far proposed include:

- New religions tend to be prophetic movements that challenge the legitimacy of the existing social order while at the same time distancing them from it (Bromley 2004).
- New religions in their formative stages particularly tend to be anti-structural, seeing "corruption" and "contradiction" in what others view as a taken-for-granted normative reality (Bromley 2004).
- New religions exist "in relatively contested spaces within society as a whole" (Melton 2004) and face ongoing potential for high levels of tension with the dominant society (Bromley 2004; Wilson 1991).
- While not unique in this regard, new religions emerge in response to charismatic leaders preaching a *new* revelation or spiritual insight

(Barker 2004). Leaders of new religions, however, favor the prophetic method of authorization, given the challenge they present to the existing social order.

- New religions are distinct from sects, in that the latter have a measure of legitimacy in the eyes of the religious establishment, having broken away from traditional faiths. As Melton (2004) suggests, "Churches view sects as different but at the same time affirm a filial relationship." New religions by contrast are "unacceptably different" from the vantage point of the mainline traditions and thereby constitute religious outsiders.
- Given their prophetic character and related anti-structural tendencies, new religions tend toward radical forms of social organization (Bromley 2004). Collectivism often prevails organizationally and relationally, especially early on in their development. Most of the established new religions in fact had their beginnings in communal forms of organization. Many religious sects by contrast, while perhaps challenging mainstream institutions and cultural values, tend to form religious subcultures, thus in important ways remaining part of society.
- Although most new religions represent offshoots from established religious traditions (Melton 2004), some are syncretistic, borrowing from more than one religious or quasi-religious tradition (Barker 2004).
- New religious movements consist predominantly of first-generation converts, at least during their formative stages (Barker 2004). Their growth thus depends heavily on converts enthusiastically proselytizing their newfound beliefs. The membership composition of other types of religious organizations is primarily made up of people born and raised in the faith (Barker 2004).
- New religions appeal to people with specific demographic characteristics, rather than people from across the demographic spectrum (Barker 2004). The sixties' new religions appealed disproportionately to white, educated, and middle-class youth. In other eras, the poor and oppressed have filled the ranks of new religious groups (Barker 2004).
- New religions are especially prone to rapid and radical changes that promote organizational transformation (Barker 2004). The volatility of new religious organizations is largely a function of intense external pressures to accommodate, combined with internal weaknesses related to inadequate resource mobilization and cultural development.

In light of the above characteristics of new religions, Bromley (2005) has developed a scheme parallel to traditional church-sect typologies. He proposes "a continuum of dominant, sectarian, and new religions based on the *degree of cultural and social alignment*" (my emphasis). Dominant religions are firmly aligned with mainstream cultural patterns and social institutions. Indeed, dominant religions are constitutive of society and take an active role in its construction and maintenance (Berger 1969; Bromley 2005). Sectarian religions reject the legitimacy and authority of the dominant churches and establish alternative organizations outside the religious mainstream. Sects collectively have widely varying degrees of alignment with societal institutions and predominant cultural values. New religions are groups that are *neither* aligned with the dominant cultural patterns nor with societal institutions. On this basis, new religions constitute a distinctive religious enterprise.

Charismatic Leadership

Charismatic authority has been central to the emergence and development of new religious movements. Yet charismatic authority is prevalent only during the initial phase of founding a new religion. The instability of charismatic authority makes it difficult to sustain organizations directed toward fulfilling the vision of a charismatic leader. In time, charismatic authority almost always falls prey to routinization and institutionalization in the interest of organizational stability. Whether the leader's charismatic authority is fully institutionalized or not, the death of a charismatic founder presents a critical turning point in the career of any new religious organization.

Most new religions had their beginnings in charismatic leadership—for example, David Berg of the Children of God/The Family, Sun Myung Moon of the Unification Church, L. Ron Hubbard of Scientology, Swami Prabhupada of ISKCON, and Guru Maharaj Ji of the Divine Light Mission. These leaders were uniformly held in awe by their early followers, who saw them as possessing extraordinary powers that set them apart from humankind generally. In the words of Max Weber (1978: 439–40), each can be considered "a prophet," or bearer of charisma who proclaims alternative if not new revelations. The prophetic method of authority, characteristic of founders of new religions, contests the legitimacy of the existing social order and seeks its transformation (Bromley 1997).

The concept of charisma as formulated by Weber applies to leaders whose authority is "endowed with supernatural, superhuman, or at least specifically exceptional powers or qualities . . . regarded as of divine origin or as exemplary" (1978: 241). Charisma represents one of three forms of authority identified by Weber, the other two being traditional and rational-legal. Traditional leaders gain authority by virtue of custom, wherein certain types of people historically ascend to positions of leadership. Rational-legal authority derives from specific offices that are formally mandated and thus authority is invested in a leadership position rather than the person who fills it. Weber saw charisma as both an attribute of individual personality and a social construction. Recent scholarship has given emphasis to the later perspective, emphasizing how charisma is both a dynamic and a collaborative process. Charisma, so defined, represents a quality attributed to someone by others who place considerable trust and faith in their leadership (Dawson 2002; Wallis 1982).

The authority the followers attribute to charismatic leadership is translated at the group level into high levels of organizational commitment, religiosity, and task performance directed toward furthering the goals of the leader and his or her organization. As Dawson concludes, charisma "is an extremely effective means of galvanizing commitment to a cause or an organization" (2002: 82). But as Weber (1978: 246) makes clear, charismatic authority is inherently unstable and remains in its "pure" form only in the short run. Given this volatility, charisma is subject to routinization, with a corresponding increase in rational-legal forms of authority.

The very effort to successfully move forward the mission of a charismatic leader perhaps inevitably requires more stable and even bureaucratic forms of organization to counter the spontaneous, ad hoc quality of charismatic authority (Wallis 1984: 108–10). The need for coordinated action requires specialists who can develop strategies, supervise followers, and delegate tasks essential to the expansion and prosperity of the group. Growth also limits the ability of charismatic leaders to maintain their previous levels of personal contact with followers, from which their authority originally grew (Dawson 2002: 86). Moreover, as members become more invested in the group, they tend to seek institutional structures that promote greater predictability and stability in their lives. This is especially true as members grow older, establish families, and require a greater degree of security. Richardson (1994: 30) refers to this as a process of "domestification." As institutionalization progresses, charismatic authority is constrained and at least partially brought under the control of formal organizational structures and rules of procedure.

In an attempt to confront and deflect processes of institutionalization, charismatic leaders employ a number of counteractive strategies. Dawson (2002: 92–94) identifies six such strategies:

1. To keep followers focused on the words and goals of a charismatic founder, the leader may shift or give different emphasis to doctrines and policies, perhaps suddenly and dramatically. Kirtanananda Swami, ISKCON guru and founder of the New Vrindaban community in West Virginia, undertook a radical change in 1987, embracing interfaith worship and practice in place of traditional Krishna Consciousness in the midst of legal problems that undermined his authority. Residents less committed to Kirtanananda's leadership left the community, although some new recruits were attracted by his religious innovations.

2. Charismatic leaders may increase demands placed on followers for sacrifice, thus affirming their authority within the group. Extreme measures of sacrifice were used by Jim Jones at Jonestown when he put followers through "suicide rehearsals" to test their commitment to his leadership. Community members remained unaware whether the "poison" they consumed was real or not.

3. Charismatic leaders may play on followers' fear of persecution by creating new and threatening enemies in order to promote a sense of crisis. Such external threats serve to promote internal solidarity and elevate a leader's standing. By 1990, Aum Shinrikyo's leader Shoko Asahara was preaching that the outside society was ruled by

the devil and that his followers were subject to attack by agents of evil (Wessinger 2000: 137).

4. Internal forces supporting institutionalization may be ridiculed, marginalized, and even ousted from the group by charismatic leaders. David Berg essentially fired 300 leaders of the Children of God and ordered them to the streets as ordinary disciples after he saw his authority being subverted by their increasing power and authoritarian style of leadership (Chancellor 2000: 10; Wallis 1984: 112–17).

5. Charismatic leaders may employ what amount to "loyalty tests" in an effort to strengthen followers' emotional ties and dependency. This may involve changes such as altering sexual practices or limiting affective relationships between members. David Koresh married or otherwise gained sexual access to all the women at the Davidian compound beginning in 1986. The commitment of Koresh's male followers was tested by their willingness to surrender their wives, lovers, and daughters to him.

6. Charismatic leaders may seek to consolidate their control and undermine the forces of routinization by relocating their groups. Beginning in the early 1970s, David Berg relocated the Children of God out of North America and remained there for a number of years in the face of growing institutionalization. Marshall Applewhite (Do) and Bonnie Nettles (Ti) kept Heaven's Gate followers on the road for decades, shifting location and residence about every six months.

While *resistance* to advancing institutionalization is perhaps a favored strategy employed by charismatic leaders, this by no means exhausts the possibilities. Wallis (1984: 110–13) delineates three others. *Acquiescence* occurs when a leader accepts a shift from being "superhuman" in the eyes of followers to a more humanlike status. The early followers of Guru Maharaj Ji of the Divine Light Mission initially viewed him as a divine incarnation of God. In time, the Perfect Master was reconstructed as a humanitarian leader and spiritual teacher (Downton 1979: 186). *Encouragement* of ongoing institutionalization occurs when leaders actively direct the process of routinization for their own advantage. L. Ron Hubbard sought to gain absolute authority within Scientology by establishing an elaborate hierarchical structure under his control (Wallis 1976). *Displacement* occurs where institutionalization proceeds without full recognition by the leader, until it is too late to reverse. During the early 1970s, a satanic cult known as The Process began to adopt more conventional patterns in an effort to gain respectability. The movement's founder, Robert de Grimston, lacked the means to stop the changes and ultimately was ousted from the group (Wallis 1984: 111–12). Palmer's (1988) analysis of Bhagwan Shree Rajneesh identified *abdication* as another potential reaction to institutionalization by charismatic leaders. Bhagwan renounced his guru status shortly before being forced out of the United States by immigration officials. Thereafter, his international communities began to disband. Although each of the above represents distinct strategies, over time charismatic leaders may well employ more than one type of response in an effort to undermine or otherwise deflect ongoing processes of institutionalization.

A major development that underscores the precariousness of charisma emerges at the death of a revered charismatic leader. The death of a charismatic leader is a critical juncture in the life of any group, community, or social movement. Some religious groups simply fade away after the passing of a charismatic founder or leader (Kanter 1972: 118; Miller 1991). Yet it appears that most religious groups weather successfully the death of a charismatic leader (Melton 1991). This seems especially likely should a group reach a level of internal stability prior to the leader's death, and where previous preparation affords a smooth transfer of spiritual and political power (Melton 1991: 9–10). Among the more established new religions, Scientology, ISKCON, The Family, the Rajneesh Foundation International/Osho, and the Siddha Yoga Dham have all experienced the death of their charismatic founders. With the exception of ISKCON, none has experienced more than limited internal conflict and defection. ISKCON, by contrast, experienced intense struggles over the spiritual and political power of its successor gurus after the death, in 1977, of Swami Prabhupada. One reason is that guru authority is hostile to effective organization, since disciples are committed primarily to their gurus rather than to an established organization (Rochford 1985: 221–55, 1998a; Shinn 1986, 1987a: 43–60). Indeed, Prabhupada's authority has yet to be successfully routinized nearly thirty years after his death, despite guru reform efforts that have included stringent bureaucratic policies meant to control the volatility of ISKCON's guru institution (see Bryant and Ekstrand 2004; Rochford 1998a; for a more positive view, see Shinn 1987b: 129). ISKCON's crisis of authority resulted in declining levels of member commitment and involvement, individual and group defection, schism, and organized challenges to the authority of ISKCON's Governing Body Commission (GBC), as well as to the guru institution (Bryant and Ekstrand 2004; Rochford 1985, 1989, 1998a, 1999a).

Sources of Organizational Development in New Religions

The major new religions of the 1960s and 1970s have undergone organizational change in the direction of accommodation with conventional society. From exclusive, communal, and high-commitment organizations, each has evolved into congregationally based movements where members have widely varying commitments and levels of involvement. Such a progression suggests that previous high-tension religious groups have become domesticated and transformed into low-tension religions. Stated differently, new religions have come to at least partially align themselves with dominant cultural patterns and social institutions.

New religion scholars have considered two overlapping issues with respect to the development of new religious movements. The first seeks to identify and analyze the factors that influence the success or failure of these new religious movements. The second focuses less on specific organizational outcomes in favor of describing social processes that promote accommodation with mainstream societies. Here, internal weaknesses associated with inadequate culture building take center stage.

An important if underdeveloped focus of sociologists interested in the fate of new and established religious organizations is on the factors that influence their success and failure (Bromley and Hammond 1987; Hall 1988; Kanter 1972; Stark 1987, 1996). Success has been defined in varying ways. Kanter (1968: 502) defines success in terms of survival. If a utopian community exists for a generation, or at least twenty-five years, it is considered successful. Stark (1987, 1996) defines success in terms of power and influence. New religious movements are successful to the extent that they "dominate one or more societies" (1987: 12). Obviously such a definition rules out the vast majority of new religions that have arisen historically, a fact that lessens the empirical usefulness of Stark's definition. Moreover, unlimited growth and societal influence often come at the expense of original teachings and organization (Wilson 1987: 30–31). Viewed from within, such changes are likely to be interpreted as evidence of failure. Kanter and Stark's treatments of success and failure are useful in that each identifies a number of key variables and issues that confront new religious movements and influence their course of development. Since religious organizations are nothing without the support of people, the question arises as to how social arrangements draw individuals into organizational roles that make them loyal, dedicated, and even obedient. Kanter (1968, 1972) proposes commitment as the necessary link between individual interests and organizational objectives. *Commitment* refers to the willingness of people to do what they can to help maintain the group because it provides what they need and is ultimately an expression of the self (Kanter 1972: 66–67).

Kanter's analysis of thirty nineteenth-century American communal groups revealed that success and failure were largely products of how strongly they built commitment (1972: 64). Successful utopian communities in her sample were based in religion; yet this was also true of a number of unsuccessful groups (1972: 136). In general, however, religious communities possessed a variety of characteristics significant to building commitment: a comprehensive value system, moral principles, shared beliefs that required conversion, charismatic leadership, sacrifice, deliberate rejection of the material (outside) world, and ritual including the use of music and singing (1972: 136–37). The presence of these characteristics led Kanter to conclude that religious groups have an edge with respect to "organizing their communities for maximum viability" (1972: 137).

Hall (1988) reanalyzed Kanter's data using sophisticated quantitative techniques and found that confession and spiritual hierarchy were commitment mechanisms that distinguished successful otherworldly sects. Confession subjects the thoughts and actions of individuals to public scrutiny and thus the self is sacrificed to the group. The presence of a spiritual hierarchy requires individuals to give up personal value standards in order to embrace the requirements of spiritual deference (Hall 1988: 686–89).

Rodney Stark (1987, 1996) has formulated the most comprehensive model addressing success and failure in new religions. Stark specifies ten internal and external factors he claims are vital to the success of new religions. The more fully a new religion fulfills each of these conditions, the greater the likelihood of success. Moreover, failure to minimally fulfill any one of the elements in the model dooms a movement to failure (Stark 1987: 13). Stark maintains that new religions are most likely to succeed to the extent that:

1. *They retain cultural continuity with the conventional faiths within the societies in which they appear.* New religions that are grounded in "familiar cultural material" (e.g., Mormons in the United States) are more likely to prosper than those that are alien to the conventional religious culture. For this reason various Hindu and Buddhist groups (e.g., ISKCON, Zen Buddhism) have found it difficult to thrive in the West.

2. *Their doctrines are nonempirical.* The lack of a supernatural basis makes nonreligious movements vulnerable to empirical disconfirmation, thus potentially threatening the commitment of adherents. Groups that rely on magic, such as Scientology, have limited potential for success because their beliefs are subject to disconfirmation (Stark and Bainbridge 1985: 263–83).

3. *They maintain a medium level of tension with the surrounding cultural environment—are strict, but not too strict.* In other words, new religious movements must be deviant but not overly so such that they become recipients of outright repression, as in the case of the Branch Davidians. Some new religions have sought to moderate elevated levels of tension by altering moral standards and lifestyle requirements, thus undermining the distinctiveness that initially attracted converts. The Family, for example, changed its controversial sexual ethos as it increasingly came under fire from critics inside and outside of the movement.

4. *They have legitimate leaders with adequate authority to ensure effectiveness. Adequate authority requires clear doctrinal justifications and members who perceive themselves as participants in the system of authority.* ISKCON lost the biggest portion of its membership in the years following Prabhupada's death in large part because his successors lacked sufficient authority in the eyes of members.

5. *They can generate a highly motivated, volunteer, religious labor force, including many willing to proselytize.* The initial growth of any new religious group depends on recruiting new converts. Although the major new religions had active missionaries that secured their early growth, many groups placed less emphasis on proselytizing as family life expanded in the 1980s (e.g., The Family, ISKCON, Unification Church). In focusing on family obligations, many members have less time to devote to movement-related activities (see Rochford 1995, on declining involvement by parents within ISKCON).

6. *They maintain a level of fertility sufficient to offset member mortality.*
Fertility rates have remained relatively high in most new religious
groups. Some in fact now have more second-generation members
than converts. Owing to the fact that presently many of the early
converts to various new religions are in their fifties and sixties, mortality rates are beginning to increase. For now, The Family has
been able to sustain numerical stability in spite of substantial
defection and an initial rise in member mortality because of high
fertility.

7. *They compete against weak, local conventional religious organizations
within a relatively unregulated religious economy.* When an established
religious tradition has a monopoly that is backed by the power of the
state, it is difficult for new faiths to thrive. This is one reason new
religions have sometimes found it difficult to flourish in parts of
Europe when there is a state-supported religion (Stark 1987: 19). In the
United States by contrast, any religious group, powerful or obscure,
retains the same legal privileges, such as tax exemptions. Existing in a
relatively favorable social environment, new religions are able to mobilize needed resources and seek converts. This is even more apparent when the conventional faiths are weakened by secularization and
substantial numbers of people are religiously inactive, and thus
available to the appeals of new religions.

8. *They sustain strong internal attachments while remaining an open social
network, able to maintain and form ties to outsiders.* Religious commitment is built and sustained by interpersonal attachments. Yet both
weak and overly strong internal ties represent potential barriers to the
efforts of new religions. Weak internal networks have limited Scientology's expansion as a *collective movement*, given its therapeutic orientation. Auditor-client relationships provide little basis for creating
enduring attachments that bind people to one other and thereby to the
movement as a whole (Stark 1987: 23). By contrast, during ISKCON's
early years, an emphasis on exclusivity within a communal context
made it difficult for members to maintain outside network ties, thus
limiting network recruitment in favor of less productive contacts with
strangers in public places (Rochford 1985).

9. *They continue to maintain sufficient tension with their environment,
remaining sufficiently strict.* Maintaining a distinctive lifestyle and
morality is key to producing high internal morale and rapid growth.
Although such a stance may result in defection by the less committed,
organizationally a greater risk exists in retaining members unwilling
to meet the high costs of membership (i.e., it produces free-riders).
Reducing strictness is often associated with second- and third-
generation members who generally seek reduced tension with the
conventional society, something readily apparent for The Family,
the Unification Church, and ISKCON (Chancellor 2000; Orme-
Collins 2002; Rochford 1999b).

10. *They adequately socialize the young to minimize both defection and the appeal of reduced strictness.* A high rate of defection by those born within a new religion can doom a movement in the absence of sufficient numbers of new converts. Yet many new religions have found it difficult to retain a large percentage of their second-generation members, even as their recruitment fortunes diminished. The Family, ISKCON, and the Unification Church have all experienced significant rates of defection by their second-generation members. In other cases, young people have maintained their affiliations even while living independent lives in the outside society as less strict congregational members. (For applications of Stark's 1987 unrevised model to the Unification Church, ISKCON, Nichiren Shoshu, Scientology, and the Children of God, see Bromley and Hammond 1987.)

Stark's model invokes the significance of religious culture in the growth of new religious groups (Stark 1996: 137), yet his model ultimately fails to develop this critical insight. Other scholars, however, have made movement culture a central focus of inquiry (Lofland 1987; Palmer and Hardman 1999; Rochford 1997, 1999b, 2000). Because new religions represent broad challenges to mainstream values and institutions, the presence of functioning *oppositional* cultures becomes vital to their long-term survival (Iannaccone 1988; Lofland 1987; Stark 1996; Wilson 1991). Belief and everyday experience can only remain aligned, and produce what Swidler (1986) refers to as "settled lives," in the context of a stable culture. Evidence suggests that in fact religious sects and movements, on the whole, produce more elaborate and robust cultures than their political counterparts (Lofland 1987: 105).

In engaging the project of cultural development, new religious communities seek to create structures, practices, and symbols meant to integrate followers while simultaneously segregating them from the perceived threats of the secular society (Rochford 1999b, 2000). Yet in virtually every case, new religions have struggled to develop institutional structures capable of sustaining members within a communal context. For the most part, this failure stems from an inability to successfully build internal "domestic cultures" (Lofland 1987: 97–98) supportive of family life. This became a serious problem for many new religions, given what Barker (2004) refers to as "inverted disproportionality," or the presence of larger numbers of children born within than first-generation converts.

The inability to develop communally based oppositional religious cultures is related to at least two factors. The first is overall mission. Some leaders and rank-and-file members alike resist the idea of shifting organizational priorities away from recruitment and missionary work. Such a posture was reversed in The Family, but only after recruitment slowed measurably and significant numbers of second-generation youths began to leave the movement (Chancellor 2000: 205–6). ISKCON leaders resisted far longer, even as recruitment dwindled in many parts of the world (Rochford 1997, 1998b). The second factor turns on economic resources. Several of the established new religions experienced financial instability during the 1980s (Chancellor 2000: 7; Rochford 1997: 70–71). This occurred when most groups already had large and growing numbers of children. Without a stable economic base, it proved difficult to adequately meet the needs of children and parents.

Lacking internal structures of support, parents and children in particular have been forced to seek employment, schooling, and recreation within the conventional culture (Chancellor 2000; Introvigne 2000: 46–47; Rochford 1997, 1999b, 2000). Not surprisingly perceptions of the outside society have changed accordingly (Chancellor 2000; Rochford 2000). Images of the "corrupt" and "evil" system become difficult to sustain when substantial numbers of first- and second-generation members alike find their everyday lives bound by conventional involvement. Moreover, this erosion of social boundaries produces shifting organizational goals. The Family (Chancellor 2000: 32), ISKCON (Rochford 1985: 271–72), Scientology (Melton 2000: 44–51), and the Unification Church (Introvigne 2000: 47) have each embraced charitable and humanitarian work on behalf of *society's* poor and needy, often in cooperation with people of other faiths.

The growth of the nuclear family in the absence of a domestic culture has also resulted in a fundamental shift in social organization. For a number of new religious groups (e.g., The Family, Unification Church, and ISKCON), the foundation of their alternative world—communalism—has largely collapsed under the weight of growing congregationalism. Members living communally now represent a distinct minority in many groups. There is now far greater diversity in levels of member commitment and involvement than was present during their earlier phases of development.

In 2001, The Family's membership included 8,900 "Charter Members" residing communally as full-time members, 3,100 "Fellow Members" living and working outside the movement, and over 64,000 "Outside Members" who range from "live-out disciples" to those whose involvement is limited to financial contributions (Shepherd and Shepherd 2002: 5–6). ISKCON and the Unification Church exhibit a similar trend in the direction of growing pluralism. A survey (N = 1,996) of ISKCON's worldwide membership in 1995–96 found that only one-third (32 percent) of the respondents identified themselves as "full-time dependent" members of ISKCON; only 17 percent of those surveyed in North America described themselves as such, with fewer than one in three (29 percent) indicating that they lived within an ISKCON temple community (see also Rochford 2000). Indirect evidence suggests a similar trend for the Unification Church. Introvigne (2000: 47) states that the church in Asia and the United States has relatively few full-time members, with a much larger congregation of "Home Church" members. The latter are largely householders living and working outside of the church's communities in support of their families. As "associate members," their commitment and involvement in the Unification Church varies widely, with some being little more than movement sympathizers (Barker 1995: 228). Given this diversity, it no longer remains clear who is and is not a "real" Unificationist, even among those affiliated with the group (Barker 1995: 227).

Teaching New Religious Organizations and Leadership

Teaching about new religious movements can be a frustrating experience, for many of the reasons cited by Eugene Gallagher in his chapter on responding to student resistance when teaching this subject. The resistance is particularly striking when addressing the topics of leadership and organization. Most students firmly subscribe to anti-cult notions that leaders of new religions are self-serving, have suspect if not evil intentions, and head organizations that are meant to exploit members rather than deliver religious enlightenment. New religious organizations thus become locations wherein naïve members are transformed into "brainwashed" clones willing to sacrifice and submit to the authority of leaders.

Part of the difficulty in confronting students' understandings of new religions is that there are elements of truth in what they think and say. Some leaders and members of their organizations have acted in deplorable and illegal ways. One immediate challenge, therefore, is to help students think through their own dismissive prejudices. This requires us as teachers to encourage students to reflect critically on their own views. As with every other field of knowledge, we must find ways to commit students to seeking more detailed, nuanced, and complex understandings about what, for many, is an emotionally loaded topic.

My suggestions related to teaching leadership and organization in new religions can be organized around four plans of action:

1. Begin by inviting students to voice their suspicions about leadership and organization in new religions in an effort to face head on the "hermeneutic of suspicion."
2. Offer class exercises that require students to collectively and concretely work through their understandings of leadership and organization within new religions.
3. Offer research assignments that require students to focus in detail on one or more new religions and to do so from varying perspectives.
4. Use guest speakers and field trips to afford students opportunities to gain understanding of leadership and organization from the inside.

The Hermeneutic of Suspicion

When it comes to controversial social problems, students almost inevitably have a point of view. In teaching about new religions, I find this an excellent place to start. Many students come to class "knowing" all too well about "the cults." Yet as any teacher knows well, entrenched points of view built on limited factual knowledge represent a threat to the learning process. In initial discussions with students, my aim is, through guided discussion, to de-stabilize rather than change their views and interpretations. My hope is that students will come away less certain in their "understandings" of new religions and thus open to learning more. Moreover, I try to transform the negativity and suspiciousness that students express into a teaching resource. Student negativity can be used to raise the broader issue of public opposition and how it may influence the survival potential of new religious groups. Moreover, recall that new religions in their formative stages are prophetic movements that challenge the existing society. As such, they perhaps inevitably confront students' taken for granted reality.

Questions and strategies to guide a beginning discussion might include:

Tell me what you know about new religious movements.

Normally this request is sufficient to get students started and has the added virtue of being neutral in tone. Be ready, however, to push on students with follow-up questions meant to get negative (and positive) views out in the open for the class to consider. Expect to hear about authoritarian and exploitative leaders, brainwashed followers, and the like. It might prove useful to have individual students initially list what they know about new religions before engaging in a class discussion. At the end of the course, the question could be asked again. This will allow students to compare their new understandings with those they held at the beginning of the course.

How do you know about new religions, what are your sources of information?

Predictably, most of what students know about new religions comes from the media. Here a teacher should explore with students how they view the media as a source of knowledge. Moreover, might the media have an interest in new religions because they are exotic and even dramatic? Can students imagine that media interest in framing a good story might well distort the character of new religions?

With the various elements of the anti-cult narrative in the open, ask students to try something that for many will likely prove difficult, if not impossible: "Place yourself inside a new religion as a committed member." "Why are you part of this new religious organization? What is it you hope to gain? How do you view the spiritual leader of your group? What are the benefits of living exclusively with other committed followers? Has your freedom been lost or regained by participating in the group? How do you see the outside conventional society?" Ask students to reflect on those characteristics of the group they found familiar or comfortable in their role as an insider. Which elements stood out as strange, uncomfortable, or even threatening to them? In what ways do student responses point to the distinctive features of new religious movements detailed earlier?

Remember that the point of this initial class discussion is to get students to consciously consider their views about new religions. The effort is primarily meant to stir their minds rather than change them. Subsequent course readings, lectures, and the like will direct students toward more complete and complex ways of thinking about new religious movements.

Class Exercises

Issues of charismatic authority and organization within new religions are often perplexing topics for students. Below I suggest ways to deal with these issues in the context of teacher-led discussions as well as group exercises.

CHARISMA. Normally people see charisma in terms of individual qualities. Like so many other fundamentally social phenomena, charisma is often viewed in terms of individual personality or character. Although Weber starts with personality, he and other scholars have stressed how charisma is fundamentally a socially produced phenomenon. Charisma thus grows out of the give and take between a leader and those who come to see him or her as embodying charismatic authority. It is important for students to see how charisma grows out of human relations rather than being based on inherent characteristics.

A teacher might get at these issues by asking students a series of questions meant to guide them in the direction of understanding charisma as a social accomplishment. Begin by asking students to define *charisma*. What are the qualities or attributes of someone we view as charismatic? Is charisma fundamentally an attribute of individual character or personality? In what ways was Martin Luther King Jr. charismatic? President John Kennedy? Adolf Hitler? David Koresh (the leader of the Branch Davidians, who died at the siege in Waco)? Does each of these leaders have similar personality characteristics that define charismatic authority? Can charisma exist in the absence of a group of people who respect and honor someone whom they view as having superhuman or exemplary qualities? Can charismatic authority exist apart from people who willingly subject themselves to it? On what basis might a charismatic leader abuse or mistreat devoted followers? Asked differently, why might followers of a charismatic leader allow themselves to be subjects of abuse?

Sociologists of religion maintain that charismatic authority is effective in the short term and is subject to routinization. Recall the various strategic responses undertaken by charismatic leaders to deal with advancing institutionalization (i.e., resistance, acquiescence, encouragement, displacement, and abdication). Following Dawson (2002), how might a charismatic leader attempt to counteract institutionalization? Ask students why they think charisma is so unstable. If charismatic leadership is unstable, how are new religions able to collectively maintain themselves? Here, the importance of organization emerges as central.

ORGANIZATION. New religions are often collectivistic and communal. Within the context of democratic and pluralistic societies, this collectivistic orientation is deemed radical. To students, organizations often stand as impediments to personal freedom. The very idea that people live in "restrictive" organizations is an immediate cause for concern and even a basis for rejecting new religions as coercive. In a fundamental sense, communalism is squarely at odds with students' commitment to individualism. Ask students to compare life in a fraternity or sorority, the military, or a sports team with that found in a communally organized new religious group. In what ways are they similar? In what ways are they different? On what basis do students view new religions as comparatively more restrictive?

Ask students to map out a plan to create a communal organization that, while dedicated to religious principles and ways of living, is truly equal and respectful of all members' rights. How would such an organization be organized? How would labor be allocated? Who would lead and what qualities would leaders have? How would the group govern itself? How would it support itself financially? The idea here is to get students thinking about the sheer difficulty of creating religious organizations dedicated to collective living that lack hierarchy and elements of social control. One can make clear that all organizations to varying degrees place limits on individual freedom, demand sacrifices, and are hierarchical. Why then are new religious organizations considered especially oppressive and coercive? Is it possible that members experience their organizations as environments that promote freedom and self-expression in part because they shelter them from the "corrupt" and "unjust" nature of the conventional world?

GROUP EXERCISE. Below is an exercise that focuses on leadership and organization in new religions. I have used different versions of this exercise in my own teaching. It asks students to consider a fabricated new religion and to do so in the guise of a new religions scholar. The later role is meant to force students into a more neutral, if not objective, stance.

> You have been asked to serve as a consultant in a potentially violent situation involving an eclectic Christian millennial group called Revelation Revealed. The group is one that sees the Bible as the inerrant word of God. The leader is a prophet who blends elements of Hinduism into his otherwise Christian theology. His followers refer to him as their guru and acknowledge that he knows the mind of God and represents Him in all ways. He has told his followers that if America reverses its evil course, a heavenly kingdom will unfold. Only by converting America's leaders and citizens to the beliefs of the "Perfect Master" can America and the world be saved.
>
> Revelation Revealed has received considerable negative publicity. Traditional Christian groups have been especially critical, claiming that the guru is little more than a cult leader looking to exploit his membership for personal gain. The media have furthered this portrayal by claiming that the guru is mentally imbalanced and dangerous. Yet, in fact, he remains mysterious even to the majority of his followers, given his preference for remaining isolated in a mountain retreat surrounded by only a handful of his most devoted disciples.

You have been asked, as a scholar of new religions, to help law-enforcement authorities understand the guru and his organization. In your initial conversation with authorities it became obvious that they viewed Revelation Revealed largely through the lens of the anti-cult master narrative.

The exercise is the following:

1. Describe the anti-cult framework that law enforcement authorities are drawn to. What characteristics of cults make the authorities especially suspicious of Revelation Revealed and its leader? On what basis does the "Perfect Master" hold authority among his devoted followers? Why are they submissive and respectful of his authority? How does the group's preference for communal living further his authority and control? Why might authorities suspect him of abusing his followers and fear the possibility of violence by members of Revelation Revealed?
2. Now try something very different. Remember you are an expert on new religions and understand well what life is like on the inside of various new religious groups. The authorities, while drawn to anti-cult images of Revelation Revealed, are open to other views and interpretations. As a scholar of religion, you realize the importance of "taking the role of the other" and walking in the shoes of a committed disciple of the guru leader of Revelation Revealed. How as an insider do you see your leader? On what basis are you attracted to him? What is he offering spiritually that makes you want to submit to his authority? Why have you and your fellow believers forsaken a conventional life to remake the world in line with the guru's spiritual insights? Why have you so willingly sacrificed for the cause, despite public criticism of your beloved master and his organization? What will America and the world be like after God's Kingdom has been established? In sum, what are the strengths and limitations associated with attempting to understand the issues of leadership and organization within Revelation Revealed, from the perspective of an informed insider?

Research-Based Projects

Having students engage in research of their own is always a positive teaching strategy. Below are two suggestions for student research projects dealing with leadership and organization. The first asks students to explore the World Wide Web to research differing perspectives of leadership and/or organization in new religions. The second requires students to research a single new religion and to analyze in some detail one issue vital to its development. The latter requires students to apply concepts and frameworks central to the study of new religions as organizations, movements, and communities. Here, scholarship on success and failure, movement development, and religious culture becomes an important element of the assignment.

WEB-BASED PROJECT. Scholars, participants in new religious groups, and critics, be they ex-members or anti-cultists, generally hold widely differing views on new religions. This assignment asks you to explore these varied views and to analyze their significance. Students are required to search the World Wide Web to locate treatments of leadership and/or organization from the perspective of each of the above three interest groups. Students should focus on a *single* new religious group for their projects. The assignment particulars are as follows:

1. Go to the Religious Movements Project Homepage (http://religious movements.lib.Virginia.edu/home.htm). Locate the "group profiles" on the home page and then review some of the many new religions listed. Choose one. Read the description provided, paying particular attention to information concerning leadership and organization. Write a one-page summary statement of your findings.
2. Next, locate a Web site run by the new religious group you have chosen to research. Again, find information dealing specifically with leadership and organization. Write a one-page summary of what you discovered.
3. Finally, locate a Web site that takes an openly critical view of your group. Possible Web sites are likely to be of two types: those organized by disgruntled ex-members and those run by anti-cult groups. Do some digging as there are some interesting Web sites out there. Again, read through the material dealing with your group, or perhaps in the case of some anti-cult Web sites, locate general statements about leadership and organization in the category "cults." Again, write a one-page summary of what you have learned.

With your three summary statements before you, think comparatively and analytically about what you found. What, if anything, do the three Web sites share in their treatments of leadership and/or organization in relation to your group? How do they differ? How do the different interests and related perspectives of the three groups shape their views of organization and/or leadership? More broadly, in what ways do these differing perspectives speak to what R. D. Laing refers to as a "politics of experience," whereby differing sides in a conflict seek to preserve and further their own prejudices? Your essay of two to three pages should be both comparative and analytical.

RESEARCH PAPER. Students are to research and produce a paper on one new religious group, movement, or community of their choosing. The paper should be eight to ten pages in length and divided into two parts. The first part is historical and descriptive. When and under what circumstances did the group emerge? Who was its founding leader and what types of people were drawn to him or her? What are the group's distinctive religious beliefs, practices, and lifestyle requirements? The second part of the paper requires students to analyze a *specific* substantive topic or issue related to leadership and/or organization significant to the group's history (e.g., shifting patterns of member commitment and related organizational change, the role and fate of charismatic leadership, problems of succession, sources of internal conflict and schism, external opposition and accommodation, internal cultural development, the second generation and organizational change, and sources of success, decline, or failure).

To help students get started with their analysis, I assign three readings: Rodney Stark's (1996) "Why Religious Movements Succeed and Fail"; Rosabeth Kanter's (1968) "Commitment and Social Organization"; and Bryan Wilson's (1991) chapter, "Sects and Society in Tension," from his book *The Social Dimensions of Sectarianism*. Students are required to locate other sources in line with the substantive focus of their papers.

Guest Speakers and Field Trips

There is no substitute for interaction with members of a new religious group. I have on a numerous occasions had guest speakers from ISKCON or other new religious groups come to my classes. What is obvious, yet striking, is the way these encounters influence students' views. Suddenly these "strange" and "alien" people become human. To further this possibility, I always ask a group of students to take guest speakers to lunch before or after the formal class presentation.

Guest speakers should be asked to talk about their perceptions of their movement's leadership and its organizational issues and concerns. Students should be required to formulate questions of their own to ask. Possible questions might include

> In what ways are they attracted to the movement's leader(s)?
> Did the leadership play a role in their decision to join the movement?
> In what ways have their opinions of the leadership changed over time?
> For what reasons have their opinions changed?
> In what ways have their commitments to the movement and its
>   leadership changed over the course of their involvement?
> Have there been specific events or incidents that have particularly influenced their commitment in positive or negative ways?
> Are there ongoing changes occurring organizationally? What are they
>   and why are they taking place?

Although difficult for many teachers and students given the academic calendar, I have found it especially effective to take students on field trips to new religious communities. Several years ago a colleague and I took twenty students on an overnight field trip to the ISKCON temple and the Hasidic Center in Boston. We spent the night at the ISKCON temple and followed much of the daily routine of the devotees. Among other things, this required students to rise at 4 A.M. to shower and be in the temple for morning worship.

Helping students to "see" leadership and organization in the field is a bit of a challenge, but possible with some guidance. I suggest giving students a list of questions to consider prior to the field trip. Examples might include the following:

- How are people in the community dressed? Is there a standard "uniform"? Are there variations of a "uniform," or are members dressed in a wide variety of clothing styles? What does clothing reveal about identity, organizational control, and separation from the dominant culture?
- Where do members live? Are they housed in properties owned or otherwise controlled by the movement? Do some members live independently and at a distance from the core community? What does this pattern of residency reveal about existing social boundaries between the group and the outside society?
- How are people making a living? Does the group support them? Do they work in businesses owned by the group? Are members employed in the outside labor market? What proportion is employed outside the group? What can we discern about the group's organization if people work primarily in jobs outside the group in support of themselves and their families?
- Is there a community school where children are educated? Are children required to attend? What proportion of children attends outside schools? Are there meaningful positions for young adults within the community, or do most seek outside employment and establish at least somewhat independent lives for themselves?
- How is the community governed? Is community leadership selected by the local membership or appointed by "higher ups" in the organization? Is there a community board responsible for overseeing the affairs of the local community? What does the response to these questions suggest about how centralized and hierarchical the organization is?
- Does the group have a charismatic leader? How do members talk about him or her? Do they seem to hold the leader in awe? Are there special rituals meant to praise the leader? Is he or she subject to worship? Are there pictures or other symbols around the community meant to glorify the leader? To what degree and in what situations do members have access to their leader? Does he or she play a central role in decision making within the group, or is there a governing board that oversees the movement's affairs? What do responses to these questions imply about the degree to which charisma has been routinized within the group?

These and other issues can be explored either though direct observation or by asking questions—something students are capable of and interested in doing. The data collected by students could serve as the basis for an extended class discussion, student presentations, or a paper.

REFERENCES

Anthony, Dick, and Thomas Robbins. 1982. "Contemporary Religious Ferment and Moral Ambiguity." In *New Religious Movements: A Perspective for Understanding Society*, ed. Eileen Barker, 243–63. New York: Edwin Mellen Press.

Bainbridge, William Sims, and Daniel Jackson. 1981. "The Rise and Decline of Transcendental Meditation." In *The Social Impact of New Religious Movements*, ed. Bryan Wilson, 135–58. New York: The Rose of Sharon Press.

Barker, Eileen. 1995. "The Unification Church." In *America's Alternative Religions*, ed. Timothy Miller, 223–29. Albany: State University of New York Press.

———. 2004. "What Are We Studying?" *Nova Religio* 8, 88–102.

Bellah, Robert. 1976. "New Religious Consciousness and the Crisis of Modernity." In *The New Religious Consciousness*, ed. Charles Glock and Robert Bellah, 333–52. Berkeley: University of California Press.

Berger, Bennett. 1981. *The Survival of a Counterculture*. Los Angeles: University of California Press.

Berger, Peter. 1969. *The Sacred Canopy*. Garden City, NY: Anchor Books.

Bromley, David. 1997. "Constructing Apocalypticism: Social and Cultural Elements of Radical Organization." In *Millennium, Messiah, and Mayhem*, ed. Thomas Robbins and Susan Palmer, 31–46. New York: Routledge.

———. 2005. "Whither New Religious Studies: Defining and Shaping a New Area of Study." *Nova Religio* 8, 83–97.

Bromley, David, and Phillip Hammond, eds. 1987. *The Future of New Religious Movements*. Macon, GA: Mercer University Press.

Bromley, David, and Anson Shupe. 1981. *Strange Gods: The Great American Cult Scare*. Boston: Beacon Press.

Bryant, Edwin, and Maria Ekstrand, eds. 2004. *The Hare Krishna Movement: The Postcharismatic Fate of a Religious Transplant*. New York: Columbia University Press.

Chancellor, James. 2000. *Life in The Family: An Oral History of the Children of God*. Syracuse, NY: Syracuse University Press.

Clark, John, Michael Langone, Robert Schecter, and R. Daily. 1981. *Destructive Cult Conversion: Theory, Research and Treatment*. Weston, MA: American Family Foundation.

Dawson, Lorne. 1998. *Comprehending Cults: The Sociology of New Religious Movements*. New York: Oxford University Press.

———. 2002. "Crises of Charismatic Legitimacy and Violent Behavior in New Religions." In *Cults, Religion and Violence*, ed. David G. Bromley and J. Gordon Melton, 80–101. New York: Cambridge University Press.

Downton, James, Jr. 1979. *Sacred Journeys: The Conversion of Young Americans to Divine Light Mission*. New York: Columbia University Press.

Enroth, Ronald. 1977. *Youth, Brainwashing, and the Extremist Cults*. Grand Rapids, MI: Zondervan.

Finke, Roger, and Rodney Stark. 1992. *The Churching of America, 1776–1990*. New Brunswick, NJ: Rutgers University Press.

Foster, Laurence. 1991. *Women, Family, and Utopia: Communal Experiments of the Shakers, the Oneida Community, and the Mormons*. Syracuse, NY: Syracuse University Press.

Gitlin, Todd. 1980. *The Whole World Is Watching: Mass Media in the Making and Unmasking of the New Left*. Berkeley: University of California Press.

Glock, Charles, and Robert Bellah, eds. 1976. *The New Religious Consciousness*. Berkeley: University of California Press.

Hall, John. 1988. "Social Organization and Pathways of Commitment: Types of Communal Groups, Rational Choice Theory, and the Kanter Thesis." *American Sociological Review* 53, 679–92.

Iannaccone, Laurence. 1988. "A Formal Model of Church and Sect." *American Journal of Sociology* 94, S241–S268.

Introvigne, Massimo. 2000. *The Unification Church*. Torino, Italy: Signature Books.

Johnson, Benton. 1963. "On Church and Sect." *American Sociological Review* 28, 539–49.

Johnson, Gregory. 1976. "The Hare Krishna in San Francisco." In *The New Religious Consciousness*, ed. Charles Glock and Robert Bellah, 31–51. Berkeley: University of California Press.

Judah, Stillson. 1974. *Hare Krishna and the Counterculture*. New York: John Wiley.

Kanter, Rosabeth Moss. 1968. "Commitment and Social Organization: A Study of Commitment Mechanism in Utopian Communities." *American Sociological Review* 33, 499–517.

———. 1972. *Commitment and Community*. Cambridge, MA: Harvard University Press.

Kent, Stephen. 2001. *From Slogans to Mantras: Social Protest and Religious Conversion in the Late Vietnam War Era*. Syracuse, NY: Syracuse University Press.

Klatch, Rebecca. 1999. *A Generation Divided: The New Left, The New Right, and the 1960s*. Berkeley: University of California Press.

Lofland, John. 1987. "Social Movement Culture and the Unification Church." In *The Future of New Religions*, ed. David G. Bromley and Phillip Hammond, 91–108. Macon, GA: Mercer University Press.

Lofland, John, and James Richardson. 1985. "Religious Movement Organizations: Elementary Forms and Dynamics." In *Protest: Studies of Collective Behavior and Social Movements*, ed. John Lofland, 179–200. New Brunswick, NJ: Transaction.

McGuire, Meredith. 1997. *Religion: The Social Context*. Belmont, CA: Wadsworth.

Melton, J. Gordon. 1991. "Introduction: When Prophets Die: The Succession Crisis in New Religions." In *When Prophets Die: The Postcharismatic Fate of New Religious Movements*, ed. Timothy Miller, 1–12. Albany: State University of New York Press.

———. 2000. *The Church of Scientology*. Torino, Italy: Signature Books.

———. 2004. "Toward a Definition of 'New Religion.'" *Nova Religio* 8, 73–87.

Miller, Timothy. 1991. *When Prophets Die: The Postcharismatic Fate of New Religious Movements*. Albany: State University of New York Press.

Nelson, Geoffrey. 1968. "The Concept of Cult." *Sociological Review* 16, 351–62.

Orme-Collins, Donna. 2002. "Death of a Moonie: Reflections of a "Blessed Child." *Cultic Studies Review* 1, 1–4.

Palmer, Susan. 1988. "Charisma and Abdication: A Study of the Leadership of Bhagwan Shree Rajneesh." *Sociological Analysis* 49, 119–35.

Palmer, Susan, and Charlotte Hardman, eds. 1999. *Children in New Religions*. New Brunswick, NJ: Rutgers University Press.

Richardson, James. 1978. "An Oppositional and General Conceptualization of Cult." *Annual Review of the Social Sciences of Religion* 2, 29–52.

———. 1994. "Update on 'The Family': Organizational Change and Development in a Controversial New Religious Group." In *Sex, Slander, and Salvation*, ed. James Lewis and J. Gordon Melton, 27–39. Stanford, CA: Center for Academic Publication.

————. 1999. "Social Control of New Religions: From 'Brainwashing' Claims to Child Abuse Accusations." In *Children in New Religions*, ed. Susan Palmer and Charlotte Hardman, 172–86. New Brunswick, NJ: Rutgers University Press.

Richardson, James, Mary Stewart, and Robert Simmonds. 1979. *Organized Miracles: A Study of a Contemporary, Youth, Communal, Fundamentalist Organization.* New Brunswick, NJ: Transaction.

Robbins, Thomas. 1988. *Cults, Converts and Charisma.* Newbury Park, CA: Sage.

Rochford, E. Burke, Jr. 1985. *Hare Krishna in America.* New Brunswick, NJ: Rutgers University Press.

————. 1987. "Dialectical Processes in the Development of Hare Krishna: Tension, Public Definition, and Strategy." In *The Future of New Religions*, ed. David Bromley and Phillip Hammond, 109–22. Macon, GA: Mercer University Press.

————. 1989. "Factionalism, Group Defection, and Schism in the Hare Krishna Movement." *Journal for the Scientific Study of Religion* 28, 162–79.

————. 1995. "Family Structure, Commitment and Involvement in the Hare Krishna Movement." *Sociology of Religion* 56, 153–75.

————. 1997. "Family Formation, Culture and Change in the Hare Krsna Movement." *ISKCON Communications Journal* 5:61–82. Available at www.iskcon.com/icj/5_2/5_2rochford.html. Accessed October 3, 2006.

————. 1998a. "Reactions of Hare Krishna Devotees to Scandals of Leaders' Misconduct." In *Wolves Within the Fold: Religious Leadership and Abuses of Power*, ed. Anson Shupe, 101–17. New Brunswick, NJ: Rutgers University Press.

————. 1998b. "Child Abuse in the Hare Krishna Movement: 1971–1986." *ISKCON Communications Journal* 6, 43–69. Available at www.iskcon.com/icj/6_1/6_1rochford.html. Accessed October 3, 2006.

————. 1999a. "Prabhupada Centennial Survey: A Summary of the Final Report." *ISKCON Communications Journal* 7, 11–26. Available at www.iskcon.com/icj/7_1/7_1rochford.html. Accessed October 3, 2006.

————. 1999b. "Education and Collective Identity: Public Schooling of Hare Krishna Youths." In *Children in New Religions*, ed. Susan Palmer and Charlotte Hardman, 29–50. New Brunswick, NJ: Rutgers University Press.

————. 2000. "Demons, Karmies, and Non-devotees: Culture, Group Boundaries, and the Development of Hare Krishna in North America and Europe." *Social Compass* 47, 169–86.

Seager, Richard. 1999. *Buddhism in America.* New York: Columbia University Press.

Shepherd, Gordon, and Gary Shepherd. 2002. "The Family in Transition: The Moral Career of a New Religious Movement." Paper presented at the CESNUR International Conference, Salt Lake and Provo, Utah, June. Available at www.cesnur.org/2002/slc/sheperd.htm.

Shinn, Larry. 1986. "Conflicting Networks: Guru and Friend in ISKCON." In *Religious Movements: Genesis, Exodus, and Numbers*, ed. Rodney Stark, 95–115. New York: Paragon.

————. 1987a. *The Dark Lord: Cult Images and the Hare Krishnas in America.* Philadelphia: Westminster Press.

————. 1987b. "The Future of an Old Man's Vision: ISKCON in the Twenty-First Century." In *The Future of New Religions*, ed. David Bromley and Phillip Hammond, 123–40. Macon, GA: Mercer University Press.

Stark, Rodney. 1987. "How New Religions Succeed: A Theoretical Model." In *The Future of New Religions*, ed. David G. Bromley and Phillip Hammond, 11–29. Macon, GA: Mercer University Press.

————. 1996. "Why Religious Movements Succeed or Fail: A Revised General Model." *Journal of Contemporary Religion* 11, 133–46.

Stark, Rodney, and William S. Bainbridge. 1985. *The Future of Religion*. Berkeley: University of California Press.

Swatos, William. 1981. "Church-Sect and Cult: Bringing Mysticism Back In." *Sociological Analysis* 42, 17–26.

Swidler, Ann. 1986. "Culture in Action: Symbols and Strategies." *American Sociological Review* 51, 73–86.

Tipton, Steven. 1982. *Getting Saved From the Sixties*. Berkeley: University of California Press.

Troeltsch, Ernst. 1931. *The Social Teachings of the Christian Churches*. New York: Macmillan.

Turner, Ralph, and Lewis Killian. 1987. *Collective Behavior*. Englewood Cliffs, NJ: Prentice-Hall.

Wallis, Roy. 1975. "The Cult and Its Transformation." In *Sectarianism: Analyses of Religious and Non-Religious Sects*, ed. Roy Wallis, 35–49. New York: John Wiley.

————. 1976. *The Road to Total Freedom: A Sociological Analysis of Scientology*. New York: Columbia University Press.

————. 1982. "The Social Construction of Charisma." *Social Compass* 29, 25–39.

————. 1984. *The Elementary Forms of the New Religious Life*. London: Routledge and Kegan Paul.

Weber, Max. 1978. *Economy and Society*. Vol. 1. Ed. Guenther Roth and Claus Wittich. Berkeley: University of California Press.

Wessinger, Catherine. 2000. *How the Millennium Comes Violently*. New York: Seven Bridges Press.

Wilson, Bryan. 1987. "Factors in the Failure of the New Religious Movements." In *The Future of New Religions*, ed. David G. Bromley and Phillip Hammond, 30–45. Macon, GA: Mercer University Press.

————. 1991. *The Social Dimensions of Sectarianism: Sect and New Religious Movements in Contemporary Society*. Oxford: Clarendon Press.

Wuthnow, Robert. 1976. "The New Religions in Social Context." In *The New Religious Consciousness*, ed. Charles Glock and Robert Bellah, 267–93. Berkeley: University of California Press.

Zaidman, Nurit. 2000. "The Integration of Indian Immigrants to Temples Run by North Americans." *Social Compass* 47, 205–19.

The Dynamics of Movement Membership: Joining and Leaving New Religious Movements

Stuart A. Wright

Questions pertaining to joining and leaving new religious movements (NRMs) frame some of the most pivotal issues for scholars. Unlike mainstream religious institutions that are sustained largely by an intergenerational base of members, NRMs must build a membership base through proselytization and recruitment. This one fact alone highlights a fundamental dilemma for NRMs and fuels the controversy that often follows them. NRMs must be effective challengers to the established social order and to traditional religious institutions in persuading potential converts to embrace an alternative path of spirituality. If and when NRMs do pose a vigorous challenge to the status quo, they typically offend conventional sensibilities and become rivals with institutional faiths for adherents. Entrenched social and religious organizations and actors exercise power to repress challengers over the contested terrain while true believers of new faiths seek to expand recruitment activities and carve out a niche for themselves in society. The dynamic that feeds the genesis of new religions is invariably wrought with conflict, controversy, and claims-making. Predictably, the new faiths are stigmatized and branded with a variety of pejorative names—heretics, infidels, heathen, and most recently, cults—all suggesting a putative threat to the social order.

In the simplest terms, NRMs seek to ensure organizational survival and success in the face of a broad array of opponents. Even if they withstand formal legal and regulatory challenges, they must still overcome informal normative obstacles to recruit and build a membership base from an unfriendly host society. Historically, new or first-generation religious movements are distinguished by a "conversionist" orientation, which both clearly symbolizes identity change and signifies entry into an elect group of believers. The experiential emphasis on conversion, the formation of a tight-knit community, the sharp delineation of in-group and out-group categories, and the development of an exclusive message and mission contribute to a distinct product and niche in the religious marketplace. NRMs promise immediate access to the transcendent and divine, offer spiritual enlightenment and inspiration, and furnish extraordinary religious myths and symbols.

An issue germane to NRM success is the mobilization of a largely secular anti-cult movement (ACM), comprising family and relatives of converts allied with social workers, psychologists, mental health specialists, and even a few scholars to employ a coercion model of affiliation. As the secular counterpart to the religious attack on cults, ACM proponents of the coercion model have endeavored to champion a scientific argument against NRM conversion, variously depicted as brainwashing, mind control, thought reform, or coercive persuasion (Clark et al. 1981; Galanti 1993; Hassan 1988; Lifton 1961, 1985; Ofshe and Singer 1986; Schein, Schneier, and Barker 1961; Singer 1979, 1986, 1995; Zimbardo and Anderson 1993). This issue has dominated much of the public debate surrounding NRMs or cults, with antagonists making claims that conversion is a product of various manipulative psychological practices inducing ego destruction, impaired psychological integration, dissociation, split personality, and overstimulation of the nervous system, resulting in a diminished capacity for rational decision making and even the loss of free will. In effect, an argument is advanced that cults apply special techniques to manufacture pseudo-conversions. Most scholars have rejected this interpretation as lacking scientific merit and empirical support, as have professional organizations such as the American Psychological Association and the American Sociological Association, which filed amicus briefs in a landmark legal case (see Anthony 1990). Despite this repudiation, however, the notion of brainwashing remains a persistent and popular belief throughout American society. (For a thorough analysis of the coercion or brainwashing model, the reader is referred to the Richardson and Introvigne chapter in this volume.)

One of the challenges facing NRM researchers will be to revisit our conceptions of conversion or affiliation in response to the changing social and demographic conditions of aging populations and maturing movements. Some new religious movements are not really new, or at least not in a first-generation sense. Much of the foundational research on NRMs has focused on the groups that were launched in the 1960s and 1970s. These studies essentially examined first-generation movements and converts and fashioned conversion models to time-specific conditions. As these movements aged, along with a core of members who stayed, important changes occurred. Second and third generations of NRM members remained; these progeny more or less "inherited" their faith, much like the offspring of traditional faiths. While NRMs may continue to emphasize bringing in new converts, the increasing importance of religious socialization of children changes the dynamics of a movement's organization. This development has important implications for any analysis of conversion, as NRMs move toward greater intergenerational dependence to build their membership base.

NRMs must not only recruit and convert potential devotees, they must also *retain* them. Retention has been a major problem for NRMs. Despite media portrayals and popular conceptions of cult brainwashing that keeps members in a state of mental or psychological captivity, research indicates that attrition rates have been quite high (Barker 1984, 1987, 1988; Beckford 1985; Bird and Reimer 1982; Galanter 1989; Goldman 1995; Levine 1984; Lewis 1986; Skonovd 1981, Solomon 1981; Taslimi, Hood, and Watson 1991; Wright 1983, 1984, 1987, 1988; Wright and Ebaugh 1993). Even during the height of countercultural youth experimentation with new religions in the early 1970s, most NRMs in the United States never achieved a membership base of more than a few thousand. Reverend Moon's Unification Church, for example, was alleged to be one of the most successful movements during this time, and yet it never attained more than 10,000 members in its American branch (Richardson 1993: 81), a modest figure by contemporary denominational standards. Studies reveal that the average length of NRM membership was about two years and that devotees were leaving at a sufficiently rapid rate to offset most of the gains through new converts. This is an important fact that was largely underreported by the media, ignored or downplayed by anti-cultists, and generally unknown to the larger public, leading to inflated estimates of NRM growth and, on occasions, wildly exaggerated claims of a cult "pandemic" (Shapiro 1977). Of course, NRMs were also reluctant to advertise high turnover rates, preferring to project an image of organizational success. Ironically, this reluctance proved to be more damaging to NRMs in the long run because the high attrition rates were the most compelling prima facia argument against the brainwashing claims that were dogging these organizations. In any case, determining how and why people leave new religious movements can also increase our understanding of how and why they become members in the first place.

Conversion/Affiliation

There have been literally hundreds of studies on conversion over the last thirty-five years, constituting a well-researched stock of knowledge that is available to us. Rambo (1982) reported 256 behavioral science entries on conversion by the early 1980s, 62 percent of which were produced after 1972. Beckford and Richardson (1983) identified 145 entries on NRM conversion around the same time, 95 percent of which were produced after 1972. While no recent systematic compilations on conversion have been published to my knowledge, a proportional growth rate would yield figures more than double those reported in the early eighties. This succinct review of NRM conversion/affiliation is divided into two sections: cultural and social structural factors affecting NRM affiliation and growth, and conversion processes and models. The key issue in the first section is the resolution of identity and moral meaning within the context of a perceived "crisis of values" precipitated by social and cultural change.

Cultural and Social Structural Factors Affecting New Religious Movement Affiliation and Growth

While NRMs ordinarily face formidable opposition and challenges to their legitimacy, cultural and social structural changes can shift or disrupt power alignments affecting elites and institutions. Social-movement theorists observe that these kinds of changes can create "openings" or "expanded opportunities" in the institutional or informal power relations that enhance movement emergence and mobilization (McAdam, McCarthy, and Zald 1996). Social actors typically lack resources and opportunities to marshal power and effect change. But cultural or social structural changes precipitating shifts in power alignments may provide expanded political opportunities that enable movements to overcome obstacles to collective action and sustain a challenge to institutional opponents. NRM emergence and mobilization can be explained in part by cultural and social structural change.

Cultural change affecting NRM opportunities has been posited as a crisis of moral meaning or cultural values (Anthony and Robbins 1981, 1982; Bellah 1976; Glock 1976; Robbins and Anthony 1972; Tipton 1982), accompanied by the emergence of a youth counterculture, widespread civil and political unrest, and the mobilization of dissident protest movements (Gitlin 1987). With changes precipitated by the civil rights movement and the resultant social disruption caused by the effort to extend equal rights to African Americans, many denizens expressed dismay at the moral contradiction of racism. This contradiction was particularly conspicuous in light of the intensive socialization and political indoctrination of the young by the country's championing "democratic values" during the Cold War years. This largely successful "democratization" effort produced a generation of idealistic youth who became disillusioned by the massive and often violent resistance to the civil rights movement.

The seeds of distrust that were planted in the 1950s and early 1960s blossomed into a full-blown counterculture by the late 1960s. As the baby boomers swelled enrollments on college campuses, students organized in support of various social causes and experimented with alternative politics, lifestyles, philosophies, and religions. Bellah (1976) contends that this period signaled a deep disruption of American civil religion, out of which a new spiritual ferment was born that prompted a search for "new myths." Tipton (1982), a student of Bellah's, echoed this argument, noting that the crisis of moral meanings gave rise to a new set of "expressive ideals" by which youth sought to guide their lives. They challenged the "utilitarian culture" by rejecting money, power, and technical knowledge as ends in themselves while celebrating love, intimacy, self-awareness, and nature. This quest for expressive ideals created opportunities for NRMs to capitalize on widespread disenchantment with traditional religious institutions while offering alternative spiritual pathways.

For observers like Bellah (1976) and Tipton (1982), the moral crisis engendered a rejection of the two pillars of American ideological self-understanding: utilitarian individualism and biblical religion. Movements of political change and lifestyle experimentation ultimately proved to be unrealistic or intrinsically unsatisfying, failing to reconcile the moral crisis. But new religious movements provided resolution of the utilitarian/instrumental demands of adulthood in conventional society (work, family, education) and the rule-orientation of religion with the counterculture's expressive ideals. In effect, the new religions provided ways to recombine the moral authority of religion with an emergent utilitarian ethic of self-awareness that resolved the value conflict, forging a new synthesis.

Robbins, Anthony, and Curtis (1975) make a similar case for the "integrative" thesis, describing four processes by which NRMs reconcile nomadic youth to mainstream culture: adaptive socialization, combination, compensation, and redirection. *Adaptive socialization* refers to the direct inculcation of values, norms, and skills that promote effective coping and adaptation to conventional institutional arrangements. *Combination* refers to the ability of NRMs to synthesize countercultural symbols and values with conventional orientations ("get high on God," "Jesus was a revolutionary"). *Compensation* points to diminished feelings of alienation from conventional, bureaucratic roles that come from substitute spiritual rewards and duties. Finally, *redirection* denotes the declining appeal of deviance, reconciling the devotee to a purposeful and constructive role within the sphere of the religious organization. The appeal of NRMs is tied to the fashioning of innovative means to manage the tensions of advanced industrial societies, providing for a reintegration of disenfranchised youth (see also Anthony and Robbins 1981; Robbins 1988).

Social structural change providing expanded opportunities for NRMs has been tied variously to family disorganization, decline of mediating structures, deinstitutionalization, secularization, and legal change. Let's examine these factors briefly.

To begin, social structural change affecting the traditional family is well established in the sociological literature. The decline in birth rates, the increased participation of women in the labor force, the enhanced geographical mobility of families, the growth in divorce and remarriage rates, and the transfer of traditional family functions to other institutions are some of the key impacts that advanced industrial societies have on traditional family structure. Some theorists see the strain on the institution of the family that arises from structurally induced changes as facilitating the growth of NRMs (Doress and Porter 1981; Galanter et al. 1979; Kaslow and Sussman 1982). Elsewhere, I have referred to this as the "family deprivation thesis" (Wright and Piper 1986) of NRM conversion. Evidence for this thesis is largely anecdotal and theoretical or derived from isolated case studies, and one empirical test of the thesis, drawing from a sample of ninety leavers and stayers of three NRMs, did not yield any support (see Wright 1987; Wright and Piper 1986). In studies using measures of reported prior closeness to family, degree of adolescent tension, and parental approval/disapproval of conversion, no significant correlations were found between family satisfaction and conversion. Converts were just as likely to report favorable experiences with families as not, and leavers were no more likely than stayers to report positive family relations.

Mediating structures refer to those groups or communities that stand between the nuclear family and the larger corporate and bureaucratic world (see Kerrine and Neuhaus 1979). With the decline of natural communities, there are fewer mediating groups to help ease the transition of the young to utilitarian, functionally specific, occupational roles. The crisis is rooted in the jolting transition from the "expressive" values, roles, and relationships of the nuclear family to the "instrumental" values, roles, and relationships of the impersonal marketplace. The eclipse of traditional mediating structures is said to be replaced by emergent "social inventions" (Coleman 1970), such as encounter groups, religio-therapeutic communities, or NRMs that serve a transitional function providing family-like bonds and affective relationships coupled with instrumental roles and expectations. NRMs often exhibit characteristics of both primary and secondary groups. They create intensive interpersonal relations resembling extended families while at the same time operating as complex bureaucratic organizations with instrumental qualities—differentiation, specialization of work roles, hierarchical structure of authority, rationally enacted rules and regulations (Beckford 1985; Bromley 1985; Richardson 1988; Robbins and Anthony 1972). Studies suggest a link between the rise of new religions and a search by young adults for "surrogate families" (Anthony and Robbins 1982; Kilbourne and Richardson 1982; Parsons 1986; Wright and D'Antonio 1993). Concurrently, it is clear that NRMs seized opportunities created by structural change, cultivating familial-like settings, symbols, and nomenclature by which to attract new converts.

Another aspect of structural change tied to NRM conversion is deinstitutionalization. According to Hunter (1981), modernity is accompanied by pervasive deinstitutionalization, a process by which private or interpersonal norms structuring courtship, marriage, child-rearing, sexuality, gender relations, consumption, and spirituality become deregulated. In the private sphere, "choice" increasingly replaces social convention, making it more difficult to navigate the troubled waters of relationships, roles, and identity. In contrast, social organization in the public sphere is becoming more regulated by massive bureaucracies in law, commerce, health care, education, labor, the military, and government. Institutions are increasingly guided by formal rationality, with little regard for personal needs. The disjuncture between public and private spheres dictates that successful role performance in the service of the institution has higher utility and value in modern society but leaves the individual with unmet personal needs. This disjuncture between the public and private spheres engenders a bifurcation of identity or self. Moreover, proliferation of secondary groups and attendant public roles stressing conformity without meaningful participation leads to further fragmentation of identity. Against this backdrop of structural strain, NRMs seize the opportunities created by deinstitutionalization by offering beliefs and practices that emphasize a "holistic" sense of self and an integrated system of meaning (see also Johnson 1981).

A related factor tied to NRM conversion and growth is secularization. There are two principal theories linking NRMs to secularization. Bryan Wilson (1976) has argued that secularization produces a corresponding rise in cults. Cults are residual forms of religion that emerge when the institutional framework of religion breaks down. Authentic religion or its awakening is diminished by expanding bureaucratic patterns of social control. New religions merely fill a void and represent exotic and "trivial" remnants that are tolerated precisely because secularization reduces religion to a consumer item; spiritual shoppers choose from a packaged array of mystiques. Stark and Bainbridge (1985) offer a different theory. They contend that secularization generates two countervailing processes: revival and innovation. *Revival* refers to the process by which sects break from churches to invigorate the shared faith tradition. *Innovation* refers to the process by which new religions are born, by either cultural import or charismatic vision. Both are important and are natural products of the religious economy, affirming pluralism and healthy competition in the spiritual marketplace.

Finally, we must be aware of a pivotal change in law that created expanded opportunities for NRMs. The passage of the Immigration Reform Act of 1965 abolished an immigration quota system that heavily favored northern Europeans. The effect of the change was a dramatic increase in the number of Asian and Latin American immigrants. Many of the new religions of the late 1960s and early 1970s were actually cultural imports that arrived with the new immigrants, particularly those of Eastern or Asian origin. The legal change in quotas initially triggered an explosion of interest among young adults in Eastern-based NRMs (Cox 1977), but since the 1980s has also fueled an influx of "immigrant churches" from Central and South America (Ebaugh and Chafetz 2000).

Conversion Processes and Models

While social science research reveals some conflicting conceptualizations of conversion, there is far greater agreement on the key issues surrounding conversion, as we shall see. Sociologists of religion generally define *conversion* as a transformation of one's identity and worldview (see McGuire 1997). However, it is often asserted or implied that NRM conversion is a more intense and substantive transformation. NRMs are more likely than conventional religions to make imposing demands of sacrifice and commitment, thus effecting a more substantial displacement of the old self and worldview, followed by adoption of a new enlightened self and meaning system. This transformation is also more likely to entail a change of appearance or dress, name, diet, lifestyle, primary group, and master attribution scheme (Downton 1979; Machalek and Snow 1993; Rambo 1993; Richardson, Stewart and Simmonds 1979; Snow and Machalek 1984; Van Zandt 1991). It is this qualitative difference in conversion that appears to fuel some of the claims of brainwashing.

One debate among scholars has been whether NRM conversion is sudden or gradual. NRM critics have suggested that cults use manipulative techniques that create an abrupt conversion and produce "sudden personality change" (Conway and Siegelman 1978). Advocates of the coercion or brainwashing model assume "suddenness" as a given feature, but sudden conversions are actually rare. The weight of empirical research has supported the idea of a more gradual process of conversion involving a series of decisions, incremental commitments, and progressive stages of psychological identification and affective attachment (Balch and Taylor 1978; Barker 1984; Downton 1979; Greil and Rudy 1984; Lofland and Stark 1965; Rambo 1993; Richardson 1978; Richardson and Stewart 1977; Snow and Machalek 1984; Straus 1976, 1979). In some cases, when conversion appeared to be sudden or abrupt, studies indicate that many converts had engaged in some measure of "seekership" that preceded the conversion (Balch and Taylor 1978; Fichter 1981; Richardson 1978; Rochford 1985).

Another issue of concern among scholars has been the extent to which the convert is an active or passive participant in the conversion process. Proponents of the coercion model assert a passive convert profile, someone who is overwhelmed by powerful external forces, with the conversion orchestrated through behavioral conditioning practices that induce conversion. These external forces, it is claimed, may cause impaired mental functioning and the destruction of the individual's natural ego defenses that diminishes logical reasoning and overrides free will (Enroth 1977; Hassan 1988; Langone 1993; Singer 1995; Tobias and Lalich 1994). Yet careful studies of NRM conversion reveal that converts often take an active role in creatively constructing a new spiritual path to "accomplish" their personal transformation (Straus 1976, 1979; Tipton 1982). Converts are more reflexively aware of their situation than anti-cultists typically claim, weighing choices, making conscious decisions about their faith, and attempting to balance their individual needs with group expectations.

An accurate understanding of conversion must also take into account the multidimensional complexion of the transformative process. Lofland and Skonovd (1981) developed a typology of "conversion motifs" to convey this point. They proposed six motifs: intellectual, mystical, experimental, affective, revivalist, and coercive. Each was assessed in terms of degree of social pressure, temporal duration, level of affective arousal, affective tone or content, and belief-participation sequence. By analyzing a broad range of conversion accounts and studies, Lofland and Skonovd demonstrated through this heuristic exercise that transformations follow varied patterns and exhibit dissimilar features. Conversion is not a single, unitary, invariable process, as has been asserted by "causal process models" (e.g., Downton 1980; Lofland and Stark 1965) or the coercion/ brainwashing model (Richardson and Introvigne, this volume). Such models are better viewed as "ideal typical natural histories" (Machalek and Snow 1985) rather than as pure descriptions of a unified causal process.

Ironically, one of the earliest attempts at causal process was co-authored by Lofland, referred to as the Lofland-Stark or "world-saver" model (1965) based on a study of the Unification Church in California. It stipulated a value-added model describing seven sequential stages through which the individual passed. The model may be summarized as follows: the conversion process begins when the potential convert experiences acute and persistent tensions within a religious problem-solving perspective, which leads the person to a self-definition of "religious seeker," after which he or she encounters the religious movement at a critical turning point in his or her life, forms an affective bond with one or more NRM members that leads to the attenuation of extra-cult ties, and subsequently the individual experiences intensive interaction with group members, which culminates in the complete transformation of identity and meaning system to produce a true believer or world-saver.

Not just anyone was attracted to this kind of religious movement, however. Lofland and Stark argue that conversion to a radically different religious worldview involves predispositional factors. Potential converts tend to be persons who feel frustrated, deprived, and under strain. They are also individuals who were previously oriented to finding religious solutions to problems and who defined themselves as religious seekers. Lofland and Stark suggest that situational factors are important in the conversion process as well. The point at which felt tensions evoke religious seeking must coincide with NRM contact. The development of an affective tie with one or more devotees is situational, since this depends in part on the perceived sincerity of gestures, styles of presentation, intrinsic feelings of liking, and the mesh of personalities during the exchange between the preconvert and the group. These new bonds also have to be sufficiently strong to compel seekers to relax extra-group ties.

Though Lofland and Stark never make any claims that their model is universally applicable to NRM conversion, it was used and tested in studies of diverse groups. Greil and Rudy (1984) provide an evaluation of ten case studies applying the Lofland-Stark model of conversion and discuss some of the problems and shortcomings of the model.

A significant contribution to the research on conversion has been made by psychiatrist Saul Levine (1984), whose work is sometimes referred to as the "identity formation thesis." Levine studied over 800 cases of youth conversion to extremist groups. He argues that these "radical departures" are actually "desperate attempts to grow up in a society that places obstacles in the way of the normal yearnings of youth" (1984: 11). The normal yearnings include obtaining increased independence from overbearing and protective parents who inhibit developmental growth into adulthood. Levine found that joiners frequently were attempting to break free of parental control to forge a post-adolescent identity and distinct self-concept. He characterizes the dilemma as a "developmental stalemate" in which a radical departure is perceived as the individual's only course of action. Yet far from rejecting parental values, converts are described as acting out the values inculcated by family and society: individualism, independence, and autonomy. What distinguishes these youth from their peers who did not join such groups is that the converts simply are unable to navigate an effective separation from parents and families, thus precipitating a more drastic measure. Levine inverts the claim that cults exploit young people by arguing that converts use the radical departure for their own ends. Once enjoined to the group, the youthful convert exploits or uses the group in the service of self-discovery and growing up. This is typically accomplished in a period of less than two years, wherein he or she takes leave of the group and returns home where these youth "are able to resume the sorts of lives their parents had hoped for them and to find gratification and significance in the middle-class world they had totally abjured" (1984: 15).

As alluded to earlier, the bulk of these studies focuses on first-generation converts to NRMs. They do not reflect changes in the organizational strategies of recruitment and the subjective patterns and experiences of conversion as NRMs have moved toward institutionalization and cultural assimilation. Evidence of more conventional patterns of intergenerational socialization of the young born into their parent's faith can be seen in a number of more recent studies. For example, Rochford (1995, 1997, 2001) has chronicled the development of ISKCON from a temple-based movement composed largely of sanyasi, or full-time devotees, to a family-oriented, household-based congregational form. This development has had far-ranging impacts on ISKCON as members have faced new challenges of work and family, shifting the emphasis from outward-directed activities (e.g., proselytizing, literature distribution, fundraising) to inward-directed, maintenance activities. Similar patterns have characterized other NRMs in second and third generations (see Berger 1999a, 1999b; Bozeman 1998; Coney 1999; Melton 1994; Mickler 1987; Palmer 1994; Palmer and Hardmann 1999; Stark 1987; Wright 1994).

Disengagement/Disaffiliation

One of the most salient features of NRMs is that they face high attrition rates. NRMs experienced their greatest growth during the late 1960s and early 1970s, a period of social and cultural experimentation (Bellah 1976; Glock 1976). But the "experimental" conversion motif (Lofland and Skonovd 1981), typifying much of youth affiliation with NRMs, was temporal and episodic, a single episode in a serial or sequential "conversion career" (Richardson 1978). Religious experimentation was not conducive to long-term commitment; rather, it was a means to pilot a broad range of experiences in pursuit of self-discovery and spiritual enlightenment. Studies show the average length of membership in NRMs to be less than two years (Barker 1988; Levine 1984; Skonovd 1981; Solomon 1981; Wright 1984, 1987). Consequently, NRMs had to survive by retaining a residual core of committed members, often just a fraction of those who passed through their doors.

Conceptualization (and operationalization) of NRM disengagement raises some of the same questions as defining *conversion*. Terms such as *defection, deconversion, disaffection, disengagement, exiting* and *apostasy* have all been used to describe this phenomenon and they reflect the complexity of the problem. Space does not permit a thorough discussion of conceptual issues, but the author has addressed the definitional problem in detail elsewhere (see Wright

1988; Wright and Ebaugh 1993). Disengagement is best understood as a multidimensional dynamic that occurs at varied levels. At the very least, we can identify the following components: affective (disaffection), cognitive (disillusionment), and social organizational (disaffiliation). For our purposes, the terms *disengagement* and *defection* are intended to encompass all three dimensions or aspects of the process. Researchers have been aware of this multidimensional quality, focusing on different reasons or motivations for leaving, various strategies of leave-taking, and mixed levels of external intervention affecting trajectories of withdrawal and postinvolvement assessments.

Disengagement/defection may be described as a process set into motion by a "triggering" factor or episode. At a cognitive level, disillusionment arises as a disruption of one's plausibility structure that affects the normal constellation of social support mechanisms. At the affective level, disaffection refers to the disruption of emotional attachments and bonds—that is, feelings of oneness, solidarity, love, or belonging. In my own research comparing matched samples of leavers and stayers ($N = 90$) in three NRMs, triggering or precipitating factors included the breakdown of social insulation, the unregulated development of dyadic relationships, the perceived lack of success in achieving world transformation, and inconsistencies between the actions of leaders and the ideals they symbolically represent (Wright 1987). Jacobs's (1989) study of forty ex-members representing sixteen NRMs reported four precipitating factors or "sources of disillusionment": conflict over regulation of intimacy and social life; conflict over time commitment, doctrine, and practice; conflict over power and status positions; and conflict over sex roles. Skonovd's (1981) study of sixty ex-members from "totalistic groups," representing a combination of NRMs and Christian fundamentalist groups, identified a "crisis milieu" triggered by factors both internal (social disruption, interpersonal conflict, physical and emotional depletion) and external (career/educational pulls, affectional pulls, removal). These studies suggest important similarities both substantively and conceptually (see Wright and Ebaugh 1993).

Triggering episodes disrupt taken-for-granted assumptions and uncritical faith, giving way to heightened doubts, disaffection, and gradual withdrawal. Analogous to marital dissolution (see Wright 1991), the person in question engineers a process of detachment that involves careful preparation for reducing the dissonance associated with leaving while quietly planning for a new life outside the group. "Strategies of leave-taking" are developed (Skonovd 1981) and linked to sources of disillusionment, opportunities for negotiation, and length of membership (Wright 1987: 67–73).

Beyond the motivational framework to explain defection, some scholars have employed role theory to describe this process (Ebaugh 1988a, 1988b; Wright and Ebaugh 1993). The assumption of role theory is that individual actions are shaped by normative expectations inhering in the social structure of groups. Defection is conceptualized as a socially structured event embedded in role relationships. Leaving entails a process of "role exiting" in which the individual disengages from role behaviors associated with belonging to a particular group and establishes an identity as an ex-member. As Ebaugh (1988b) notes, being an "ex" is a unique role in an adversarial group, affording such role occupants special status as a former insider. It is the incorporation of the "ex" status that gives meaning to the new identity and role.

Another consideration in the study of disaffiliation is the mode of exit. The vast majority of leavers do so voluntarily, though some are the product of intervention by outside agents. Coercive intervention, or "deprogramming," involves abduction and forced confinement and was a popular method supported by anti-cult groups at least through the 1980s. Bromley (1988) has conducted the most extensive study of deprogramming based on a sample of 396 cases of Unification Church members between 1973 and 1986. He found the number of deprogrammings peaked in 1976 ($N = 108$) and then sharply declined afterward. There was a slight increase after the Jonestown mass suicides in 1978, but never anything approaching the 1976 peak. He attributed the decline to legal difficulties accompanying the dubious practices of deprogrammers to force recantations of faith and impose involuntary confinement. Several other findings are of note. Bromley discovered that parents were more likely to pursue deprogrammings of their daughters than their sons, suggesting greater tolerance of male nonconformity. He also found that the overall success rate of deprogramming was about 64 percent, while slightly more than one-third of deprogrammed subjects (36 percent) returned to the movement. About half of those deprogrammed were in the movement for one year or less. The success of deprogramming declined as the length of membership in the movement increased.

The rationale for deprogramming was based on the assumption that converts were "programmed" (i.e., brainwashed), an argument buttressed in part by selective accounts of some ex-members. However, research eventually revealed that claims of brainwashing were made almost exclusively by deprogrammed ex-members and rarely by voluntary defectors (Barker, 1984; Beckford, 1985; Lewis, 1986; Solomon, 1981; Wright, 1984, 1987). Indeed, Wright (1984) found that two-thirds (67 percent) of voluntary defectors in his sample said they were "wiser for the experience" while 91 percent rejected the brainwashing explanation altogether. Barker (1984) contends that an essential part of the deprogramming process is to convince members they have been brainwashed, coloring the way deprogrammed ex-members construct their accounts.

As deprogrammers and ACM organizations ran into mounting legal obstacles, advocates of intervention turned to less coercive means of dissuasion. Various forms of mediated disaffiliation were developed by the ACM and segments of the therapeutic community, who joined forces to create a quasi-professional industry of "exit counselors" or "exit therapists." Today ACM proponents are more likely to employ therapeutic concepts and language to discredit cults, offering "rehabilitation" or "recovery" services through counseling or referrals to residential "treatment" centers (Hassan 1988; Langone 1993).

One final consideration here is a special form of exit: apostasy (Bromley 1998). A critical distinction can be made between the typical leave-taker and the apostate. The leave-taker may be defined as the individual who makes a decision to terminate his or her commitment and disaffiliates in a nonpublic act of personal reflection and deed. Some degree of anguish or difficulty may characterize this decision, but the leave-taker does not assume a public role of recrimination and is able to effectively integrate previous experiences into a holistic concept of self and identity. The apostate, on the other hand, is defined as a defector who is aligned with an oppositional coalition in an effort to broaden a dispute with the former group and who embraces a posture of confrontation by making public claims. The apostate essentially carves out a moral or professional career as an "ex," capitalizing on opportunities of status enhancement through affiliation with the oppositional groups (Wright 1998). Consequently, apostates tend to join forces with anti-cult organizations to leverage claims against NRMs while forging a new occupational or professional role as deprogrammer, counselor, exit therapist, conference speaker, administrative officer, or some combination of the above (see Giambalvo 1992; Hassan 1988; Langone 1993; Ross and Langone 1988; Ryan 1993), ensuring a kind of institutionalization of apostasy. The role of the apostate in the dispute broadening process helps to explain the negative public image of NRMs. (See the Richardson and Introvigne chapter for perspectives on media coverage of NRMs.)

Teaching/Learning Strategies

There are a number of ways in which teaching a college course about new religions can be enhanced and made more effective. In this section, I discuss ways to compel analytical thinking and fuel debate. The primary means to accomplish this goal is through the assignment of manageable research exercises that can be conducted within the framework of the course and help illustrate key concepts, models, and theories.

Mapping the Local New Religious Movement Landscape

If you are teaching a course on new religions for the first time, consider creating both a directory and a map of new religions in your city. This is a more challenging task than it might appear. It could easily be a class project that consumes the entire semester. The initial endeavor will be unique in this regard, so allow ample time for the class to complete the work (subsequent classes will simply revise and update). In moderate to large metropolitan areas, the creation of a directory can be begun by culling NRMs from a list of religious organizations or churches in the phone book's yellow pages. In some cases, it will not be self-evident that organizations are new religions. For those that are "cultural imports," or at least have exotic-sounding names, placement on a preliminary list may be readily apparent. But those NRMs within the conventional nomenclature of the Judeo-Christian tradition that are unaffiliated with a larger denominational entity pose a different challenge. "Independent" churches or religious organizations may or may not qualify as NRMs, depending largely on the definition. Herein, students will discover an important step in doing social science. Determination of placement on the NRM directory list immediately raises the pivotal problem of definition.

From a teaching standpoint, you can use this opportunity in the classroom to discuss and explore key definitional issues and parameters. What is a new religion? How and in what ways is it new? In sociological terms, *newness* is a relative term. Some "new" religions are now fifty years old (e.g., Unification Church, Scientology). A half-century-old religion may be new by historical standards, but when do we cease calling a religion new? Some new religions appear to be simply modifications or revisions of established religions (e.g., Boston Church of Christ, The Way International, Jesus People USA). How substantial does a modification or alteration of an existing tradition have to be in order to qualify as new? And how does this kind of group differ from a sect? This exercise should engender healthy debate and discussion. Out of this discussion, the class should formulate an operational definition. Instructors should keep in mind that scholars have not resolved this problem satisfactorily, so the operational definition will be less than ideal (see Melton 2004). But such is the nature of our enterprise. Have the class create a set of criteria consistent with the operational definition.

After formulating an operational definition and a set of criteria, the class faces the logistical task of identifying the NRMs that qualify. This involves collection of data by students and use of an assessment instrument based on the criteria developed. There is some flexibility here. Students can build the directory by gathering information through interviews with religious leaders or officials, visiting religious services, and/or observing practices and behavior. Interviews conducted by phone are probably preferable in the creation of the directory, for several reasons. Telephone interviews are less daunting to the timid, do not require travel, are less time-consuming, and are logistically more manageable. Given the limited investments some students can make in a single course, this approach is probably best.

Some basic guidelines about telephone interviewing should be covered in class. Students should be cautioned that NRM officials may attempt to downplay or minimize deviance. The management of organizational image and identity is a strategic objective for stigmatized groups. Student interviewers must be prepared to probe beyond packaged information or superfluous responses. The assessment instrument should contain questions that help penetrate vague or evasive responses and determine definitional boundaries. These initial contacts will also serve another important function: obtaining permission to make follow-up calls to qualifying NRMs. As part of the mapping task, students can ask telephone interviewees to confirm address listings in the phone book and even requesting directions to the church. Patterns of spatial location and clustering on the map may reveal important sociological insights and should be discussed.

Exploring Conversion Accounts

Upon completion of a NRM directory and map, students use their contacts with the groups in the directory to set up interviews with converts. One way to teach students about conversion is through the direct experience of interviewing converts. Ideally, face-to-face interviews provide the most enriching educational experience. But university policy or possibly concerns about risks to students may deter the use of this method. Telephone interviews can be conducted in lieu of face-to-face interviews. A seminal task here is the construction of a separate interview questionnaire for converts, and the questionnaire should probably be a single instrument designed and used by the class as a whole. The advantage of a standardized questionnaire is that the data obtained can then be compared in a uniform manner. The questions can explore some of the research already discussed, though it will not be possible to evaluate all of the theories or ideas covered in this chapter. As instructor you may want to select one or two theories or hypotheses to examine; however, there are some things to consider in making this selection. For example, cultural and social structural factors influencing NRM conversion (e.g., the Bellah-Tipton thesis, the Robbins et al. integrative thesis, deinstitutionalization, etc.) will prove difficult to assess in class. These larger social forces are too abstract and unwieldy to examine unless they are broken down into smaller components. On the other hand, the surrogate family claim, or the "family deprivation" thesis of conversion, which focuses on narrower questions about adolescence and familial relationships, is a manageable research project. Questionnaire items assessing family deprivation are reproduced in Wright and Piper (1986).

Examining conversion issues at the micro level is certainly more applicable to this kind of exercise. Determining whether conversion is sudden or gradual, for example, is a realistic and workable assignment for students. Exploring the extent to which the individual plays a passive or active role in the conversion process is also a manageable objective. If you want to pursue a more ambitious project, have students assess the causal-process models formulated by Lofland and Stark (1965) and/or Downton (1979). You could conduct a comparison of these models and determine which is a better fit with the data, or students could suggest modifications or combinations of each to formulate their own model. Another option is to examine the conversion motifs formulated by Lofland and Skonovd (1981). Students could apply this typology to the conversion accounts they collect and assess the heuristic value of the motifs.

One project that is quite manageable addresses the issues surrounding the second generation of NRM members. As described previously, second-generation members basically inherit their religion rather than experience conversion firsthand. In this manner, "conversion" is more like socialization or the culmination of religious training. For students to explore the generational differences asserted, they can compare first- and second-generation accounts of conversion. This project could be constructed in several different ways. Each student could be given the assignment of collecting both kinds of interviews. Or the class could be divided into two groups, with group A assigned to collect interviews with first-generation converts and group B with second-generation converts. These accounts then can be assembled and analyzed to assess how well the generational distinctions hold. Such comparisons should also foster some discussion among students of parallels to their own experiences and religious choices.

By doing these exercises, students can gain valuable research experience, get firsthand exposure to the people and issues they are studying, and become more intellectually engaged in the debates surrounding NRMs. Of course, it is left to the discretion of the instructor to determine the extent of student participation in research activity and how these data might be used and shared in class. Some educators may want to give students only brief exposure to data collection and use the exercises to leverage better critical thinking and class discussion. Others may want to push their students toward a refinement of their research skills and systematic analysis. This course is offered at my institution as a senior-level sociology class for which familiarity with research methods and data analysis is expected.

If conducting interviews is not an option for the class, or if you want to augment the exercises, extend an invitation to a local NRM member to speak to the class about his or her conversion. NRM members are often willing to speak in these venues. Keep in mind that the dynamics of a public conversion account may differ from one given in personal interview. For example, the convert will be aware of audience receptivity and response to a personal account that may, in turn, affect the delivery or pitch. Students may also be emboldened to ask questions in the company of others that they might otherwise be reluctant to pose in a telephone interview. The convert will be alert to the fact that he or she may face some enmity, or will sense that he or she is not "preaching to the choir." On the other hand, face-to-face interaction (as opposed to the anonymity of the telephone interview) may humanize the NRM devotee for some students. This dynamic notwithstanding, the guest conversion account should be viewed as an important educational tool. If possible, extend the invitation to several different NRM members, for comparative purposes. Also, you might want to vary the invitations to converts representing different NRMs, and even to second-generation members, in order to evaluate the merit of empirical concepts, models, and theories. You may also want to have students prepare for speakers by assigning them readings on "conversion rhetorics" and the problems associated with retrospective accounts (McGuire 1997: 74–75; Rambo 1993).

Finally, a fallback strategy is to assign students to read published accounts of conversion that have been included in the research literature (e.g., Downton 1979; Levine 1984; McMullen 2000; Wilson and Dobbelaere 1994).

Exploring Disengagement and Withdrawal

Unlike NRM converts, who congregate together in churches, temples, and meeting halls and are readily identifiable, ex-members of NRMs are diffuse and often inaccessible. Consequently, making a map or directory of NRM leavers is not realistic. Occasionally, ex-members form networks or organizations, but these are sometimes adversarial entities under the auspices of the ACM (see Goldberg and Goldberg 1982; Hassan 1988). Also, some networks of ex-members are not only ACM activists but also have professional careers as deprogrammers or exit counselors (Wright 1998). For this reason, the challenge is to locate independent ex-members. One suggestion involves asking current members if they are still in touch with some ex-members. I found this to be the case in many of my interviews with NRM members (Wright 1987). A request could then be made for a telephone number. A network of respondents built through contacts provided by friends or acquaintances is called a "snowball sample." Some members will be reticent to give out phone numbers without obtaining permission from the former member. This courtesy is understandable, and students should respect this arrangement while firmly pursuing the necessary contact information. Once permission is secured and contact is made, interviews can be conducted in the same manner as with converts. You may want to divide the assignments into interviews with converts and defectors, for purposes of comparison.

If such an exercise is assigned, a different interview instrument will have to be constructed. The instrument should include some conversion items but also should have items that explore issues and questions addressing disengagement. Triggering factors or sources of disillusionment have been a focus of researchers, and these could be investigated by students as well to determine if similar patterns arise. Multidimensional aspects of withdrawal could be examined (affective, cognitive, social organizational), as well as the causal-process model of defection (Skonovd 1981, 1983). Questions about the strategies used for leave-taking could be posed and compared with previous studies. Students will want to make a distinction between voluntary leavers and deprogrammed members, given the sharp differences in postinvolvement attitudes by these ex-member.

If tracking down defectors is an unworkable assignment, you may want to consider extending invitations to selected ex-members to speak to the class. Students should still be able to locate ex-members using the method described above. Or you can take the initiative to contact NRM organizations and identify ex-members if no class interview assignment is made. Once these contacts are made and some relationships are established, the process does not have to be repeated each semester. I have found that former members are often willing to come back without much cajoling. Indeed, some express a deep sense of gratification in being able to address college students. They feel they have important experiences to share and not a lot of venues in which to share them. As with speakers who are converts, you may want to vary the invitations to ex-members to represent a wider range of NRMs and be able to compare defection accounts. Some caution should be taken, however, to avoid "professional exes" who make a career out of a putative victimization. While some ex-members have been wronged by the abusive practices of some NRM leaders, you should make a distinction between these essentially private individuals with a story and professional exes who are essentially "shopping" their services as therapists or career apostates on a moral crusade (see Wright 1998). Finally, students should be aware that problems associated with retrospective accounts and conversion rhetorics also apply to disengagement and withdrawal (see Wright and Ebaugh 1993). Should access to former members be problematic, you can refer students to published accounts of disengagement and withdrawal (Jacobs 1989; Skonovd 1981; Wright 1987).

REFERENCES

Anthony, Dick. 1990. "Religious Movements and Brainwashing Litigation: Evaluating Key Testimony." In *In Gods We Trust*, 2nd ed., ed. Thomas Robbins and Dick Anthony, 295–344. New Brunswick, NJ: Transaction.
Anthony, Dick, and Thomas Robbins. 1981. "Cultural Crisis and Contemporary Religion." In *In Gods We Trust*, 1st ed., ed. Thomas Robbins and Dick Anthony, 9–31. New Brunswick, NJ: Transaction.
———. 1982. "Contemporary Religious Ferment and Moral Ambiguity." In *New Religious Movements: A Perspective for Understanding Society*, ed. Eileen Barker, 243–63. New York: Edwin Mellen Press.
Balch, Robert W., and David Taylor. 1978. "Seekers and Saucers: The Role of the Cultic Milieu in Joining a UFO Cult." In *Conversion Careers: In and Out of the New Religions*, ed. James T. Richardson, 839–60. Beverly Hills, CA: Sage.
Barker, Eileen. 1984. *The Making of a Moonie: Choice or Brainwashing?* Oxford: Blackwell.
———. 1987. "Quo Vadis? The Unification Church." In *The Future of New Religious Movements*, ed. David G. Bromley and Philip E. Hammond, 141–52. Macon. GA: Mercer University Press.
———. 1988. "Defection from the Unification Church: Some Statistics and Distinctions." In *Falling from the Faith*, ed. David G. Bromley, 166–84. Newbury Park, CA: Sage.
Beckford, James A. 1985. *Cult Controversies: The Societal Response to New Religious Movements*. London: Tavistock.
Beckford, James A., and James T. Richardson. 1983. "A Bibliography of New Religious Movements in the United States and Europe." *Social Compass* 30, 111–35.
Bellah, Robert N. 1976. "The New Religious Consciousness and the Crisis of Modernity. In *The New Religious Consciousness*, ed. Charles Y. Glock and Robert N. Bellah, 335–52. Berkeley: University of California Press.
Berger, Helen. 1999a. *A Community of Witches*. Columbia: University of South Carolina Press.
———. 1999b. "Witches: The Next Generation." In *Children in New Religions*, ed. Susan J. Palmer and Charlotte E. Hardman, 11–28. New Brunswick, NJ: Rutgers University Press.
Bird, Frederick, and William Reimer. 1982. "Participation Rates in New Religious Movements and Para-Religious Movements." *Journal for the Scientific Study of Religion* 21, 1–14.
Bozeman, John. 1998. "Field Notes: Radical Reorganization in the Church Universal and Triumphant." *Nova Religio* 1, 293–97.
Bromley, David G. 1985. "Financing the Millennium: The Economic Structure of the Unificationist Movement." *Journal for the Scientific Study of Religion* 24, 253–75.

————. 1988. "Deprogramming as a Mode of Exit from New Religious Movements: The Case of the Unificationist Movement." In *Falling From the Faith: The Causes and Consequences of Religious Apostasy*, ed. David G. Bromley, 185–204. Newbury Park, CA: Sage.

————, ed. *The Politics of Religious Apostasy*. Westport, CT: Praeger.

Clark, John G., Michael D. Langone, Robert E. Schecter, and R. Daily. 1981. *Destructive Cult Conversion: Theory, Research and Treatment*. Weston, MA: American Family Foundation.

Coleman, James. 1970. "Social Inventions." *Social Forces* 49, 163–73.

Coney, Judith. 1999. "Growing up as Mother's Children: Socializing a Second Generation in Sahaja Yoga." In *Children in New Religions*, ed. Susan J. Palmer and Charlotte E. Hardman, 108–23. New Brunswick, NJ: Rutgers University Press.

Conway, Flo, and Jim Siegelman. 1978. *Snapping: America's Epidemic of Sudden Personality Change*. Philadelphia: Lippincott.

Cox, Harvey. 1977. *Turning East*. New York: Touchstone.

Doress, Irving, and Jack N. Porter. 1981. "Kids in Cults." In *In Gods We Trust*, ed. Thomas Robbins and Dick Anthony, 297–302. New Brunswick, NJ: Transaction.

Downton, James V. 1979. *Sacred Journeys: The Conversion of Young Americans to Divine Light Mission*. New York: Columbia University Press.

————. 1980. "An Evolutionary Theory of Spiritual Conversion and Commitment: The Case of the Divine Light Mission." *Journal for the Scientific Study of Religion* 19, 381–96.

Ebaugh, Helen Rose. 1988a. *Becoming an Ex: The Process of Role Exit*. Chicago: University of Chicago Press.

————. 1998b. "Leaving Catholic Convents: Toward a Theory of Disengagement." In *Falling From the Faith*, ed. David G. Bromley, 100–121. Newbury Park, CA: Sage.

Ebaugh, Helen Rose, and Janet Saltzman Chafetz. 2000. *Religion and the New Immigrants*. New York: Altamira.

Enroth, Ronald. 1977. *Youth, Brainwashing and Extremist Cults*. Grand Rapids, MI: Zondervan.

Fichter, Joseph. 1981. "Youth in Search of the Sacred." In *The Social Impact of New Religions*, ed. Bryan Wilson, 21–42. New York: Edwin Mellen Press.

Galanter, Marc. 1989. *Cults: Faith, Healing, and Coercion*. New York: Oxford University Press.

Galanter, Marc, Richard Babkin, Judith Rabkin, and Alexander Deutsch. 1979. "The Moonies: A Psychological Study of Conversion and Membership in a Contemporary Religious Sect." *American Journal of Psychiatry* 136, 165–70.

Galanti, Geri-Ann. 1993. "Reflections on 'Brainwashing.'" In *Recovery from Cults*, ed. Michael D. Langone, 85–103. New York: Norton.

Giambalvo, Carol. 1992. *Exit Counseling: A Family Intervention*. Bonita Springs, FL: American Family Foundation.

Gitlin, Todd. 1987. *The Sixties: Years of Hope, Days of Rage*. New York: Bantam.

Glock, Charles Y. 1976. "Consciousness Among Youth: An Interpretation." In *The New Religious Consciousness*, ed. Charles Y. Glock and Robert N. Bellah, 353–66. Berkeley: University of California Press.

Goldberg, Lorna, and William Goldberg. 1982. "Group Work with Former Cultists." *Social Work* 27, 165–70.

Goldman, Marion. 1995. "Continuity in Collapse: Departures from Shiloh." *Journal for the Scientific Study of Religion* 34, 342–53.

Greil, Arthur L., and David R. Rudy. 1984. "What Have We Learned From Process Models of Conversion? An Examination of Ten Studies." *Sociological Focus* 17, 306–23.

Hassan, Steven. 1988. *Combating Cult Mind Control*. Rochester, VT: Park Street Press.

Hunter, James. 1981. "The New Religions: Demodernization and the Protest Against Modernity." In *The Social Impact of New Religious Movements*, ed. Bryan Wilson, 1–20. New York: Edwin Mellen Press.

Jacobs, Janet. 1989. *Divine Disenchantment: Deconverting from New Religions*. Bloomington: Indiana University Press.

Johnson, Benton. 1981. "A Sociological Perspective on New Religions." In *In Gods We Trust*, ed. Thomas Robbins and Dick Anthony, 51–66. New Brunswick, NJ: Transaction.

Kaslow, Florence, and Marvin Sussman. 1982. *Cults and the Family*. New York: Haworth.

Kerrine, Theodore, and Richard John Neuhaus. 1979. "Mediating Structures: A Paradigm for Democratic Pluralism." *Annals of the American Association for Political and Social Science* 446, 10–18.

Kilbourne, Brock, and James T. Richardson. 1982. "Cults vs. Families: A Case of a Misattribution of Cause." In *Cults and the Family*, ed. Florence Kaslow and Marvin Sussman, 81–100. New York: Haworth.

Langone, Michael D. 1993. *Recovery from Cults: Help for Victims of Psychological and Spiritual Abuse*. New York: Norton.

Levine, Saul. 1984. *Radical Departures: Desperate Detours to Growing Up*. New York: Harcourt, Brace & Jovanovich.

Lewis, James R. 1986. "Reconstructing the 'Cult' Experience." *Sociological Analysis* 47, 151–59.

Lifton, Robert J. 1961. *Thought Reform and the Psychology of Totalism*. New York: Norton.

———. 1985. "Cult Processes, Religious Totalism and Civil Liberties." In *Cults, Culture and the Law*, ed. Thomas Robbins, William Shepherd, and James McBride, 59–70. Chico, CA: Scholars Press.

Lofland, John, and Norman Skonovd. 1981. "Conversion Motifs." *Journal for the Scientific Study of Religion* 20, 373–85.

Lofland, John, and Rodney Stark. 1965. "Becoming a World-Saver: A Theory of Conversion to a Deviant Perspective." *American Sociological Review* 30, 863–74.

Machalek, Richard, and David A. Snow. 1985. "Neglected Issues in the Study of Conversions." In *Scientific Research on New Religious Movements*, ed. Brock Kilbourne, 123–30. San Francisco: Pacific Division AAAS.

———. 1993. "Conversion to New Religious Movements." In *The Handbook on Cults and Sects in America*. Part B, ed. David G. Bromley and Jeffrey K. Hadden, 53–74. Greenwich, CT: JAI Press.

Marx, John H., and David L. Ellison. 1975. "Sensitivity Training and Communes: Contemporary Quests for Community." *Pacific Sociological Review* 18, 442–62.

McAdam, Doug, John McCarthy, and Mayer N. Zald. 1996. *Comparative Perspectives on Social Movements*. New York: Cambridge University Press.

McGuire, Meredith B. 1997. *Religion: The Social Context*. Fourth Edition. Belmont, CA: Wadsworth.

McMullen, Michael. 2000. *The Bahai: The Religious Construction of a Global Identity*. New Brunswick, NJ: Rutgers University Press.

Melton, J. Gordon. 1994. "The Church Universal and Triumphant: Its Heritage and Thoughtworld." In *The Church Universal & Triumphant in Scholarly Perspective*, ed.

James R. Lewis and J. Gordon Melton, 1–20. Stanford, CA: Center for Academic Publishing.

———. 2004. "Toward a Definition of 'New Religion.'" *Nova Religio* 8, 73–87.

Mickler, Michael. 1987. "Future Prospects of the Unification Church." In *The Future of New Religious Movements*, ed. David G. Bromley and Phillip E. Hammond, 175–86. Macon, GA: Mercer University Press.

Ofshe, Richard, and Margaret Singer. 1986. "Attacks on Peripheral versus Central Elements of Self and the Impact of Thought Reforming Techniques." *Cultic Studies Journal* 3, 2–24.

Palmer, Susan J. 1994. "Heaven's Children: The Children of God's Second Generation." In *Sex, Slander and Salvation: Investigating The Family/Children of God*, ed. James R. Lewis, 1–26. Stanford, CA: Center for Academic Publishing.

Palmer, Susan, and Charlotte Hardman, eds. 1999. *Children in New Religions*. New Brunswick, NJ: Rutgers University Press.

Parsons, Arthur. 1986. "Messianic Personalism: A Role Analysis of the Unification Church." *Journal for the Scientific Study of Religion* 25, 141–61.

Rambo, Lewis R. 1982. "Bibliography: Current Research on Religious Conversion." *Religious Studies Review* 8, 146–59.

———. 1993. *Understanding Religious Conversion*. New Haven: Yale University Press.

Richardson, James T. 1978. *Conversion Careers: In and Out of the New Religions*. Beverly Hills, CA: Sage.

———, ed. 1988. *Money and Power in the New Religions*. New York: Edwin Mellen Press.

———. 1993. "A Social Psychological Critique of 'Brainwashing' Claims about Recruitment to New Religions." In *Handbook on Cults and Sects in America*. Part B, ed. David G. Bromley and Jeffrey K. Hadden, 75–98. Greenwich, CT: JAI Press.

Richardson, James T., and Mary H. Stewart. 1977. "Conversion Process Models and the Jesus Movement." In *Conversion Careers*, ed. James T. Richardson, 24–42. Beverly Hills, CA: Sage.

Richardson, James, Mary H. Stewart, and Robert B. Simmonds. *Organized Miracles: A Study of a Contemporary, Youth, Communal, Fundamentalist Organization*. New Brunswick, NJ: Transaction.

Robbins, Thomas. 1988. *Cults, Converts and Charisma*. Newbury Park, CA: Sage.

Robbins, Thomas, and Dick Anthony. 1972. "Getting Straight with Meher Baba: A Study of Drug Rehabilitation, Mysticism and Post-Adolescent Role Conflict." *Journal for the Scientific Study of Religion* 11, 122–40.

Robbins, Thomas, Dick Anthony, and Thomas Curtis. 1975. "Youth Culture Religious Movements: Evaluating the Integrative Hypothesis." *Sociological Quarterly* 16, 48–64.

Rochford, E. Burke, Jr. 1985. *Hare Krishna in America*. New Brunswick, NJ: Rutgers University Press.

———. 1995. "Family Structure, Commitment and Involvement in the Hare Krishna Movement." *Sociology of Religion* 56, 153–76.

———. 1997. "Family Formation, Culture, and Change in the Hare Krishna Movement." *ISKCON Communication Journal* 5, 61–82.

———. 2001. "The Changing Face of ISKCON: Family, Congregationalism and Privatization." *ISKCON Communications Journal* 9, 1–12.

Ross, Joan Carol, and Michael D. Langone. 1988. *Cults: What Parents Should Know*. Weston, MA: American Family Foundation.

Ryan, Patrick. 1993. "A Personal Account: Eastern Mediation Group." In *Recovery from Cults*, ed. Michael D. Langone, 129–39. New York: Norton.

Schein, Edwin, Inge Schneier, and Curtis H. Barker. 1961. *Coercive Persuasion*. New York: Norton.

Shapiro, Eli. 1977. "Destructive Cultism." *American Family Physician* 15, 80–83.

Singer, Margaret T. 1979. "Coming out of the Cults." *Psychology Today* 8, 72–82.

———. 1986. "Consultation with Families of Cultists." In *The Family Therapist as Systems Consultant*. ed. L. I. Wynne, S. H. McDavid, and T. Weber, 270–83. New York: Guilford.

———. 1995. *Cults in Our Midst*. San Francisco: Jossey-Bass.

Skonovd, L. Norman. 1981. *Apostasy: The Process of Defection from Religious Totalism*. Ph.D. dissertation. Ann Arbor, MI: University Microfilms International.

———. 1983. "Leaving the Cultic Religious Milieu." In *The Brainwashing/Deprogramming Controversy*, ed. David G. Bromley and James T. Richardson, 91–105. New York: Edwin Mellen Press.

Snow, David A., and Richard Machalek. 1984. "The Sociology of Conversion." *Annual Review of Sociology* 10, 167–90.

Solomon, Trudy L. 1981. "Integrating the Moonie Experience: A Survey of Ex-Members of the Unification Church." In *In Gods We Trust*, ed. Thomas Robbins and Dick Anthony, 275–96. New Brunswick, NJ: Transaction.

Stark, Rodney. 1987. "How New Religions Succeed: A Theoretical Model." In *The Future of New Religious Movements*, ed. David G. Bromley and Phillip E. Hammond, 11–29. Macon, GA: Mercer University Press.

Stark, Rodney, and William Sims Bainbridge. 1985. *The Future of Religion: Secularization, Revival and Cult Formation*. Berkeley: University of California Press.

Straus, Roger. 1976. "Changing Oneself: Seekers and the Creative Transformation of Life Experience." In *Doing Social Life*, ed. John Lofland, 252–73. New York: John Wiley.

———. 1979. "Religious Conversion as a Personal and Collective Accomplishment." *Sociological Analysis* 40, 158–65.

Taslimi, Cheryl Rowe, Ralph W. Hood, Jr., and P. J. Watson. 1991. "Assessment of Former Members of Shiloh: The Adjective Check List 17 Years Later." *Journal for the Scientific Study of Religion* 30, 306–11.

Tipton, Steven M. 1979. "New Religious Movements and the Problem of Modern Ethic." In *Religious Change and Continuity*, ed. H. Johnson, 286–312. San Francisco: Jossey-Bass.

———. 1982. *Getting Saved from the Sixties*. Berkeley: University of California Press.

Tobias, Madeleine, and Janja Lalich. 1994. *Captive Hearts, Captive Minds*. Alameda, CA: Hunter House.

Van Zandt, David E. 1991. *Living in the Children of God*. Princeton, NJ: Princeton University Press.

Wilson, Bryan. 1976. *Contemporary Transformations of Religion*. New York: Oxford University Press.

Wilson, Bryan, and Karel Dobbelaere. 1982. *Religion in Sociological Perspective*. New York: Oxford University Press.

———. 1994. *A Time to Chant: The Soka Gakkai Bukkhists in Britain*. New York: Oxford University Press.

Wright, Stuart A. 1983. "Defection from New Religious Movements: A Test of Some Theoretical Propositions." In *The Brainwashing/ Deprogramming Controversy*, ed. David G. Bromley and James T. Richardson, 106–21. New York: Edwin Mellen Press.

————. 1984. "Post-Involvement Attitudes of Voluntary Defectors from New Religious Movements." *Journal for the Scientific Study of Religion* 23, 172–82.

————. 1987. *Leaving Cults: The Dynamics of Defection*. Washington, DC: Society for the Scientific Study of Religion.

————. 1988. "Leaving New Religious Movements: Issues, Theory and Research." In *Falling from the Faith*, ed. David G. Bromley, 143–65. Newbury Park, CA: Sage.

————. 1991. "Reconceptualizing Cult Coercion: A Comparative Analysis of Divorce and Apostasy." *Social Forces* 70, 125–45.

————. 1994. "From Children of God to The Family: Movement Adaptation and Survival." In *Sex, Slander and Salvation*, ed. James R. Lewis and J. Gordon Melton, 121–28. Stanford, CA: Center for Academic Publishing.

————. 1998. "Exploring Factors that Shape the Apostate Role." In *The Politics of Religious Apostasy*, ed. David G. Bromley, 95–114. Westport, CT: Praeger.

Wright, Stuart A., and William D'Antonio. 1993. "Families and New Religions." In *The Handbook on Cults and Sects in America*, Part A, ed. David G. Bromley and Jeffrey K. Hadden, 219–240. Westport, CT: JAI Press.

Wright, Stuart A., and Helen Rose Ebaugh. 1993. "Leaving New Religions." In *The Handbook on Cults and Sects in America*, Part B., ed. David G. Bromley and Jeffrey K. Hadden, 117–38. Westport, CT: JAI Press.

Wright, Stuart A., and Elizabeth S. Piper. 1986. "Families and Cults: Familial Factors Related to Youth Leaving or Remaining in Deviant Religious Groups." *Journal of Marriage and Family* 48, 15–25.

Zimbardo, Phillip, and Susan Anderson. 1993. "Understanding Mind Control: Exotic and Mundane Mental Manipulations." In *Recovery from Cults*, ed. Michael D. Langone, 104–28. New York: Norton.

Gender in New Religions

Sarah M. Pike

New religious movements (NRMs) have typically emerged and
thrived in times of social upheaval, during which normative gender
roles are challenged. The industrializing mid-nineteenth century
and the women's suffrage movement provided the context for the
emergence of Mormonism, Christian Science, Seventh-Day Adventism, Spiritualism, and Theosophy (with the exception of Mormonism,
all founded by women). Over 100 years later, the feminist movement
and sexual revolution of the 1960s and 1970s resulted in several
decades of widespread religious experimentation, when many of today's new religions gained large numbers of converts (for a discussion of NRMs as experiments, see Dawson's chapter in this volume).
In the mid-nineteenth century and again in the 1970s, men and
women joined NRMs to take part in social experimentation. They
turned to NRMs that challenged socially legitimated gender roles and
offered new models for ideal relations between the sexes. Some men
and women found empowerment in biblically based patriarchal
structures and others in free love, but all of them were seeking
something that they believed does not exist in more mainstream
religious traditions.

The feminist movement of the late twentieth century coincided
with the upsurge in new religions. It resulted in at least three perspectives that have influenced scholarship on gender and religion in
general, and on gender roles in NRMs in particular. The first perspective is that religions dominated by men are inherently oppressive
to women and should be dismantled (Daly 1973). In this view, women can be disempowered only by religions with traditional gender roles, male deities, and male leadership. A second influential
view developed alongside this radical application of feminism and

argued for a reassessment of and reform from *within* male-dominated traditions. In reaction to these feminist critiques, a third approach argued that women often find meaning and power in religions that seem on the surface to offer them only subjugation, but on closer examination empower them in subtle ways. Anthropologists (Abu-Lughod 1993) and religious studies scholars using ethnographic methods (Griffith 1997) are among those who have championed this third perspective. Their research suggests that women's choices to join religions that appear to be oppressive and male-dominated should not be rejected out of hand, but rather more carefully examined through case studies.

There are two general approaches to the study of gender in NRMs that have been shaped by these feminist perspectives on religion. The first is a negative evaluation of NRMs as abusive to women, a view sometimes found in the accounts of women who left NRMs and who, looking back, are highly critical of their experiences, or among families who see their daughters and sisters as "brainwashed" by power-hungry gurus. Such a view falls in line with those feminist scholars who reject outright religions with charismatic male leaders and female followers. New religions of the mid-nineteenth century and of the 1960s and 1970s drew criticism as well as curiosity from outsiders for the same reasons as they attracted converts. Their critics often focused on unconventional gender roles and sexual practices; polygamy, celibacy, and sexual relations outside marriage were particularly problematic. Historians Paul E. Johnson and Sean Wilentz's The *Kingdom of Matthias: A Story of Sex and Salvation in 19th-Century America* (1994) exemplifies scholarship on the abuses of power in a nineteenth-century NRM that at first seemed to offer expanded roles to women. Critical perspectives argue that insiders typically gloss over inequities and real abuses of power that occur within their communities (see Janet Jacobs's discussion of abuse in this volume). Insiders, on the other hand, complain that critics unfairly judge their religions.

While these interpretations of gender roles in NRMs tend to emphasize the abuse of power by men over women, the second approach suggests that power relations in new religions are complex and rarely reducible to the simplistic image of male gurus and passive female followers, although such a dynamic can be an aspect of some NRMs. Mary McCormick Maaga (1998) draws attention to the unquestioned assumption among outside critics that all-powerful male leaders exert absolute control over their female followers and rob them of agency and power. Likewise, R. Marie Griffith's ethnography of conservative evangelical women (1997) explores the ways in which some women experience an apparently oppressive and unequal situation as empowering. This second approach does not assume that there is anything necessarily oppressive about a particular gender arrangement. Instead, it focuses on how women have made meaning from their experiences in NRMs and how they have worked within particular power structures. One variation of this experiential approach is the view that NRMs are laboratories for individual and collective experimentation with gender roles (see Dawson in this volume and Palmer 1993). A balanced study of NRMs requires both approaches: an analysis of sexist and abusive practices accompanied by attention to the many possible ways that men and women *experience* their roles in a particular movement.

New religions offer a range of roles for men and women that are shaped by a variety of factors, including mythology, theology, the roles and teachings of the founder and leaders, and the demographic background of participants. There are several ways of experimenting with gender roles that are common in new religions. Sociologist Susan Palmer identifies three models: sex polarity, sex complementarity, and sex unity (1994). These can be more specifically described as the following four types: (1) traditional models in which males are in leadership roles and women are responsible for the household and childrearing; (2) reversals of the dominant male leader/submissive female follower dichotomy so that women exercise leadership over men; (3) partner-ship models that take several forms, from male priests and female priestesses seen to be completely equal to divine couples where the man is the leader/ founder but his partner exercises considerable power as well; and (4) move-ments such as some forms of neo-paganism that collapse boundaries between male and female, encouraging men to explore their feminine side, for exam-ple, or the androgynous model of gender put forth by Heaven's Gate.

These four types of gender roles characterize nineteenth-century NRMs as well as NRMs that came of age in the 1960s and 1970s. If we approach NRMs as providing opportunities for experimentation with sex and gender, their in-novations are most visible in the following three areas: (1) conceptions of deity and language used to talk about the divine; (2) leadership and organizational structure; (3) sexuality, marriage, and family. These are the areas that best re-veal the complexity of men's and women's experiences in NRMs. Under each of these headings we will briefly look at examples of nineteenth-century new religions and then in more detail at those NRMs that emerged in the second half of the twentieth century.

Conceptions of Deity

The conceptions of deity in NRMs usually fall into four categories that roughly correspond to the four types of gender roles: (1) a monotheistic male god in continuity with Christianity, Judaism, or Islam; (2) a complete reversal of these traditions, such as a female form of deity; (3) a divine pair (Shakers and Unificationist); and (4) a universal force or power beyond gender. There are, of course, many NRMs without any concept of a deity, such as UFO groups that locate supernatural power in advanced alien civilizations.

Nineteenth-century new religions revised familiar models of the Christian god and developed completely new conceptions of the divine. The Mormons believed in the male god of the Hebrew Bible, whereas Elizabeth Cady Stan-ton's *Woman's Bible* reversed this image with its critique of male god talk and exploration of the gender of Elohim. The Shakers (United Society of Believers) described a dual godhead that was equal parts male and female, and they modeled their leadership roles on their understanding of the divine. Shaker founder Mother Ann Lee established a tradition of brothers and sisters running Shaker communities as equal but separate partners. Just as their god had two sides, the community incorporated dualities in all realms of life, even to the point of designing separate entrances and stairways for men and for women to enter their buildings. Theosophists, on the other hand, rejected any kind of anthropomorphic god and saw the divine as a "Universal Divine Principle."

Like the Mormons, some more recent NRMs believe in a god modeled on the patriarchal god of the Hebrew Bible and New Testament. Others turn to Asian deities, such as the Hindu god Krishna in the case of ISKCON (International Society for Krishna Consciousness). Stories of Krishna place him at the center of the lives of his female devotees, and although he has a female counterpart, ISKCON devotees consider him to be a masculine god embodying men's calling to a spiritual life. The Love Family, a communal NRM founded by Love Israel, also based their theology on the biblical God. They even modeled their communal structure on the Hebrew patriarchs, with men made in the image of God. The Love Family leaders turned to biblical scriptures to justify their continuity with the ancient practice of polygamy and gave men in the community far more power than women in most aspects of communal life.

Feminist critiques of religion have often focused on what they call male "god talk." The response of some NRMs to these critiques is to substitute goddess for god, reversing the polarity. When the feminist movement of the 1970s picked up momentum, women began leaving organized religions, searching for alternative forms of spirituality, imagining new forms of deity, and converting to NRMs (Goldenberg 1979). One of the most highly publicized NRMs that has attracted many women seeking female forms of deity is neo-paganism. Many spiritual feminists and neo-pagans base their values on a woman-centered theology. Some of them believe that adopting stories and images of ancient goddess-worshiping matriarchies will help to bring about changes in gender roles (Eller 1993). Many witches and other neo-pagans believe in the "Triple Goddess" of maiden, mother, and crone that originated with the first neo-pagans in mid-twentieth-century England. In their view, sexuality, pregnancy, labor, delivery, and breastfeeding are ways that women embody the Goddess in the biological events of their lives, making the physical body sacred. Starhawk (1989: 23) makes this connection explicit: "Deity is seen in our own forms, whether female or male, because the Goddess has her male aspect. Sexuality is a sacrament." Raelians also reverse the usual polarity by seeing women as saviors of the world and men as the destructive forces that have brought humanity to a planetary crisis (www.sowoman.org). An extreme example of gender role reversal is when men instead of women are excluded from religious life. Some new religions restrict participation to women only, as has sometimes been the case in the feminist spirituality movement (Eller 1993) and among some Dianic Wiccans (Griffin 2000).

Instead of putting male or female deities one above the other, some NRMs, like their nineteenth-century predecessors the Shakers, teach that God is both male and female. Unificationists believe that the biblical God encompasses both masculine and feminine aspects of his/her nature and is the "one true parent" who is both mother and father to humanity. This understanding of God is reflected in the Church's focus on men and women as partners—brothers and sisters working together to perfect their spiritual lives.

In their attempts to create alternatives to existing religions, other NRMs see the divine as beyond gender. The Raelians, for instance, look to the extraterrestrial and androgynous race of beings, the Elohim, as their model. Although androgyny is held up as an ideal, in the Raelian creation story, the alien Yahweh is male, a father to his son Raël (Palmer 1994). Heaven's Gate members similarly imagined extraterrestrials as androgynous and modeled their lifestyles after the ideal of androgyny.

Like other religious people, participants in NRMs live their theology in diverse ways. Understandings of the divine profoundly shape their religious lives, and the human realm, especially in communal NRMs, often reflects the cosmic order. The roles that NRMs institute for men and women can be modeled on their understandings of deity—father or mother, dual or plural. NRMs with male gods and no feminine sense of the divine tend to cast men as spiritual leaders and women in subservient roles. While NRMs with a dominant male god are more likely to restrict women's roles, those that believe in a goddess, dual godhead, or divinity beyond gender are often, but not always, characterized by more equality between men and women, especially in the area of leadership.

Leadership

Like images of the divine, leaders of NRMs model gender roles for their followers. Most religions feature male founders or charismatic leaders and female congregants or followers who often fill places of worship in larger proportions than men. Leadership in NRMs tends to follow four models: (1) male charismatic leaders; (2) female leaders; (3) male charismatic leaders with women as complementary leaders, but in secondary roles; or (4) female and male leaders on an equal basis.

During what historian Jon Butler calls the "spiritual hothouse" of the nineteenth century, both men and women founded NRMs that eventually became established American religions (1990). Joseph Smith was the nineteenth-century founder and leader of the Mormons, and to this day, males continue to fill the most powerful positions in their church. Mary Baker Eddy started Christian Science, and her *Science and Health* (1875/1971) continues to be the central Christian Science text. Spiritualism, which began with the Fox sisters in 1848, was characterized by female mediums and continues to feature women as well as men in leadership roles. Although Mother Ann Lee, the founder of the Shakers, died in 1784, the Shakers reached their height (their greatest number of members and communities) in the nineteenth century. Shaker communities enjoyed a century-long tradition (through the late twentieth century) of female elders who, alongside male elders, had an equal hand in running their communities' affairs.

Many of the high-profile new religions that gained strength in the 1960s and 1970s have been led by charismatic male leaders following the pattern set by religions that privilege the male divine. These include Jim Jones (Peoples Temple), Rajneesh (Rajneesh or Osho movement), Raël (Raelian movement), David Koresh (Branch Davidians), Swami Prabupada (ISKCON), Reverend Sun Myung Moon (Unificationist movement), David Berg (Children of God), and Love Israel (the Love Family). Sociologist Elizabeth Puttick (1997) points out that in new religions that are based on a master-disciple relationship, as many of them are, charismatic leaders take on fatherly roles for their disciples, especially their female disciples. Joining a new religion often requires absolute devotion to the guru or leader. Devotees tend to submit to the guru's authority as a child submits to a parent's will. In the case of Bhagwan Shree Rajneesh (also known as Osho), many devotees thought he represented "the ideal father" who was gentle and nurturing. But according to other devotees, he could also manifest the negative, authoritarian aspects of fatherhood. When new religions, like more established religions and other social institutions, place men (priests, ministers, etc.) in positions of authority over women who are instructed to unquestioningly obey them, abusive behavior becomes a possibility. In some instances members' submission includes sexual submission to the teacher (Boucher 1988/1993).

New religions often legitimate hierarchical gender roles by turning to sacred texts—in the case of the Love Family, the Hebrew Bible. In the Love Family, women served men in many ways and were not among the community's formal leadership. According to Robert Balch's ethnographic study of the community (1998), women acquired power only through their relationships with men on the group's council of elders. The construction of spiritually powerful masculinity embodied in leaders and founders is one of the characteristics that many of these new religions share with other religions characterized by male leadership.

Although men are typically the founders and figureheads of new religions that emerged in the 1960s and 1970s, there are some significant exceptions. Starhawk (neo-paganism), Elizabeth Clare Prophet (Church Universal and Triumphant), and Gurumayi (Siddha Yoga) are all female leaders whose followers look to them for inspiration and guidance. Catherine Wessinger (1993) lists four characteristics of NRMs that tend to elevate women to leadership roles: nonmasculine deity, no idea of the Fall, the absence of traditionally ordained clergy, and a broadened view of gender roles. The neo-pagan and New Age movements share these characteristics. Neo-pagans and New Agers tend to argue for men's and women's equality and downplay absolute devotion to charismatic leaders. These NRMs are unusual for their large numbers of female leaders; women founded or play prominent roles in some of the most important New Age and neo-pagan organizations. Two of the most famous New Age teachings, the Seth material and the Course in Miracles, were channeled through female mediums, Jane Roberts and Helen Schucman, respectively.

Ironically, in these instances, women find power through submission in their roles as channels who are simply conductors for male (and occasionally female) messengers.

Reversals in traditional gender roles can also occur because of the charisma of the particular women who take charge of movements that were originally headed by men. An example of this reversal of gender roles, whereby a male founder designates women as his rightful heirs to the leadership, is the Brahma Kumaris. Women have played prominent roles in this movement because their traditional feminine qualities are valued (www.bkwsu.com). Dada Lekhraj, the religion's founder, who later became known as Brahma Baba, formed a managing committee of eight young women to head his movement. He eventually signed over his assets to them and gave them a trust to administer. The Brahma Kumaris continue to be characterized by a largely female leadership, although men also sometimes assume leadership roles (Howell 1998). When women function as spiritual leaders, there is a reversal of the usual polarity, with the result that women are seen as spiritually superior.

Female leadership in new religions can take many forms. Some women start their own religions while others inherit their positions from male leaders. When male founders of new religions die, leadership sometimes falls to their female partners. Like their male predecessors, these women become high-profile representatives for their religious communities. For instance, Siddha Yoga's Gurumayi Chidvilasananda was chosen to carry on the Siddha Yoga lineage of Swami Muktananda, who died in 1982. (Gurumayi is an exception in a movement that typically saw men as spiritually superior; see www.siddhayoga .org.) The Family International (originally the Children of God) founder David Berg's second wife Maria played a central role in the movement and succeeded her husband as leader after his death in 1994. She became the spiritual center of the community and continued to uphold Berg's teachings. These are just a few examples of the ways that new religions offer women opportunities to take on leadership roles.

As in more established religions, women's spiritual and organizational leadership in the new religions can be controversial. When women become leaders, the definition of gender roles is challenged. Men sometimes have difficulty taking directions from women because they are unaccustomed to a loss of power. Similarly, some men in the Osho movement were frustrated with Osho's message that they needed to develop their feminine side. One of Elizabeth Puttick's interviewees complained that "the concept of being female has a negative side to me, a suggestion of weakness." Another observed that "many of us have chosen to move into femininity at the expense of masculinity" (1997: 95). On the other hand, women who assume mothering roles or act "like men" often reaffirm standard gender understandings in order to gain acceptance.

As new religions expand their membership and organizational complexity and because their founders cannot be everywhere at once, women often have the opportunity to assume secondary leadership roles as managers and missionaries. Several women, including two sisters, Carolyn Moore Layton and Annie Moore, were prominent members of the inner circle of the Peoples

Temple; these women acquired more power and authority in the community as Jim Jones's health deteriorated. Likewise, when Rajneesh was busy elsewhere, his secretary Ma Anand Sheela assumed a secondary leadership role and became the leader of the movement's Rajneeshpuram community in Oregon. Soon, Sheela set all the commune's policies and was the group's spokeswoman. She eventually left in disgrace when the community was disbanded. Sheela was charged with criminal activities, fled the country, was disowned by Rajneesh, and ultimately served some prison time. As this latter example suggests, it is not only men who abuse powerful positions in their communities; female leaders of NRMs have also been accused of being controlling and abusive.

In NRMs dominated by male leaders, women are sometimes given important missionary roles and are sent out to recruit new members. The first Unificationist movement missionary to the United States was Dr. Young Oon Kim ("Miss Kim"). She was largely responsible for developing Unificationist communities before Rev. Moon himself went on a speaking mission in the United States in the early 1970s. But as Elizabeth Puttick (1997: 6) points out, "It is an issue as to how far women can be empowered in the context of absolute surrender to a male master." Rev. Moon was unquestionably the head of the Unificationist movement, just as Rajneesh remained spiritual master for the women in his movement who became spiritual and organizational leaders, and Jim Jones continued to be seen as the Peoples Temple's leader even when his inner circle was basically running Jonestown.

Equal partnerships in leadership are rare in NRMs, just as they are in more established religions. Some neo-pagan groups, especially witchcraft covens, have priests and priestesses who are equally powerful. These groups usually believe in a divine pair of god and goddess and the complementarity of masculine and feminine characteristics. Janet and Stewart Farrar (1984, 1987), authors of numerous books about contemporary witchcraft, teach and facilitate rituals together as equal partners.

In most NRMs, men usually claim the most powerful roles, just as they do in the broader society. However, the absence of established traditions of leadership can open opportunities for women, especially in secondary leadership roles. The Rajneesh or Osho movement, Brahma Kumaris, and neo-pagan movement are among the few new religions that consistently have had more women than men in leadership roles, even though two of these movements were founded by men. But most other new religions have featured more male than female leaders, mirroring the trend in the majority of world religions.

Sex, Marriage, and the Family

As social changes during the mid-nineteenth century and the 1960s called into question traditional understandings of gender roles, one of the important ways that women and men responded was through sexual experimentation. Sexual practices in particular can have a powerful impact on gender roles because sexuality is so often seen as an expression of ideal gender identity. Sexuality is also the area most ripe for abuse of power and one in which women are particularly vulnerable. NRMs have included sexual and marriage practices that have been empowering to women, and others that have been abusive or oppressive.

Sexual behavior, marriage, and family life in NRMs are shaped by interpretations of past history, sacred texts, current social contexts, and utopian ideals. On one end of the spectrum of sexual choice is celibacy, often used to channel sexual energy into spiritual practice, while on the other end is polyamory (multiple lovers). Experimental sexual and marital practices in NRMs fall into roughly four categories: (1) a male-dominated plural marriage model that is often based on ancient texts (early Mormons, Branch Davidians) and follows the pattern of religions with a male divine and male leadership; (2) a reversal of traditional practices characterized by free love, homosexual relationships, or extramarital affairs (the nineteenth-century Oneida community, some neo-pagans, Raelians) that often, but not always, allow women more freedom; (3) celibacy; and (4) traditional heterosexual marriages but with some variations that diverge from the norm.

New religions of the mid-nineteenth century included diverse sexual practices such as Mormon polygamy, Shaker celibacy, and Perfectionist "plural marriage." These examples suggest that new marriage and sexual practices are not simply a product of the 1960s—that new religions have always been innovative in this area. Mormonism provides a good example of how experimentation with sex roles can be a phase in a movement's history (Foster 1981). Joseph Smith and other early Mormons modeled their teachings about polygamy on the patriarchs of the Hebrew Bible. Smith believed that it was God's intention for him to take multiple wives, but the Church now forbids polygamy, though it still supports men's superior role (for more information on diverse experiences of and responses to polygamy, see Embry 1987).

Oneida Perfectionists also turned to theology and textual sources to legitimate sexual experimentation, but for them heavenly practice meant free love. The Perfectionist community (established in 1848) was a nineteenth-century experiment in group marriage based on John Humphrey Noyes's interpretation of biblical teachings. Noyes interpreted the Bible as saying that legal marriage would be abandoned in heaven and love would be universalized in the afterlife, with its important physical aspects intact. He saw Perfectionism as a way to realize this divinely ordained pattern on earth (Foster 1981). At Oneida, men and women alike were free to choose sexual partners and traditional marriage was shunned. Likewise, Noyes attempted to liberate women from what he saw as the burden of giving birth and raising children by teaching male continence or "celibate intercourse." The Perfectionists practiced what Noyes called "complex marriage," in which individual sexual loyalties had to be sacrificed for the good of the entire community.

The Shakers are an early example of a religious community requiring celibacy for both men and women. Founder Ann Lee interpreted the Bible to say that there would be no sexual relations in heaven. Like Noyes, she taught her followers to imitate the heavenly model in earthly practice. Many new religions promote the symbolic value of motherhood, even when they discourage actual women from giving birth; the Shakers are an early example of this tendency. The Shakers' founder, Ann Lee, was called "Mother Ann" because she was seen as their spiritual mother, nurturing them along their spiritual path. Sally Kitch argues that the Shakers saw "the metaphor of spiritual motherhood [as] a positive symbol for women because it transforms qualities that have been perceived as liabilities of female gender symbolism into strengths. ... The metaphor of spiritual motherhood reveals the cultural value hidden in traditional female characteristics, personalities and experiences" (quoted in Sered 1994: 76). Shaker women found that celibacy gave them freedom from the pain of labor and childbirth, and it allowed them to focus on their spiritual family rather than raising biological children. In the midst of nineteenth-century social and sexual experimentation, Mormon, Shaker, and Perfectionist men and women all put into practice their ideals of the right relations between the sexes.

More recent NRMs also promote a variety of sexual practices, including polygamy, open marriage, and celibacy. Love Israel, founder of the Love Family, like Joseph Smith before him, legitimated his sexual practices with reference to the lives of the biblical patriarchs. The Love Family's structure was based on a "golden pyramid," with Love Israel at the top. Israel also had special privileges, including sexual relationships with multiple women, while his followers were required to be celibate. According to Robert Balch (1998), before 1971 everyone in the group was celibate except for Love Israel and a few women. By the end of the 1970s, new members were required to be celibate for at least a year before they were granted permission from community elders to enter into sexual relationships. Male elders in the community exercised the most sexual freedom and often practiced polygamy. Women were expected to submit to their husbands, even when this meant tolerating their husbands' additional sexual liaisons.

At the opposite end of the sex and marriage spectrum, sexual freedom in NRMs is often a reaction to traditional views of sexuality. Raelians are very explicit in their condemnation of Christianity for being negative toward sexuality and women. Raelians tend to be open to varieties of sexual expression, including bisexual and homosexual experiences. Instead of looking to biblical teachings about the afterlife, Canadian NRM founder Raël believes that extraterrestrials have a plan for humans and that humans must transform their lives in preparation for the future. Raelians are encouraged to be bisexual, explore behavior associated with the opposite gender, and participate in free love (Palmer 1993).

Sexual practices in NRMs often involve a critique of the ways in which other religions limit sexual expression and institute rigid gender roles. Participants in new religions who advocate sexual freedom are convinced that transformation of the body, sexuality, and gender roles is a precondition for changing society. Neo-pagans and New Agers also criticize the sexual restrictions of monotheistic religion and place sexuality in the realm of the sacred.

They reconstruct the histories of ancient goddess-worshiping matriarchies, borrow sacred sexual techniques from Tibetan Buddhist Tantric traditions, and reclaim roles previously seen as negative, such as the "sacred prostitute." In general, neo-pagans and New Agers tend to be tolerant, if not actively supportive, of sexual diversity. Neo-pagan priestess Starhawk sees all forms of sexual expression as potentially sacred: "In Witchcraft, 'All acts of love and pleasure are My Rituals.' Sexuality, as a direct expression of the life force, is seen as numinous and sacred. . . . Marriage is a deep commitment, a magical, spiritual, and psychic bond. But it is only one possibility out of many for loving, sexual expression" (1979/1989: 91). Sexual freedom is important to many neo-pagans because they believe that sexuality is both natural and sacred. *Freedom* is translated to mean the right to choose a homosexual relationship, to have multiple lovers, to be celibate, or to commit to a monogamous heterosexual relationship. Neo-paganism and feminist spirituality have attracted large numbers of lesbians and gay men who have found themselves invited to openly express their affection for same-sex partners (Pike 2001). For these NRMs, sexuality can be an expression of and is inseparable from religious identity.

Participants in NRMs also choose celibacy for religious reasons. Some new religions based on Hindu traditions, such as Siddha Yoga, allow women as well as men to become renunciants. Among the Brahma Kumaris, both women and men are urged to practice celibate lifestyles in order to progress spiritually (Howell 1998; Palmer 1993). New forms of Buddhism established in the United States have also attracted women to celibate and monastic lifestyles. New religions that offer a celibate lifestyle to women as well as men expand women's roles into a sphere often taken to be exclusively male.

Unlike the Shakers, who taught life-long celibacy, more recent NRMs may promote celibacy as a stage in spiritual development. But celibacy in NRMs is not always equally available to men and women. For instance, many men who joined Krishna Consciousness in its early years sought to live as celibates because they believed celibacy had higher spiritual value. They also wanted to imitate the Hindu stages of life during which men renounce their families and lead lives of celibate spiritual devotion. In some movements where male celibacy is highly valued, as in Krishna Consciousness, women are seen as inferior and a threat to male spiritual progress and men's commitment to celibacy (Muster 1997; Palmer 1994). Nori Muster, a former ISKCON member, describes her first impression: "Unfortunately, women remained on the sidelines of the ISKCON utopia. Unless spoken to, they were not allowed to look at men or talk to them. They had no voice whatsoever in social affairs. Subhananda said this was to protect the chastity of the men dressed in saffron, who were practicing celibacy. At the temple, women had to cover their heads with a shawl and their legs with a long skirt or, preferably, wear a sari" (Muster 1997: 11). According to Muster, on occasion ISKCON women were made to sit at the back of the room behind the men as a sign of their spiritual inferiority and to prevent them from being a distraction. These cases suggest that celibacy in NRMs has an indeterminant effect on gender. When it is restricted to men, it can elevate men's roles and subordinate women's roles in the religious community.

Although experimentation with polygamy, celibacy, and sexual freedom are more common, marriage practices in NRMs often diverge from the social norm. An NRM marriage can include heterosexual marriage that mimics marriage in the outside society, but some groups encourage their members to express themselves in new ways. During the 1970s, some participants in The Family International (Children of God) experimented with multiple partners, a practice they called "sharing." They were encouraged by their leader and founder, David Berg, who taught that sexual expression was a God-given pleasure (Chancellor 2000). Thirty years later, The Family's Web site still encourages members to live out these teachings if they choose to (www.thefamily .org). Berg also taught that masturbation, nudity, and children's sexual expression were "natural," but his biblical interpretations forbid homosexuality. Maria, Berg's wife, modeled his teaching on "sharing" when she witnessed to a man by having sex with him. The Family's Web site explains Berg's view on this kind of "sharing." James Chancellor's study concludes that, although these practices could be abused, many women as well as men have found them liberating.

The Unificationist movement also holds up traditional heterosexual marriage as its ideal, but Unificationists experience a range of sexual and family roles, including celibacy, monogamous marriage, parenthood, and sibling-like relationships with other adults. Church members undergo periods of celibacy because Unificationists believe that Adam and Eve were tempted by Lucifer and then passed on their fallen nature to their descendents. Consequently, contemporary men and women must purify themselves before they are ready to be perfect parents. During the earlier years of movement, they typically lived at least six years of a monastic-like celibate lifestyle to purify themselves before engaging in sexual activity within marriage. Even after marrying, men and women live separately and remain celibate for several years, acting as brother and sister toward each other. Only after this phase of purification are they seen to be ready to consummate their relationship and become parents. Unificationist mass weddings often include thousands of participants and are called "Blessings" because Reverend Moon blesses the participants—a blessing that purifies couples of their sinful nature and re-creates them as true children of God (Barker 1984). Sometimes Rev. Moon even chooses partners by "matching" them at mass meetings. But these arrangements are not necessarily binding; members can turn down the partners he chooses for them if they want to. After a period of celibacy for both partners, married couples are expected to assume traditional gender roles, with the woman often, but not always, taking care of the household. In this way, NRMs like the Unificationist movement incorporate both unusual practices (long periods of celibacy in marriage) and marriages that follow the social norm.

Women and men in the Rajneesh movement were unlikely to choose celibacy or traditional marriage. Instead, Rajneesh encouraged them not to marry or to have children. Sociologist Marion Goldman, who interviewed many former members of Rajneeshpuram years after the commune had disbanded, found that women overwhelmingly valued their experiences in Rajneesh-puram. Even though many of them did not remain involved in the Osho move-ment, they saw their time in the movement as significant in their lives. Goldman asked women who had followed Osho's directive not to have children if they later regretted this choice, and she found that they overwhelmingly did not: "They believed that they were not meant to mother, and some of them talked about problems with their current stepchildren, nieces, or nephews. Bhagwan's many warnings about how bearing children made self-actualization difficult compelled two of them to have abortions during their twenties and thirties. . . . Although their accounts held some sadness, none of [them] believed that motherhood would have been good for her" (1999: 262). These women credited Rajneesh with liberating them from traditional role expectations. Because of his encouragement, they were able to give top priority to spiritual growth and self-realization.

NRMs demonstrate many variations on motherhood and parenting. Neo-pagans and spiritual feminists use metaphors of motherhood and birth in re-lation to goddesses as well as real women. For them, a woman's maternal role is a positive and sacred experience. Other NRMs "liberate" women from the bonds of motherhood with celibacy and birth control. Still others cast women as traditional mothers and use motherhood as a way to restrict women from leadership roles and limit their spiritual progress.

Many NRMs are strikingly different, however, in their emphasis on the communal family over the traditional mother and father roles. The Peoples Temple, Branch Davidians, Love Family, and other new religions that have created communal living situations have called upon other adults, sometimes elders, to help with childrearing, childcare, and schooling. Identification with a larger communal family may actually replace motherhood and fatherhood, with the result that both men and women can actively pursue spiritual growth and communal identity. Single mothers were attracted to the Peoples Temple, as were older single women, in part because of its supportive communal structures (Maaga 1998). Raelians and Rajneesh devotees discourage parent-hood, encourage birth control, and disassociate sexual activity from reproduc-tion. Because they plan to clone humans in the future, reproducing in the old-fashioned way is unnecessary for Raelians.

Communal living arrangements potentially transform the roles of parents and families in new religions. Participants in the Osho or Rajneesh movement felt that their lives as parents were made easier in communal settings. They were taught not to procreate because Rajneesh believed that families were de-structive and dysfunctional. Contraception, abortion, and sterilization were all practiced by participants in the Osho movement. Some women left their chil-dren behind when they went to Rajneesh's ashram in India, and they felt this was justifiable because of the importance placed on spiritual growth. Rajneesh intended his communities to be monastic in the sense that the members put spiritual devotion before family. However this trend shifted over the years as increasingly more women in the Osho movement chose to become mothers

(Puttick 1997). Elizabeth Puttick notes that the men she interviewed who had fathered children were divorced and none had custody or regular contact with his children. Although no children were born in the Rajneesh communes in the United States (Rajneeshpuram) and England (Medina), children did accompany their parents to these communities, but were reared communally. Rajneesh devotees and many other participants in communal NRMs found communal life to be an attractive alternative to the nuclear family model.

NRMs with male founders and male deities are more likely to institute traditional family models, with men in charge and women in subordinate positions. Polygamy tends to restrict women's power in NRMs and sexual freedom tends to increase it. But scholars have found that even in NRMs that seem at first glance to restrict women's roles, sexual practices may have liberating results. Although sexual experimentation in NRMs promises new gender roles for the future, ideals do not always reflect the reality of participants' experiences. New religions often reaffirm traditional gender roles even while theoretically promoting new forms of sexual expression and gender identity. Women may, for example, be encouraged to use their sexual attraction as a way of exercising power. The Family's practice of "Flirty Fishing" is the most clear-cut example of this. For a phase of their development beginning around 1974, The Family sent women out to proselytize in the streets by seducing men. Some women even became fund-raisers who worked as prostitutes by finding male sponsors to give them money and other valuables in exchange for sex. Flirty Fishing was seen as a way to reach people who would not otherwise be open to The Family's religious message. Not surprisingly, this practice attracted a lot of negative attention. Like many sexual experiments in new religions, it was just that—an experiment in new ways to put religious ideals into practice. For a number of reasons, including the prevalence of sexually transmitted diseases and especially the AIDS scare of the 1980s, Flirty Fishing was abandoned and other forms of recruitment took its place. Nevertheless, according to the many interviews conducted by James Chancellor, the practice of Flirty Fishing "moved many women into the center of family life and offered them extraordinary opportunity and status" (2000: 115). In this case, women's sexuality was valued and even sacralized, but women's roles were still constrained by their biological identity. Specific case studies complicate these generalizations and allow for more nuanced views of the divergence within and between NRMs. The next section suggests ways to teach both the general trends in NRM gender relations and some of the exceptions to them.

Teaching about Gender and New Religions

Gender in new religions is a sensitive topic for students, as it is one of the issues around which the most conflict and tension occurs between the new religions and the outside society. By focusing on the ways in which new religions experiment with, invert, uphold, and challenge gender norms, students' own assumptions about gender, sex, families, and parenting may seem to be under attack. I try to make the beliefs and practices of new religions less threatening by humanizing them as much as possible and by exploring with students some case studies that help them make sense of how and why participants in these new religions are attracted to alternative gender roles and find them meaningful.

My approach to teaching about gender in NRMs includes four strategies: (1) begin with student assumptions about men's and women's roles in religion in general, and specifically in NRMS, using the categories of conceptions of deity, leadership, sexuality, marriage, and family; (2) involve students in class exercises that allow them to explore the ways in which these categories apply to specific case studies; (3) assign research projects that require students to explore gender roles in NRMs in some depth; and (4) arrange field trips and guest speakers to bring students into face-to-face contact with participants in NRMs.

Student Assumptions about Men's and Women's Roles

The first part of this chapter is divided into categories that can be used to teach about different factors that impact or are shaped by gender in new religions: conceptions of deity, leadership, sexuality, marriage and family. I recommend starting with student assumptions about contemporary gender roles in religions that are more familiar. The first step is to ask students to use these categories to analyze a religion that they know. A set of questions for students to consider might include some of the following:

- Is/are the deity/ies in this religion male or female? By what names are they called (e.g., "Lord," "Great Mother") and what language is used to describe them ? How do they shape men's and women's roles in the religion?
- Who are the leaders or people in powerful positions in the religion? Do men and women have equal access to leadership roles? Why or why not?
- What are the religion's teachings concerning sexuality, including topics such as premarital sex, birth control, homosexuality, abortion, polygamy? Is sex seen as something sacred or sinful? Are rules governing men's and women's sexual practices different or the same? Why or why not?
- What are the religion's views regarding marriage and family life? Are boys and girls socialized into the religion differently or similarly?

I then raise questions comparing the familiar religion to what they know about NRMs—"How do you think NRMs differ in these areas from the religions that are more familiar to you?" At this point we typically discuss assumptions about sexual abuse and sexual control in religions they have heard about in the news, such as the Branch Davidians. I find it useful to get student preconceptions on the table and to create an open and tolerant environment in which they can voice their understandings of NRMs before they read any course materials. As the discussion proceeds I encourage them to ask several critical questions: "In what ways do the media represent gender issues (David

Koresh's teen brides, for instance)?" "What is the story the reporters are trying to tell you?" "What different story might an insider tell?"

Class Exercises with Case Studies

I combine teacher-led discussion exercises with assignments that allow students to test their views within a small-group context. An effective method for introducing students to these strange and different religious worlds is to have them read personal accounts or memoirs of what life is like for the men and women who join NRMs. By reading personal stories and anecdotes comparatively, students can also begin to understand the range of men's and women's experiences in these unfamiliar religions. The following four potential sources do a good job of conveying women's experiences of gender roles in NRMs:

> Feminist sociologist Elizabeth Puttick's study of *Women in New Religions* (1997)
> Former Hare Krishna Nori Muster's *Betrayal of the Spirit* (1997)
> Rebecca Moore's account of her two sisters' involvement in the inner leadership circle of the Peoples Temple, *The Jonestown Letters* (1986)
> Marion Goldman's study of women in the Osho movement, *Passionate Journeys* (1999)

I might assign these case studies to four separate groups of students for homework and ask them to come to class prepared to discuss the readings. I ask them to consider some or all of the following questions:

- What aspects of the person's life before they joined the NRM seems to have led them to join?
- What are the NRM's conceptions of deity, leadership roles, and teachings about sexuality, marriage, and family?
- What were some of the negative experiences they had in the religion because of their gender and how did they deal with them?
- In what ways did they find aspects of the NRM attractive for themselves as women?
- In what ways do women's experiences differ from men's in this religion?
- If they left the NRM, what caused them to leave and what did they take away with them?
- What meanings did they place on their experience in the NRM?

The goal of these exercises should be to humanize participants in new religions as much as possible, to show both the positive aspects of their lives in the new religions and the constraints with which they have chosen to live. Again, it is useful to compare these situations with the constraints that women in more established religions also live with—for example, the fact that women cannot be Catholic priests. Like Krishna Consciousness, Catholicism tends to relegate women's and men's roles to different spheres, giving men more spiritual power with the underlying assumption that they are closer to God.

After this kind of small group activity I might use a guided class exercise of students' becoming men or women who join an NRM; this encourages students to identify with the people they are reading about to at least some extent. I might ask students to imagine themselves as new recruits in one of the religions they read about in the case studies and to write a brief personal account considering the following questions (see Eugene Gallagher's chapter in this volume about how to accomplish this effectively in class):

- What religion, if any, did you grow up in and what factors caused you to join this NRM?
- Why did you join the NRM and what did it offer you?
- How did your friends and family react and how did you respond to them?
- What expectations did you have about gender roles in this NRM and what was the reality of these roles?

After they have taken some time to write their accounts, I ask for volunteers to read them aloud and we discuss some of the issues that emerge. I've also found it useful to conduct exercises that delve more deeply into a particular area of gendered experience in NRMs. For example, the sex lives of religious people are likely to attract student interest and thus offer an opportunity to teach about beliefs and practices concerning gender. Sexual improprieties have been common among the accusations against new religions yet often have no basis in reality. But NRMs, like many religions, include instances of sexually abusive behavior as well as sexual empowerment and sometimes diverge in practice from stated ideals. It may be helpful to point out the many examples of sexual impropriety in more accepted religions to give students a context in which to view cases involving new religions.

Students should be encouraged to look at the range of sexual practices across NRMs, from celibacy to polygamy. Examples can be drawn from the four case studies listed above as well sources like James Chancellor's book on The Family International (2000). Chancellor includes many personal accounts of how men and women experienced unorthodox sexual practices taught by David Berg, such as "sharing" partners and "Flirty Fishing." There is both evidence of how Berg's teachings could be used to exploit women and fond memories by former participants of how they were liberated and empowered by these experiences. In this exercise, students might respond to some of the following questions:

- What are the religious justifications for the practice (free love, celibacy, polygamy, etc.) in this particular religion?
- What are both positive and negative aspects of this practice, in your opinion?
- What are both positive and negative aspects of the practice from the point of view of participants?
- How are sexual practices shaped by understandings of gender and what effect do they have on gender roles, if any?

Research Projects

I require both Web-based and more traditional library assignments that allow students to spend time in the company of NRMs (for other ideas about research assignments, see Cowan's chapter in this volume). I give written assignments in which students investigate gender roles in one nineteenth-century NRM and one twentieth-century/twenty-first-century NRM. They might be required to draw from a range of views, including news stories, insiders' accounts, an anti-cult or negative perspective, and at least one academic source that seems to be relatively objective or balanced. Students should be asked comparative questions in order to make sense of the many different perspectives on any particular NRM. Again, the categories of conceptions of deity, leadership, and sex/marriage/family can help students organize a view of the NRM's basic beliefs and practices that affect gender roles.

Among the best sources currently available for the study of insiders' perspectives on new religions are Internet sites. I ask students to choose one of several Web sites to research. The Unificationist movement's site (www.unification.org), for instance, includes a long, but accessible explanation of their beliefs about sexuality and marriage. The Family's home page (www.thefamily.org) describes their version of open marriage or "sharing" and puts it in the context of Christian beliefs. The Raelian movement's site about women (www.sowoman.org) includes descriptions of their positions on abortion, masturbation, and other issues related to gender and sexuality, as well as personal testimonies from both men and women about how their involvement with the movement has changed their lives.

Field Trips and Guest Speakers

There is no good substitute for face-to-face contact with participants in NRMs. Many NRMs are more than willing to send representatives to college classes. I usually suggest that they give a short (twenty- to thirty-minute) presentation in order to leave plenty of time for questions. I make a point of talking to the visitor beforehand and explaining my goals for the class. I let him or her know that I have encouraged students to come prepared with questions about men's and women's roles in the religion, among other things.

For field trips, I provide questions ahead of time and ask students to write a detailed account of what they observed immediately following their visit. I typically ask some of the following questions:

- What objects or symbols of the religion's deity were evident, if any? Was/were the deity/ies depicted as male, female, or neither? What language was used to describe it/them?
- What were men's and women's different roles in the service or ritual activity? What divisions of labor did you notice? Did men and women in the audience/congregation seem to have similar roles or was their participation somehow differentiated?

- How were men and women arranged in the space? Were they separated in any way and if so, was there any difference in how they were positioned vis-à-vis the main activities of the service or ritual? What were participants wearing and were there any apparent differences based on gender, age or relative importance in the ritual?

REFERENCES

Abu-Lughod, Lila. 1993. *Writing Women's Worlds: Bedouin Stories.* Berkeley: University of California Press.

Balch, Robert W. 1998. "The Love Family: Its Formative Years." In *Sects, Cults, and Spiritual Communities,* ed. William Zellner and Marc Petrowsky, 63–94. Westport, CT: Praeger.

Barker, Eileen. 1984. *The Making of a Moonie: Choice or Brainwashing.* Oxford: Basil Blackwell.

Berger, Helen A., Evan A. Leach, and Leigh S. Shaffer. 2003. *Voices from the Pagan Census: A National Survey of Witches and Neo-Pagans in the United States.* Columbia: University of South Carolina.

Boucher, Sandy. 1988/1993. *Turning the Wheel: American Women Creating the New Buddhism.* Boston: Beacon Press.

Butler, Jon. 1990. *Awash in a Sea of Faith: Christianizing the American People.* Cambridge, MA: Harvard University Press.

Chancellor, James D. 2000. *Life in The Family: An Oral History of the Children of God.* Syracuse, NY: Syracuse University Press.

Daly, Mary. 1973. *Beyond God the Father: Toward a Philosophy of Women's Liberation.* Boston: Beacon Press.

Eddy, Mary Baker. 1875/1971. *Science and Health, with Key to the Scriptures.* Boston, MA: First Church of Christ, Scientist.

Eller, Cynthia. 1993. *Living in the Lap of the Goddess: The Feminist Spirituality Movement in America.* New York: Crossroads.

Embry, Jessie. 1987. *Mormon Polygamous Families.* Salt Lake City: University of Utah Press.

Farrar, Janet, and Stewart Farrar. 1984. *The Witches' Way: Principles, Rituals and Beliefs of Modern Witchcraft.* Blaine, WA: Phoenix Publishing.

————. 1987. *Witches' Bible Compleat.* New York: Magickal Childe Publishers.

Foster, Lawrence. 1981. *Religion and Sexuality: The Shakers, the Mormons, and the Oneida Community.* Urbana: University of Illinois Press.

Goldenberg, Naomi. 1979. *The Changing of the Gods: Feminism and the End of Traditional Religions.* Boston: Beacon Press.

Goldman, Marion. 1999. *Passionate Journeys: Why Successful Women Joined a Cult.* Ann Arbor: University of Michigan Press.

Griffin, Wendy, ed. 2000. *Daughters of the Goddess: Studies of Healing, Identity, and Empowerment.* Walnut Creek, CA: AltaMira Press.

Griffith, R. Marie. 1997. *God's Daughters: Evangelical Women and the Power of Submission.* Berkeley: University of California Press.

Howell, Julia Day. 1998. "Gender Role Experimentation in New Religious Movements: Clarification of the Brahma Kumari Case." *Journal for the Scientific Study of Religion* 37, 453–62.

Johnson, Paul E., and Sean Wilentz. 1994. *The Kingdom of Matthias: A Story of Sex and Salvation in 19th-Century America.* New York: Oxford University Press.

Maaga, Mary McCormick. 1998. *Hearing the Voices of Jonestown: Putting a Human Face on an American Tragedy.* Syracuse, NY: Syracuse University Press.

Moore, Rebecca. 1986. *The Jonestown Letters: Correspondence of the Moore Family, 1970–1985.* Lewiston, NY: Edwin Mellen Press.

Muster, Nori J. 1997. *Betrayal of the Spirit: My Life behind the Headlines of the Hare Krishna Movement.* Urbana: University of Illinois Press.

Palmer, Susan J. 1993. "Women's 'Cocoon Work' in New Religious Movements: Sexual Experimentation and Feminine Rites of Passage." *Journal for the Scientific Study of Religion* 32, 343–56.

———. 1994. *Moon Sisters, Krishna Mothers, Rajneesh Lovers: Women's Roles in New Religions.* Syracuse, NY: Syracuse University Press.

Pike, Sarah. 2001. *Earthly Bodies, Magical Selves: Contemporary Pagans and the Search for Community.* Berkeley: University of California Press.

Puttick, Elizabeth. 1997. *Women in New Religions: In Search of Community, Sexuality, and Spiritual Power.* New York: St. Martin's.

Sered, Susan Starr. 1994. *Priestess, Mother, Sacred Sister: Religions Dominated by Women.* New York: Oxford University Press.

Starhawk. 1979/1989. *The Spiral Dance: A Rebirth of the Ancient Religion of the Great Goddess.* San Francisco: Harper & Row.

———. 1982. *Dreaming the Dark: Magic, Sex, and Politics.* Boston: Beacon Press.

Wessinger, Catherine, ed. 1993. *Women's Leadership in Marginal Religions: Explorations Outside the Mainstream.* Urbana: University of Illinois Press.

INTERNET SITES

Alternative Considerations of Jonestown and the People's Temple. http://jonestown.sdsu.edu

Brahma Kumaris World Spiritual Organization. www.bkswu.com

The Family International. www.thefamily.org

International Society for Krishna Consciousness. www.iskcon.org

Osho (Bhagwan Shree Rajneesh) movement. www.oshoworld.com/index.asp

The Raelian Message. www.rael.org

The Raelians' pro-women Web site (which includes testimonies by women and men about the importance of the feminine). www.sowoman.org

The Siddha Yoga movement. www.siddhayoga.org

Starhawk. www.starhawk.org

The Summit Lighthouse (Elizabeth Prophet). www.tsl.org

The Unificationist movement. www.unification.org

Abuse in New Religious Movements: Challenges for the Sociology of Religion

Janet Jacobs

The study of new religious movements (NRMs) is a diverse field of research that explores the varied ways in which conversion to and affiliation with alternative religious groups function in contemporary society. From the outset, the study of new religions offered insights into the cultural dislocations of the 1960s and 1970s that led large numbers of disaffected youth to seek alternative spiritual paths (Tipton 1982). Within the field of sociology, the rise in religious seekership was explained as a search for meaning and moral structure in a hypocritical and materialistic society (Marx and Ellison 1975; Tipton 1982). While a vast majority of this scholarship emphasized the significance especially of non-Western religious groups (for example, Divine Light Mission and Hare Krishna), a number of studies looked at Christian-based movements that, like Eastern-oriented communities, offered spiritual alternatives to mainstream religious culture (Wallis 1978).

Scholars pointed out that, in addition to promising a more intimate and closer relationship to God and/or the divine, these movements filled important social needs, including those of friendship, social acceptance, and love (Jacobs 1984; Lofland 1978; Lofland and Stark 1965). As new forms of spiritual relationship, the religious movements of the 1960s and 1970s offered intimacy and community in an increasingly technological and alienating world (Marx and Ellison 1975). Many of these movements thus functioned as surrogate families, in which emotional as well as spiritual attachments were encouraged and developed (Robbins and Anthony 1972). Along with the relational and familial approaches, other social theories (see Lorne Dawson's chapter in this volume) have focused on the roles played by secularization, innovation, experimentation, and social change in the creation and development of religious alternatives.

While the sociological literature tended to emphasize the meaning and value of NRMs in modern society, a competing body of literature emerged within the field of social psychology. Here, researchers were more inclined to point out the "deviant" nature of religious affiliation, constructing theories of conversion that highlighted the personality traits of religious followers, many of whom were portrayed as unstable and dysfunctional (Conway and Seligman 1978; Levine 1984). Some of the more thoughtful and sophisticated literature in this area applied theories of thought reform and psychoanalysis to religious conversion. Within this theoretical framework, new religious movements were viewed as totalistic environments that fostered extremist ideologies and behaviors grounded in rigid and uncompromising definitions of right and wrong, good and evil. According to this perspective, converts were attracted especially to charismatic leaders who represented an idealized parent figure (Lifton 1987).

In conjunction with this psychological orientation, fears of brainwashing and mind control became popularized as families sought to remove children or other relatives from groups perceived to be totalistic and thus dangerous (Streiker 1984). It was during this time that psychological deprogramming emerged as a means to counter the effects of religious totalism. In response to the psychological orientations, which were often popularized in the media, sociologists increasingly focused on issues of rational choice, religious freedom, and the effects of demonizing new religious movements as violent and deviant (Bromley and Hadden 1993).

Amid the controversies and social conflicts that came to be associated with the study of new religions, feminist critiques of the movements contributed additional insights that further problematized the study of new religions in contemporary society. Initially, the feminist perspective on NRMs focused on gender roles and gender hierarchies in the development of alternative religious communities. As early as 1978, Emily Culpepper discussed the patriarchal aspects of conversion to new religious movements, suggesting that few of these groups offered any real alternative to traditional, male-dominated religious organizations:

> The roles for women within such movements are heavily traditional, patriarchal ones—usually urging a norm of heterosexist, reproductive, nuclear family goals. The theology is frequently explicitly or implicitly woman-hating. . . . For the female membership, what is offered is in reality a new/old religious reinforcement of the conventional oppressive female roles which are so up for criticism and reevaluation in contemporary society. (Culpepper 1978: 220–21)

Soon after Culpepper's critique appeared, other feminist scholars began to interrogate the role that gender played both in conversion to and deconversion from religious groups (Jacobs 1984, 1989; Rose 1997). Within this area of research, questions of women's status were examined with regard to religious theologies that associated women with the flesh and men with the spirit, and

that were thus geared to regulating and controlling female behavior and sexuality within the movements (Goldman 1995; Isaacson 1995; Jacobs 1989). At
the same time, issues of sexual exploitation complicated the study of gender, as
ethnographic data revealed the extent to which women were expected to serve
the sexual needs of male devotees and their leaders, as well as to use their sexuality to recruit new members (Davidman and Jacobs 1993). By the 1980s, feminist researchers studying the new religious movements took a new and more
critical stance, pointing out the failure of these movements to protect devotees
from violence and abuse.

That critical approach shown in the feminist literature was the foundation
for the study of abuse in new religious movements, an area of research that
covers a wide range of behaviors including physical and sexual violence. In the
early stages of the research, reports of devotees described demands for obedience and submission in which followers were forced to grovel at the feet of a
guru or to show their faith through a willingness to endure physical punishment and various forms of public humiliation. Other accounts of religious
"commitment" spoke of child abuse, threat of bodily harm, and isolation and
ostracism for anyone breaking rules and any acts of disobedience (Jacobs 1989;
Rochford 1985). As one devotee of a charismatic Christian group explained,

> Pastor Jim was feared and revered. He was the leader of the thing.
> He was responsible for bringing them together. Pastor Jim's word
> was law. And if there was a question of how I raise my child, he was a
> strong disciplinarian. You can beat those kids black and blue, that's
> all right. They are going to be the better for it.... The women were
> submissive. They take the Bible view of it, plain and simple. And
> if someone disobeyed, spank them or give them a bloody nose, that's
> all right. He was the man responsible for organizing it. (Jacobs 1989:
> 94)

Followers of other movements such as the Hare Krishna spoke of the fear
they experienced in challenging the leadership of the group in the aftermath
of the Swami's death. "I knew the board was capable of violence," one devotee
reported. "I felt very threatened there" (Jacobs 1989: 58).

As the research on violence in NRMs grew in scope and definition, a
troubling pattern of gendered abuse began to emerge. This pattern of abuse
included the sexual abuse of children, incest, rape, battering, forced prostitution, the demand for sexual favors in exchange for "spiritual rewards," and
the sexual transmission of disease to the consorts of religious leaders (Balch
1991; Jacobs 1989; Puttick 1997; Spickard 1995). Although not all movements
were characterized by such abuses, a large number of groups, including The
Family (formerly known as the Children of God), the Love Family, Osho, and
various Buddhist communities, manifested one or more of these forms of
violence within their religious and social culture. As the data reveal, patterns
of abuse are evident in small as well as large communities, Eastern as well as
Western-based groups, and in those organizations that have both single and

multiple religious and social units. Rather than size, geographic proximity, or a shared belief in a common god figure, what links these groups is a charismatic social structure that is patriarchal in nature.

Typically, movements with abusive histories seem to share the following characteristics:

- The presence of a strong male charismatic leader
- A structured hierarchy of command that is vested in an elite corps of male followers
- A set of beliefs that reinforces traditional notions of female submission and male superiority
- Disciplinary and devotional practices that adhere to rigid gender norms and behaviors
- In many but not all cases, a family-based social structure that casts the leader as a paternal figure whose authority is absolute and uncontested.

It is these structural characteristics, embedded in the power dynamics of patriarchal social relations, that place women and children especially at risk for violence and abuse. The Branch Davidians, under the leadership of David Koresh, offer perhaps the most compelling example of how charismatic male authority can lead to the abuse of women and girls. In what is undoubtedly one of the most publicized cases of sexual violence, Keri Jewell, a fourteen-year-old follower of the Branch Davidians, testified before Congress that she had been raped at the age of ten by Koresh. Jewell reported that Koresh's authority was not contested by parents or other adult devotees who, while aware of the abuse, did nothing to protect the children from Koresh's violence. Similar accusations against religious leaders and male devotees in other groups confirm that, rather than an anomaly, Koresh's behavior was symptomatic of a pattern of sexual abuse that characterizes the developing cultures of numerous and diverse NRMs.

Findings such as these have caused a controversy within the sociology of religion, particularly among those scholars who emphasize the virtues rather than the problems of new religious movements. For the most part, the sociological literature on NRMs has avoided the difficult questions of gendered violence and sexual exploitation, emphasizing instead the constructive and functional aspects of religious commitment. In an effort to protect religious freedom and to counter the stigma typically associated with alternative religious groups, scholars in the sociology of religion have often been reluctant to recognize and discuss the abusive practices of these movements, despite the violence identified in the research. At academic conferences and in reviews of the literature, feminist scholars who have brought these abuses to the attention of their colleagues have been heavily critiqued and the accounts of their informants have come under attack and are viewed with suspicion.

Resistance to the study of abuse and violence in NRMs has resulted in a narrow representation of religious communities in the research and a trivialization of the experiences of devotees who have been violated and abused while members of these groups. As a number of chapters in this volume suggest, many scholars in the field maintain that violence represents a minor though sensationalized aspect of alternative religious culture—"the exception rather than the norm" of religious commitment. This view, which has been consistently reproduced in the literature, relies on a definition of violence that focuses on mass suicide and collective murder. Other forms of violation— extreme disciplinary actions or sexually abusive behaviors, for example—have, by comparison, rarely been taken seriously or treated with any importance. The absence of discourse on varied aspects of religious violence—particularly those abuses that are gender-based—is especially troubling in light of abuse patterns that place women and girls at risk. The material presented in this chapter is intended to fill this gap in sociological studies and to offer a more nuanced and critically challenging perspective on religious movements, one that will help students understand and appreciate the power dynamics of gendered violence in religious communities. My discussion of abuse in new religious movements will focus first on theoretical approaches to the study of violence and then on strategies for effectively teaching this difficult and troubling aspect of religious commitment.

Theoretical Approaches to the Study of Gendered Violence: Patriarchy and the Structural Dynamics of Abuse in New Religious Movements

Numerous theories have been used to help explain and understand the proliferation of gendered violence in Western society. A number of these theoretical approaches can be applied to the study of sexual violence in NRMs as well. Theories that trace the effects of male dominance on gender relations, male sexual violence and control in the family, and the sexual objectification of women in society are especially useful for teaching about abuse. Although new religious movements have not exclusively been founded and led by men (see, for example, Catherine Wessinger's 1990 study of the Siddha Yoga movement), the vast majority of movements in which abuse has been most frequent are those that are male dominated. Because of the relationship between patriarchy and the proliferation of gendered violence in new religious movements, theories of male dominance and the rise of patriarchal social institutions provide a useful framework for situating religious groups within the larger study of patriarchy and violence against women. Here, the work of Frederich Engels is both informative and insightful. In his classic groundbreaking text, *The Origin of the Family, Private Property, and the State* (1884), Engels elaborates a theory of male dominance and female subordination from an evolutionary perspective. According to Engels, the shift from a hunter-gatherer culture to an agricultural-based economy based on private property led to a system of power and dominance wherein men gained control over land, tools, and ultimately women and children, whose dependence on male providers left them both vulnerable and powerless. This new economic arrangement gave rise to the patriarchal family, which in turn became the foundation for development of other social institutions such as religion and government, which reinforced notions of male supremacy (Engels 1884).

Relating the study of abuse in NRMs to Engels's theory of patriarchy is especially effective for encouraging an understanding of contemporary authoritarian religious communities. As described above, many of these groups reflect the values, norms, and religious belief systems that characterize the social relations of power Engels identified over a century ago when he sought to explain the secondary status of women in European industrial society. The diminishing status of women, as described by Engels, became institutionalized by religious cultures that defined women as property and objects of exchange in biblical narratives; these narratives characterized the "contents" of a man's household as his wives, male and female slaves, large and small cattle, and other property (Exodus 20:14). According to Engels, these biblical laws led to the development of the state's legal codes and social norms that gave men total control over marriage, virginity, and sexual access to women and children.

Engels thus provides a theoretical framework for understanding the structural characteristics and gendered norms of contemporary authoritarian movements that reproduce earlier religious cultures in which women are treated as the property of charismatic leaders and as sexual commodities. A powerful example of this phenomenon is found in the history of the Love Family. Founded by Israel Love in the 1970s, the culture of the movement soon became defined by Love's desire for power and possessions, including sexual control over female devotees:

> Given his exceptional status in the Family, it should not be surprising that Love took advantage of his unusual power and privilege. . . . As the Family grew and prospered, Love's lifestyle became increasingly extravagant. He took long vacations, bought several airplanes, and moved into a luxurious house on Queen Anne Hill furnished with beautiful paintings by Family artists and expensive antique furniture. Love enjoyed the best food, the finest wine and a retinue of devoted servants. His household included the most talented musicians and the most attractive women, many of whom had sex with him on a regular basis. (Balch 1995: 171)

The notion of women as property is thus especially relevant for an analysis of the sexual abuse of young women and girls in movements such as the Branch Davidians and the Love Family.

Expanding on Engels's theory of patriarchy and control over women, Judith Herman's work on incest provides yet another theoretical approach through which to understand the dynamics of sexual abuse in NRMs. In her most widely read text, *Father-Daughter Incest* (1981), Herman offers this insight into patriarchy and gendered norms of family violence:

In patriarchal societies, including Western society, the rights of ownership and exchange of women within the family are vested primarily
in the father.... Only under male supremacy do women become objects of exchange. Only male supremacy determines that men have
the right to give women for marriage or concubinage, while women
have no comparable rights either in men or themselves. Only under
male supremacy do incest taboos become agreements among men
regarding the disposition of women.... The man who has the power
to give a woman away also has the power to take her for himself.
(Herman 1981: 60–92)

If we apply Herman's analysis to NRMs, we see that charismatic leaders
assume the role of a divine father who, in violating the women and children
under his control, is exercising the privilege of male entitlement that has for
centuries characterized male-dominated societies. At Jonestown, for example,
Pastor Jim Jones referred to himself as the all-knowing Father or Dad to whom
all devotees owed obedience and to whom all could confess their deepest fears
and desires. In his role as a rigid but "loving" parent, Jones cited the teachings
of Saint Paul as a rationale for engaging in and demanding sexual service from
his female followers (Jones 1989). Similarly, the leader and highly revered
father figure of an Eastern-based group regularly engaged in sex with the
children of his devotees. Interviews with the followers in this movement revealed that the leader believed it was both his right and his responsibility to
help these children "toward enlightenment" by initiating them into the sex-
based meditation of his spiritual practice (Jacobs 1989).

Another approach to understanding abuse in new religious movements
is to examine those theories that consider the relationship between violence
against women and the objectification and sexualization of women in society
more generally. Moving outside the purview of familial patriarchy, these theoretical models focus on patriarchal relations across institutions that perpetuate
gendered violence. Here, scholars such as Allan G. Johnson provide a useful
paradigm for exploring patriarchy as a generalized system of male dominance:

At its core, patriarchy is a set of symbols and ideas that make up a
culture embodied by everything from the content of everyday conversation to literature and film. Patriarchal culture includes ideas
about the nature of things, including men, women, and humanity,
with manhood and masculinity most closely associated with being
human and womanhood and femininity relegated to the marginal
position of the "other." ... Going deeper into patriarchal culture, we
find a complex web of ideas that define reality and what's considered
good and desirable. To see the world through patriarchal eyes is to
believe that women and men are profoundly different in their basic
natures, that hierarchy is the only alternative to chaos, and that
men were made in the image of God with whom they enjoy a special
relationship. (Johnson 2000: 30)

Johnson's analysis helps to explain patriarchy as a system that attributes godlike qualities to male leaders who, in violating the members of their communities, are empowered to modify the codes of moral conduct that might otherwise call their behaviors into question. As one devotee of a Hindu-based group described this phenomenon:

> He was like God to me. I was his disciple and his child. I trusted him completely. He told me that he knew what I needed for my spiritual growth and I believed him. When he said he wanted to have sex with me, I hesitated at first but then he assured me that this was the right path. (Jacobs 2000: 121)

Within this theoretical framework, the work of Katherine Mackinnon (1994) is also useful for understanding the dynamics of gendered violence in NRMs. In her well-known theories of sexuality and male dominance, Mackinnon examines the social context through which men exercise power over women and girls:

> Masculinity precedes male as femininity precedes female, and male sexual desire defines both. Specifically, "woman" is defined by what male desire requires for arousal and satisfaction and is socially tautologous with "female sexuality" and the "female sex." In the permissible ways a woman can be treated, the ways that are socially considered not violations but appropriate to her nature, one finds the particulars to be male sexual interests and requirements . . . such that sexuality equals heterosexuality equals the sexuality of (male) dominance and (female) submission. (Mackinnon 1994: 261)

Mackinnon's theory further elaborates the ways in which male norms of sexual behavior and the primacy of male sexual desire pose a danger to women whose needs and safety are subordinated to those of men. According to Mackinnon, the "unequal sexuality" that characterizes patriarchal gender relations helps to explain the underlying norms of female compliance and the subsequent violence that inform so much of the sexual abuse in contemporary society, including that which is found in NRMs.

Strategies for Teaching about Abuse in New Religious Movements

Having articulated the problem of abuse in NRMs and the theoretical models for understanding the proliferation of violence against female devotees, I now suggest a number of strategies for teaching this painful and challenging material in the classroom. First and foremost, it is significant to recognize that curriculum materials and classroom discussions that focus on gendered violence are often difficult to teach, both because of the sensitive nature of the topic and because of the potential for retraumatization among students with abusive histories. Studies of college students indicate that a sizable number of women have experienced some form of sexual abuse in their lives (Russell 1983; Swisher and Wekesser 1994). It is therefore important to prepare students for the discussion and, if need be, to offer students optional ways to study the material if the topic proves too painful or troubling.

Second, graphic discussions of rape, incest, and other humiliating and violent sexual abuses, while effective for illustrating the reality and seriousness of the social problem, nevertheless raise the possibility of voyeurism and titillation in class discussion. I therefore caution against using visual representations—photographs or films—that may exploit those who have been victimized. In my experience, the use of violent sexual imagery to teach about violence against women diverts attention away from the causes of the violence and toward the bodily representations of those who have been violated and degraded.

Third, with topics such as sexual abuse, there is a tendency among students to trivialize the violence or to blame the victim. It is therefore especially important that these responses be attended to in the classroom as soon as they arise so that a safe and respectful environment for all students is maintained. To minimize the tendency toward victim blaming, it is particularly helpful to introduce the theoretical material (as outlined above) from the outset, and to repeatedly remind students that violence in religious movements is not an isolated phenomenon but exists within the larger context of gendered power relations in a patriarchal culture. This approach will help shift the dialogue away from notions of devotee or leader pathology and to larger questions of how and why the problem of violence against women remains such a significant aspect of gender relations in modern society. To bring this point across, students might be asked to consider the differences and similarities between sexual abuse in religious groups and sexual harassment and violence in other social organizations, such as families, schools, offices, and mainstream religious denominations. Challenging students to view these movements and their abusive behaviors through the lens of more general institutional violence can lead to a provocative and critically important dialogue on how norms of gendered violence are a prevalent part of social life, both within and outside religious movements. This perspective on abuse will not only help diffuse the phenomenon of victim blaming but also will lessen the tendency for students to single out religious movements as sites of deviance and anti-social behavior.

Once the social context of gendered violence has been adequately addressed, an effective teaching tool for examining religious movements is to use case studies. In this regard, The Family offers an especially insightful example of the types of abuses that exist in NRMs and the manifestations of male power and control that can lead to violence against female devotees. As a new religious movement, The Family first emerged in the 1970s under the leadership of David Berg, a charismatic figure who became known to the group as Father David Moses. As the founder and leader of this Christian-based religious community, Berg espoused and promulgated a theology of conversion and belief that encouraged adultery, group sex, sexual relations with children, and incest (Puttick 1997). These beliefs and ideologies were documented and disseminated through a series of letters in which Berg advised his follow-ers that "there is no such thing anymore as a Biblical Law against adultery, as long as it is done in Love, because the 'Law of Love' supersedes all other laws" (Puttick 1997: 123). Not only did Berg espouse adultery and sexual rela-tions with children, but he created a system for attracting followers that re-quired female devotees, including his wife, to prostitute themselves. Berg called this practice "Flirty Fishing." He referred to potential converts as fish and female followers were designated as the bait. Berg told the women and girls in the movement that, in prostituting themselves for The Family, they would be like Jesus:

> The fish can't understand crucifixion, they can't understand Jesus. But they can understand the ultimate creation of God, a woman.... Every one of you girls who spreads out your arms and legs on the bed of those men are just like Jesus, exactly like Jesus. (Puttick 1997: 52)

According to the scholar Elizabeth Puttick (1997), Flirty Fishing eventu-ally expanded to include other forms of prostitution, in which female devotees worked in escort services and as call girls to support the religious community—practices that were eventually eliminated because of fears surrounding disease and the spread of AIDS. As a result of numerous court cases involving ac-cusations of abuse in Australia and Great Britain, The Family eventually agreed to revise and reject Berg's theological position on sexual relations with children.

As a case study, The Family illustrates the types of gender norms and ideologies that Engels, Herman, Johnson, and Mackinnon address in their the-ories of patriarchy and control over female sexuality. The Family's patriarchal form of charismatic leadership is a useful basis for exploring paternalism and sexual violence; the sexual objectification of women in society; and the com-modification of women's sexuality. Teaching about this group is also an effec-tive way to draw parallels between the values espoused by an abusive religious community and the values of the culture as a whole. In a society where women's bodies are used to sell a plethora of products from clothes to alcoholic bever-ages, should practices such as Flirty Fishing really seem so shocking or surprising? What makes Flirty Fishing so abhorrent in the first place? Is it because women's sexuality is being used to sell religion rather than cars? Or because the women themselves are being treated as commodities? Questions such as these challenge students to think critically about the sexual practices of NRMs specifically as well as to think more universally about the sexualization of women in society.

The case history of The Family also raises important questions with regard to Mackinnon's theory of unequal sexuality and the norms of male-female sexual behavior that place women and girls at risk for abuse. Using Mack-innon's argument on male sexual dominance as a framework for studying The Family, the meaning of *consent* can be examined from the point of view of the norms of female compliance and sexual submission. If, for example, female devotees "consent" to serve the movement (and the leader) through prostitution or participation in group sex, should these practices be considered abusive, coercive, or simply a matter of personal choice? Certainly, Mackinnon would argue that consent within the current system of male sexual dominance is not consent at all, but a form of socialized submission that leads to exploitation and abuse. A good source of discussion topics for the class is to ask students whether they agree with Mackinnon's interpretation, or whether Flirty Fishing and required group sex can be understood as freedom of religion among those who choose to follow a leader such as Berg. Along the same lines, students can be encouraged to examine the reasons women might join such movements, and what aspects of patriarchal culture socialize women to join sexually exploitive and abusive relationships within the context of religious conversion. Although these are highly sensitive and challenging issues to address in the classroom, they are fundamental to understanding the perpetuation of norms of violence in religious culture.

Finally, the literature on The Family offers valuable insights into the way in which the sexualization of women in NRMs was trivialized in the early research in this field. Assigning readings such as Roy Wallis's article on "Recruiting Christian Manpower" (1978) can lead students into a discussion of the values and attitudes that scholars of religion have historically brought to the study of alternative communities, especially with respect to the issues that affect women and children. In his initial analysis of The Family, Wallis referred to Flirty Fishing as an "innovative strategy" while describing Berg as a leader with strong "sexual appetites":

> How can this amazing innovation in religious recruitment be accounted for, and how is it justified by the Children of God . . . ?
> The letters of 'Father Moses David' have always adopted a rather robust style of writing in which sexual analogy plays a considerable part even on nonsexual matters, but although the origins of such developments within the Family [Children of God] such as the institution of plural wives, trial marriages, etc., can be accounted for partly in terms of Mo's own sexual appetites, again they provide no explanation for the distribution of sexual resources beyond the confines of the Family. (Wallis 1978: 72)

Using Wallis's study as a basis for analysis and class discussion, students can consider the effects of valorizing the leader's sexuality in a scholarly study while at the same time characterizing the female devotees as "sexual resources." What are the consequences of this form of gender objectification in social scientific inquiry, and what biases are evident in describing Flirty Fishing as "an amazing innovation"? Discussions such as these are effective teaching tools for getting students to see their own biases with respect to notions of female sexuality and perceptions of sexual abuse. Through a reading of Wallis's article, students can gain a greater understanding of the ways in which assumptions of neutrality in the social sciences have perpetuated cultural ideologies that are harmful to women and children.

Other case material can also prove fruitful for exploring the complex issues that inform the study of violence and abuse in NRMs. Another valuable exercise for critical thinking is to use incidents such as the assault on the Branch Davidian Compound in Waco, Texas, to examine when and what types of interventions are necessary and/or appropriate to protect devotees from harm. Students can be asked to consider whether the actions of the government were in fact justified by the evidence of rape and other forms of internal violence, or did the government overreact to the dangers that the group actually posed? In broaching this topic for discussion, I find that a debate format is an extremely good teaching tool. Debate topics can range from pro-government to anti-government arguments, with students divided into opposing advocacy groups and some students assigned a middle-of-the-road position. Similarly, the ethics and legality of deprogramming can be the subject for a lively and stimulating debate. Under what conditions would students authorize or enlist professional deprogrammers to rescue family members from potentially dangerous communities? Are these types of interventions ever warranted and should they be legal if the safety of a devotee is at risk? How can families accurately assess the risk to their children and what other measures could they take to seek help for what they perceive to be a dangerous situation?

Because many of these questions have yet to be resolved, fostering these debates and dialogues in the classroom allows students to grapple with timely and relevant sociological concepts. According to Anthony, Robbins, and Barrie-Anthony (2002), mass suicides and homicides in a small number of the groups have in recent years led to the creation of restrictive laws, particularly in France, that limit the rights and freedoms of the vast majority of nonviolent movements. At the same time, other scholars, including myself, argue that NRMs, like all other social organizations, must be held accountable for the promulgation of beliefs and practices that endanger and violate devotees. Although these issues may engender difficult and sometimes contentious classroom discussions, the study of abuse in new religious movements is fertile ground for creating dialogue and promoting skills of critical thinking and social analysis. As the recent scandals in the Catholic Church reveal, authoritarian religious cultures of all orientations place followers at risk for violations by those in power. Perhaps more than any other lesson, it is this understanding of abuse within NRMs that makes the study of religious violence such an important topic for students to explore in the sociology of religion.

REFERENCES

Aidala, Angela. 1985. "Social Change, Gender Roles, and New Religious Movements." *Sociological Analysis* 46, 287–314.
Anthony, Dick, Thomas Robbins, and Steven Barrie-Anthony. 2002. "Cult and Anticult Totalism: Reciprocal Escalation and Violence." *Terrorism and Political Violence* 14, 212–39.

Balch, Robert. 1991. "Charismatic Leadership and the Corruption of Power." Unpublished paper.

———. 1995. "Charisma and Corruption in the Love Family." In *Sex, Lies, and Sanctity: Religion and Deviance in Contemporary North America*, ed. Mary Jo Neitz and Marion S. Goldman, 155–79. Greenwich, CT: JAI Press.

Bromley, David G., and Jeffrey K. Hadden, eds. 1993. *Handbook on Cults and Sects in America*, 2 vols. Greenwich, CT: JAI Press.

Conway, Frederick, and J. Seligman. 1978. *Snapping: The Epidemic of Sudden Personality Change*. New York: J. B. Lippincott.

Culpepper, Emily. 1978. "The Spiritual Movement of Radical Feminist Consciousness." In *Understanding New Religions*, ed. George Baker and Jacob Needleman, 220–34. New York: Seabury Press.

Davidman, Lynn, and Janet Jacobs. 1993. "Feminist Perspectives on New Religious Movements." In *The Handbook on Cults and Sects in America*, Part B, ed. David G. Bromley and Jeffrey K. Hadden, 173–90. Greenwich, CT: JAI Press.

Engels, Frederich. 1884. *The Origins of the Family, Private Property, and the State*. New York: International Publishers.

Goldman, Marion. 1995. "From Promiscuity to Celibacy: Women and Sexual Regulation at Rajneeshpuram." In *Sex, Lies and Sanctity: Religion and Deviance in Contemporary North America*, ed. Mary Jo Neitz and Marion Goldman, 203–19. Greenwich, CT: JAI Press.

Herman, Judith. 1981. *Father-Daughter Incest*. Cambridge, MA: Harvard University Press.

Isaacson, Lynne. 1995. "Rule Making and Rule Breaking in a Jesus Community." In *Sex, Lies and Sanctity: Religion and Deviance in Contemporary North America*, ed. Mary Jo Neitz and Marion Goldman, 181–201. Greenwich, CT: JAI Press.

Jacobs, Janet. 1984. "The Economy of Love in Religious Commitment: The Deconversion of Women from Nontraditional Religious Movements." *Journal for the Scientific Study of Religion* 23, 294–307.

———. 1989. *Divine Disenchantment: Deconverting from New Religions*. Bloomington: University of Indiana Press.

———. 2000. "Charisma, Male Entitlement and the Abuse of Power." In *Bad Pastors: Clergy Misconduct in Modern America*, ed. Anson Shupe, William A. Stacey, and Susan E. Darnell, 113–30. New York: New York University Press.

Johnson, Allan. 2000. "Patriarchy, the System." In *Women's Lives: Multicultural Perspectives*, ed. Gwyn Kirk and Margo Okazawa-Rey, 24–34. Toronto: Mayfield.

Jones, Constance. 1989. "Exemplary Dualism and Authoritarianism at Jonestown." In *New Religious Movements, Mass Suicide, and Peoples Temple*, ed. Rebecca Moore and Fielding McGehee III, 209–27. Lewiston, NY: Edwin Mellen Press.

Levine, Saul. 1984. *Radical Departures: Desperate Detours to Growing Up*. New York: Harcourt, Brace and Jovanovich.

Lifton, Robert. 1987. *The Future of Immortality and Other Essays for a Nuclear Age*. New York: Basic Books.

Lofland, John. 1978. "Becoming a World Saver Revisited." In *Conversion Careers: In and Out of New Religions*, ed. James Richardson, 10–23. Beverly Hills, CA: Sage.

Lofland, John, and Rodney Stark. 1965. "Becoming a World Saver: A Theory of Conversion to a Deviant Perspective." *American Sociological Review* 30, 862–74.

Mackinnon, Catherine. 1994. "Sexuality." In *Theorizing Feminism: Parallel Trends in the Humanities and Social Sciences*, ed. Anne Herrmann and Abigail Stewart, 257–87. Boulder, CO: Westview Press.

Marx, John D., and David L. Ellison. 1975. "Sensitivity Training and Communes: Contemporary Quests for Community." *Pacific Sociological Review* 18, 441–60.

Puttick, Elizabeth. 1997. *Women in New Religions*. New York: St. Martin's.

Robbins, Thomas, and Dick Anthony. 1972. "Getting Straight with Meher Baha: A Study of Drug Rehabilitation, Mysticism, and Post Adolescent Role Conflict." *Journal for the Scientific Study of Religion* 11, 122–40.

Rochford, E. Burke, Jr. 1985. *Hare Krishna in America*. New Brunswick, NJ: Rutgers University Press.

Russell, Diana. 1983. "The Incidence and Prevalence of Intrafamilial and Extrafamilial Sexual Abuse of Female Children." *Child Abuse and Neglect* 7, 133–46.

Spickard, James. 1995. "When None Call It Evil: A Sociological Framework for Evaluating Abuse in Religions." In *Sex, Lies, and Sanctity: Religion and Deviance in Contemporary North America*, ed. Mary Jo Neitz and Marion S. Goldman, 251–68. Greenwich, CT: JAI Press.

Streiker, Lowell. 1984. *Brainwashing, Cults, and Deprogramming in the 1980s*. New York: Doubleday.

Swisher, Karen, and Carol Wekesser, eds. 1994. *Violence against Women*. San Diego, CA: Greenhaven Press.

Tipton, Steven. 1982. *Getting Saved from the Sixties*. Berkeley: University of California Press.

Wallis, Roy. 1978. "Recruiting Christian Manpower." *Society* 15, 72–74.

Wegner, Judith. 1988. *Chattel or Person? The Status of Women in the Mishnah*. New York: Oxford University Press.

Wessinger, Catherine. 1990. "The Legitimation of Feminine Authority: The Siddha Yoga Case." Paper presented at the annual meeting of the Society for the Scientific Study of Religion, Virginia Beach, Virginia.

New Religious Movements and Violence

Thomas Robbins and John R. Hall

Contemporary interest in violence involving new religious movements (NRMs) is an understandable consequence of various sensational incidents in recent decades. "Benchmark cases," note Bromley and Melton (2002: 2–3), "consist of the Manson Family murders in 1969, the Peoples Temple murder-suicides in Jonestown [Guyana] in 1978, the Branch Davidian murder-suicides at Mt. Carmel outside Waco in 1993, the Solar Temple murder-suicides in Switzerland and Canada in 1994, the Aum Shinrikyo murders in Tokyo in 1995, and the Heaven's Gate collective suicides in California in 1997." The murder-suicides involving the Movement for the Restoration of the Ten Commandments in Uganda in 2000 probably also should be included, although the destruction of the group was so complete that there is little information on which to base analysis. In this essay, we discuss the basic explanatory issues that arise in connection with these and other episodes of collective violence involving NRMs and esoteric spiritual movements. We then consider how to teach about the issues involved.

Explaining Violence: Cases, Theories, Factors

To introduce the substantive issues relevant to teaching about NRMs and violence, we first survey the kinds of incidents involved, next briefly summarize three alternative theoretical approaches to explaining such incidents, and then turn to detailed consideration of the causal factors and social processes held to be at work.

Benchmark Cases

Religion is hardly a stranger to violence. Europe, for example, has witnessed numerous incidents over the centuries, including the medieval crusades, lethal persecutions of heretics and "witches," and incidents during the Protestant Reformation. Most spectacularly, among the persecuted Old Believer sect in late seventeenth- and early eighteenth-century Muscovy, thousands perished in a series of mass-suicide immolations (Robbins 2000).

- The earliest spectacular episode of cult violence in recent decades involved murders committed in the late 1960s near Hollywood by followers given orders by Charles Manson, a charismatic drifter who had a history of brushes with the law. Manson's "religious" status was ambiguous and the body count was very low compared to later events, but the incident became a bellwether.
- Almost a decade later, in 1978, leftist minister Jim Jones's Peoples Temple communal settlement of nearly 1,000 people in Jonestown, Guyana, received an unwelcome visit from a delegation of journalists and "concerned relatives" led by U.S. congressman Leo Ryan, who had received alarming reports about "concentration camp" conditions there. Sharpshooters from Jonestown murdered Congressman Ryan, three newsmen, and a defector shortly after they left Jonestown. The community, fearing reprisals and adhering to a rehearsed script, staged a mass suicide in which 913 people died (largely but not in all cases voluntarily), most of them by drinking a poisoned fruit-flavored punch (Hall 2004b; Maaga 1998).
- The Branch Davidian sect was a fringe offshoot of the Seventh-Day Adventist Church led by the messianic young David Koresh. He and his followers amassed a stockpile of weapons at their Mount Carmel compound near Waco, Texas. In February 1993, agents of the U.S. Bureau of Alcohol, Tobacco, and Firearms, tipped off by sect opponents, initiated a raid of the compound to search for weapons and possibly make arrests. But the Davidians received advance warning of the raid, and the poorly planned "dynamic entry" by federal agents precipitated a shootout in which a number of BATF agents and sect members died, leaving Koresh, other Davidians, and several agents wounded. FBI agents replaced the BATF agents, and a siege ensued. During an assault by the FBI meant to end the siege some seven weeks later, over eighty persons perished when the compound burned to the ground in a fire that was probably (there is some dissensus) set by the Davidians (Hall, Schuyler, and Trinh 2000).
- The Order of the Solar Temple was a somewhat different group— mystical illuminati living in Quebec and Western Europe, led by the older mystagogue Joseph DiMambro and the youthful New Age homeopathic doctor Luc Jouret. Threatened with internal dissent and apostasy, and perceiving external opposition signaled by some arrests

and a government investigation, the group engaged in murder and collective suicide in France and Switzerland in 1994 and 1995. In some instances, believers committed suicide months after the leaders already had died. The Templars claimed to be undertaking a "transit" to the dog star Sirius and to eternal life (Hall and Schuyler 1998; Introvigne and Mayer 2002).

- In 1995, members of Shoku Asahara's Aum Shinrikyo (Supreme Truth) sect introduced poison gas into the Tokyo subway system. "This attack was intended primarily as a preemptive strike against the police," who were belatedly investigating murders and less drastic violent acts that the group was alleged to have carried out against both members and opponents (Reader 2000b: 204). Asahara had come to perceive a vast conspiracy of the American and Japanese governments, Jews, Freemasons, and others against his movement.
- In 1997, thirty-nine members of a UFO cult, Heaven's Gate, poisoned themselves in a suburb of San Diego. The arrival of a comet had convinced the leader, Do, that a spacecraft was ready to transport them from Earth to a Heavenly Kingdom in which they would be reunited with co-leader Ti, who had died in 1985.
- As for the least understood episode, in March 2000 in Uganda, the leaders of an apocalyptic group that recruited primarily former Roman Catholics, the Movement for the Restoration of the Ten Commandments systematically orchestrated the murder through poison, stabbing, and strangulation of approximately 400 members, many of them dissidents who had requested return of their donations. In a second phase of killings, participants gathered in a barricaded building for a party that culminated in an explosion and a fire (Melton and Bromley 2002b).

The violence in these benchmark cases is horrific. However, large-scale violence involving modern NRMs is relatively rare. Among thousands of novel movements, "the vast majority," notes James Richardson, "does not teach or practice violence, even if they accept millennial beliefs" (2001: 109). Confrontations of some sort between unconventional sects and the state are not infrequent, notes Stuart Wright, but out of 130 episodes in the 1990s, "only three of the cases . . . culminated in collective religious violence" (Wright 2002: 12).

Certain observers (e.g., Singer and Lalich 1995) have tended to exaggerate proneness to violence on the part of novel cults, asserting that such groups are intrinsically unstable and prone to violence. Charismatic leadership, which characterizes many new movements, is often associated with violence. Although this view is not entirely erroneous, it requires qualification. "Since a high proportion of new religious movements begin with a charismatic leader and a small band of followers, and since most established groups often preserve a measure of charismatic authority, it is problematic to assert a direct causal relationship between charismatic leadership and violence" (Melton and Bromley 2002a: 46).

Generalized assertions are further complicated by the difficulty of distinguishing between new movements and more established or institutionalized religions. Most "new" religions are not entirely novel. They are likely to have borrowed key cultural and organizational elements from one or another existing tradition. Thus, Hare Krishna is a Hindu sect, Aum Shinrikyo draws largely on Buddhism with an admixture of Christian elements, and the Branch Davidians are ultimately an offshoot of the Seventh-Day Adventist Church. It is also important to note that established religions themselves are sometimes directly involved in violence (Hall 2003). The ambiguous contrasts between new religions and established traditions complicate any approach that links new religions per se to violence.

Nor is the violence solely in one direction. In the United States, there have certainly been cases of spectacular violence carried out by emergent religious movements—for example, the infamous Mountain Meadows Massacre by Mormons of settlers traveling across Utah Territory in the 1840s, the power struggle waged against competitors by Ervil LeBaron's polygamist Church of the Lamb, and conflicts between the Nation of Islam and rival organizations. But these rare instances are widely outnumbered by cases of violence perpetrated *against* new groups—for example, Quakers publicly hanged in colonial New England and the famous massacre of spirit dancers associated with a Native American revitalization movement at Wounded Knee. At present, over 2,000 religious groups operate in the United States, at least half of which have come into existence since 1960, along with many "quasi-religious" New Age and religiotherapy groups. Nevertheless, since 1960 fewer than two dozen U.S. groups have been involved in suicide or homicide events producing multiple deaths. On the other hand, there are numerous cases in which new movements have been the victims of armed attack, member abduction, or police harassment. The usual response of targeted groups is not to strike out violently but to initiate civil and criminal legal proceedings.

Why, then, is there such a strong connection between NRMs and violence in the public mind? In large part, the answer has to do with how the general public learns about NRMs. As Bromley (2004) has noted, new religious movements often encounter immediate, intense opposition from a variety of sources, including established religions mounting a counter-cult movement and secular anti-cult movements. Both kinds of opposition tend to characterize new movements as dangerously unstable and predisposed to violence. In turn, the number and significance of major episodes of new religious violence have become magnified by institutional and media responses and by public opinion. Violent episodes involving participants as either victims or perpetrators in novel religious movements are generally deemed more newsworthy and more directly connected to their religious organizations than are incidents involving persons with more traditional religious affiliations. Moreover, unsubstantiated rumors of impending violence by new religions often receive substantial media attention, while there are less likely to be reports about disconfirmed rumors, such as those concerning Chen Tao, a Taiwanese millennialist movement in Texas or the Concerned Christians in Colorado (Melton and Bromley 2002a). A misleading impression of substantial violence has thus been generated by selective attention to actual or alleged violent incidents, and by the tendency to attribute the causes of violence to the "cultic" quality of NRMs. By contrast, mainline religious groups are less likely to be perceived as implicated in problematic behavior on the part of members or ex-members. Yet fringe members of these groups may sometimes take part in violence connected to social issues such as abortion or racial integration. In short, violence is stereotypically generalized in relation to NRMs disproportionately to its actual occurrence. Nevertheless, episodes of violence involving NRMs are distinctive and sometimes stunning, and they cry out for explanation.

Theoretical Explanations of Movement Violence

A central theoretical issue concerns whether *internal* or *external* factors are the primary causes of violent episodes. Does collective violence arise as a function of the deviant organizational and social psychological features of so-called cults, or is the external social response to controversial movements the key factor that leads to violence, both by and against stigmatized groups? Behind this issue is a second one: what meanings do participants in such groups—and people outside them—give to their actions? And how do such meanings shape unfolding events that involve violence?

In accounting for violence, some scholars, as well as journalists and anticult activists, have emphasized the importance of internal movement traits. Others, both scholars and "cult apologists," have given more emphasis to external contextual factors. Today, most scholars recognize that neither internal nor external factors are typically causally sufficient in themselves, and that they usually interact to produce violent outcomes. Assuming such interaction and excluding one-sided explanations, we briefly describe three alternative explanatory approaches.

The first, a model proposed by psychiatrist Marc Galanter (1999), is based on analysis of the Peoples Temple, the Branch Davidians, and Heaven's Gate. It identifies three internal conditions that interact with one external contingency to increase the potential for violence: (1) the *isolation* of the group, (2) the *grandiosity and paranoia* of the leader, (3) the leader's *absolute dominion* over his followers, and (4) *government mismanagement* of interaction with the group. Geographic or behavioral isolation (a trait shared by many nonviolent communal sects) cuts the group and its leadership off from external feedback and monitoring of group actions, increasing the likelihood of extreme behavior by members operating exclusively on the basis of their own internally constructed definitions of situations. Such isolation may be reinforced by the second factor, grandiose paranoia of the leader, which conditions the third factor, a leader's effort to maintain absolute control over his movement. Galanter's external factor, government mismanagement, represents a rather broad category of public acts (and negligence). Most notably, violence can be provoked by undue aggressiveness and repression by state officials, or by the clumsiness of state intervention—for example, alleged blunders of the BATF and FBI in confronting the Davidians at Mt. Carmel (Hall, Schuyler, and Trinh 2000).

The second approach, advanced by Hall, Schuyler, and Trinh (2000), uses analysis of how apocalyptic meanings play out in unfolding historical time to compare incidents involving the Peoples Temple, the Branch Davidians, the Solar Temple, Aum Shinrikyo, and Heaven's Gate. The authors propose that an apocalyptic worldview, charismatic leadership, and strong solidarity heighten the potential for violence. However, actual violence is held to occur on the basis of distinctive cultural structures of apocalyptic meaning. Their analysis suggests two alternative ideal-typical trajectories. In a "warring apocalypse of religious conflict," a spiral of escalating tension emerges between a movement group and external opponents, the latter who succeed at recruiting journalists and government officials to their cause. In the alternative trajectory, a "mystical apocalypse of deathly transcendence" emerges if a retreatist "mystical" group such as Heaven's Gate elects collective suicide. From the group's perspective, it moves to an eternal realm of existence.

The third approach is David Bromley's model of "dramatic denouements" (2002). Bromley envisions movement–society conflicts as unfolding social interactions that potentially move through three stages: (1) latent tension, (2) nascent conflict, and (3) intensified conflict. At each stage the parties in conflict have the options of further contestation, accommodation, or retreat. Given the alternatives, most conflicts do not reach the high intensity that can trigger mass violence. However, if conflict does intensify, the contesting parties tend to radicalize, heightening their mobilization and seeking to form coalitions with third parties against an assumed common enemy, now perceived to be dangerous or sinister rather than merely troublesome. These conditions may yield a "dramatic denouement"—a climactic moment in which one or both parties embark on a decisive "project of final reckoning" intended to restore their sense of moral order. Such projects take the form of either (1) an exodus or collective withdrawal from the sphere of conflict (e.g., the Mormons' migrating from Illinois to unsettled Utah, the Peoples Temple relocating to Jonestown in tropical Guyana); or (2) a battle in which one or more contenders rejects the mutual existence of both parties and seeks to restore moral order through coercion. Either way, each side presumes moral superiority and repudiates the continued existence of both parties in the same social space.

Because all three of these approaches incorporate both internal and external types of factors, we now consider such factors in greater detail.

Internal Group Characteristics Facilitating Violence

Religious movements that become caught up in violence often share key features as social groups, including apocalypticism, charismatic leadership, totalistic organization, and internal conflict. After considering such features, we will briefly note the limitations of explanations based solely on group characteristics.

APOCALYPTICISM. Wessinger (1997) has analyzed apocalyptic expectations as embodying ideas of "catastrophic millennialism," in which evil is perceived as rampant in a world where everything is getting worse. For salvation and the elimination of evil, "the world as we know it has to be destroyed and created anew by God" (Wessinger 1997: 50; cf. Hall 1978: 68–82). Religious movements that become involved in violent episodes almost always promote millenarian or apocalyptic worldviews that call for participants to live extraordinary lives. Sometimes, apocalyptic movement participants may draw antinomian implications, in part because the posited end of the established order implies that received norms and institutions are not binding in the face of a "higher cause." Strongly apocalyptic movements also may anticipate that violence and persecution will be directed against their own group as the vanguard of the new order, and therefore go into a "survivalist" mode, stockpiling arms and engaging in paramilitary practices.

EXEMPLARY DUALISM. Anthony and Robbins (1978) have specified a basic motif that predominates in some apocalyptic movements. In what they term exemplary dualism, contemporary sociopolitical or socioreligious forces are perceived in terms of an absolute contrast between good and evil. Conflicts that might otherwise appear mundane become imbued with ultimate meaning. Thus, the besieged Branch Davidians regarded federal agents as the biblical Babylonians, or forces of darkness. Similarly, Constance Jones notes that Peoples Temple leader Jim Jones saw "the United States, its institutions, and even its standards of beauty... as the 'beast'—totally irredeemable—to be overcome by the redeeming remnant," thus preparing Temple members "for sacrifice, struggle, and an apocalyptic final showdown" (Jones 1989: 212). On quite a different front, Kaplan (2001: 491) argues, the extremist fringe of the antiabortion movement concluded that "abortion was symptomatic of the fact these were indeed the Last Days and that God's judgment on a fallen world was rapidly approaching."

Generally speaking, the actions of apocalyptic groups depend on how they position themselves in relation to apocalyptic time, and this positioning can shift over the course of a group's history. Some post-apocalyptic groups style themselves as having survived or otherwise escaped the apocalypse, to a "heaven-on-earth." But if movements position themselves before the apocalypse, they may seek to convert others to salvation before the end days, or they may prepare for struggle against "the Beast" (Hall 1978; Hall, Schuyler, and Trinh 2000). In the United States, Christian apocalyptic movements are usually theologically "premillennial," teaching that the Second Coming of Christ must precede the Millennial Kingdom because sinful humanity is not capable of creating the kingdom on it own. In the time of the "Tribulation," the tyrannical Antichrist will rule by violence until he is overthrown by Christ. Pre-Tribulationist pre-millennialists expect to be "raptured," or taken to Jesus before the Tribulation. By contrast, post-Tribulationists expect that their own salvation will come only after the Tribulation, which they must endure. This latter theology puts a premium on discipline, group cohesion, and preparation for violent conflict. Post-Tribulationist groups are more likely to be communal, totalist, paramilitarist, and "survivalist" (cf. Barkun 1997). Christian Identity fundamentalists, who adhere to racist beliefs demonizing Jews and degrading blacks, are equivalent to post-Tribulationists. They view the United States as already controlled by a demonic "Zionist occupation government," and "have no hope of supernatural escape via the rapture." Thus they stockpile "arms and supplies as they await the end" (Kaplan 2001: 483). At the extreme, a pre-apocalyptic religious movement may declare a "holy war" against the established order (Hall 2004a).

PROPHECY AND CHARISMATIC LEADERSHIP. To gain legitimacy with an audience, apocalyptic prophecies typically require a messianic prophet. Yet movements led by messianic prophets are often volatile because, as Max Weber observed, charismatic authority is inherently precarious, since it lacks written codes or customary practices and it depends on a charismatic leader's special "gift of grace," which may appear ephemeral. The unstable character of charisma has been said to increase the potential for violence. Thus, Johnson (1979) analyzes how Peoples Temple leader Jim Jones sensed his authority to be slipping, and how his responses led to new threats to his charisma. In a different way, Palmer (1996) has explained the decline of the Solar Temple on the basis of the diminishing charisma of the aging and quite possibly ill Joseph DiMambro.

Other research suggests that charismatic leaders may become unbalanced as their movements develop if they lack egalitarian interaction with colleagues who can provide critical feedback. They can also become isolated and thus may succumb more easily to dark impulses (Wallis and Bruce 1986). Charismatic leaders sometimes become distinctly authoritarian. In turn, Robert Lifton suggests, authoritarian gurus are psychologically sustained by "functional megalomania." The guru depends on the support of disciples to maintain his stability. His "self often teeters on the edge of fragmentation, paranoia, and overall psychological breakdown" (Lifton 1999: 13). Such breakdown of the leader's identity almost by definition increases volatility, though not necessarily violence.

Whatever we make of such arguments, it is important to keep in mind that charisma is not inevitably associated with violence; indeed, there have been very important nonviolent charismatic leaders such as Gandhi and Martin Luther King. Dawson (2002: 81) asserts that it is not charismatic leadership per se but rather its *mismanagement* that leads to dangerous volatility. This is a valid point, for there are multiple pathways by which charisma becomes routinized. However, it is also important to recognize, as Dawson acknowledges, that institutional mismanagement itself is ultimately "rooted in the problematic legitimacy of charisma" (2002: 81).

LACK OF INSTITUTIONALIZATION. Charismatic authority in its pure form is incompatible with institutional restraints on the arbitrary caprice of the leader. Almost by definition it resists accountability beyond its immediate audience.

Even within the range of accountibility within a group, members may gradually become conditioned to accept arbitrary and bizarre behavior on the part of their leader. These circumstances, Wallis and Bruce (1986) argue, weaken any constraints on deviant practices and even violence in movements with pronounced charismatic leadership—for example, Synanon, the Peoples Temple, and the Manson Family.

Volatility can also stem from a *lack of institutionalized supports* for charismatic leaders, who experience "a more or less permanent legitimation crisis" (Dawson 2002: 255). As charismatic movements institutionalize, they may develop an administrative staff that strives to expand its authority. The leader sometimes resists this tendency by "crisis mongering," thus keeping the movement in turmoil such that stable institutional structures cannot be consolidated.

However, institutionalization also may have the opposite effect, diminishing the movement's volatility. Comparing the ill-fated Peoples Temple with the controversial Unification Church, Galanter (1999: 121–25) argues that, although the latter movement experienced substantial tension at its boundaries, volatility was inhibited by both decentralization and the emergence of a middle-management cadre that insulated the rank and file from the impulsivity of the leader. Larger sects such as Scientology or the Unification Church have not become violent in part because they have developed bureaucratic structures that mute the impact of a leader's eccentricities. However, since the Peoples Temple developed both an administrative staff and a bureaucratic structure (Hall 2004b: chap. 6), such features in themselves clearly do not prevent violence.

TOTALISTIC ENCAPSULATION. The likelihood of violence may be enhanced by a totalistic organizational pattern, which tends to isolate participants from the broader society and insulate them from non-movement influences. According to Lifton (1999), encapsulated members may become "overcommitted" to the group. Sensational claims of cultist mind control tend to misrepresent this phenomenon, which seems better explained by the social situations that sects can set up. Totalist "milieu control" reinforces the arbitrary commands of the leader, which "encapsulated" participants cannot easily resist. Totalistic movements exert pressure on members to identify with the group and to conform to narrow group norms at the expense of wider cultural standards. As a researcher who studied the murderous Aum Shinrikyo cult suggests, when members become more committed to such a group, its religious authority rather than converts' earlier values increasingly guide their behavior (Pye 1996). Nonconforming members will generally defect or be expelled. Those who remain in a group weaken their extra-group ties and thus their potential "normative dissonance" (Mills 1982). In turn, inhibitions against extreme behavior may erode if such behavior is directed at stigmatized enemies of the group.

SOCIAL SYSTEM DYNAMICS. Overall, Galanter (1999) has argued, factors that increase the possibility of violence may be understood in relation to a theoretical framework that characterizes a religious movement as a social system. Galanter analyzes what he alternatively terms "cults" and "charismatic groups." Like any social system, such groups depend on fulfillment of key system functions such as boundary control, feedback, internal monitoring, and goal attainment. To be self-regulating, a group system requires an element of negative or critical feedback. However, in the short term, negative feedback may challenge group beliefs and thereby lead to the demoralization of members. There is thus in most functioning social groups a temptation to suppress negative feedback, even though such suppression would ultimately undermine the system. This contradiction—intrinsic to social systems—may be particularly potent in ideological groups, which necessarily put a premium on solidarity and consensus.

As social systems, religious movements often have a distinctive goal that organizes a good deal of group activity—making converts. Sometimes, however, a movement may become disinclined to pursue aggressive outreach, and it will shift efforts from outreach to internal monitoring and surveillance. This development often increases tension at the group's boundaries—that is through conflict with forces in the group's environment. The actions of religious communal movements such as the Peoples Temple that suddenly decamp and withdraw to an isolated retreat may both reflect and increase boundary tension. Hall (2004b: chap. 10) and Galanter (1999) argue that at Jonestown, growth in external monitoring of the Peoples Temple increased Jim Jones's paranoia and precipitated increased internal monitoring and security measures. Themes of apocalyptic doom became increasingly prominent. Negative feedback was more and more discouraged. The group's leadership increasingly worked to prevent penetration of the system's boundaries. Congressman Ryan, visiting in the company of journalists and the delegation of "concerned relatives," appeared to signal the disruption of the group's boundary control, and the events during this visit precipitated the final catastrophe.

Our survey of research analyzing internal factors demonstrates what Richardson (2001: 108–109) has observed, that "violence is usually viewed as a characteristic of group culture." Richardson, who is critical of this approach, characterizes it as "characterological." Perhaps its key explanatory weakness is that highlighted traits such as apocalypticism or charismatic leadership are shared by a significantly larger set of movements than the subset of violent groups. Thus, such explanations in and of themselves are insufficient. For this reason, it is important to consider other explanations.

PERSECUTION, EXTERNAL TENSIONS, AND RELATIONAL DYNAMICS. "Given the high level of tension with society under which some unconventional groups have been forced to operate," notes Gordon Melton, "it is not surprising that the violent tendencies of some cult leaders have emerged." Violence generally erupts, he continues, "only after a period of heightened conflict" in which "both sides" have contributed to escalation (1985: 57–58). Nor are the internal features of a group discussed above immune from external influence. Thus, in his analysis of the nineteenth-century Mormon Wars, Grant Underwood (2000: 55) maintains that persecution is the most vital factor "propelling a

movement to emphasize an apocalyptic rhetoric of judgment and ven-
geance. . . . Persecution is . . . the incubator of apocalypticism."

The role of external conflict and persecution in violent confrontations
has been explicitly theorized in interactionist accounts that explore the relational dynamics between movements and their environments. Scholars pursuing this line of analysis observe that new movements often engage in deviant
practices, both of religion and of lifestyle. They may employ unconventional
means to raise funds, recruit followers, maintain their organization, and defend themselves. In doing so they tend to attract negative reactions from
outsiders, which in turn increase tension. Thus, "violence is usually embedded
in the relationship between new religions and their opponents, and should not
be viewed as something necessarily inherent in the structure and organization
of either" (Richardson 2001: 22).

APOCALYPSE, RELIGIOUS CONFLICT, AND TRANSCENDENCE. Hall, Schuyler,
and Trinh's broadly interactionist analysis incorporates both internalist and
externalist considerations. To focus on explaining violence, the authors disavow
either apologetics or passing judgment. They identify two alternative apocalyptic cultural structures at work in the cases of Jonestown, the Branch Davidians,
Aum Shinrikyo, the Solar Temple, and Heaven's Gate. One is predominantly
external, the other, predominantly internal. According to their model of
"apocalyptic religious conflict," violence is especially likely in solidary apocalyptic groups. However, these widely shared features do not in themselves
explain the violence. Rather, violence tends to emerge out of escalating conflict between a group and external opponents situated within an encompassing
established social order. Alliances emerge between apostates and distraught
relatives and the broader cultural opponents of cults, who together work to
bring to their cause news reporters, government officials, and politicians. If a
movement's leaders perceive external challenges as threatening their legitimacy, their prophecy, and the very capacity for movement continuation, they
may refuse to submit to external definitions of reality or authority, strike out
violently against opponents, and then carry out a collective suicide.

Although there are differences in the specifics of how conflict with outsiders unfolds, the model offers a useful basis for understanding four cases:
the Peoples Temple, the Branch Davidians, Aum Shinrikyo, and the Solar
Temple. However, aspects of two cases do not approximate the model of apocalyptic conflict. In the Solar Temple, there was indeed external opposition, but
it "did not pose any imminent threat," and some believers undertook the
ritualized collective suicide that their leaders called "the Transit" months after
the initial carnage in which the leaders died. As for Heaven's Gate, the group
"did not direct any violence outward, and their deaths lacked any obvious
connection to external conflict" (Hall, Schuyler, and Trinh 2000: 12–14). As
Bromley (2002: 40) observes, the relative salience of internal and external
factors varies from case to case: "The Branch Davidians represent the best
example of the primacy of external factors and Heaven's Gate . . . the primacy of
internal factors." Using an inductive method, Hall and his colleague propose

an alternative cultural structure of apocalyptic meaning at work in the absence of strong external conflict. In what they term "a mystical apocalypse of deathly transcendence, . . . flight from the Apocalypse on Earth through the ritualized practice of collective suicide would supposedly achieve other-worldly grace." In this analysis, the Solar Temple reflects a mixture of cultural structures, with aspects of both apocalyptic conflict and mystical apocalyptic transcendence in evidence, while Heaven's Gate more closely approximates the latter structure alone (2000: 192; on Heaven's Gate, cf. Davis 2000).

DEVIANCE AMPLIFICATION AND DRAMATIC DENOUEMENTS. When controversial, novel, or esoteric movements become embroiled in conflict, they often are labeled or stigmatized. Some scholars have argued that such developments heighten the potential for violence. This process has been theorized using the interactionist concept of *deviance amplification*—a spiraling process of escalating hostility between a culturally deviant group and agents of the wider society. According to this theory, if both parties become enmeshed in escalating mutual recrimination, an explosive denouement is increasingly likely to ensue unless a process of de-amplification intervenes. Michael Barkun (1997) has applied this approach to conflicts involving Scientology and Christian Identity churches.

Explosive culminations of the spirals of deviance amplification are delineated in David Bromley's model of *dramatic denouements*, discussed above, as "those rare moments when antagonistic human groups seek extraordinary climactic clarity and closure" (2002: 40). Essential to dramatic denouements is the emergence of reciprocal stereotyping in which opponents depict cults as authoritarian, unstable, and naturally violent, while within NRMs, external social-control agents become viewed as inherently persecutory and repressive. Alarmist reciprocal stereotypes of "dangerous cults" and authoritarian repression push both controversial movements and official control agents, as well as "concerned citizens" and volunteer activists, toward increasingly apocalyptic outlooks (Bromley 2002; Hall, Schuyler, and Trinh 2000). Such polarization produces threatening acts, symbolic degradation of opponents, and further internal radicalization. In turn, Bromley argues, the movement relationship to the wider society is destabilized as a result of increased secrecy, the elimination of potentially mediating third parties, and organizational consolidation or fragmentation. If unchecked, conflict between a movement and elements of the wider social order reaches a point where one or both parties decide that their core identity is so threatened that dynamic action is necessary. The "dispute escalation" may now result in bloodshed, and a violent catastrophe is a possible outcome.

Bromley analyzed both instances of explosive escalation and the alternative outcome, accommodation. Although belligerent stereotypes enhance the likelihood of violence, beleaguered movements typically initiate some mode of accommodation "in response to both internal pressures toward a more settled lifestyle and contestation by oppositional and regulatory groups" (Bromley 2002: 24). Accommodating groups may eliminate, reduce, or mitigate provocative behaviors such as sexual experimentation, paramilitarism, and regimented totalism.

MOVEMENT FRAGILITY AND VIOLENCE. Catherine Wessinger (2000) argues that certain groups develop a condition of "fragility" that gives them a particular susceptibility to violent encounters. Although fragility might be regarded as an internal factor, it seems empirical that apocalyptic beliefs, charismatic leadership, totalistic organization, and other internal factors interact with external environmental pressures to produce fragility. Thus, what Wessinger terms "catastrophic millennialism" is generally linked to "radical dualism." Catastrophic millennialists see evil pervading the world, and often feel a strong imperative to confront and confound evil forces. But this is not simply a sentiment internal to apocalyptic religious movements. "The 1993 confrontation between the Branch Davidians and law enforcement agents involved dualistic thinking on both sides—the Branch Davidians regarded the federal agents as agents of demonic Babylon and FBI agents regarding Davidian leader David Koresh as a demonic criminal and con man." Radical dualism can easily slide into paranoia, and millenarian dualism can have "the effect of dehumanizing the other outside the group." In the midst of a fierce struggle, apocalyptic dualists may "even sanction the murder of those who are dehumanized" (Wessinger 2002: 133). Factors contributing to a movement's fragility may include intragroup dissidence; undermining of the leader's charisma or psychological stability; failure of the movement to attain its goals, including recruitment; traumatic key defections; and intensified tension at the group's boundary (external conflict). In Wessinger's view (2002: 222), this pattern is exemplified by the demise of the Order of the Social Temple.

The Relation between Internal and External Factors in Explanations of Violence

Both internal and external factors seem relevant to explaining violence connected with NRMs, including, in the trajectory of conflict, escalatory vs. accommodative outcomes. Today most scholars—in contrast to some journalists and activists—acknowledge that the two kinds of factors dynamically interact. Nevertheless, there are subtle differences in emphasis. For certain cases, sociologists such as Bromley, Hall, and Richardson have pointed to the salience of the external provocative societal response to stigmatized cults. However, as Massimo Introvigne comments in his study of the Solar Temple suicides, "when internal factors are sufficiently strong, even moderate opposition is transformed into a narrative of persecution" (Introvigne 2000: 157). Hall, Schuyler, and Trinh agree, directly pursuing the question raised by their analysis of the Solar Temple of whether there could be "religious mass suicide in the absence of apocalyptic confrontation" (2000: 148).

Interactionist concepts such as deviance amplification, stigmatization, apocalyptic religious conflict, and dramatic denouements remind us that violence is usually situationally contingent rather than structurally inevitable. It tends to be a product of the interaction of parties with partly conflicting or incompatible goals. However, occasionally, individuals and groups may act out violence with little in the way of environmental influences and regardless of the nuances of social response. To date, there is no single general explanation of violence associated with NRMs. Rather, multiple factors and trajectories have been identified.

Teaching about New Religious Movements and Violence

As we have seen, the issue of violence in new religious movements has provoked great public controversies and a diverse scholarship. There is also an abundance of accessible historical documents, videos, and other materials. Thus, the basic resources for teaching are at hand. Yet the controversies have consequences for the question of *how* to teach about religion and violence. On the one hand, teaching about violence requires sensitivity to students' preconceptions and feelings that the subject matter may bring to the surface. On the other hand, violence—broadly defined—is at the heart of many controversies about new religious movements and, considering the topic, can encourage students' development of critical thinking and analytic skills. Overall, the sensitivity of the issues and the scholarly debates around new religions and violence can raise existential challenges to students' identities and worldviews. Therefore, successful pedagogy depends on, first, a thoughtful philosophy of the classroom. On this basis, it is then possible to consider (1) framing the issue of violence, (2) topical themes, and (3) special pedagogical tools.

A Philosophy of Teaching about NRMs and Violence

Any course is more likely to succeed when a classroom atmosphere encourages students to engage in open discussion based on a standard of civic participation and respect for others. Students all too easily undergo a cognitive withdrawal if they regard an approach to a subject as threatening; or alternatively, they can be presumptuous about the truths they hold to be self-evident and other students can feel shut out (see the chapter by Eugene Gallagher in this volume). The trick, then, is to coax students out of the safe place of silence while acculturating them to civic norms of classroom discussion.

General exercises for courses on religion can be especially important when addressing a vexed topic such as violence. One simple exercise is to have students write down unsigned brief statements about their beliefs concerning religion and the divine, and then shuffle the answers and read them back to the class. Typically, students thereby confront the radical diversity of views existing among their peers.

A course instructor is also well served by setting several goals for a module or course on violence and NRMs. These goals can be divided into basic pedagogical ones and substantive goals related to the specific curriculum. *Basic goals* ought to be addressed early on:

- Get students to recognize how controversial the subject is.
- Have students examine their own preconceptions and stereotypes—for example, about cults.
- Teach students to read critically across authors and disciplines.

More *substantive goals* concern what knowledge and understandings are taken away from the course or module, and they thus ought to be mapped across the entire course or module.

- Consider the problem of how to define *violence* and understand how differences in definitions yield alternative understandings of violence that occurs in relation to NRMs.
- Demonstrate that different disciplines and intellectual approaches (for example, religious studies, history, psychology, and sociology) ask different questions, even about the "same" phenomenon of violence.
- Use historical and cross-cultural comparison to deepen students' understanding of how violence in relation to NRMs is connected to larger social structures and processes.
- Move beyond classifying theories and explanations of religious violence to evaluate empirically the specific mechanisms and processes they propose.
- Explore the question of whether violence is "intrinsic" to NRMs or, for that matter, religion more generally.
- Consider the issue of exceptionalism—that is, how and in what ways NRMs are highly unusual phenomena or, conversely, what parallels there are such that violence happens for similar reasons in relation to NRMs as it does elsewhere.

There are many ways for a course or module to meet these goals. Here, we propose possible strategies. For a successful course, the *basic* goals listed above require attention at the beginning; we therefore consider that a central framing issue be addressed early on. *Substantive* goals can then be approached via what we will call topical themes and pedagogical tools.

Framing the Issue of Violence

As Gallagher (this volume) points out, students often come to a course on NRMs bearing a "hermeneutic of suspicion" regarding cults. Violence often figures prominently in fueling this predisposition, and thus the study of violence offers a teaching moment for moving toward establishing a classroom atmosphere in which such a predisposition can be bracketed in the interests of open and rigorous discussion. Framing the issue of violence at the outset can encourage this shift.

Although defining *violence* might seem simple, it turns out to be a vexed task, for definitions of violence are often confounded with the question of whether violence is legitimate or not, and legitimacy is a social construction. The taking of another person's life has a different valence according to whether the killing is deemed murder, war, accident, self-defense, capital punishment, or negligence. Also, conceptions of violence are often culturally freighted, such that people operating within their own cultural framework do not regard certain actions (e.g., circumcision, spanking of children, foot-binding, dental braces) as violent, whereas similar actions outside their own culture will seem violent (Jackman 2001). Definitions are further confounded by questions about physical versus verbal or psychological violence, about whether desecration of sacred symbols is violence, about the threat of violence via intimidation, and about whether social manipulation constitutes violence.

Violence is a subject in its own right. However, it is also the basic framing topic for considering NRMs and violence. To initiate a course or module, one of three alternative devices might be used:

1. Propose a definition of *violence* and ask students to consider whether a given action qualifies as violence under the definition. One strategy would be to use Jackman's somewhat controversial definition that violence encompasses "actions that inflict, threaten, or cause injury." Violent *actions*, she continues, may be "corporal, written, or verbal," and the *injuries* may be "corporal, psychological, material, or social" (2001: 443).

2. Ask students to write an (unsigned) definition of *violence* that they think should be used in the course, then collect and redistribute the definitions, and discuss them. You can energize the discussion by drawing on conventional definitions that focus on physical harm to persons and, sometimes, property or by putting forward Jackman's definition.

3. Devise a list of actions that might occur in relation to a NRM, with checkboxes for "violent? no/yes," and "acceptable? no/yes." For example, the following items might be included:
   • Pressuring a nonmember to join group
   • Promising nonmember material/spiritual rewards for joining
   • Requiring public or private confession of actions against group rules or values
   • Giving public verbal chastisement to participant for wrongdoing
   • Publicly distributing written chastisement
   • Requiring isolation from friends as punishment
   • Performing mild physical punishment, such as spanking
   • Exerting social pressure on a member not to leave the group
   • Physically preventing a member from leaving the group
   • Engaging in voluntary self-chastisement
   • Engaging in voluntary infliction of physical pain to oneself
   • Providing opportunities for another person voluntarily to place himself or herself in physical danger, or even danger of death
   • Requiring or forcing another person to place himself or herself in physical danger, or even danger of death
   • Physically harming a member who fails to conform to group norms

- Physically harming an outside person who is engaged in a forceful attempt to remove a member from the group against the member's will

Ask students to complete the checklist. Collect and collate the responses, or simply engage the students in a discussion of the rationales for their answers, raising possible definitions of *violence* along the way.

With any of these exercises, lively discussion likely will bring students to understand the complexity of the issues. Major points from the discussion can be noted and used later as benchmarks that connect to teaching moments in the discussion of particular cases, theories, or explanations. The point ought not to be reaching any definitive conclusion but, rather, establishing a classroom atmosphere in which students can approach the question of violence in an intellectually open and honest way. In broader courses, it may be easy to connect the framing issue of violence to previous course discussions; in a stand-alone course on religion and violence, teaching moments should come to the fore in the subsequent treatment of topical themes.

Topical Themes

Classroom consideration of NRMs and violence is open to a variety of treatments, depending on the character of the course, the length of time devoted to the subject, the size of the class, and how course activities and assignments are organized. Here, we assume that the course has had an initial framing discussion about violence. In what follows, we lay out a general list of topical themes. You might decide to treat all the themes fully within a course or, in a shorter module, avoid trying to pack too much in and treat certain topical themes as preparatory, then focus on a particular theme. Whatever themes get treated, they need to be addressed in ways that bring in alternative scholarly viewpoints.

HISTORICAL AND COMPARATIVE PERSPECTIVES. Most students initially will not associate religion with violence, partly because they rarely have experienced such a correlation personally, as an understandable consequence of the relative containment of religion as a settled institutional pattern within (post)modern societies. It is therefore useful to initiate the study of religious movements and violence by raising, however briefly, historical and comparative cases. Hall's (2003) overview differentiates alternative types of violence associated with religion historically—for example, violence that occurs as an outcome of competition between religious groups—and the religious sanctification of violence undertaken by a colonial state or empire. Some kinds of violence—for example, psychological abuse of members—can occur in both institutionally settled religions and emergent religious movements. Most important for our purposes, emergent religious movements often come into both personal and institutional conflict with a wider society that sometimes results in violence—for example, struggles over the allegiance of group members, efforts by proclaimed agents of a society at large to regulate or suppress a movement, and religious-movement violence toward either the wider society or its own members.

There is a wealth of scholarship on historical and comparative cases (Candland 1992; Hall 2003). The key here is to draw on accessible and teachable studies. Of particular note, Brian Wilson's (1973) study of millennialism points to many instances of violence, while Robbins (2000) examines a case—the Old Believers in late seventeenth-century Russia—that has relevance for contemporary collective suicides. Walzer's (1965) classic study of the Protestant Reformation is replete with discussions of violence, and Behringer (1987/1997) provides one of many fascinating studies of witchcraft persecution. For cross-cultural comparison, Peter Partner (1997) offers a readable account of holy wars in Christianity and Islam. For North America specifically, studies about Mormons and their persecution is a useful historical case. With lectures (and possibly readings) on one or two such historical and comparative cases, an instructor can open students up to seeing seemingly familiar cases in a different light.

BASIC QUESTIONS ABOUT RELIGIOUS MOVEMENTS AND VIOLENCE. Having established some historical and comparative context for considering violence, the next pedagogical step is to lay out basic clusters of questions about violence and NRMs to keep in mind when exploring contemporary cases and explanations. Raising these questions does not require answering them, nor need it entail reference to specific readings or cases, except perhaps by example. Instead, the questions serve as benchmarks against which subsequent discussions of cases and explanations can be compared. Indeed, a simple and effective teaching strategy is to pose the questions to the students and have a freewheeling debate, perhaps asking students to link their views and arguments to discussions of historical and comparative cases. Three basic clusters of questions seem important to address:

1. For any particular kind of violence, is it something that happens more widely that also happens in NRMs? Or is it something quite distinctive to NRMs that is highly unlikely to happen outside such groups (and if so, why)? If such violence can be found more widely—for example, in more conventional kinds of religious groups or in other kinds of organizations—are there particular features of NRMs that make such violence more likely to happen in relation to NRMs? What features?

2. Are NRMs as a *general* category of social group especially prone to violence of a particular kind? If so, what are the features of NRMs that make them violence-prone? Or is violence relatively rare in NRMs? In other words, what is the overall rate of (a given type of) violence in NRMs?

3. Are there different types of NRMs, with some types having certain characteristics that make them especially likely to experience (a given type of) violence? Or do all NRMs share certain characteristics that make them equally prone to violence?

Raising these questions should accomplish two related pedagogical goals: first, to ensure that students consider violence associated with NRMs in relation to the overall universe of NRMs (and indeed, other kinds of both religious and nonreligious organizations), rather than sampling on the dependent variable by looking just at cases of NRM violence; and second, to openly consider the tremendous variation in NRMs and whether certain specific characteristics or types are associated with violence.

CONTEMPORARY CASES OF EXTREME VIOLENCE. Most undergraduates more readily address analytic and theoretic issues by studying particular cases, especially if the cases are already well known or situated within culturally familiar circumstances. Therefore, the comparative study of contemporary cases of violence works well as the core of a module or course on NRMs and violence. Given the substantial scholarship on contemporary cases, it is a relatively simple matter to pick two to five cases and develop an in-depth analysis of each. Using lectures alone, an instructor could treat one case per class meeting. Or, with discussion and supplementary course materials such as readings, videos, films, or tape recordings, the number of class meetings devoted to a particular case can be expanded. Indeed, it would be possible to base an entire course on core discussions of two or three cases of violence—for example, using materials on the Peoples Temple and Jonestown (Hall 2004b; http://jonestown .sdsu.edu), the Branch Davidians (Wright 1995); the Solar Temple (Lewis 2005); or Aum Shinrikyo (Reader 2000b). Alternatively, a survey of cases can employ one of the comparative studies—for example, Wessinger (2000) or Hall, Schuyler, and Trinh (2000).

ALTERNATIVE EXPLANATIONS OF VIOLENCE. It is relatively easy to layer onto the comparative study of contemporary cases discussion of how to account for violence. Indeed, most of the case studies and comparative works explicitly or implicitly advance explanations, and thus consideration of cases ought to address what the explanations are and whether they accord with evidence. For large-scale violence, the central issue considered in the literature—discussed in the first part of this chapter—concerns the importance of *internal* propensities of NRM groups (e.g., charismatic leadership, apocalyptic ideology, group fragility) versus *external* factors (including violence or proto-violence against a group) versus *interactive* processes. One way to draw students out concerning alternative explanations is to ask them whether any given factor is *necessary* (the violence would not happen without the presence of this factor, though this factor alone might not bring violence about) or *sufficient* (this factor in itself makes violence virtually inevitable). In these discussions, the instructor can provoke debate by introducing as examples groups that possess certain characteristics without violence occurring (e.g., the highly apocalyptic Shakers, or groups with failed prophecy and no violence, or NRMs such as Scientology that experience very strong cultural opposition from society at large without becoming violent).

PERSISTING AND EMERGING ISSUES. Beyond the topical themes considered so far, there are a number of issues that might be considered to conclude a course or module on NRMs and violence. Because these themes go beyond widely cited scholarship, an instructor could simply raise them briefly in a concluding lecture, drawing on recent relevant scholarly or news publications. Four issues seem particularly worth raising:

1. Millennialism. In popular culture, especially popular religious culture, calendrical time is often pegged to apocalyptic events that are depicted as violent. Has this sort of expectation been borne out? For example, was the millennial moment of 2001 associated with violence in NRMs? Is or is not calendrical time important? Why?

2. Temporal variation. The incidents of large-scale violence associated with NRMs in the industrialized world seem to ebb and flow. Are there factors (such as the degree of competition among religions, the maturing and institutionalization of NRMs, the erosion of the anti-cult movement, and institutional learning of both NRMs and state authorities) that explain variation in the number of incidents of violence over time?

3. Historicity and globalization. Although many of the relatively recent benchmark cases of violence connected with NRMs happened within industrial countries in North America, Europe, and Japan, a number of other societies also have experienced either persecution of NRMs (e.g., Falun Gong in China and evangelizing sects in Russia), violence within NRMs (e.g., the Movement for the Restoration of the Ten Commandments in Uganda in 2000), or other kinds of violence (e.g., violence as a tool of competition between emerging sects in China; see Kahn 2004). Thus, the question arises: is violence associated with NRMs connected to broader historical dynamics of social change? (See the chapter by Lorne Dawson in this volume.)

4. Religion and terrorism. Especially in the wake of the 9/11 terrorist attacks, a multidisciplinary debate has intensified about the relation between religion—notably Islam—and terrorism (Appleby 2000; Hall 2004a; Juergensmeyer 2000; Lifton 2003; Lincoln 2003). However, many political scientists and sociologists remain skeptical that religion has anything to do with terrorism per se. Thus, a course on NRMs and violence might consider whether its discussions yield insights into contemporary "religious terrorism."

Pedagogical Tools

By exploring topical themes, we have sought to show a way that various aspects of a discussion of violence and NRMs can be arrayed. Each of the themes just considered is open to relatively brief treatment or expansive development. Yet effective teaching requires aligning themes with a packaged set of readings and class activities that consolidate the module or course.

Bundling materials and activities for a course or module on NRMs and violence is not a radically different pedagogical project from other kinds of course preparation. The key matter concerns how to array a mix of lectures, discussions, exercises, readings, media screenings, and other course activities in relation to a set of course meetings. We have already discussed how to frame a course and its thematic content. Here we simply add to that mix several specific ideas about course materials and activities.

READINGS. Readings, of course, ought to be a central feature of college courses. Given today's student, the challenge is to include academic writings that challenge students intellectually while not putting them off by abstract or stilted style. Analytic discussion of actual events "on the ground" is the typical focus of a course on violence, and this orientation easily engages students. Given the range in quality of writings about NRMs—especially popular writings—the most formidable challenge here is to educate students in their critical use. The choice of required and suggested readings for a course will set the tone. However, if students are asked to conduct independent library research, they typically select various nonscholarly books and articles—ones that an instructor might well regard as *objects* of analysis (e.g., a book titled *Evil Web: A True Story of Cult Abuse and Courage*) rather than *research* studies. Nonacademic writings can be useful, but they often need to be treated as data rather than analysis—that is, as historical and cultural materials that are objects of study.

One effective way to structure students' elective reading selections is to ask them, for any paper or project, to develop an initial list of *analytic scholarly sources*, defined as books published by university presses (and major academically oriented presses) and scholarly journals that include footnotes or references. Just getting students to make this distinction can be a major task and achievement! Yet the goal should hardly be to exclude nonacademic writings. There is now a wealth of materials generated from: personal experiences, the increasing bureaucratic orientation of many NRMs, litigation, news coverage, the public controversies, and interests in documentary, docudrama, and other types of narrative engagements with the subject of NRMs and violence. More than many other subjects, then, the study of NRMs and violence lends itself to using a variety of materials, including:

- NRM documents about theology, eschatology, organization, history, etc., as well as more time- and event-related documents ranging from newsletters to letters to editors, court documents, and correspondence
- Family- and cultural-opponent documents, including both general ones and those concerning specific groups and conflicts with those groups
- Newspaper articles
- Official reports by government bodies, associations, and the like
- Films and television programs, sometimes available on CD

Often, such materials can be found on the Internet (see the chapter by Douglas Cowan in this volume).

CASE-STUDY ARCHIVAL ANALYSIS. Another useful pedagogical tool is to provide students with a set of archival documents about a particular group, and then ask them to analyze and discuss the documents, either in a short paper or in a classroom discussion. This exercise requires students to step outside their own preconceptions and approach an issue with a fresh mind, so it is best used before students read scholarly discussions of the group. The instructor then can follow up with scholarly readings and engage the students in relating the archival evidence to the readings.

The key to success with such an exercise is to find a good set of archival materials about a particular incident of violence. Fortunately, one Web site, "Alternative Considerations of Jonestown and Peoples Temple" (http://jones town.sdsu.edu), features an on-line archive of primary sources and tape recordings transcripts under its "About Jonestown" link.

A FILM/DISCUSSION UNIT. Popular films are of interest for how they represent violence associated with NRMs (for the general issue of NRM public images, see the chapter by Richardson and Introvigne in this volume). Although showing a DVD early in the course is probably not a good idea, using one after basic analytic issues have been raised can help concretize discussion. There are two possibilities widely available through video stores or on-line via a Google search. The more analytically respectable film is the documentary *Waco: The Rules of Engagement* (1997). By contrast, *Guyana Tragedy* (1980), with a cast that includes Powers Boothe, James Earl Jones, and Meg Foster, is a popularized dramatic rendering of the murders and mass suicide at Jonestown.

REALISTIC SCENARIOS. A useful way to draw students into a discussion of societal responses to concerns about violence in NRMs is to organize a classroom exercise in which students play social roles in relation to a fictional but realistic situation. For example, an instructor might hold a "dangerous cult" exercise. In it, students are told that a number of members of a shadowy cult known as God's Chosen Few have committed suicide at their isolated compound in Idaho. Students are then appointed to competing FBI task forces, each given a mandate to define a "dangerous cult" to distinguish it from other kinds of religious organizations and come up with plans for dealing with such groups, including whether and how they should be monitored, by whom, when intervention should be carried out, and by whom. Students from the different task forces then report on their conclusions and discuss them with other teams. Similar exercises could be designed based on scenarios involving distraught parents whose children have joined an NRM that they believe is drifting toward violence, or members of an NRM who feel themselves persecuted by outsiders.

Conclusion

Use of the teaching strategies and pedagogical tools described above will vary according to course or module length, enrollment, and other considerations, but given the controversial issues explored in the first part of this chapter, we think that a variety of course activities ought to be included, and even lectures should be done in a format that encourages questions and discussion. Perhaps students will become inspired to a sociological imagination about religion, and even pursue the further study of these complex processes. We certainly hope so.

REFERENCES

Anthony, Dick, and Thomas Robbins. 1978. "The Effect of Detente on the Growth of New Religions: Reverend Moon and the Unification Church." In *Understanding New Religions*, ed. Jacob Needleman and George Baker, 80–100. New York: Seabury.

———. 1995. "Religious Totalism, Violence, and Exemplary Dualism." *Terrorism and Political Violence* 7, 10–50.

———. 1997. "Religious Totalism, Exemplary Dualism, and the Waco Tragedy." In *Millennium, Messiahs, and Mayhem*, ed. Thomas Robbins and Susan Palmer, 161–84. New York: Routledge.

Appleby, R. Scott. 2000. *The Ambivalence of the Sacred: Religion, Violence, and Reconciliation*. Lanham, MD: Rowman & Littlefield.

Barkun, Michael. 1997. "Millenarians and Violence: The Christian Identity Movement." In *Millennium, Messiahs, and Mayhem*, ed. Thomas Robbins and Susan Palmer, 247–60. New York: Routledge.

Behringer, Wolfgang. 1987/1997. *Witchcraft Persecutions in Bavaria: Popular Magic, Religious Zealotry, and Reason of State in Early Modern Europe*. Cambridge, UK: Cambridge University Press.

Bromley, David. 2002. "Dramatic Denouements." In *Cults, Religions, and Violence*, ed. David G. Bromley and J. Gordon Melton, 11–41. Cambridge, UK: Cambridge University Press.

———. 2004. "New Religious Movements and Episodes of Collective Violence." In *Oxford Handbook of New Religious Movements*, ed. James Lewis, 143–62. New York: Oxford University Press.

Bromley, David G., and J. Gordon Melton. 2002. "Violence and Religion in Perspective." In *Cults, Religion, and Violence*, ed. David G. Bromley and J. Gordon Melton, 1–10. Cambridge, UK: Cambridge University Press.

Candland, Christopher. 1992. *The Spirit of Violence: An Interdisciplinary Bibliography of Violence and Religion*. New York: Harry Frank Guggenheim Foundation.

Davis, Winston. 2000. "Heaven's Gate: A Study in Religious Obedience." *Nova Religio* 3, 241–67.

Dawson, Lorne. 1998. *Comprehending Cults: The Sociology of Religious Movements*. Toronto: Oxford University Press.

———. 2002. "Crises of Charismatic Legitimacy and Violent Behavior in New Religious Movements." In *Cults, Religion, and Violence*, ed. David G. Bromley and J. Gordon Melton, 80–101. Cambridge, UK: Cambridge University Press.

Galanter, Marc. 1999. *Cults: Faith, Healing, and Coercion*, rev. ed. New York: Oxford University Press.

Hall, John R. 1978. *The Ways Out: Utopian Communal Groups in an Age of Babylon*. London: Routledge and Kegan Paul.

———. 2000a. "The Apocalypse at Jonestown." In *Apocalypse Observed*, ed. John Hall, Philip Schuyler, and Salvaine Trinh, 49–75. New York: Routledge.

————. 2000b. "From Jonestown to Waco." In *Apocalypse Observed*, ed. John Hall, Philip Schuyler, and Salvaine Trinh, 15–44. New York: Routledge.

————. 2003. "Religion and Violence: Social Processes in Comparative Perspective." In *Handbook for the Sociology of Religion*, ed. Michele Dillon, 359–81. Cambridge, UK: Cambridge University Press.

————. 2004a. "Apocalypse 9/11." In *New Religious Movements in the Twenty-First Century: Legal, Political, and Social Challenges in Global Perspective*, ed. Phillip C. Lucas and Thomas Robbins, 265–82. London: Routledge.

————. 2004b. *Gone from the Promised Land: Jonestown in American Cultural History*, 2nd ed. New Brunswick, NJ: Transaction.

Hall, John R., and Philip Schuyler. 1998. "Apostasy, Apocalypse, and Religious Violence." In *The Politics of Religious Apostasy*, ed. David G. Bromley, 141–70. Greenwood, CT: Praeger.

————. 2000. "The Mystical Apocalypse of the Solar Temple." In *Apocalypse Observed*, ed. John R. Hall, Philip Schuyler, and Salvaine Trinh, 111–49. New York: Routledge.

Hall, John R., Philip Schuyler, and Salvaine Trinh. 2000. *Apocalypse Observed: Religious Movements in North America, Europe, and Japan*. New York: Routledge.

Introvigne, Massimo. 2000. "The Magic of Death: The Suicide of the Solar Temple." In *Millennialism, Persecution, and Violence*, ed. Catherine Wessinger, 287–321. Syracuse, NY: Syracuse University Press.

Introvigne, Massimo, and Jean Francois Mayer. 2002. "Occult Masters and the Temple of Doom." In *Cults, Religion, and Violence*, ed. David G. Bromley and J. Gordon Melton, 170–88. Cambridge, UK: Cambridge University Press.

Jackman, Mary R. 2001. "License to Kill: Violence and Legitimacy in Expropriative Social Relations." In *The Psychology of Legitimacy: Emerging Perspectives on Ideology, Justice, and Intergroup Relations*, ed. John T. Jost and Brenda Major, 437–67. New York: Cambridge University Press.

Johnson, Doyle P. 1979. "Dilemmas of Charismatic Leadership." *Sociological Analysis* 40, 315–23.

Jones, Constance. 1989. "Exemplary Dualism and Authoritarianism at Jonestown." In *New Religious Movements, Mass Suicide, and the Peoples Temple*, ed. Rebecca Moore and Fielding McGhee, 209–30. New York: Edwin Mellen Press.

Juergensmeyer, Mark. 2000. *Terror in the Mind of God: The Global Rise of Religious Violence*. Berkeley: University of California Press.

Kahn, Joseph. 2004. "Violence Taints Religion's Solace for China's Poor." *New York Times*, November 25.

Kaplan, Jeffrey. 1995. "Absolute Rescue." *Terrorism and Political Violence* 7, 128–63.

————. 2001. "The Roots of Religious Violence in America." In *Misunderstanding Cults*, ed. Benjamin Zablocki and Thomas Robbins, 478–514. Toronto: University of Toronto Press.

Lewis, James R. 2005. "The Solar Temple 'Transits': Beyond the Millennialist Hypothesis." In *Controversial New Religions*, ed. James R. Lewis and Jesper Aagaard Petersen, 295–317. New York: Oxford University Press.

Lifton, Robert. 1999. *Destroying the World to Save It: Aum Shinrikyo, Apocalypticism, and the New Global Terrorism*. New York: Holt.

————. 2003. *Superpower Syndrome: America's Apocalyptic Confrontation with the World*. New York: Thunder's Mouth Press.

Lincoln, Bruce. 2003. *Holy Terrors: Thinking about Religion after September 11*. Chicago: University of Chicago Press.

Maaga, Mary. 1998. *Hearing the Voices of Jonestown*. Syracuse, NY: Syracuse University Press.

Melton, J. Gordon. 1985. "Violence and the Cults." *Nebraska Humanist* 8, 51–61.

Melton, J. Gordon, and David G. Bromley. 2002a. "Challenging Misconceptions about the New Religions-Violence Connection." In *Cults, Religion, and Violence*, ed. David G. Bromley and J. Gordon Melton, 42–56. Cambridge, UK: Cambridge University Press.

———. 2002b. "Lessons from the Past, Perspective for the Future." In *Cults, Religion, and Violence*, ed. David Bromley and J. Gordon Melton, 229–44. Cambridge, UK: Cambridge University Press.

Mills, Edgar. 1982. "Cult Extremism." In *Violence and Religious Commitment*, ed. Kenneth Levi, 75–87. University Park: Pennsylvania. State University Press.

Palmer, Susan. 1996. "Purity and Danger in the Solar Temple." *Journal of Contemporary Religion* 11, 303–18.

Partner, Peter. 1997. *God of Battles: Holy Wars of Christianity and Islam*. New York: HarperCollins.

Pye, Michael. 1996. "Aum Shinrikyo." *Religion* 26, 261–70.

Reader, Ian. 2000a. "Imagined Persecution: Aum Shinrikyo, Millennialism, and the Legitimation of Violence." In *Millennialism, Persecution, and Violence*, ed. Catherine Wessinger, 158–84. Syracuse, NY: Syracuse University Press.

———. 2000b. *Religious Violence in Contemporary Japan: The Case of Aum Shinrikyo*. Honolulu: University of Hawaii Press.

———. 2002. "Dramatic Confrontations: Aum Shinrikyo against the World." In *Cults, Religion, and Violence*, ed. David G. Bromley and J. Gordon Melton, 189–208. Cambridge, UK: Cambridge University Press.

Richardson, James. 2001. "Minority Religions in the Context of Violence." *Terrorism and Political Violence* 13, 103–33.

Robbins, Thomas. 2000. "Apocalypse, Persecution, and Self-Immolation." In *Millennialism, Persecution, and Violence*, ed. Catherine Wessinger, 205–219. Syracuse, NY: Syracuse University Press.

———. 2002. "Volatility in Religious Movements." In *Cults, Religion, and Violence*, ed. David G. Bromley and J. Gordon Melton, 57–79. Cambridge, UK: Cambridge University Press.

Robbins, Thomas, and Dick Anthony. 1995. "Sects and Violence: Factors Enhancing the Violence of Marginal Religious Movements." In *Armageddon in Waco*, ed. Stuart Wright, 236–59. Chicago: University of Chicago Press.

Selengut, Charles. 2003. *Sacred Fury: Understanding Religious Violence*. Walnut Creek, CA: Altamira Press.

Singer, Margaret, and Janja Lalich. 1995. *Cults in Our Midst*. San Francisco: Jossey-Bass.

Storrs, Anthony. 1997. *Feet of Clay: A Study of Gurus*. New York: Free Press.

Strozier, Charles. 1994. *Apocalypse: On the Psychology of Fundamentalism*. Boston: Beacon Press.

Tabor, James, and Eugene Gallagher. 1995. *Why Waco? Cults and the Battles for Religious Freedom in America*. Berkeley: University of California Press.

Underwood, Grant. 2000. "Millennialism, Persecution, and Violence: The Mormons." In *Millennialism, Persecution, and Violence*, ed. Catherine Wessinger, 43–61. Syracuse, NY: Syracuse University Press.

Wallis, Roy, and Steve Bruce. 1986. "Sex, Violence and Religion." In *Sociological Theory, Religion, and Collective Action*, ed. Roy Wallis and Steve Bruce, 115–27. Belfast: Queens University.

Walzer, Michael. 1965. *The Revolution of the Saints: A Study in the Origins of Radical Politics.* Cambridge, MA: Harvard University Press.

Wessinger, Catherine. 1997. "Millennialism with and without Mayhem." In *Millennialism, Messiahs, and Mayhem,* ed. Thomas Robbins and Susan Palmer, 47–60. New York: Routledge.

———. 2000. *How the Millennium Comes Violently: From Jonestown to Heaven's Gate.* New York: Seven Bridges.

———. 2002. "New Religious Movements and Conflicts with Law Enforcement." In *New Religious Movements and Religious Liberty in America,* ed. Derek Davis and Barry Hankins, 89–106. Waco, TX: Baylor University Press.

Wilson, Bryan. 1973. *Magic and the Millennium.* London: Heinemann.

Wright, Stuart, ed. 1995. *Armageddon in Waco.* Chicago: University of Chicago Press.

———. 2002. "Public Agency Involvement in Government-Religious Confrontations." In *Cults, Religion, and Violence,* ed. David G. Bromley and J. Gordon Melton, 102–122. Cambridge, UK: Cambridge University Press.

PART III

Resources for Teaching New Religious Movements

Responding to Resistance in Teaching about New Religious Movements

Eugene V. Gallagher

In discussing how the mass media "manufactured consent" about David Koresh and the Branch Davidians during and after the deadly fifty-one-day siege of the Mount Carmel Center in 1993, James T. Richardson observed that "the media are the most significant mediating structure between the mass public and marginal religions" (1995: 156). The general popularity of media stories about "destructive cults" reinforces a "subtle feedback loop" that not only shapes general public opinion but also influences the tacit expectations that students bring to the study of new religious movements (NRMs; Shupe and Hadden 1995: 194). In the spring semester of 2004, one of my students gave colloquial expression to the pervasiveness of the dominant anti-cult narrative when he reacted to reading a scholarly analysis of the Branch Davidians by acknowledging that "prior to reading the book, I shared the same sentiments as millions—that David Koresh was a few beers short of a 30-pack" (Macy 2004). As that comment suggests, the widespread credibility granted to the common anti-cult narrative poses a distinctive, but not unique, challenge to those who teach about new religious movements.

I have worked at a small liberal arts college and taught a course on new religious movements in the United States virtually every year since 1980. In my experience, most students arrive in class already equipped with a simple but powerful interpretive framework. Much more frequently than in other courses in the study of religion, they come prepared to exercise early and vigorously a pre-theoretical "hermeneutic of suspicion" that inclines them to discount the sincerity, seriousness, and even sanity of those whom they will be studying. Like many in the general public, they "know" that leaders of "cults" are not "really" religious but rather power-mad and psychologically unstable master manipulators who seek only their own benefit. They also "know" that those who join "cults" cannot have done so with a full understanding and deep appreciation of what they were getting into but must instead have been lost or aimless individuals who were particularly vulnerable to a wily leader. Finally, they also "know" that little if any good can come of "cult" membership and that those who join are liable to suffer personal harm or even do harm to others. In short, most students come to the study of new religious movements with a set of assumptions that conform very closely to the standard alarmist portrait of cults presented by prominent anti-cult activists like Steven Hassan, Rick Ross, and Margaret Singer (Hassan 2000; Ross 2004; Singer 1995).

The general anti-cult stereotype reaches students through a variety of channels, including popular entertainment media. Students have frequently asked me, for example, if I was familiar with Adam Sandler's portrait of cult life in "Joining the Cult," from his CD *What the Hell Happened to Me?* In that piece, three weeks after Sandler persuades a friend to join a cult led by "Russell" with the promise of free clothes, free food, and free haircuts, not to mention "hot girls," the following exchange ensues. When Sandler asks his friend if his decision has made him happy, his friend replies that it is the best thing he ever did. But Sandler then ups the ante by asking his friend if he harbors any anger at the cult for making him kill his father. With unshakable faith, his friend replies that it was, of course, the only way to save his father. Such bits of popular culture prepare students to expect the study of new religious movements to provide high entertainment value but also make them less likely to expect genuine spiritual insight, carefully considered commitment, or ideals whose value is worth serious contemplation. Students do not typically arrive in class prepared to take new religious movements seriously, *on their own terms.*

Students' resistance to taking new, alternative, or marginal religions seriously leads them to short-circuit the processes of analyzing and interpreting others' religious experience by preemptively dismissing the subjects' own self-understandings. Wayne Proudfoot, however, has insisted that "where it is the subject's experience which is the object of study, that experience must be identified under a description that can plausibly be attributed to him" (1985: 195). But the standard anti-cult narrative does not offer a description of their religious experience that members of new or alternative religious groups typically find plausible and therefore fails to meet Proudfoot's basic test of descriptive adequacy. Thus, the particular pedagogical challenge for those who teach about new religions is to develop teaching strategies, readings, and other assignments that encourage students to accept, at least provisionally, the notion that "the subject's self-ascription is normative for describing the experience" (Proudfoot 1985: 194) and to endeavor to describe that self-understanding in its full complexity.

Other than this volume, there are no sustained treatments of the particular challenges of teaching in college classrooms about new religious movements. But the phenomenon of student resistance to taking certain subjects seriously is certainly not limited to the study of new religious movements. The extensive literature on race and multiculturalism in the classroom, for example, frequently addresses the topic of student resistance (Tuitt 2003; Wlodowski and Ginsburg 1995) and the literature on discussion as a way of learning offers multiple suggestions about how carefully constructed and managed class discussions can prompt students to recognize and take seriously differences of many sorts (Brookfield and Preskill 1999). Nor is the damaging impact of stereotypes limited to the study of new religious movements or even to the broader study of religion. Particularly when a course addresses subject matter unfamiliar to most college students, teachers frequently encounter implicit expectations that obstruct rather than facilitate students' understanding of the material at hand.

Those concerned with teaching about diversity or multiculturalism issues have been at the forefront in fashioning pedagogical strategies that challenge students to recognize, consider critically, and reformulate the implicit assumptions that they bring to the classroom (Fox 2001; Tuitt 2003). Within the academic study of religion, those teaching the religions of Africa, for example, have long noted how students' implicit expectations of the material have posed serious impediments to their efforts (Hackett 1993), and similar concern has been directed to the teaching of Islam, both at the college and K–12 levels (Alavi 2001; Douglas 2000).

Some scholars have also emphasized that distorting presuppositions may not only be held by students but may also be constitutive of the academic study of religion itself. Miriam Peskowitz, for example, has argued that "the problem is a culture that even though well meaning is one in which a white Protestant ethos is still hegemonic and Christianity's others cannot feel welcome" (1997: 716). A powerful set of expectations, some implicit and some more explicit, are thus arrayed against taking new religious movements seriously as expressions of human religious life. First, there is the pervasive fear of destructive "cults," instigated by the efforts of anti-cult activists, fueled by spectacular incidents involving a handful of groups, validated by largely uncritical repetition in the news media, and augmented by caricatures in popular entertainment where exotic others are often presented as targets of humor. Second, there is the widespread failure of K–12 education in the United States to devote sustained attention to the academic study of religion. As one observer lamented, "everywhere, the curriculum fails to take religion seriously" (Beauchamp 2002: 4). That failure leaves most college and university students unprepared to engage in the academic study of religion and inclined to see the study of religion as something quite different from their study of literature, history, science, or art. Students have typically had little practice or training in studying religion as a human phenomenon.

If "most resistance appears to stem from apprehensions about vulnerability or control" (Wlodowski and Ginsburg 1995: 59) and "student resistance says more about self-perceptions" (Weimer 2002: 152), the reluctance of students to take new religious movements seriously becomes more understandable. Most students simply arrive at college without the extensive training in the study of religion that they have had in history and English, for example. That such lack of preparation could produce uncertainty or apprehensiveness about how to address religious phenomena, especially new, marginal, alternative or otherwise unconventional religions, in academic terms is entirely understandable. The standard anti-cult narrative, so aggressively marketed by many of its media-savvy proponents, stands ready to offer students a simple and easily applied interpretative approach to unfamiliar material. By filling a vacuum, it can reduce any anxiety they might experience about making sense of new material. In three simple steps—the leader is a nut; the followers are sheep; and they are all in harm's way—the anti-cult caricature allows students to convert the challengingly unknown into the comfortably known. Finally, the inherent tendency of the academic study of religion, as a discipline, to take Protestant Christianity as a model for all religion also complicates efforts in the classroom to take many new religious movements seriously *as religions* and not as doctrinal deviations or entertaining or frightening curiosities.

In what follows I will draw some suggestions from the general literature on teaching and learning, discussions of race and diversity in the classroom, and observations about teaching the academic study of religion to sketch out some pedagogical resources and strategies for teaching about new religious movements in ways that can overcome or at least mitigate student resistance to taking them seriously as "irreducible experiments in being human" (Chidester 1988: 1). I will first discuss the systematic application of methodological belief as a strategy for getting students to uncover what participants in new religious movements find meaningful, satisfying, and even compelling about their religious lives. Next, following the lead of many scholars on race, class, and gender, I will focus on the roles that analysis of rhetoric can play in facilitating the understanding both of new religious movements and the social opposition to them. In that section I will also examine the role of the teacher as a facilitator and participant in the cooperative construction of meaningful knowledge in the classroom. Finally, I will address more directly the actual practice of teaching about new religious movements. Although my comments will focus on teaching about new religious movements within the context of the academic study of religion, they may have usefulness in other disciplinary contexts as well. They may even have broader applicability since, in a sense, the entire contemporary cult controversy can be conceived as a teaching enterprise. In public discourse about cults, commentators strive to address specific audiences and inform them, sway their opinions, and provoke them to action. Much of that teaching is carried out in the pages of newspapers and popular magazines, on Web sites and electronic discussion lists, and on television and radio. Virtually none of it is informed by careful consideration of pedagogical goals, practices, and values, but all of it contributes to the assumptions that students bring to the classroom. Academic teaching about new religious movements thus needs also to be aware that it does not hold a monopoly on the teaching enterprise, even as it seeks to ground itself in approaches and strategies that promote accurate, deep, and lasting learning that has a significant impact on students who recognize its value in their own lives (Fink 2003).

Doubting and Believing

The central challenge in teaching about new religious movements is students' predisposition not to take them seriously on their own terms as religions. Although that pre-theoretical interpretive bias has been nourished by the mass media, it also finds support in the central roles that skepticism, critique, and dis-assembly play in academic discourse. But Peter Elbow has argued that although the pervasive academic employment of a hermeneutic of suspicion, which he traces to Descartes' efforts to establish a solid methodological base "by trying systematically to doubt *everything*," has frequently yielded deep insights and new knowledge, such "methodological doubting" needs to be balanced by an equally rigorous process of "methodological believing" (1986). He proposes that "thinking is not trustworthy unless it also includes methodological belief: the equally systematic, disciplined, and conscious attempt to believe everything no matter how unlikely or repellent it might seem-to find virtues and strengths we might otherwise miss" (Elbow 1986: 257). Where methodological doubting distances its practitioners from the material at hand, exposes flaws and weaknesses, and uncovers hidden assumptions, biases, and interests, methodological believing can connect its practitioners to the material, reveal strengths and insights, and identify new perspectives, connections, and values. Elbow suggests that methodological belief can be employed "to find a valid sense in words, . . . to transmit an experience, [to] enlarge a vision" (1986: 278, 261). He refers to both methodological doubt and methodological belief as constituting "games," emphasizing that both are approaches that can be tried out on the material at hand "in a casual, exploratory, heuristic way" or temporary stances that can be adopted to see what they might yield. But they are not necessarily permanent commitments to maintain a particular viewpoint beyond its methodological uses. In short, both games invite their participants to entertain, seriously but for a limited time, a range of possibilities and to enter imaginatively into another world. Elbow's methodological belief, then, is one way of meeting Proudfoot's criterion of descriptive adequacy, of describing a religious experience in terms that could plausibly be attributed to the subject.

When playing the believing game, Elbow suggests that participants pose such questions as "what's interesting or helpful about the view? What are some intriguing features that others might not have noticed? What would you notice if you believed this view? If it were true? In what senses or under what conditions might this idea be true?" (1986: 275).

Elbow is fully aware, however, that practicing methodological belief is not necessarily an easy task. He observes that "the believing game is *harder* to learn in debates or discussions where people are already too invested or polarized into dug-in positions. It is also harder to use (at first, anyway) on issues where it looks as though there is a single, "correct" answer to be had: people are too likely to feel they are being asked to entertain views which can be 'proved' wrong" (Elbow 1986: 274). Such cautions would also be appropriate for those teaching about new religious movements. Although students' acceptance of the standard anti-cult argument tends to be broad but shallow, those who have had some sort of personal experience (e.g., through near or distant family members or friends) are liable to endorse that argument more fervently. In addition, only the hardier nonconformist students are likely to have an instinctive appreciation for the situation of religious minorities. As with other games, it takes substantial practice to learn the rules and to improve one's skills in methodological belief. For it to have its full impact, the "believing game" needs to be practiced frequently throughout a course.

Carefully constructed and deftly managed discussions can encourage methodological belief. Stephen Brookfield and Stephen Preskill argue, for example, that "discussions that involve students who speak in different voices, express varied viewpoints, and use different expressive forms help students learn about the contested nature of knowledge" (1999: 23). Although they have in mind primarily race, class, and gender, Brookfield and Preskill also note that discussions can facilitate students' recognition of their own analytical and interpretive assumptions *as assumptions*, as different choices that they have made about how to view and understand certain things. They argue further that heightened student awareness of such differences can have other beneficial effects. They assert that "part of the process of confronting differences is to disclose the ways in which dominant groups and prevailing cultural traditions have silenced certain voices and to explore how these traditions have functioned to prevent their contributing to the conversation" (Brookfield and Preskill 1999: 27–28). Similarly, various proponents of "equity pedagogy" aim to help students to become reflective participants in the discussions of a democratic society by developing pedagogical strategies that ensure that all voices—minority and majority alike—can be heard and taken seriously in their classrooms (Tuitt 2003). Those observations suggest that classroom discussions can be an arena in which methodological belief is profitably exercised not only to uncover what actual participants in new religious movements understand to be their compelling characteristics but also to address the ways in which new religious movements may perceive themselves to be silenced or misconstrued by dominant groups. Methodological belief would thus lead directly to enhancing students' appreciation of the dynamic interactions between new religious movements and their social environments, including the sources and effects of the tensions between new religions and their cultural opponents (Hall, Schuyler, and Trinh 2000; Stark and Bainbridge 1985).

If those teaching about new religious movements have as one of their goals providing a descriptively adequate account of those movements as a baseline for further analysis and interpretation, then appropriately designed discussions can become settings for identifying and examining the assumptions that make such accurate descriptions difficult to achieve. Because discussions focus on the individual learner, "overcoming the resistance is not something the teacher does for the students; it is something the teacher works to help students accomplish for themselves" (Weimer 2002: 159). Although many educational theorists assume that varied viewpoints will necessarily surface in discussions, it is also helpful to introduce, as the topic for discussions, material that itself already contains multiple viewpoints. In the case of new religious movements, there is a rich array of materials that do just that, many of them from sources in popular culture with which students may already be familiar.

Rhetoric

Generally sooner than later, any discussion about new religious movements has to engage the disparate vocabularies used to identify and interpret the subject matter. That is both unavoidable and appropriate because "addressing the politics of representation starts with an attention to language itself" (Rosenfelt 1997). As other essays in this collection have amply demonstrated, in the broader public discussion of new religious movements, the term *cult* has effectively been removed from its former limited, technical range of meanings and invested with a new set of meanings that carry strongly negative connotations (Richardson 1998). Anti-cult activists frequently accuse academics, who prefer the term *new religious movement*, of being "cult apologists." Similar skirmishes have taken place about terms such as *deprogramming, coercive persuasion, conversion,* and *charisma,* among others (Zablocki and Robbins 2001). The "politics of representation" implicit in such contested language offers an ideal opportunity for the application of Elbow's methodological belief, particularly because methodological doubt so strongly animates how participants in the conflict evaluate each other's positions. The rhetoric employed by participants in the contemporary "cult wars" is directly related to the participants' perceptions of what is real, true, and good. Because the believing game encourages "the act of seeing the strength in someone else's position and the weakness in one's own" it can offer students a way of identifying the animating values behind the various rhetorics and comprehensive views of the world that they express (Elbow 1986: 289). It offers students a way of moving beyond the facile assertion that "one person's cult is another's new religion," for example, to a more complex understanding of the perceptions, values, and social relationships that shape anyone's reactions to a particular new religious movement.

Elbow's general observation about the "believing game" is appropriate for understanding the contested terminology in the study of new religious movements. He writes that methodological belief "is particularly useful for eliciting and understanding ideas that are at the limits of what we can imagine or explain-ideas that the doubting game usually sees as completely dubious" (Elbow 2000: 77). Whether the limits of one's imagination are tested by the fervent worship of members of the International Society for Krishna Consciousness or the fulminations of the ostensibly secular anti-cult movement against "destructive cults," or the more forthrightly religious objections to erroneous or heretical religions made by counter-cult ministers, the questions at the heart of Elbow's believing game at least open the possibility of developing an adequate description of positions that one does not hold oneself and hence of developing a more complex understanding of the politics of representation at work in contemporary discussions of new religious movements.

Both methodological belief and methodological doubt involve a careful scrutiny of language. Elbow contends that "the effort to believe is almost always an effort to find a *valid sense* in words where before there was no sense or an invalid sense" (1986: 280). Elbow argues, however, that while "methodological doubt represents the human struggle to free ourselves from parochial closed-mindedness, . . . it doesn't go far enough. Methodological doubt caters too comfortably to our natural impulse to protect and retain the views we already hold" (1986: 263). Thus, in contrast to the classic deployment of a hermeneutic of suspicion by Marx, Nietzsche, and Freud, and the more contemporary efforts to unmask the hidden hegemonic impulses in language coded by race, gender, or class (Morey and Kitano 1997; Ricoeur 1973), students' doubts about new religious movements have the effect of reinforcing views they already hold about what is "really" religious, or self-evidently "normal," or obviously socially acceptable.

On the other hand, methodological belief, with its systematic efforts to identify valid sense in what individual speakers are saying, leads students "genuinely to enter into unfamiliar or threatening ideas instead of just arguing against them without experiencing them or feeling their force. It thus carries us *further* in our developmental journey away from mere credulity" (Elbow 1986: 263). In teaching about new religious movements, it is methodological belief, rather than doubt, that has the potential to reveal the discursive structures that privilege certain types of expression and experience while consigning others to a realm literally beyond believability, and to restore voices from the margins that have been silenced by self-appointed guardians of a conformist majority. As an interpretive strategy, methodological belief promises to recover a more descriptively adequate sense of the diversity of human religious activity. As Elbow puts it, the believing game "fights group-think by privileging minority opinions and giving them *more* power against the monolithic majority" (1986: 283).

Ironically, Elbow himself demonstrates in a few of his own offhand comments both the need for employing methodological belief and the difficulty of doing it evenhandedly. In considering the potential negative effects of excessive credulity, he refers to persons who are "particularly susceptible to some dangerously seductive view (such as racism, anti-Semitism, Moonie-ism, IQ-ism, or nationalism" and shortly thereafter suggests that people who are "peculiarly susceptible to beliefs, especially to 'total' beliefs . . . gravitate to cults" (1986: 283). Elbow's implicit endorsement of the anti-cult stereotype shows that even a strong advocate of methodological belief can fail to apply it consistently, and it also demonstrates again how so many different sources, even ones particularly attentive to the nuances of the teaching and learning processes, combine to shape the pre-theoretical expectations that students bring to the study of new religious movements. But Elbow himself, I imagine, would delight in having his strategy of methodological belief be used to bring to the surface some of his own unexamined assumptions.

Elbow's strategies for training students to be attentive listeners, and perceptive readers who are at least initially willing and able to entertain multiple interpretations of any material they encounter, imply what Richard Miller, Laurie Patton, and Stephen Webb (1994) have called a "rhetorical model" of teaching. Recalling that in classical philosophy, rhetoric "denotes a mode of discourse that aims to convince an audience to take seriously, if not embrace, a certain point of view," they argue that rhetorical teaching aims "neither to improve technique nor simply to make students more knowledgeable, but to empower individual voices and to provide a space for practicing critical skills and reflective inquiry about matters of personal and public importance" (Miller et al. 1994: 820, 821). They contend that rhetorical teaching will promote active learning and energetic student engagement with issues and contribute to the formation of habits of mind that will be of lasting value both inside and outside the classroom. Just as the strategy of methodological belief challenges students to change the way they approach the study of new religions, the rhetorical paradigm of teaching challenges teachers to change their self-definition and practice. Teachers will need to conceive of themselves, not primarily as experts in course management or as transmitters of knowledge; rather, they will situate themselves as fellow learners with their students, all of whom are striving to construct persuasive and trustworthy knowledge out of their specific encounters with common subject matter and with each other. The rhetorical paradigm invites teachers to see themselves, as well as their students, "as persons with our own assumptions, uncertainties, arguments, levity, and commitments" (Miller et al. 1994: 821). In order to come seriously to grips with the diversity of viewpoints in such a classroom, teachers and students alike would need to employ something like Elbow's believing game. In the process, students and teachers would become more familiar and, if all goes well, more proficient at the fundamental "processes and habits of democratic discourse," a development that would benefit them outside the classroom as well (Brookfield and Preskill 1999: 23).

Teaching as envisioned by Elbow and Miller et al. puts more at risk for both students and teachers. But, its proponents assert, there is much more to be gained in such active learning (Sutherland and Bonwell 1996). On their part, students have to accept substantial responsibility for their own learning and engage in collective efforts to make meaning rather than passively receive information delivered by authoritative lecturers. But responsibility for changing students' approach to learning is shared by students and their teachers. Maryellen Weimer observes that "many college students today are the antithesis of autonomous, independent, self-regulating learners, and I believe that faculty have had a hand in making them so. But we are equally able to take actions that set in motion a different set of learning parameters" (2002: 118). In order to promote active learning, teachers have to abandon to some extent the comfort zone of their disciplinary expertise and experience and enter the same intellectual fray as their students, where their own assumptions, convictions, and even identities are open to critical inspection. Students will need to abandon the comfortable passivity that all too easily can characterize their response to teaching.

Weimer argues that a shift in teachers' understanding of their own roles is not optional but necessary. She writes that "our continued insistence on always being at the center of classroom activities directly compromises attempts we make to be learner-centered. We must move aside, often and regularly" (Weimer 2002: 74). The nature of that transformation was memorably captured in an article that recommended that a teacher should no longer be a "sage on the stage" but rather a "guide on the side" (King 1993). But that change does not entail a teacher's completely abandoning responsibility for "running" a course. Arguing that structure is a crucial element in all courses, Judith Miller, James Groccia, and John Wilkes (1996) observe that "a common mistake of teachers in first adopting an active learning strategy is to relinquish structure along with control, and the common result is for students to feel frustrated and disoriented" (1996: 17). They see multiple opportunities for a teacher to exercise influence in matters such as course design, construction of assignments, and managing the flow of activity both inside and outside of the classroom.

In addition to the metaphor of the guide, others have proposed that the role of the teacher in active learning is more like a gardener, a midwife, a coach, or a conductor of an orchestra. Weimer argues that the diverse metaphors all point to similar functions. In her view, "learner-centered teachers connect students and resources. They design activities and assignments that engage learners. They facilitate learning in individual and collective contexts. Their vast experience models for novice learners how difficult material can be accessed, explored and understood" (2002: 76). The fundamental benefit in such a reconception of the teacher's role is that it creates opportunities for teachers and students to demonstrate, through specific accomplishments, that learning has actually taken place rather than simply presuming that it has occurred through some sort of invisible alchemy.

Discussion is one of the primary tools that can be used to promote active learning, but discussions are inherently much harder to direct, shape, and bring to an appropriate and anticipated conclusion than are lectures because "at the heart of discussion is the open and unpredictable creation of meanings through collaborative inquiry" (Brookfield and Preskill 1999: 25). The design and guidance of effective discussions demands from teachers an array of skills that are not necessarily cultivated when they learn to be effective lecturers. Perhaps the most important skill that a teacher can bring to classroom discussions is the ability to listen to the comments of each individual carefully, critically, and with an awareness of his or her potential contributions to reaching the goals of the exercise. Borrowing a characterization of the director of a play, J. Scott Johnson proposes that the teacher become "an audience of one." He remarks that "when playing the role of an audience of one, I may appear to be doing nothing to the casual outside observer, but by the intensity of my concentration, by the focus of my attention, I will be communicating to the students what they need to know" (Johnson et al. 1996: 95). Johnson adds that in directing student learning, "as an attentive audience, I take whatever they bring to the classroom and mold it through careful criticism. I reflect their input, individually and collectively, so they can better see themselves and what they are learning" (1996: 95). The type of alert and critical listening that Johnson advocates suggests that teachers need to bring to student comments in discussions the same attentiveness to the subtleties and nuances of language as they bring to the analysis of data in their own scholarly work. If in the process they treat their students' comments and observations with the same care and gravity with which they approach their own objects of study, they will have encouraged students to take both what they themselves and their fellow students have to say with a greater degree of seriousness. By doing that they will have taken substantial steps toward creating the type of classroom in which discussions actually do promote the mastery of techniques and the cultivation of habits of mind that foster learning in all students, no matter what preparation, proclivities, talents, or identities they bring to the classroom.

Practice

Tip O'Neill's well-known adage that "all politics is local" applies to teaching with equal force. The processes of teaching and learning are indelibly shaped by the specific "ecosystems" of their institutional, curricular, and departmental settings; by the demands placed on particular courses by various constituencies; and by the particular identities, abilities, and levels of interest that both teachers and students bring to the classroom. Consequently, there is no single way to teach anything and for both teachers and students there is no substitute for being reflective practitioners. For students, part of taking responsibility for their own learning is figuring out which strategies for reading, studying, writing, and speaking work best for them. Likewise, teachers need always to be thinking about which strategies will work best to encourage specific students to achieve the goals stipulated for a specific classroom session, assignment, or course. But for such reflection to have its greatest potential for positive impact it should not take place in isolation. Students need to be encouraged to enter into productive exchanges with their teachers and fellow students about *how* they learn best and, consequently, figure out how they can make their way through a course in ways that capitalize on their strengths, give them appropriate opportunities to demonstrate their accomplishments, and encourage them to accept new challenges and experiment with new ways of learning. Similarly, as teachers reflect on, refine, and augment their array of strategies for promoting student learning, they can learn not only from their own experiments and their colleagues but also from the extensive contemporary literature on teaching and learning.

In this section I will focus on how a few basic principles of course design can help teachers respond to the specific challenges involved in teaching about new religious movements. Fully aware that they will need to be adapted to other settings, I will also describe a few activities that I have used to promote learning about specific dimensions of new religious movements.

Although specialists in instructional development have devised a variety for paradigms for effective course design, they all address three fundamental questions. In constructing a course, or an assignment or class session, teachers need to consider *what* they want to accomplish, *how* they intend to accomplish it, and *how they will know* if they have been successful. Course design should ultimately respond to a simple question: how should students be different as a result of completing this specific activity? Typical goals include having students become familiar with the characteristic subject matter and modes of inquiry of individual disciplines, master specific content, apply what they have learned to concrete problems or issues, develop certain skills or competencies, or integrate what they have learned into a broader pattern of knowledge. Whatever they may be, it is of paramount importance that the goals of a course be clearly and specifically articulated, directly related to the specific activities that make up the work of the course, and open to assessment that both evaluates a student's current achievement and points the way to improvement.

As an example, I will list a recent articulation of the goals for my own course and offer some commentary on them. REL 346, Cults and Conversion in Modern America, is an advanced course in the study of religion that has as a prerequisite REL 101, The Study of Religion, an introductory course that uses a selection of theoretical literature to investigate the contours of five different religious traditions. REL 346 typically enrolls forty to fifty students, nearly all of whom are juniors and seniors; as many as a quarter of them may be majors or minors in religious studies. Some manage to avoid the prerequisite by applying their study of anthropology, sociology, psychology, American studies, or other potentially related fields. The syllabus lists six general goals:

1. To develop an understanding of the multiple contexts in which new or alternative religious movements currently exist in the United States.
2. To develop an ability to apply theoretical concepts to the interpretation of new and alternative religions.
3. To develop a familiarity with at least some of the groups that are frequently mentioned as alternative or new religions or cults.
4. To develop a sense of the historical context of contemporary cult controversies.
5. To develop the ability to make persuasive comparisons, generalizations, and judgments.
6. To refine general skills of information retrieval and evaluation, critical reading, argumentative writing, and oral presentation. (Gallagher 2003)

Those goals are also designed to reinforce an understanding that in all of its dimensions the course involves three fundamental and interrelated intellectual operations: description (what is it?), analysis (how does it work?), and interpretation (what does it mean/why does it matter?). Each of the goals is designed to involve at least one of those operations. For example, an adequate description of any new religious movement in the contemporary United States has to take account of the often controversial context in which they exist (goal no.1) but also must include a thorough familiarity with, among other things, the origins, history, fundamental practices and beliefs, leadership and membership of the group (goal no. 3), a task that is often complicated by the context of controversy that surrounds many groups.

Because students are largely unaware of the interpretive presuppositions they typically bring to a course on new religious movements, I've often tried an exercise on the first day of class that brings those assumptions to light. Giving students the fictional caution that it is the only information that scholars have been able discover, I present to them a short text and ask them to describe the religious practices and beliefs that are suggested in it, the nature of the group implied by it, and the character of its relationships with its social environment. My favorite text for this discussion is short but fairly provocative. It reads: "For there are eunuchs who have been so from birth, and there are eunuchs who have been made eunuchs by other men, and there are eunuchs who have made themselves eunuchs for the sake of the kingdom of heaven. He who is able to receive this, let him receive it." Although I always request that anyone who knows the source of the text not disclose it at the outset, I have never had anyone identify it immediately. In the ensuing discussion students typically conjure up a rigid, elitist, world-denying group of celibates, perhaps tyrannized by a demanding charismatic leader, who exist in significant tension with the rest of society. Students vividly imagine the conflicts that would be precipitated within families and broader social groups if someone were to become a member. They often express bewilderment about why someone would resort to such dramatic curtailment of sexuality and sometimes wonder about what else the members of the hypothetical group would deny themselves. As the conversation unfolds, they become more eager to determine which "cult" has produced the text; most frequently they mention "those UFO people," meaning the Heaven's Gate group. They are invariably surprised and unsettled to find that the text was taken from the Gospel according to Matthew 19:12. Their surprise is founded, I believe, on the impression that they have made a category mistake; earliest Christianity, they presume, cannot have anything to do with contemporary cults. The jarring collision between the presupposition that Christianity represents one type of (benign) religion and new religious movements are a distinctive other (dangerous) type begins to make them aware of the prejudgments that they bring to the classroom, alerts them to the possibility of a much wider range of comparisons, and raises the possibility that apparently neutral descriptive language may actually have a polemical dimension or even purpose. With that initial exercise in de-familiarization accomplished, I adjourn class until the next session.

In order to get a variety of issues out on the table, and to capitalize on the unsettling effect of our first exercise, I have typically shown a video or film on the second day of class. After initially relying on current articles from newspapers or news magazines, for some years I used an MTV news special on cults. More recently, even though it runs nearly two hours, I've used the feature film *Holy Smoke* (Campion 2000). That full-length theatrical release centers on the affiliation of an Australian girl, played by Kate Winslet, with a fictional Indian group led by "Baba." The girl's troubled and often amusingly dysfunctional family quickly engages an American "cult exiter," played by Harvey Keitel, to accomplish her departure from the group. Although it sometimes skirts close to the caricatures of the anti-cult narrative, the film is notable for the complexities and ambiguities of its characters' relationships to new religious movements in general, to their families, and to each other. When they view the film, students know that they will have to complete a five- to seven-page group paper for the next class session, during which they will present their analysis orally and discuss it with the other students. That assignment gives me a way to get students to talk to each other and to me about the issues that they see emerging as they begin their study of new religious movements. It also gives me an early reading on the assumptions and interests that they bring to the course. The group format for the paper reminds students that they will be expected to engage each other in serious discussions throughout the course, both inside and outside the classroom.

Because *Holy Smoke* vividly introduces students to the notion that new religious movements can be controversial, I typically have followed the film with other brief examples of "cult" controversies. I've recently used the readily available reports by the U.S. FBI and the Canadian Intelligence Service that addressed fears of cult activity during the year 2000 (Kaplan 2002) to introduce the idea that law enforcement has sometimes taken an interest in new religions. Most recently, I've added a class session on a 1781 pamphlet that a former member had written against the Shakers (Rathbun 1781). My goal in examining that material is to cultivate a sense of the full range of parties who have been interested in new religious movements, the nature of their interests, the reasons they have given for their interests, the actions that have both taken and urged on others, and the rationales they have given for their actions. In short, I try to direct students' attention to how participants in disputes about new religious movements have themselves used the processes of description, analysis, and interpretation so that students can discern the particular values that animate their judgments. Elbow's "methodological belief" offers a strategy for getting students to take seriously the conflicting opinions about new religious movements on their own terms; and analysis of the "politics of representation" implicit in the rhetorics of members of new religious movements, their cultural opponents, and other external observers alerts students to the processes by which different meanings can be constructed from some of the same materials. Brief role-playing exercises (e.g., As a Shaker, how would you respond to Rathbun's criticism? If your sibling joined Baba's group, how would you react? If you found the practices of a group alarming or distasteful, how would you respond? For what reasons would you be willing to renounce sexuality?) can be used to ease students into methodological belief (Elbow 1986).

The goals for my course have been formulated intentionally to subject students' taken-for-granted knowledge about new religious movements to critical scrutiny from the first class session onwards. Tackling head-on the controversial contexts in which many new religions exist (goal no. 1) immediately introduces students to the notion that there are multiple points of view about new religions. Reading Peter Berger on the processes of "world-building and world-maintenance" (goal no. 2) gives students a way of thinking about how such points of view are developed and what purposes they might serve. Requiring students to view specific groups from the inside (goal no. 3) encourages them to undertake comparisons between how groups are portrayed by their "cultural opponents" and how they are portrayed by their leader(s) and their members and to reflect on the differences in those portrayals and their etiologies. Readings in the general theory of religion, as well as in theoretically informed treatments of new religious movements, such as Stark and Bainbridge's (1985) treatment of secularization, sectarianism, and the formation of cults (goal no. 2), prepares students to identify the theoretical assumptions that are implicit in any analytical or interpretative statements about new religions, from the seemingly casual observation that "they're nuts" to more sustained examinations of individual groups or the general phenomenon of new religious movements. Similarly, some familiarity with the history of new religious movements before their own lifetimes—even the notion that there actually *is* a history to new religious movements in the United States (goal no. 4)— prepares students to evaluate critically claims about the unprecedented nature of new religious movements in the contemporary United States and to chart a more complex genealogy of religious innovation in the United States. At least in my practice, then, responding to student resistance to taking new religious movements seriously *as religions* involves situating student's pre-theoretical assumptions and judgments in a variety of comparative, historical, and theoretical contexts that offer alternative understandings of what students purport to "know," either implicitly or explicitly, when they enter the classroom. Such strategies for loosening the hold of students' assumptions can clear the way for systematic application of methodological belief to a variety of case studies.

One advantage of organizing most of the course as a series of case studies is that it gives the course the flexibility to respond to unanticipated events. Both the Branch Davidian standoff and the Heaven's Gate suicides, for example, happened while I was teaching the course. In both cases, I was able to drop a case study and substitute investigation of the unfolding stories without much disturbing the continuity of the course. Such moments of connection between students' academic work and events in the world outside the classroom vividly reinforce the value of the study of new religious movements.

Having familiarized themselves with a variety of interpretive perspectives on new religious movements and an array of case studies, students should be better prepared to understand that any evaluative statement about a new religion is an argument, a rhetorical attempt to persuade an audience that something is or is not the case. Training in argument is one of the fundamental goals of higher education. As Jonathan Z. Smith put it, "it is argument, in particular argument about interpretations, that marks the distinctive mode of speech that characterizes college" (1988: 729). In the case of new religious movements, arguments quickly spill out of the classroom into the realm of public opinion where, for example, some voices have argued for extensive regulation of new religious movements (Singer 1995). If, as Smith contends, "argument exists for the purpose of clarifying choices and ... choices are always consequential [and] require the acceptance of responsibility," the study of new religious movements is well suited to introduce students to the types of arguments they will encounter as participants in the democratic society of the United States.

The particular type of resistance that students often manifest in learning about new religious movements is the product of identifiable social forces. It poses challenges to teachers that are not unlike those faced in teaching about other controversial topics, including race and gender. Sustained reflection on the practice of teaching in one's own specific context can do much to aid teachers in mitigating or overcoming that resistance, but the contemporary literature on teaching and learning, in various ways, offers both theoretical grounding and practical guidance for teaching about new religious movements in ways that promote significant and lasting student learning.

REFERENCES

Alavi, Karima. 2001. "At Risk of Prejudice: Teaching Tolerance about Muslim Americans." *Social Education* 65, 344–48.

Beauchamp, Marcia. 2002. "Guidelines on Religion in Public Schools: An Historic Moment." *Spotlight on Teaching* 17, pp. 2, 4,10.

Berger, Peter. 1967. *The Sacred Canopy: Elements of a Sociological Theory of Religion.* Garden City, NY: Doubleday.

Brookfield, Stephen D., and Stephen Preskill. 1999. *Discussion as a Way of Teaching: Tools and Techniques for Democratic Classrooms.* San Francisco: Jossey-Bass.

Campion, Jane, dir. 2000. *Holy Smoke.* DVD. Miramax.

Chidester, David. 1988. *Salvation and Suicide: An Interpretation of Jim Jones, the Peoples Temple, and Jonestown.* Bloomington: University of Indiana Press.

Douglass, Susan L. in collaboration with the First Amendment Center. 2000. *Teaching about Religion in National and State Social Studies Standards.* Fountain Valley, CA, and Nashville, TN: Council on Islamic Education and First Amendment Center.

Elbow, Peter. 1986. "Methodological Doubting and Believing: Contraries in Inquiry." In Peter Elbow, *Embracing Contraries: Explorations in Learning and Teaching,* 254–304. New York: Oxford University Press.

————. 2000. "The Believing Game—A Challenge after Twenty-Five Years." In Peter Elbow, *Everyone Can Write: Essays towards a Hopeful Theory of Writing and Teaching Writing,* 76–80. New York: Oxford University Press.

Fink, L. Dee. 2003. *Creating Significant Learning Experiences: An Integrated Approach to Designing College Courses.* San Francisco: Jossey-Bass.

Fox, Helen. 2001. *"When Race Breaks Out": Conversations about Race and Racism in College Classrooms.* New York: Peter Lang.

Gallagher, Eugene V. 2003. "Cults and Conversion in Modern America." REL 346 course offered at Connecticut College, Spring semester, 2003. Available at www .aarweb.org/syllabus/syllabi/g/gallagher/1JN2D-Gallagher.pdf. Accessed June 6, 2004.

Hackett, Rosalind I. J. 1993. Teaching African Religions. *Spotlight on Teaching.* Available at www.aarweb.org/publications/spotlight/previous/1-2/01-02-01teac.asp. Accessed June 6, 2004.

Hall, John R., Philip Schuyler, and Salvaine Trinh. 2000. *Apocalypse Observed: Religious Movements and Violence in North America, Europe, and Japan.* New York: Routledge.

Hassan, Steven. 2000. *Releasing the Bonds: Empowering People to Think for Themselves.* Somerville, MA: Freedom of Mind Press.

Johnson, J. Scott, Jennifer Kellen, Greg Seibert, and Celia Shaughnessy. 1996. "No Middle Ground? Men Teaching Feminism." In *Teaching What You're Not: Identity Politics in Higher Education,* ed. Katherine J. Mayberry, 85–103. New York: New York University Press.

Kaplan, Jeffrey, ed. 2002. *Millennial Violence: Past, Present, and Future.* London: Frank Cass.

King, Alison. 1993. "From Sage on the Stage to Guide on the Side." *College Teaching* 41, 30–35.

Macy, Alex. 2004. E-mail posting for REL 346, "Cults and Conversion in Modern America." Connecticut College, March 6, 2004.

Miller, Judith E., James E. Groccia, and John M. Wilkes. 1996. "Providing Structure: The Critical Element." In *Using Active Learning in College Classes,* ed. Tracey Sutherland and Charles Bonwell, 17–30. San Francisco: Jossey-Bass.

Miller, Richard B., Laurie L. Patton, and Stephen H. Webb. 1994. "Rhetoric, Pedagogy, and the Study of Religions." *Journal of the American Academy of Religion.* 62, 819–50.

Morey, Ann, and Margie Kitano. 1997. *Multicultural Course Transformation in Higher Education: A Broader Truth.* Boston: Allyn & Bacon.

Peskowitz, Miriam. 1997. "Identification Questions." *Journal of the American Academy of Religion* 65, 707–26.

Proudfoot, Wayne. 1985. *Religious Experience.* Berkeley: University of California Press.

Rathbun, Valentine. 1781. *An Account of the Matter, Form, and Manner of a New and Strange Religion, Taught and Propagated by a Number of Europeans, Living in a Place Called Nisqueunia, in the State of New-York.* Providence, RI: Bennett Wheeler.

Richardson, James T. 1995. "Manufacturing Consent about Koresh: A Structural Analysis of the Role of the Media in the Waco Tragedy." In *Armageddon in Waco: Critical Perspectives on the Branch Davidian Conflict,* ed. Stuart A. Wright, 153–76. Chicago: University of Chicago Press.

———. 1998. "Definitions of Cult: From Sociological-Technical to Popular-Negative." In *Cults in Context: Readings in the Study of New Religious Movements,* ed. Lorne L. Dawson, 29–38. New Brunswick, NJ: Transaction.

Ricoeur, Paul. 1973. "The Critique of Religion." *Union Seminary Quarterly Review* 28, 205–12.

Rosenfelt, Deborah S. 1997. "Doing Multiculturalism: Conceptualizing Curricular Change." In *Multicultural Course Transformation in Higher Education,* ed. Ann Intili Morey and Margie K. Kitano, 35–55. Boston: Allyn & Bacon.

Ross, Rick. 2004. Web site for the Ross Institute. Available at www.rickross.com. Accessed June 6, 2004.

Sandler, Adam. 1996. *What the Hell Happened to Me?* CD. Warner Brothers.

Shupe, Anson, and Jeffrey K. Hadden. 1995. "Cops, News Copy, and Public Opinion: Legitimacy and the Social Construction of Evil in Waco." In *Armageddon in Waco,* ed. Stuart Wright, 177–202. Chicago: University of Chicago Press.

Singer, Margaret Thaler, with Janja Lalich. 1995. *Cults in Our Midst: The Hidden Menace in Our Everyday Lives.* San Francisco: Jossey-Bass.

Smith, Jonathan Z. 1988. "Narratives into Problems: The College Introductory Course and the Study of Religion." *Journal of the American Academy of Religion* 56, 727–39.

Stark, Rodney, and William Sims Bainbridge. 1985. *The Future of Religion: Secularization, Revival, and Cult Formation*. Berkeley: University of California Press.

Sutherland, Tracey E., and Charles C. Bonwell, eds. *Using Active Learning in College Classes: A Range of Options for Faculty*. San Francisco: Jossey-Bass.

Tuitt, Frank. 2003. "Afterword: Realizing a More Inclusive Pedagogy." In *Race and Higher Education: Rethinking Pedagogy in Diverse College Classrooms*, ed. Annie Howell and Frank Tuitt, 243–64. Cambridge, MA: Harvard Educational Review.

Weimer, Maryellen. 2002. *Learner-Centered Teaching: Five Key Changes to Practice*. San Francisco: Jossey-Bass.

Wlodowski, Raymond J., and Margery B. Ginsberg. 1995. *Diversity and Motivation: Culturally Responsive Teaching*. San Francisco: Jossey-Bass.

Zablocki, Benjamin, and Thomas Robbins, eds. 2001. *Misunderstanding Cults: Searching for Objectivity in a Controversial Field*. Toronto: University of Toronto Press.

Teaching New Religious Movements on the World Wide Web

Douglas E. Cowan

As a cultural and social phenomenon, the Internet has become so much a part of life for university students and instructors that it is sometimes difficult to imagine what we did before the advent of the World Wide Web, how we communicated without e-mail or conducted research without almost instantaneous access to information. Although it does appear to be slowing somewhat, the growth rate of Internet participation over the past decade is staggering—16 million users in 1995, 378 million in 2000, and more than 500 million in 2002 (Dawson and Cowan 2004: 5). Given this, it is not surprising that the Web is also a very active religious environment. Indeed, few commentators have failed to note that religious information of all types is prominent online.

Broadly construed, religious activity on the Internet occurs along a continuum bounded at one end by *religion online* and at the other by *online religion*. Conceived originally by Christopher Helland as a dyad (2000; cf. Hadden and Cowan 2000), *religion online* means use of the Internet as a vehicle for providing information about or by religious groups, movements, and traditions. Religious organizations ranging from small, local congregations to large, denominational administrations upload Web sites to increase communication with existing members, extend their outreach to potential members, and not infrequently, counter what they consider misleading information posted by critics. *Online religion*, on the other hand, regards the World Wide Web as an interactive venue for religious practice, ritual, observance, and innovation. That is, rather than simply seek information online, adherents use the Web as an integral part of their religious lives. Chat rooms turn into scripture study classrooms or prayer groups; Web cameras provide geographically removed adherents the opportunity for religious practices like ritual adoration (Young 2004) or "virtual" pilgrimage (Bunt 2000; Macwilliams 2004); and, with the emergence of groups such as the "cybercoven" and the "cyberchurch," some religionists are trying to move their entire ritual working group life online (Cowan 2005). Since Helland's initial distinction, however, it has become clear that religion online and online religion are, more often than not, theoretical endpoints rather than identifiable positions in empirical space (Dawson and Cowan 2004). Though examples that cluster closer to the religion online end of the continuum are considerably more common, as the various cultures of cyberspace have evolved, the nature of the space between these two poles has changed, creating an environment in which Web-based religious activity involves (and in some cases requires) some measure of both *religion online* and *online religion*. If scripture study is considered by a group as religious practice, for example, then the chat rooms and discussion forums in which these studies take place both provide religious information to participants (religion online) and allow participants to practice their religion in a computer-mediated environment (online religion).

More to the point for this volume, the World Wide Web is also a very active *new religious* environment, and I know of no new religious movement that is absent from the Web entirely. Because the structure of the Internet does not inherently favor one religious tradition over another, in many ways the thousands of different NRMs that do participate online do so little differently than more culturally dominant traditions. They upload Web sites explaining (and advertising) their various traditions; they host (or are the subject of) a wide range of Internet discussion forums; and while some try to translate offline religious behavior online, others are content simply to have a minimal Internet presence. The United Nuwaubian Nation of Moors, for example (www.geocities .com/Area51/Corridor/4978/unnm.html), maintains only the most basic Web site, whereas others, like the Raelian religion (www.rael.org) and the Temple of Set (www.xeper.org), have large, elaborate sites that can provide researchers and students with a wealth of information about the movement. Since it is unlikely that more than a few students (or instructors) will have direct personal experience with many new religious movements (NRMs), the World Wide Web presents an unprecedented opportunity for this fascinating religious dimension to enter the classroom.

New Religious Movements on the World Wide Web

Broadly speaking, the same cultural dynamics by which new religious movements are marked offline translate into the online world. That is, although they are an established, often vibrant part of the religious landscape, at the same time they are the target of intense criticism and social opposition. They provide millions of adherents with fulfilling religious lives, yet the fear with which at least some people regard them regularly leads to charges of unscrupulous recruiting practices such as "brainwashing" and "thought control."

In this section, I will consider three central issues related to NRMs and the Internet, each increasing in terms of the specificity with which it applies directly to new religious movements. First is the question of computer-mediated religious practice and the possibility of online religious community. Though this applies to more traditional religions as well as NRMs, one of the basic debates about all religious life on the Internet is whether offline religious sensibilities and behavior can ever be adequately translated into a computer-mediated environment and how (or whether) they are changed in the translation. The second issue is the matter of the Internet as a controversial information space. Because the cultural legitimacy of new religious movements is inherently more contested than that of dominant traditions, there are far more countermovement Web sites opposing NRMs than there are sites dedicated to countering the influence of, say, the Methodists or the Disciples of Christ. Learning to distinguish among different information types and sources is crucial to using the Internet responsibly. The third issue, and the one most specifically related to NRMs, is fear of the Web as a recruiting tool in the hands of unscrupulous new religious leaders. Since one of the principal scholarly debates about NRMs has been the process by which potential adherents encounter, participate in, and for the most part ultimately leave these groups, whether the Internet acts to facilitate recruitment is in some dispute.

The New Religious Community on the World Wide Web

One of the most important debates about all religious movements on the Internet is whether or not an authentic religious *community* can ever develop online, and if it can, how such a community might differ (if, indeed, it does) from a similar offline group. That is, is there a new form of religious community emerging, one bounded more by affinity and shared electronic connection than by proximity and shared physical boundaries? Although churches, temples, mosques, synagogues, covens, groves, and kindred all create Web sites to advertise their real-world presence, the fact remains that few seek to move that presence online in a way that would replace offline interaction. Online modern pagan working groups like the JaguarMoon Cybercoven (www.jaguarmoon.org) may attempt to provide for all of their members' religious needs over the Internet, but the offline Wiccan coven is in no danger of disappearing. Despite this, significant debate has occurred among scholars of the Internet whether an authentic online community is even a possibility in a computer-mediated environment. Some have dismissed the idea, arguing as Joseph Lockard does, that rather than the new Internet reality, any notion of a virtual community has become "a new governing myth" (1997: 229) of the World Wide Web. Mark Slouka (1995) and Clifford Stoll (1999) concur, contending that computer-mediated interaction actually "assaults" and "undermines" authentic community.

Others, however, have suggested that if the ways in which community is conceptualized categorically exclude what is happening on the Internet, then perhaps the analytic category itself has become inadequate (Cowan and Hadden 2004b). As Lorne Dawson points out in one of the most succinct discussions of the problem, regardless of the particular form it takes or is alleged to take, "it is simply assumed too often that 'community' is present [or not], without really specifying why or how" (2004: 77). That is, Dawson asks, how would we know if we encountered a community online? What criteria would we use to assess it? On the one hand, must we admit that something is a community simply because those involved say that it is? On the other hand, if we deny that some online group is a community, what then do we call it?

Drawing on the work of a number of scholars, Dawson has proposed six identifiers of online community that, once again, mirror similar conditions offline: "(1) interactivity, (2) stability of membership, (3) stability of identity, (4) netizenship and social control, (5) personal concern, and (6) occurrence in a public space" (Dawson 2004: 83). While the last of Dawson's characteristics could be the most problematic theoretically, especially in terms of the offline emergence of modern pagan covens and secretive magical lodges as some-times very private communities, as a whole they indicate a useful analytic frame-work within which to examine and evaluate online activity. With the exception of a requirement that it occur in some manner of public space, each of Dawson's identifiers characterizes *intentional* versus *accidental* patterns of association—social groups as opposed to social aggregates. This differs from Tönnies's *Gesellschaft* by virtue of the fact that they are not limited to (and may not even include) the contractual and exchange relations that he regarded as central to the concept, but resemble more Georg Simmel's conditions of disclosure and reciprocity within secret societies, dynamic attributes by which conceptual sep-aration as a primary group is established, social relations within the group are strengthened and extended, and group identity and loyalty is maintained in the face of the social pull of other groups to which participants may belong (cf. Cowan 2005).

New Religious Information on the World Wide Web

This "social pull of other groups" brings us to the issue of the World Wide Web as a contested information space—what I have called elsewhere a "meta-technological paradox": "more information available more quickly than ever before in human history but with fewer controls on the quality, accuracy, and propriety of that information" (Cowan 2004: 258). While there is no debate that the Web is the most readily accessible source of information on new religious movements, as a general rule, peer review is nonexistent online and misinformation ranges from honestly held delusions to deliberate fraud. Since the Web is often the first (and the last) place students go for information, however, they must be educated on how to evaluate the information they obtain, and separate the academically useful wheat from the seemingly end-less stream of electronic chaff.

This is particularly true in the case of new religious movements, the cul-tural legitimacy of which is often very hotly contested. Of the thousands of NRMs that exist in the world at any one time, only a relative handful are ever discussed in the various print resources—academic or otherwise—to which students have ready access, and the Internet is, by default, the only source of information available. The issue then becomes how credible the information is that they obtain online.

In broad strokes, Web-based information about new religious movements breaks down into four categories: (1) Web sites that are in favor of the NRMs in question, whether official or unofficial sites; (2) Web sites that are opposed to these NRMs, whether uploaded by dedicated countermovement groups or concerned individuals; (3) research and resource sites that seek to provide information about NRMs without necessarily privileging one side or the other, including online academic journals and sites such as the Religious Movements Homepage project (www.religiousmovements.org); and (4) discussion venues, whether asynchronous (i.e., threaded discussion forums like www.alt.religion .scientology or the myriad Yahoo! and MSN groups) or quasi-synchronous (i.e., chat rooms). Each of these presents particular pedagogical opportunities and challenges.

First, for many groups the Internet has become a relatively easy way to disseminate religious teachings, practices, and sacred texts—some of which are, for all practical purposes, now available only online. Research into the Church of Satan, for example, is made considerably easier because thousands of pages of primary source material have been uploaded, including Michael Aquino's history of the Church of Satan, which prints out at nearly 1,000 pages and is readily available as a PDF download (www.xeper.org/maquino). In this category, though, it is important to distinguish between official and unofficial Web sites, to recognize the different levels of authority with which site operators might speak, and to be sensitive to the presence of particular organizational agendas. Some groups, like the Church of Scientology, maintain strict control over all aspects of religious belief and practice, and regard alternative interpretations or unauthorized transmission of their teachings as problematic at best, criminal at worst. Web sites posted by Scientologists are required to follow strict guidelines in the online use of church symbols, texts, and trademarks, and the Church of Scientology has been accused of providing members with Web design software pre-installed with censorware that automatically suppresses anti-Scientology sites during Internet searches (Brown 1998). Modern paganisms, on the other hand, which have no overarching *magisterium* and whose beliefs are often wildly eclectic and personally gnostic, present an "official" face only in the sense of institutional Web sites that are attached to particular groups—the Church of the Goddess (www.cog.org), for example, or the Church of All Worlds (www.caw.org). Unlike Scientology, the vast majority of modern pagan sites are unofficial and are developed by individual adherents as a way of expressing their particular vision of modern paganism.

The second category is populated by dedicated countermovement sites. While some of these are the product of disgruntled former members, others are the online presence of individuals or groups in the secular anti-cult (e.g., the American Family Foundation at www.csj.org) or the evangelical Christian counter-cult (e.g., the Christian Apologetics and Research Ministry at www .carm.org) movement. (For a discussion of the similarities and differences between these two movements, see Cowan 2002, 2003.) While these sites often contain information on a wide range of NRMs, site content must always be considered in the context of the purpose for which it has been uploaded. With particular reference to the Church of Scientology, for example, I have argued that the Web is "becoming an unrestrained venue for movement/countermovement propaganda" (Cowan 2004: 258), and countermovement information is often managed and manipulated to present the worst possible picture of the new religious landscape.

The third category includes secondary research sources such as peer-reviewed academic journals available through online providers like ATLA, JSTOR, and EBSCOHost; full-text media reports accessed through Lexis-Nexis, and dedicated Internet resource and research sites such as the Religious Movements Homepage Project (www.religiousmovements.org; see Hadden 2000), the Ontario Consultants on Religious Tolerance (www.religioustolerance.org; see B. A. Robinson 2000), the Center for Studies on New Religions (www.cesnur .org), the American Religion Data Archive (www.thearda.com; see Finke, Mc-Kinney, and Bahr 2000), and the Internet Sacred Text Archive (www.sacred-texts.com). Used in conjunction with online movement and countermovement sources, these provide students with essential components in the process of research triangulation.

Finally, and in my opinion among the most important sites for online ethnography, are the discussion venues. These include chat rooms, moderated discussion forums, personal blogs, and the popular alt.-type unmoderated e-mail lists. Here, students can observe (and participate in) discussions about a number of new religious movements, as well as track the history of different debates, the ebb and flow of online discussions, and the dynamics of forum participation, commitment, and attrition. Many of the discussion forums on Yahoo!, for example, have publicly accessible archives of all messages posted since the beginning of the forum.

One of the significant debates that informs each of these categories is over the propriety of uploading material that some new religions want to keep for initiates only. Originally, the philosophy of Internet usage tended to favor the notion of full and free access to any information uploaded to the Web, regardless of where it came from or who had proprietary rights over it. This is clearly illustrated on the modern pagan Internet, for example, in the rampant cutting, pasting, and reloading of material with little if any concern for intellectual property rights. In recent years, however, some NRMs have seen religiously sensitive material find its way onto the Net and then proliferate in a way that has proved impossible to control. This has been a particular problem for the Church of Scientology, which has witnessed numerous countermovement groups upload its esoterica in an ongoing attempt to persuade Internet visitors of what these groups regard as the dangers of Scientology. The Church of Scientology, on the other hand, has responded with a series of lawsuits seeking injunctions against the Internet republication of this material (see Cowan 2004).

New Religious Recruiting on the World Wide Web

This brings us to the question of the Internet as a recruiting space and the claims that unsuspecting Web visitors will be drawn into a cult by unscrupulous Web masters and gurus. Consider the example of Heaven's Gate.

In March 1997, as thirty-nine bodies were removed from a rented mansion in Rancho Santa Fe, California, media reports began to suggest that the World Wide Web, by then only a few years old, was somehow involved in these bizarre deaths. Labeled by some "the computer cult," Heaven's Gate had some members who had operated a moderately successful Web design business, communicated their final message via their own Web site (www.heavensgate.com), and sought to interact with other Web participants in discussion forums and chat rooms. Because of this, a number of commentators were quick to lay at least part of the blame for their suicides on the Internet. Repeated in national and religious media, these claims quickly tapped into public misperceptions about new religious movements in general and raised particular debate about whether the Internet could be used by controversial groups to recruit unsuspecting new members.

Though the *New York Times* was careful to avoid blaming the Internet unequivocally for the Heaven's Gate suicides, it did quote alleged cult expert Rick Ross, who opined that "the Internet has proven a powerful recruitment tool for cults" and that "Heaven's Gate was emblematic of a growing number of small, computer-connected cults that have flourished in the last decade" (quoted in Markoff 1997: A-20). A week later, in an article entitled "Blaming the Web," *Newsweek* featured evangelical counter-cult apologist Tal Brooke, who believes that "the Net can be an effective cult recruiting tool. It's like fishing with a lure" (quoted in Levy 1997: 46). Some scholars concurred with this assessment. Hugh Urban, for example, argues that Heaven's Gate "was one of the first [religious sects] to emerge as a true religion of and for the computer age" (2000: 282). Reflecting the same popular, though at that point untested, fears of the World Wide Web as a vast recruiting office for new religious movements, he continues that "the Net is an ideal means of mass proselytization and rapid conversion—a missionary device that operates instantly, globally, and anonymously" (2000: 283).

It did not take long, however, for these claims to be challenged. A week after their initial report, *Newsweek* profiled one of the surviving members of the group, noting that most of "the messages posted by Heaven's Gate on the Internet were being greeted by scorn and derision" (Miller 1997: 29). Less than two months after the suicides, the authors of an article in *Computers Today* argued that the deaths generated far more interest in the Heaven's Gate Web site than the group itself had been able to do prior to their "Earth exit" (Srilatha and Agarwhal 1997). Communications scholar Wendy Gale Robinson (1997) contends that "the press acted irresponsibly by pointing the finger at the Net," and that "there is nothing in [Heaven's Gate] literature and the interviews with surviving cult members to support the idea that they felt part of cyberculture or that the Internet was anything more than a digital bulletin board on which to affix their messages."

While there is no doubt that the Heaven's Gate group did use the Internet to communicate its message, the important questions are how much influence sites like these actually have and whether the Internet could be used as a recruiting tool by new religious movements. Drawing on the emerging scholarship of Internet culture and the wealth of social scientific literature on recruitment processes and affiliation with new religious movements, Lorne Dawson and Jennifer Hennebry (1999) argue that the available empirical evidence supports neither the conclusion that Heaven's Gate was recruiting via the Internet nor the more basic contention that the World Wide Web is a particularly effective recruiting environment.

An important factor in the debate about the Internet as a potential recruitment tool that must be borne in mind is the elective nature of Internet participation. The World Wide Web is voluntary space in which visitors can operate with considerably less personal investment than in the offline world and from which they can disengage (or be disengaged) with relative ease. Prior to the Internet, for example, if someone wanted to investigate Scientology as a potential religious choice, contact required both physical proximity to a Scientology organization and sufficient interest to overcome any reticence about visiting the offices of what has often been labeled a cult. Few would contest, on the other hand, that visiting www.scientology.org presents a considerably lower threshold of risk, and hence investment. Cultural fears, however, are hard to dispel, no matter how much countervailing evidence is marshaled (Glassner 1999). In their research into the growth of modern paganism among teenagers, for example, Lynn Schofield Clark (2003), and Helen Berger and Douglas Ezzy (2004) point out that the "mass media and the Christian Right continue to suggest that the Internet is, among other things, seducing young people into new religious movements" (2004: 175).

Teaching about New Religious Movements and the World Wide Web

Although little of what I will present in this section applies solely to new religious movements, the World Wide Web does offer some distinct advantages for instructors who teach NRM courses. Here, I will briefly touch on three of these advantages, then offer some practical suggestions for using the Internet as a research and teaching tool. Each of these suggestions is informed by the basic pedagogical principles underpinning my own course on new religious movements: that students will (1) experience an introduction to the broad spectrum of religious beliefs that exist (and flourish) outside the cultural mainstream; (2) encounter a variety of methods for understanding and analyzing new religious movements in society; and (3) confront at least some of the ways in which dominant religious and secular cultures have responded to the burgeoning presence of NRMs.

The first pedagogical advantage of the Internet is its fluidity. New religious movements are constantly emerging, developing, changing, maturing, and in many cases simply disappearing from view, and whether these dynamics are dramatic or mundane, the fluid nature of the Internet allows for their rapid online reflection almost as they take place. In March 2000, for example, when hundreds of bodies belonging to members of the Movement for the Restoration of the Ten Commandments of God were discovered burned in a church in a remote area of southern Uganda, the Center for Studies on New Religions (www.cesnur.org) began within hours to collect and upload media reports from a number of international sources, as well as initial reactions and analyses from prominent NRM scholars. A year later, and on the other side of the world, when the Reorganized Church of Jesus Christ of Latter-day Saints officially changed its name to the Community of Christ (www.cofchrist.org), the Internet was one of the principal means by which that was communicated to congregations (and potential members) around the world. And, finally, appalled at what it regards as the debasement of the teachings of Srila Prabhupada (the founder of the International Society for Krishna Consciousness), the ISKCON Revival Movement (www.iskconirm.org) uses the Internet extensively to push for reform, renewal, and a return to what it believes are the true principles of Krishna Consciousness. In each of these cases—and dozens more could easily be assembled—the World Wide Web affords students an opportunity learn about NRMs in ways unheard of little more than a decade ago.

A second significant issue in the academic study and teaching of NRMs has always been access to the movements themselves. Instructors whose primary field is not NRMs may feel unprepared to take students to a Hare Krishna temple or a Church of Scientology org (branch). They may not know how to make the initial contact leading to a visit or have insufficient time in a survey course to make such a visit. Now, since more and more college and university classrooms are being equipped with Internet technology, students and instructors can read the official teachings of different groups online, take virtual tours of group venues, and follow at least some of the controversies in which many new religious movements remain embroiled. On the official Web sites of the International Society for Krishna Consciousness (www.iskcon.com and www.krishna.com), students can listen to audio files of the Hare Krishna *mahamantra*, spiritual talks by a number of ISKCON leaders, and devotional music structured around *harinama-sankirtana*—the public chanting of mantra that is often accompanied by music, dancing, and literature distribution. Students can download articles from the *ISKCON Communications Journal*, an internal publication intended to promote dialogue among devotees, as well as the official ISKCON magazine, *Back to Godhead*. They can visit pages devoted to ISKCON centers around the world, many of which include virtual tours of the temple grounds and buildings. Although it is true that a virtual tour often means little more than a set of pictures showing the buildings or property, prior to the advent of the Internet even these were not available to most instructors.

Despite concerns about the veracity of the information one encounters online, a third issue is that the World Wide Web is home to a number of important resources for scholars and teachers of new religious movements. The CESNUR Web site mentioned above (www.cesnur.org) archives hundreds of media reports on new religious happenings around the world, as well as dozens of academic papers written by a wide variety of NRM scholars on topics ranging from the brainwashing controversy to the religious implications of *Buffy the Vampire Slayer*. The Ontario Consultants on Religious Tolerance (www.religioustolerance.org) maintain a massive Web site devoted to "religious freedom, tolerance and diversity as positive cultural values," and include over 2,500 essays and articles on religious movements from Asatru to Zoroastrianism. And, finally, one of the largest information sites on new religious movements is the Religious Movements Homepage Project (www.religiousmovements.org), begun (and run until his death in 2003) by Jeffrey K. Hadden, a professor of sociology at the University of Virginia. Recognizing the pedagogical opportunities represented by the Internet, Hadden and his students developed detailed profiles on over two hundred new religious movements. Each profile provides visitors with a brief historical overview of the group, its leaders, beliefs, and practices, and any controversies in which it has been involved. Each profile also contains a set of Internet hyperlinks and a bibliography of scholarly and popular resources on the group. For anyone who find the prospect of using Internet technology in the classroom somewhat daunting, I recommend Hadden's own account of the Religious Movements Homepage, "Confessions of a Recovering Technophobe" (Hadden 2000).

The benefits of the World Wide Web in the classroom have to be balanced against the pedagogical challenges it presents. Besides the obvious problem of plagiarism from the Internet, students using the Web for research are confronted with a plethora of information they are often ill-equipped to evaluate critically. This is only compounded by the problem that much of the information available online is superficial and replicative, rather than substantial and original. Recognizing that students must be taught how (and how not) to use the Internet to conduct research, and how to evaluate information they find online, is one of the most important tasks facing any instructor who would use the World Wide Web in his or her classroom.

Though these may seem obvious to many readers, based on questions I have been asked by colleagues about the value of this Web site or that, I offer the following preliminary guidelines on evaluating Web-based information: First, look for the name of the site operator or developer, not just an e-mail address. Try to find out who is behind the information. If there is an "About Us" link, read that page carefully because it often reveals important details that can bear on how seriously one ought (or ought not) to take the material presented. For example, though the Christian Apologetics and Research Ministry (www.carm.org) is a very impressive counter-cult Web site, it is by and large the sole project of one man with a Master of Divinity degree. This is not to say, of course, that nothing on the site is credible or useful, merely that it ought not be confused with information offered by those more academically prepared for the task of discussing new religious movements.

Second, ask students whether they would credence information found online if it came from an offline source. That is, if students were handed a photocopied flyer on the street entitled "Bob's Cult Report," how much weight would they lend it in their research? Though the online version may be more slick, in terms of the information provided there may be little difference between the two. Third, and especially in terms of information related to new religious movements, always insist on research triangulation. The operant definition of *cult* used by the secular anti-cult movement, for example, is substantially different from that which informs either the evangelical counter-cult movement or the social scientific study of religion, while new religious movements themselves are understandably appalled when the term is applied to them at all. In order to understand and evaluate which language is being spoken, it is important for students to know whose voice is speaking from the World Wide Web.

Exploring New Religious Communities Online

Hundreds, if not thousands, of Yahoo!- or MSN-based discussion forums style themselves "online communities." Since a great many of these maintain publicly accessible message archives, they provide an excellent opportunity for students to explore the issues raised in the debate over the authenticity of online communities. Close examination of these archives can reveal important aspects of the construction and maintenance of religious belief through sympathetic conversation, the interplay of challenge and apologetic when what we might call "information antagonists" come to the same discussion venue, and the creation (or at least the appearance of) a religious community online.

On Yahoo!, for example (http://groups.yahoo.com), discussion groups can be searched by name and individual archives examined by date, subject thread, member participation, total message traffic, number of posts per month, and message content. Following Dawson's criteria for identifying the presence of online community—(1) interactivity, (2) stability of membership, (3) stability of identity, (4) netizenship and social control, (5) personal concern, and (6) occurrence in a public space (2004: 83)—students can use these discussion archives to perform detailed ethnographic analyses. How interactive *are* the discussions? One of the things I found while researching modern pagan use of the Internet (Cowan 2005) was that, of the hundreds of Yahoo! discussion groups dedicated to modern pagan topics, only a relative few see more than marginal participation among members. Many consist of little more than forum operators posting "shovelware" (Internet material common to a number of sites and simply cut, pasted, and reloaded onto one's own site) and asking for a response from anyone who might happen to see their messages. How stable is the membership over time, and what does that membership mean? That is, can something legitimately be called an online community if it has 300 members, of which only ten people post regularly to the discussion forum? And how well do those members who do post messages know (or attempt to know) their fellow list members? Is there evidence of personal concern that they are invested in the lives and experiences of those with whom they share the forum? If it is not the case that something called a community either exists or it doesn't, blinking into being when a sufficient number of characteristics are present and disappearing the moment it falls below some theoretical threshold of viability, what can these forums tell students about the reality and the rhetoric of online communication? Depending on the particular forums chosen, this project fulfills all three of the underpinning pedagogical principles of my new religious movements course.

(Ir)responsible Information on the World Wide Web

One of the problems I encounter regularly with students' use of the Internet is that when it comes to the World Wide Web in general, and new religious movements in particular, they rarely know enough to know that they don't really know anything at all. Thus, countermovement Web sites are often quoted in student papers as though they are authoritative sources about the religious group in question, and students rarely question the provenance or the purpose of the information they encounter. While I recognize that this is often little more than a combination of Internet search engines that rank countermovement sites higher than official sites, and student unwillingness to dig deeper than absolutely necessary when completing an assignment, this problem can be turned to creative pedagogical advantage.

Recalling the three categories of NRM information available online—Web sites that are positively disposed, negatively disposed, and research orientated—as an introductory exercise in this area, I often have my students search the Internet and bring to class what they regard as useful examples of each category. Not only does this illustrate the methodological principle of research triangulation, it also provides an opportunity for students to examine their own assumptions about why they chose the Web sites they did, why they identified this group or that as a cult, and why they located Web sites in particular informational categories. To give just one obvious example, devout Christian students are often far less likely to credence the information on official movement sites such as www.witchvox.com or www.scientology.org than they are material found on evangelical counter-cult sites like www.carm.org or www.apologeticsindex.com. Since a fundamental component of every NRM course is to help students learn to think critically and analytically about the topic, highlighting these choices in class discussion discloses both their own assumptions about new religious movements and the assumptions of the broader culture.

Not surprisingly, one group that has never failed to turn up multiple times during this exercise is Heaven's Gate. This incident is particularly useful for exploring the construction and development of rumor-panics about new religious movements, something that can easily segue into class discussions about similar rumor-panics over brainwashing or Satanic ritual abuse. Fear of technology and the inability of humankind to control that which it has created have been cultural staples at least since we entered the atomic age in 1945. When combined with a popular suspicion of new religious movements that is aggravated by media coverage on a regular basis, this fear is only heightened by claims that a mysterious new technology like the World Wide Web has the power to increase a cult's influence. Because so few Internet participants understand in even the most rudimentary way how the technology functions, however, and because so few outside the relatively restricted world of NRM scholarship have considered the empirical reality of proselytization and conversion, students learn that ignorance is one of the principal foundations on which such popular fears are constructed.

COMPARING PROPAGANDAS ON THE INTERNET. A more in-depth exploration of these dynamics involves a detailed comparison of the information presented on a number of different movements, countermovements, and research Web sites. By parsing the similarities and differences in the information they find, students can learn to recognize the distinctions and make the critiques that are crucial to the academic study of new religious movements—notably the differences between (1) the variety of emic and etic voices; (2) official and unofficial institutional positions; and (3) falsifiable and nonfalsifiable religious and social structural claims made regularly by religious movements and countermovements alike.

Divided into groups based on the size of the class, students are given a single new religious movement to research online, then they present a critical analysis of the information they found. Rather than study a number of groups on a single site, each group explores numerous sites looking for information on one particular religious movement. How, specifically, does information presented about the Church of Jesus Christ of Latter-day Saints on its official site (www.lds.org) differ from a dedicated religious countermovement sites like Saints Alive in Jesus (www.saintsalive.com)? How does the definition of a cult on a Christian counter-cult site like Apologetics Index (www.apologeticsindex .com) differ from that used on secular anti-cult sites like the American Family Foundation (www.csj.org)? Are there groups that are targeted by one type of countermovement that are ignored by the other? And how are all of these sites different from scholarly sites like the Religious Movements Homepage (www .religiousmovements.org) or the Center for Study on New Religions (www .cesnur.org)?

This exercise not only exposes students in more depth to a variety of new religious movements, it also hones their ability to make more careful and nuanced evaluations of the information available on these sites. For example, while official sites often contain glowing testimonials from happy, healthy new religionists, countermovement sites almost invariably offer testimony from ex-members. In many cases, these latter voices would be silenced but for the Internet, and learning how to weight them with the analytic balance necessary is an important component of the pedagogic process. Also, because students almost inevitably find the same information on a number of sites, they learn how information on the Web is interconnected, interrelated, and often simply replicated over and over. While this may seem a rather obvious point, with the often confusing welter of hyperlinks with which a student is confronted on Web sites and search engines, it is a point easily lost.

The World Wide Web as a Research Tool

Few teachers, at whatever level of education, are unaware of the enormous plagiarism problem posed by the Internet. Rarely does a semester go by when I am not forced to confront a student who has ignored my warnings about that particular temptation. This does not address, however, the legitimate use of the Internet in student research and writing. In closing, then, I offer what has turned out to be my arc of permissibility in challenging students to use the Web for their research.

Like many of us, I began by simply requiring that students cite the Uniform Resource Locator (URL), or Internet address, for any Web pages they quoted and then reference the material in a standard bibliographic format. I quickly realized, however, that tracking down Web sites to check quotes and citations was more work than was reasonable, so I started requiring that students print out hard copies of any pages from which they quoted material and include them with their papers. A variety of problems ensued with this approach. Some students included the Web pages in the total page count for their research paper, others simply ignored my instructions, and a few pled last-minute printer failure. More problematic here, though, is the dumbing down of research skills that is encouraged by using the Internet alone. Every semester, at both the undergraduate and graduate level, there are research papers and class presentations whose preparers have gone no further than the Internet for their source materials: no books, no journal articles, and, almost inevitably, no scholarship.

Although I encourage students to use the Internet for an initial reconnaissance of their research topics—indeed, many university libraries have discontinued their subscriptions to the standard print indices of scholarly journals—the pedagogic challenge is to help students understand that they must (1) use the Web responsibly, and (2) not limit their researches to the Web. To this end, all my syllabi now contain a disclaimer about Internet research, which reads in part:

> While students are permitted to use the Internet to conduct research, citation of the Internet in research papers is permissible only under the following conditions: (1) Primary research sources are Internet-based and *only* (or only reasonably) available online—for example, you are writing *about* the Internet. (2) Secondary research sources are available online; this includes newspaper articles accessed through Lexis-Nexis, online peer-reviewed journals, and full-text articles from peer-reviewed journals accessed through databases such as JSTOR, EBSCOHost, and ATLA.

In practice, the first caveat breaks down into two parts: (1) using the Internet to conduct research into new religious movements—something I have already discussed—and (2) researching the presence and behavior of new religious movements as active Internet participants. If (1) is the Internet as a vast, if uneven library, then (2) is the World Wide Web as a sociological or anthropological field site. While I often encourage students to approach Internet research as interactive fieldwork, I also provide them with careful guidelines about disclosure and research ethics. These will be similar, I suspect, to instructions provided by most teachers, but they have added significance on the Web.

If students are analyzing discussion-forum content gathered from publicly accessible archives, there is little ethical difficulty that I can see. Participants who join forums with public archives are aware of this fact, and they have chosen to upload their communications into a public space. Though they are more technologically advanced now than a decade ago, it is not insignificant that these forums used to be called "bulletin board services"—the computer-mediated equivalent of writing a note on a piece of paper and tacking it up at the supermarket for anyone passing by to read. This dynamic changes significantly, however, when students request to conduct research interactively—as participant observers as opposed to simply readers of posted messages.

Although it has been used to unpack often very different understandings of identity, anonymity, and the Internet, numerous commentators have referenced Peter Steiner's now famous cartoon from the July 5, 1993, *New Yorker*, in which one dog with a paw on a computer keyboard says to another dog sitting on the floor, "On the Internet, nobody knows you're a dog." Put in the terms of this discussion, "In an online Wiccan chat room, nobody knows you're a sociology student . . . but they should." Responsible research in this context means more than just not copying the work of others. It means not pretending to be something one is not.

In addition to being illegal, making various claims to online identity can be unethical or immoral, a fact that should not go unimpressed on students. Writing *Cyberhenge*, for example, presented numerous opportunities to engage in unethical research practices (Cowan 2005). Presenting myself as a modern pagan seeker, I could easily have joined any number of online Wicca 101 classes. I could have claimed to be a young woman from a First Nations background seeking to integrate my native spirituality with aspects of Wicca. I could have presented myself as an elderly man looking for spiritual solace in the twilight years of my life. Or, as an even more egregious experiment that builds on a number of examples I have found on the Web, I could have invented my own modern pagan lineage, borrowed the same shovelware used by many other sites, and simply started my own Wicca 101 class. If these gross distortions of identity are regarded as problematic offline, why should the situation be considered substantively different or more desirable online?

My instructions to students in this context are simple. First, disclose *your* identity. While some new religionists are reluctant to discuss their beliefs and practices with nonmembers, especially if they have not fully disclosed their own new religious affiliation to friends and family, many others are flattered that researchers are taking an interest in them and they are more than willing to share details of their spiritual journeys. Second, protect *their* identity.

Respect your sources, and unless informants specifically give you permission to use their real names, use pseudonyms.

Another overarching caveat on use of the Internet in student research concerns secondary sources. A number of scholarly and media resources are now available online, and academic databases such as JSTOR and the EBSCOHost sites often provide links to full-text versions of articles. Lexis-Nexis allows students to conduct media searches quickly and thoroughly, often from their home computers. Students are permitted to use these because they represent the journal stacks at the library that have been translated online.

If secondary research sources are simply taken from ordinary Web sites, however, these secondary sources, whether scholarly or corroborative, *must* be cited in the presentation or the research paper. For example, if a student is doing a project on Vodoun, I will not accept as secondary research the material simply taken from practitioner Web sites; it must be corroborated by other sources. I also do not generally permit students to cite online versions of offline material that is readily available in the library; that is, they *cannot* cite online versions of the Ante-Nicene Patristics. They must go to the library and properly cite book, chapter, and page number(s). While the Internet can be a tremendous boon to scholarship, I fear that it is also responsible for creating one of the laziest generations of students and scholars in the history of higher education, and I do what I can in each class to stem that particular tide.

INTERNET SOURCES

Primary Sites

Church of All Worlds: www.caw.org.
Church of Jesus Christ of Latter-day Saints: www.lds.org.
Church of the Goddess: www.cog.org.
Church of Scientology: www.scientology.org.
Community of Christ: www.cofchrist.org.
Heaven's Gate: www.heavensgate.com.
International Society for Krishna Consciousness: www.iskcon.com; www.krishna.com.
ISKCON Revival Movement: www.iskconirm.org.
JaguarMoon Cybercoven: www.jaguarmoon.org.
Raelian Religion: www.rael.org.
Temple of Set: www.xeper.org.
United Nuwaubian Nation of Moors: www.geocities.com/Area51/Corridor/4978/unnm.html.
Witches' Voice: www.witchvox.com.

Countermovement Sites

American Family Foundation: www.csj.org.
Apologetics Index: www.apologeticsindex.com.
Christian Apologetics and Research Ministry: www.carm.org.
Saints Alive in Jesus: www.saintsalive.com.
Watchman Fellowship: www.watchman.org.

New Religious Research Sites

American Religion Data Archive: www.thearda.com.
Center for Studies on New Religions: www.cesnur.org.
Information Network Focus on Religious Movements: www.inform.ac.
Internet Sacred Texts Archives: www.sacred-texts.com.
Ontario Consultants on Religious Tolerance: www.religioustolerance.org.
Religious Movements Homepage Project: www.religiousmovements.org.

REFERENCES

Berger, Helen, and Douglas Ezzy. 2004. "The Internet as Virtual Spiritual Commu-
nity: Teen Witches in the United States and Australia." In *Religion Online: Finding
Faith on the Internet*, ed. Lorne L. Dawson and Douglas E. Cowan, 189–203. New
York: Routledge.
Brown, Janelle. 1998. "A Web of Their Own." *Salon*. Available at http://archive.salon
.com// 21st/feature/1998/07/15feature.htm. Accessed August 3, 2004.
Bunt, Gary R. 2000. "Surfing Islam: Ayatollahs, Shayks, and Hajjis on the Super-
highway." In *Religion on the Internet: Research Prospects and Promises*, ed. Jeffrey K.
Hadden and Douglas E. Cowan, 127–51. London and Amsterdam: JAI Press/
Elsevier Science.
Clark, Lynn Schofield. 2003. *From Angels to Aliens: Teenagers, the Media, and the
Supernatural*. New York: Oxford University Press.
Cowan, Douglas E. 2000. "Religion, Rhetoric, and Scholarship: Managing Vested
Interest in E-Space." In *Religion on the Internet: Research Prospects and Promises*,
ed. Jeffrey K. Hadden and Douglas E. Cowan, 101–24. London and Amsterdam:
JAI Press/Elsevier Science.
———. 2002. "Exits and Migrations: Foregrounding the Christian Counter-Cult."
Journal of Contemporary Religion 17, 339–54.
———. 2003. *Bearing False Witness? An Introduction to the Christian Countercult*.
Westport, CT: Praeger.
———. 2004. "Contested Spaces: Movement, Countermovement, and E-Space Propaganda." In *Religion Online: Finding Faith on the Internet*, ed. Lorne L. Dawson
and Douglas E. Cowan, 255–71. New York: Routledge.
———. 2005. *Cyberhenge: Modern Pagans on the Internet*. New York: Routledge.
Cowan, Douglas E., and Jeffrey K. Hadden. 2004a. "God, Guns, and Grist for the
Media's Mill: Constructing the Narratives of New Religious Movements and
Violence." *Nova Religio* 8, 64–82.
———. 2004b. "Virtually Religious: New Religious Movements and the World Wide
Web." In *The Oxford Handbook of New Religious Movements*, ed. James R. Lewis,
119–40. New York: Oxford University Press.
Dawson, Lorne L. 2004. "Religion and the Quest for Virtual Community." In *Religion
Online: Finding Faith on the Internet*, ed. Lorne L. Dawson and Douglas E. Cowan,
25–54. New York: Routledge.
Dawson, Lorne L., and Douglas E. Cowan 2004. "Introduction." In *Religion Online:
Finding Faith on the Internet*, ed. Lorne L. Dawson and Douglas E. Cowan, 1–16.
New York: Routledge.
Dawson, Lorne L., and Jennifer Hennebry. 1999. "New Religions and the Internet:
Recruiting in a New Public Space." *Journal of Contemporary Religion* 14, 17–39.

Finke, Roger, Jennifer McKinney, and Matt Bahr. 2000. "Doing Research and
    Teaching with the American Religion Data Archive." In *Religion on the Internet:
    Research Prospects and Promises*, ed. Jeffrey K. Hadden and Douglas E. Cowan,
    81–99. London and Amsterdam: JAI Press/Elsevier Science.
Glassner, Barry. 1999. *The Culture of Fear: Why Americans Are Afraid of the Wrong
    Things*. New York: Basic Books.
Hadden, Jeffrey K. 2000. "Confessions of a Recovering Technophobe: A Brief History
    of the Religious Movements Homepage Project." In *Religion on the Internet:
    Research Prospects and Promises*, ed. Jeffrey K. Hadden and Douglas E. Cowan,
    345–62. London and Amsterdam: JAI Press/Elsevier Science.
Hadden, Jeffrey K., and Douglas E. Cowan. 2000. "The Promised Land or Electronic
    Chaos? Toward Understanding Religion on the Internet." In *Religion on the In-
    ternet: Research Prospects and Promises*, ed. Jeffrey K. Hadden and Douglas E.
    Cowan, 3–21. London and Amsterdam: JAI Press/Elsevier Science.
Helland, Christopher. 2000. "Online Religion/Religion Online and Virtual Commu-
    nitas." In *Religion on the Internet: Research Prospects and Promises*, ed. Jeffrey Hadden
    and Douglas Cowan, 205–24. London and Amsterdam: JAI Press/Elsevier Science.
Levy, Steven. 1997. "Blaming the Web." *Newsweek*, April 7, pp. 46–47.
Lockard, Joseph. 1997. "Progressive Politics, Electronic Individualism, and the
    Myth of Virtual Community." In *Internet Culture*, ed. David Porter, 219–32.
    New York: Routledge.
Macwilliams, Mark. 2004. "Virtual Pilgrimage to Ireland's Croagh Patrick." In *Religion
    Online: Finding Faith on the Internet*, ed. Lorne L. Dawson and Douglas E. Cowan,
    223–37. New York: Routledge.
Markoff, John. 1997. "Death in a Cult: The Technology." *New York Times*, March 28,
    p. A-20.
Miller, Mark. 1997. "Secrets of the Cult." *Newsweek*, April 14, p. 29.
Robinson, Bruce A. 2000. "Evolution of a Web Site Devoted to Tolerance." In *Religion
    on the Internet: Research Prospects and Promises*, ed. Jeffrey K. Hadden and
    Douglas E. Cowan, 309–23. London and Amsterdam: JAI Press/Elsevier Science.
Robinson, Joanne Maguire. 2000. "Mapping a 'Cyberlimen': A Test Case for the Study
    of Electronic Discussion Boards in Religious Studies Classes." In *Religion on the
    Internet: Research Prospects and Promises*, ed. Jeffrey K. Hadden and Douglas E.
    Cowan, 325–44. London and Amsterdam: JAI Press/Elsevier Science.
Robinson, Wendy Gale. 1997. "Heaven's Gate: The End?" *Journal of Computer-
    Mediated Communication* 3(3). Available at www.ascusc.org/jcmc/vol3/issue3/
    robinson.html. Accessed June 2, 2004.
Slouka, Mark. 1995. *War of the Worlds: Cyberspace and the High-Tech Assault on Reality*.
    New York: Basic Books.
Srilatha, D., and Agarwhal, Sarita. 1997. "Experience the Occult, as 'Heaven's Gate'
    Opens." *Computers Today*, May 1, p. 95.
Stoll, Clifford. 1999. *High-Tech Heretic: Reflections of a Computer Contrarian*.
    New York: Anchor.
Urban, Hugh. 2000. "The Devil at Heaven's Gate: Rethinking the Study of Religion
    in the Age of Cyber-Space." *Nova Religio* 3, 269–302.
Young, Glenn A. 2004. "Reading and Praying Online: The Continuity of Religion
    Online and Online Religion in Internet Christianity." In *Religion Online: Finding
    Faith on the Internet*, ed. Lorne L. Dawson and Douglas E. Cowan, 93–105.
    New York: Routledge.

Charting the Information Field: Cult-Watching Groups and the Construction of Images of New Religious Movements

Eileen Barker

Religious pluralism is by no means a new phenomenon, but with increasing globalization, migration, the expansion of the mass media, and most recently the spread of the Internet, the visibility of new religious movements (NRMs) would seem to have reached an unprecedented level in the West. But not only are we presented with alternative religions offering us different truths, different ways of living, and different means of achieving different visions of salvation, we are also bombarded with radically different depictions of these movements. Together the depictions have generated a marketplace in which alternative images of reality compete for acceptance by the general populace, particularly by those in positions of power who might be able to enhance or diminish the power of these religions. While new religious movements are offering alternative sets of beliefs and practices to all who are willing to listen to their accounts of themselves, other people are presenting alternative constructions of these movements' beliefs and practices that differ not only from the NRMs but also from each other.

There are, however, limits to the potential confusion we may find ourselves confronting. While it is true that no two individuals ever see social phenomena in exactly the same way, there are always some aspects of a social phenomenon that will be shared by pretty well everyone; for example, while a father might see the Unificationist Church as exploiting his daughter, and the daughter may see it as offering liberation, both will agree that it is a movement created in Korea by a man known as Sun Myung Moon and that its beliefs are based on a text known as *Divine Principle*.

It is also true that we can discern systematic differences among different people and what they perceive. Furthermore, it is possible to discern more or less regular patterns in how the suppliers and consumers of these different images take account, not only of their own particular interests but also of competing images as they construct and refine their own images. And, as in previous periods of history, like-minded individuals have formed cult-watching groups (CWGs) with the aim of promoting their own views and mobilizing support for their particular perspectives.

The resulting cacophony can, to say the least, be confusing for the uninitiated who are faced with accounts that seem so much at variance with each other. However, by scrutinizing the incongruent images of NRMs that confront us, teachers can address some of the fundamental questions underpinning the pedagogical enterprise:

- How can we teach students to critically assess and evaluate the profusion of information they are presented with, not only in the classroom but also in every other aspect of their lives?
- How can they learn to distinguish blatant untruths, fallacious arguments, or empty rhetoric from reliable data and rational thought?
- How can they develop the capacity to recognize ways in which they might be manipulated (directly or indirectly, consciously or subconsciously) so that they see the world through one pair of glasses rather than another?
- How might they come to recognize that other people can sincerely and legitimately hold views that differ from their own?

One way of approaching the disparity among images constructed by the various CWGs is by recognizing that these images are frequently asking different questions. Once this situation is appreciated, the answers become somewhat less confusing; quite a few of the seemingly conflicting statements are more comprehensible. Put another way, if we can understand where a particular group "is coming from," we might be better equipped to assess the way it depicts various movements.

To pursue this further, I shall construct some ideal-typical models of CWGs on the basis of the question each group asks. The question is usually motivated by the group's underlying interests and the policy toward NRMs that it advocates. These interests, in turn, are linked to the methodology the group employs—the sources upon which it depends for building its image of the NRMs—and the aspects of each movement that it is likely to select and, just as importantly, to repudiate, avoid, or ignore when it constructs and projects its image of the movement.

Ideal-Types of Cult-Watching Groups

The sociologist Max Weber (1949) popularized the "ideal-type" as a conceptual tool, constructed for the purpose of comparison. It provides a model or template against which the confused and confusing institutions and processes found in reality can be compared to an "ideal" structure or pattern of behavior. This tool enables us to see how close (or how far) different phenomena are from the ideal-type and in what particular ways they differ from it and, thus, from each other. The ideal-type may also lead to testable hypotheses by suggesting that certain variables are likely to be found co-existing while other characteristics are less likely to be found together. In this way, the ideal-type helps us to create some order out of the constantly shifting and complex realities of social life.

It should be stressed that the ideal-type does not claim to represent reality. It should be judged as more or less useful, rather than more or less true. Furthermore, the "ideal" aspect of the ideal-type does not describe a characteristic that is ideal in the sense of its being the best in any evaluative way. It is, rather, ideal in the sense that it is representing a particular characteristic (or characteristics) so that the degree of presence or absence of that characteristic (or characteristics) is more apparent.

As CWGs, like all phenomena, have different characteristics that can be selected to describe them, we need to select a characteristic or variable that will be useful insofar as it is likely that other characteristics or features might follow from its presence (or absence). For our purposes, we are interested in the characteristics of CWGs that will help us assess the reliability of their information for a particular purpose. That purpose could be to alert others to the movement's dangers or to its positive features; it could be to assess the movement's theological accuracy or ethical value; or it could be to obtain an objective and balanced overview of its beliefs and practices.

New Religious Movements

It might seem that a new religious movement is in some ways the most reliable, but in other ways the least reliable, source of information about itself. It is, of course, the members and their interactions that provide the "primary construction" of an NRM that the CWGs claim to describe. By "being," the NRM is the reality that all the varied "secondary constructions" claim to represent (Barker 1995). Surely, one might ask, the NRM must know better than outsiders what it is like? And in many respects this is undoubtedly true. There are, however, problems with this situation.

First, there are many aspects of any movement and new converts are likely to "see" a very different movement from those in a position of leadership. Second, even if we were to grant that insiders might construct images of their movements that bear more resemblance to each other than they do to outsiders' images, we still have to recognize that the members are constructing *their* picture—that is, they will be selecting certain characteristics but not others.

This is not to suggest that NRMs typically lie about themselves (though some do). There have certainly been false images of NRMs constructed by both the movements and their opponents. Some religions have been known to advocate dishonesty as part of their policy, examples being the "heavenly deception" advocated by sections of the Unification Church, the "transcendental trickery" of some ISKCON devotees, and the sanctioning of what some term lies through the Roman Catholic Church's Doctrine of Mental Reservation. More commonly, however, it is through selecting and/or stressing some things rather than others that the different pictures emerge.

None of the ideal-types we shall discuss is, to take a trivial example, likely to include an account of members of NRMs cleaning their teeth in the morning. The ideal-types are far more likely to address issues considered to be of greater significance. So far as NRMs are concerned, they will be offering a response to the question, "What is so good, exclusive, new, special, and right about the movement?" Their interest is quite likely to persuade nonmembers—and members—that they are the best and that they alone have the Truth. They will focus on their successes, while it is unlikely that they will parade their failures. So far as possible, any skeletons will remain locked in the cupboard.

Being the creators and perpetuators of their movements, it might seem superfluous for an NRM to turn to any other authority in its description of itself, yet it is by no means uncommon for the movements to woo and seek endorsements from public figures who are considered to be more persuasive than the movements themselves, in the light of the negative coverage they receive in the media and elsewhere. Photographs are taken of the leader shaking hands or in conversation with world leaders, or failing that, with a local dignitary such as a mayor—although few of these notables will know much about the NRM, its beliefs or practices. Sometimes scholars are quoted (often out of context); sometimes academic institutions are persuaded to grant honorary degrees to the founders of the new faith. Obviously, testimonies by converts are of how their lives have been enriched; testimonies from former members who have become disillusioned with the movement are unlikely to feature.

Cult-Awareness Groups

The ideal-type of a cult-awareness group (CAG) is in some ways a mirror image of the NRM. For the CAG, the underlying question is, "What do the movements do that is actually or potentially harmful to their own members, to other people, and/or to society in general?" Given this concern, it is not surprising that a subsidiary question is, "How can we control the movements?" Nor is it surprising that the images produced by CAGs concentrate on the more negative aspects of these movements and tend to ignore not only any positive but also any "normal" aspects of the movements, which they are likely to label as "destructive cults."

As outlined in the chapter by Richardson and Introvigne, there were a number of parents in the early 1970s who formed cult-awareness groups (collectively referred to as the anti-cult movement) in North America and Western Europe; they were concerned about their (adult) children's suddenly converting and giving up promising careers and futures to follow a charismatic leader who, the parents believed, was exploiting their sons and daughters. The parents did, however, face several difficulties in their attempts to mobilize action against NRMs through their accounts of the movements. One problem was that their children were blissfully unaware of the harm to which they were being subjected. On the contrary, they were defining their new movement in the glowing terms we might expect from an enthusiastic convert. Clearly it was necessary for the CAGs to have a good reason for painting such a different picture. Another problem that CAGs faced was the widely accepted belief in the West that people have a right to religious freedom, a belief firmly endorsed by the United Nations' Universal Declaration of Human Rights and other internationally accepted resolutions.

An answer to these problems was provided by a popular explanation for the apparently inexplicable conversions: the so-called brainwashing thesis. According to brainwashing logic, the converts were not *really* happy, nor had they made a free choice to join the NRM. Rather, something had been done to them—they had been subjected to irresistible and irreversible techniques that had rendered them incapable of resistance or escape or of recognizing their own best interests. The thesis, which appeared to have the further advantage of absolving both parents and converts from any responsibility (let alone culpability), was strengthened by professional deprogrammers, who had a financial interest in persuading the parents that, if they wanted to see their sons or daughters again, they would have to pay thousands (sometimes tens of thousands) of dollars or pounds to arrange for their adult children to be forcibly (and illegally) kidnapped and involuntarily held until they renounced their faith.

In other words, one of the major harms that cult-awareness groups include either explicitly or implicitly in their portrayals of NRMs is that the converts (some insist on the more passive term *recruits*) are hapless victims, lured into the movements against their will and now subjected to all manner of dangerous processes and prepared to perform all manner of undesirable actions against what would "normally" be their better judgment. The images constructed by CAGs thus tend to use the passive voice when speaking of the grass-roots membership: "X was done to the recruit," "The victim was made to do Y," or "The victim has to be rescued," rather than "The convert decided to do this or that." None of the movement's features that might have seemed attractive to the convert are mentioned. Or, if they are, they are described in such as way as to appear to be some sort of duplicity. Actions that in other circumstances might be labeled "good deeds" (such as helping the poor or elderly) are described as, at best, "public relations exercises," or, at worst, devious manipulations for some nefarious goal (the leadership, as opposed to the hapless victims, being able to define the situation to their own advantage).

The brainwashing thesis also allows CAGs to declare that they fully support the principle of religious freedom for all, and that it is the NRMs that have taken away their members' freedom. However, although many NRMs (like other proselytizing believers such as Evangelical Christians) do put pressure on people to accept their beliefs and way of life, all the evidence suggests that their techniques of mind control are not all that efficient. Only a small proportion of those who are subjected to the movements' attempts to influence them actually agree to join, and the majority of those who do succumb are likely to leave within a year or two (Bromley 1988). Both the NRMs and the CAGs have tended to keep quiet or even deny that the turnover in NRM membership is higher than for most traditional religions. The NRMs do not want to advertise the fact that converts become disillusioned with the movement, and the CAGs do not want to advertise the fact that converts not only can, but frequently do, leave of their own accord. In fact, many NRMs now have difficulty keeping more than a minority of the children who they have brought up and socialized in their movement.

NRMs have, of course, caused harm; and CAGs can be seen as performing a valuable role in alerting potential converts, and the world at large, to actual and potential dangers. When, however, their claims become too stringent, their images can lose some of their salience. Both police and government officials have told me that they rarely get useful information from groups that closely resemble the CAG ideal-type, as they already know what they will be told about any NRM about which they seek information. What they will be offered, they say, is a string of negative attributes such as brainwashing, splitting up families, financial malpractice, political intrigue, and criminal tendencies that range from selling goods without a peddler's license to mass murder.

It is a common practice of the CAG ideal-type to generalize from the genuine dangers of a few specific cases, suggesting that these are common features of all NRMs. Thus, one reads or hears the phrase "Cults break up families" or "Cults train their members to commit suicide," rather than that this particular movement, at this place and time, had two members who killed themselves.

A related tactic is to imply guilt through association, the association often being invoked by little more than the negative baggage that comes with the label "cult." After the tragic happening in 1978, when over 900 members of the Peoples Temple committed suicide or were murdered, references to the Peoples Temple could be found in nearly every mention of NRMs. A quarter of a century later, the Peoples Temple deaths are still frequently mentioned, together with the events associated with the Solar Temple, Heaven's Gate, the Branch Davidians, and Aum Shinrikyo. The point here is not that these were not horrific occurrences, but that hundreds of law-abiding NRMs have also existed over the past half-century, and that all NRMs are all being tarred with the same brush.

There is a further twist to the CAG ideal-type generalization in that it implies that the negative actions attributed to NRMs are not to be found in more traditional religions. For example, those who repeatedly state that "cults break up families" get indignant at the suggestion that Jesus did such a thing; if biblical verses such as Luke 14:26 or Matthew 10:35–36 are quoted, one may be told that His words have to be understood in a different context, yet such elucidation is less likely to be extended to the NRMs.

Again, following from the question "What harm do the movements do?" we should not be surprised that the principal source of information for CAGs' depictions of NRMs are people with negative experiences in the movements or with some political or financial interest in perpetuating a harmful image. Originally this circle of people consisted of concerned relatives and friends of members, and later it incorporated former members, particularly those who had been "deprogrammed" and taught to see their "cult experience" in negative terms (Lewis 1986). The ideal-typical CAG is likely to refuse to have any association with the NRMs themselves, insisting that (1) the movements would only lie to them, (2) they could be in danger of succumbing to mind-control techniques, and/or (3) they would risk giving the movements credibility by recognizing them in any way.

While NRMs try to improve their image through endorsements by high-status personnel, CAGs try to denigrate anyone who proposes an image of the movements at variance with their own. Members of NRMs are dismissed as either brainwashed or deceptive. Scholars who have studied the NRMs and are not unequivocally against the movements are defined as "cult apologists" or are smeared with *ad hominem* arguments. In other words, what the scholars write is not criticized with evidence but, rather, is denied or dismissed through a slur (be it true or false) that has no bearing on the truth.

Counter-Cult Groups

Members of our next ideal-type ask the question, "What do the movements believe that is wrong?" The counter-cult groups (CCGs) differ from CAGs in that, rather than being concerned about the NRMs' actions, they are troubled by their teachings. They are often, but by no means exclusively, conservative Christians who feel strongly that they need to protect their interpretation of Scripture, and that people who have different interpretations are heretics or infidels who may be bound for (and perhaps have to be saved from) eternal damnation. Most of the debate is of a nonempirical nature; and in the final analysis, the truth of the claims that are being made are a question of faith.

It is important that students recognize the difference between theological claims and claims of a testable nature. A good starting point is the definition by Karl Popper (1963: chap. 1) of a scientific statement as one that is empirically falsifiable. At the same time, it is also important to recognize that pointing out to believers that a theological statement has apparently been falsified and/or contains a logically fallacious argument will not necessarily dissuade them from their belief. The supernatural can, by definition, overcome the rules of nature, and even of logic (as might appear to the nonbeliever contemplating the doctrines of transubstantiation, the virgin birth, or the Trinity). This makes it difficult to have a conclusive argument with someone who is arguing on theological grounds. You might point out that the Scripture does not say X (or that it also says Y, which might seem to contradict X), or you might point out that the world did not end on the date predicted by the NRM. The believers might, however, reply that something *did* happen, but in the spirit world, or that the catastrophe was averted because of the believers' prayers or actions, or that there is some other explanation for the apparent failure of the prophecy.

Research-Oriented Groups

The basic question that members of research-oriented groups (ROGs) pose is, "What are the movements like?" This question encompasses a whole series of subsidiary questions such as: What are their beliefs and practices? Who is likely to join them and how likely are they to remain members? What kind of lifestyle do they adopt? What authority structures and communication networks are used in the organization of the movement? What are their attitudes toward women, children, education, sex, marriage, medicine, death, the outside society? Are members expected to eat certain kinds of food, wear certain kinds of clothes, or listen to certain kinds of music? How do they differ internally in different settings? How do they change over time? How do they interact with other sections of society, such as relatives, former friends, the media, government bodies, other religions, and/or the law? And how do these and other sections of the public react to the movements?

In trying to construct as balanced and objective a picture as possible, ROGs include descriptions of actions, whether they are considered good or bad, and beliefs, whether they are considered right or wrong. But unlike CAGs and CCGs, ROGs try to avoid pronouncing on the truth or falsity of the movements' theological or ideological doctrines, and they attempt to adopt a value-free stance so far as morality is concerned. This is not to say, of course, that they are not concerned with questions that are relevant to value judgments—*value freedom*, referring to the objectivity of the data, and *value relevance*, referring to the usefulness for implementing certain value positions (Weber 1949). Thus, while social scientists, *qua* citizens, can decide to investigate certain questions that they consider important, and to use the results of that investigation for ethical or political ends, their actual research (description, analysis, and explanation) should be free of their own subjective value judgments and reflect only the object of study. Of course, this is more easily said than done, but the social sciences have developed several techniques aimed at pursuing such a goal.

While acknowledging that definitions are a necessary means of communication, ROGs also recognize that exactly how these are delineated is arbitrary (or, at least, socially relative), rather than reflecting some God-given truth. They are, thus, likely to refrain from asserting whether or not a particular movement is a "real" religion. They may, however, be interested in charting the ways in which players in the "cult scene" use, and sometimes manipulate, definitions and labels to further their own interests. A NRM might, for example, want to be defined as a religion in order to gain tax exemption, or not be defined as a religion so that it can teach its practices in public schools in the United States; Christian CCGs will assert that an NRM that in many ways shares its own beliefs is not a Christian movement; CAGs will say that an NRM claiming religious persecution is not a real religion but a cult.

ROGs tend to consist of scholars whose interest in the NRMs is more professional than personal, the majority having been trained in one or other of the social sciences, such as the sociology of religion, history of religions, anthropology, or religious studies, and it is the methodology of the social sciences that ideal-typically informs their pictures of the movements. This means that they are likely to engage in a number of techniques (such as interview, questionnaire, participant observation, and the content analysis of literature), and to approach NRMs from a variety of angles, taking account of the different perspectives to build up a multidimensional picture. This will involve studying both members and nonmembers of the movements.

If social scientists want to make a generalization, they will need, ideal-typically (1) to avoid bias by obtaining a random sample (when each individual has an equal probability of being selected for interview or questionnaire), and (2) to make use of a control group (Barker 1995). This means that, unlike most of the other types of cult-watching groups, the ROG will include a study of people who have no connection with the NRMs. Although this might at first seem somewhat perverse, the reason is that the scientific method is based on comparison as a means of finding out "what goes with what" or, to put it another way, science attempts to establish the ways in which different variables are correlated (or, just as important, not correlated) with each other. There can be quite a strong association between two things—say, a cult and suicide—in the public mind, when, objectively speaking, there might be no association (or possibly a negative one) between the two.

Taking this example, one might read perfectly accurate accounts under headlines such as "Cult Member Commits Suicide" on two or three occasions and come to the not unreasonable conclusion that there is a connection between being a member of an NRM and committing suicide. Recognizing that visibility is not the same thing as actuality, and that the media are unlikely to produce headlines announcing "Methodist Commits Suicide"—that, indeed, even if the suicide is reported, any mainstream religious affiliation is unlikely to be mentioned at all—the social scientist would want to find out what the rate of suicide was for nonmembers of a similar age and background as members. It is not inconceivable that it turns out that the suicide rate of nonmembers was twice that of members. If this were the case, the ROG might then ask what it is about the movement that could prevent, rather than encourage, its members to kill themselves. Of course, it may be that those with nonsuicidal tendencies are less likely to join the movement in the first place, but at least the question will have been raised, rather than there being an all-too-ready assumption that suicide is typical of the movement and atypical of the rest of society.

By the late 1970s, a number of scholars who had been studying the NRMs out of an academic interest were becoming increasingly aware that the images of the movements that they were constructing were not only radically different from but also being attacked by cult-watching groups and some of the media (as well as by disgruntled NRMs). In particular, they found themselves at odds with CAGs over issues related to brainwashing, the use of value-laden concepts, and generalizations and assumptions of negative behaviors being associated with NRMs in ways that, it was assumed, they were not associated with older religions, other social institutions, and/or the population at large. As a consequence of this, a number of ROGs emerged, some of which entered the political arena by trying to promote their images as alternatives to those being marketed by other CWGs.

Several of these ROGs are loose affiliations of academics, such as the Swedish FINYAR (www.finyar.se), German REMID (www.remid.de), Hungarian VIK (Centre for Information on Religion), and Lithuanian NRTIC (New Religions Research and Information Centre) (http://en.religija.lt). Groups such as J. Gordon Melton's Institute for the Study of American Religion (www .americanreligion.org), and Massimo Introvigne's CESNUR publish informative encyclopedias and books; CESNUR also organizes a series of international conferences and runs a Web site with a wealth of material concerning the NRMs (www.cesnur.org); another invaluable ROG Web site was established by the late Jeffrey Hadden and is now edited by Douglas Cowan (http:// religiousmovements.lib.virginia.edu/home.htm). At this point I must declare an interest because, in the late 1980s, I founded an ROG called Inform (www .inform.ac), which had the support of the British government and mainstream churches. Inform's primary aim is to provide information about minority religions that is as objective and up-to-date as possible. Like most other ROGs, Inform has been, and continues to be, attacked by various CAGs, CCGs, and NRMs—all of whom question its approach, labeling it a "cult apologist" in the case of the former two types and "anti-cultist" in the case of the latter (Barker 2001). It remains, however, the only CWG for which the British government is willing to provide financial support.

Human Rights Groups

Ideal-typical human rights groups (HRGs) ask the question, "In what ways are NRMs discriminated against?" Their interest is in safeguarding the rights of the movements if these are transgressed by individuals, groups, or governments. They report on discriminatory legislation, unjust applications of the law, intolerant acts, and unfair treatment and/or depictions of the movements.

The concerns of many of the HRGs are not confined to NRMs, but encompass minority ethnic and political groups as well. They may know relatively little about the movements, their main interest being in what happens to them rather than in what they believe or do. They should, however, be mentioned as they not infrequently clash with the CAGs, and there are some HRGs, such as Human Rights Without Frontiers, that focus primarily on minority religions. Some HRGs are directly associated with NRMs, one example being the Foundation for Religious Freedom (FRF). Older minority religions also run HRGs, but a number of these (like several inter-faith groups) prefer, sometimes quite explicitly, to dissociate themselves from the newer religions, concentrating instead on protecting their own freedoms.

Cult-Defender Groups

Cult-defender groups (CDGs) can be seen as a mirror image of the CAGs and CCGs. They ask, "What is good and true about NRMs?" CDGs tend to have an interest in exposing how the movements have been discriminated against by "bad" CAGs and "wrong" CCGs, and how the media have distorted the truth about the movements. CDGs are frequently closely associated with the NRMs themselves, with members sometimes working for the group in some organizational capacity. There are, indeed, some CDGs that are almost entirely run by one or more NRMs, one example being the New CAN. The Old CAN (Cult Awareness Network) was a CAG that was declared bankrupt as the consequence of a court case resulting from an incident involving forcible deprogramming. The Church of Scientology (in association with the FRF) bought the CAN name and telephone number, and the New CAN now supplies inquirers with its construal of NRMs which, unsurprisingly, differs radically from that of the Old CAN.

The Media

Although not a cult-watching group in the same way as the ideal-types outlined above, the media are undoubtedly the most influential constructors of images of NRMs in that they are the main, if not the only, source of information about the movements for the overwhelming majority of people; consequently, they play an important role in the cult scene. A separate chapter in this volume (by Richardson and Introvigne) covers the media in detail, but I would like to consider them here from a slightly different angle, as a significant number of them ideal-typically share certain features that can alert us to some characteristics in their constructions of NRMs, despite the fact that the reliability of these depictions varies enormously.

First, the media's primary interest is to attract and keep an audience of readers, viewers, and listeners, so members of the media ask the question, "What will make a good story?" With good reason, it is commonly assumed that the largest proportion of a potential audience will be attracted by a story that is about something new and exotic, rather than the familiar and everyday. In many ways, bad news is good news for the media. A story about a bizarre and/or destructive cult that has unconventional sexual practices and/or commits criminal actions and/or brainwashes innocent victims is more likely to attract an audience than one about a young student who, while continuing to live with his parents, has converted to a new religion and is doing quite well in his studies.

Furthermore, the media tend to work under the pressures of time and space, for both the production and the presentation of their story. They often have only a few days (sometimes only a few hours) to put together their report.

They do not always have time to check facts, let alone to investigate different points of view. The minutes that they are on air or the number of words they are allotted are strictly limited, allowing for little in the way of qualification or the provision of citations.

The media are, moreover, generally of a transitory nature in the sense that their presentations are relatively unavailable for checking after the initial impression has been made. Thus a particular picture, sound bite, or association of ideas might stick in the listeners', readers', or viewers' memory, while the more general context and any qualifications are forgotten. Sometimes, despite the fact that no false statements are made, a completely fallacious image can be given. A striking example was a television film about the Soka Gakkai in the United Kingdom that was "topped and tailed" by pictures of rescuers taking victims of sarin gas from the Tokyo underground. The only factual link between the two movements was that they had both originated in Japan. Despite the fact that the story named members of Aum Shinrikyo as responsible for the outrage, for the students who talked to me after viewing the program, the media's lumping together of the two NRMs left a vivid impression that the pacific UK members of Soka Gakkai were associated with such lethal behavior.

This ideal-typical depiction of the media suggests that the media will likely have a symbiotic relationship with cult-awareness groups. The media accept CAG images of NRMs more readily than those of the other CWGs, since the CAGs are most likely to construct uncomplicated stories of "dangerous cults" and thereby provide the more sensational exposés that can attract an audience. While counter-cult groups also produce negative images of NRMs, details about how their beliefs deviate from the Truth are likely to be of interest only to those who already accept the Truth professed by the CCGs. Images constructed by cult defenders are unlikely to be acceptable in a climate typically disposed to be suspicious of, if not openly antagonistic toward, NRMs; and ROGs, quite apart from offering a less sensational (potentially boring) story, tend to go in for long-winded qualifications rather than catchy sound bites.

The Caring Professions

The caring professions (social workers, therapists, counselors, and exit counselors) are not normally concerned about NRMs, but some who have treated former NRM members have consequently offered their constructions of the movements in the public marketplace of competing images. These images have been of particular salience with reference to ritual Satanic abuse, but are not confined to such cases. For the ideal-typical social worker or therapist, the key question is, "How can the former member be helped?" This can lead to collaboration between the client and the therapist or the social worker in the construction of a narrative that will make sense to the client and allow him or her to get on with life. In extreme cases, therapists or social workers might not only interpret but actually create a client's experiences through, perhaps, the use of leading questions.

Obviously enough, dealing with case studies of individuals who have been harmed (or encouraged to feel that they have been harmed) is not likely to yield a balanced picture of the movement. It is possible, of course, that the movement does even more harm than the therapist is aware of; either way, the construction certainly does not involve the use of random samples or a control group. The point is that, however much the therapist or social worker is successful in helping the client recover from an experience in the NRM, merely talking to the client will give rise to a one-sided and partial picture of the movement. In some ways, it is like a divorce lawyer relying exclusively on his clients' accounts to construct a picture of the institution of marriage.

Lawyers

When lawyers take part in a court of law, especially in countries that, like the United States or the United Kingdom rely on an adversarial (as opposed to an inquisitorial) system, they have to argue for one of two opposing versions of the facts. The final outcome is that one version is accepted and the other rejected. The question that is being addressed is, "How can the court be persuaded to pronounce that the defendant is guilty (or innocent) of a particular offense?" In such circumstances, there are strict rules about what is considered admissible evidence. Even expert witnesses are limited in what they can say by the questions that they are asked about a specific aspect of the case, which is unlikely to be concerned about the movement as a whole. Furthermore, the final judgment will be an all-or-nothing verdict, whereas in reality guilt and truth are rarely that straightforward.

Problems arise when the outcome of a court case is presented as proof that an NRM that has been found guilty on a particular count is also judged to be guilty of actions that were not considered by the court—or, conversely, when a movement that has been found not guilty claims that this proves it is as pure as the driven snow on several other counts. It is, furthermore, possible in cases of acquittal that there just was not sufficient evidence presented at the trial to convict "beyond all reasonable doubt." In other words, the statement "it has been proved in a court of law" should be treated with caution.

Some Important Caveats

Although this chapter has attempted to show some of the reasons that an awareness of the methodology of the social sciences might result in a more reliable and balanced account of NRMs than that given by some CWGs, it should not be taken as an apologetic for ROGs. Again it must be stressed that the ideal-typical caricatures are more or less useful tools; they are not meant to represent reality but to sensitize us to potential features of these groups. No actual group will reflect a type precisely, but some will be more similar to one type and dissimilar to another type than other groups. Real groups frequently span more than one ideal-type (several CCGs have accumulated a considerable amount of useful information on the activities of the movements as well as their beliefs); and real groups almost invariably comprise a wide range of individuals who disagree with each other quite vehemently about a number of issues. Furthermore, real groups have changed over time, with for example some CAGs becoming increasingly professionalized and moving in certain respects away from the CAG type toward that of an ROG. At the same time, some ROGs have become increasingly concerned with the potential harm of the NRMs and have focused their research to take on such questions than hitherto, while including an awareness of the relationship between the movements and wider society. Attempts have been made at reconciling some of the differences in approach. These may amount to little more than presenting opposing arguments within one volume (Zablocki and Robbins 2002), but some genuine attempts have pointed to similarities among the different types while pointing out differences within their own type (Langone 2005).

It certainly should not be thought that groups that seem closer to one ideal-type are "better" or even "more useful" than those nearer another ideal-type. Each ideal-type can perform more or less positive and negative functions for individuals and for society as a whole. CAGs can alert us to harmful activities, CCGs can help to delineate theological truths from heresy for those who share their faith. And some of the members of these groups, while making it clear that they do not agree with an NRM's theological position, will fight for the movement's right to hold its own beliefs. There are excellent investigative reporters in the media, some of whom spend months or even years meticulously researching an NRM (see, for example, Fitzgerald 1986). There are established academics, well schooled in the methods of social science, who, nonetheless, produce slipshod accounts of the NRMs. Members of the caring professions are more likely to help clients to face reality than construct false memories, and if called upon to make a public statement, take great care not to generalize about a movement on the basis of information from a few former members.

It is, moreover, possible that conjuring up an image that might seem inappropriate in one situation can appear decidedly appropriate in another. Take, for example, the term *cult*. Most scholars have spoken out against use of the term because of its strongly negative (but usually nonspecific) general connotations (as opposed to use in sociological discourse). I have, however, heard former members of NRMs, who were both upset and bewildered by their experience in a movement, exclaiming what a great relief it was to be told that they had been in a cult. It gave them a starting point from which to re-evaluate their position and an opportunity to distance themselves from the movement and create a narrative that not only made sense but allowed them to move forward with their lives.

Some Suggestions for Teaching

It is undoubtedly true that one of the reasons teaching students about NRMs is problematical is that we know so little about many of the hundreds of movements that have emerged in the West during the past few decades. But perhaps an even greater problem lies in the fact that there is so *much* information "out there" that is contradictory, unreliable, and/or partial in its depiction of particular movements and of the cult scene in general. Somehow we have to help our students to pick their way through the mass of conflicting claims and judgments that fill the competing images of NRMs constructed by a wide variety of individuals and organizations. Of course, just making students aware that there *are* all these conflicting images is our first and possibly most important task. Then, once they have been alerted to how the information in one television report or from one particular Web site is only one way of seeing the movements, they can raise questions about how and why the images differ.

As with much of the educational enterprise, learning is likely to be most effective when students are guided to question, discover, and experience for themselves. The rest of this chapter consists of some suggestions in the form of a few exercises that can facilitate the active involvement of students in (1) recognizing, (2) analyzing, (3) understanding, and (4) critically assessing the ways images of new religions are constructed.

Selection in Descriptions

A relatively simple introduction to the potential variety in the construction of social reality is to ask students to write down what you are doing as you sit or stand in front of the class. Alternatives are to ask them to write down what is happening in the classroom or to show them a picture. Writing is better than asking them to describe out loud, as the first speaker is likely to define the kind of description that subsequent speakers will use. With any luck, when the written accounts are read out, you will be able to demonstrate the students' different assumptions of time periods and levels of analysis (physiological, psychological, or social). Some will give straightforward reports of what they see; some will describe things that they cannot actually see but assume from the fact that you are there (your heart is pumping the blood); some will impute feelings (you are bored), or motives (you are trying to get us to think), or invoke a wider social context (playing the role of the teacher; earning money; contributing to the educational system). I once was told I was dying, which was, of course, perfectly true—I just hoped it was a long-term description!

Encourage the students to analyze the differences in their accounts and to categorize the various aspects that can be selected. Asking them which was the "real" description might produce the argument that they are all real. You might then ask which accounts they were more certain were true (How did they know you were trying to teach them something? What if you were really thinking about what you would be doing that evening? Could both accounts be true? How could they find out?). You might also point out that there were some things you were definitely *not* doing (you were not, presumably, standing on your head). Asking them which is the "best" description might lead them to ask "best for what/whom?"

A similar exercise involves showing the students an action-packed film and asking them to describe what happened. This time you might encourage them to recognize the social pressures in the construction of a description by (1) asking them to write down an account independently, then (2) constructing a group account.

Using Ideal-Types for Comparative Analysis

Having familiarized the students with the idea that people's constructions of reality can differ from one another, you might introduce the concept of Weber's ideal-type and invite them to classify some of the NRM images with which they are already familiar.

Encourage the students to speculate about how information coming from different sources can more or less systematically give rise to different perspectives and ask them to speculate what difference it might make if the information came from people with the following:

I. Direct knowledge, such as
   (A) Members (note that leaders may differ in their accounts from grassroots members, and that converts might differ in their perspectives from second- or subsequent-generation members)
   (B) Ex-members
   (C) Relatives and friends/teachers who have seen changes in converts
II. Those with second-hand information, such as
   (A) The media
   (B) Other religions
   (C) Local, national, or international governments and other official authorities such as law enforcers
   (D) Therapists/social workers/mental health specialists
   (E) Academics
   (F) Members of various kinds of cult-watching groups

Then present the types of CWGs outlined in the earlier part of this chapter and ask them to decide in what ways these help us (and fall short of helping us) to understand and assess the different depictions of NRMs. An earlier version of the typology (Barker 2002) has a table of the five main types, which could be copied or downloaded (www.cesnur.org/2001/london2001/barker.htm), then adapted for the exercise. You can illustrate a variety of perspectives by recommending they look at the following Web sites (those that are connected with an ampersand provide more or less conflicting perspectives):

www.watchman.org/ & www.mormon.org
www.rickross.com/ & www.cultawarenessnetwork.org/dbase/bios/
   rross.html
religiousmovements.lib.virginia.edu/ & www.csj.org
www.cultinformation.org.uk/home.html & www.religioustolerance.org
www.movingon.org/ & www.thefamily.org

www.hrwf.net/ & www.miviludes.gouv.fr/rubrique.php3?id_
   rubrique=93
www.scientology.org/ & www.xenu.net/ & www.religioustolerance.org/
   scientol.htm
www.vatican.va/roman_curia/pontifical_councils/interelg/documents/
   rc_pc_interelg_doc_20030203_new-age_en.html & www
   .paganfederation.org/pfinfo.htm
www.findhorn.org/about_us/commonground_new.php

Another possibility is to have one half of the class look at one Web site and the other half at the corresponding site, and then have the two groups discuss what they think a movement is really like before viewing the alternative site.

Field Visits

It is more than likely that there are some NRMs with centers near the school and that they would be willing to host a visit from the class. Some of these NRMs might provide the opportunity of observing a service (ISKCON holds regular services open to the public); others would entail sitting round talking to members as a group or individually. The students are likely to gain more from such visits if they have been given some basic information about the movement and previously discussed their expectations. After the visit, the students can be asked to write short accounts of their visit and then engage in a general discussion about what they saw and heard and what their impressions were, particularly to comment on anything that surprised them and *why* it might have surprised them.

Among the questions and issues that can be raised are what the students think they learned about the authority structure in the movement; the group's attitude toward race and gender and toward nonmembers; the physical surroundings; the kinds of clothes worn; the friendliness and openness of the members; and "how they differ from *and* how they resemble us." The discussion can also focus on what it was possible to learn by visiting the movement that the students would not have learned by just reading about it, and what they could *not* learn about the movement as the result of a single visit. In what ways (if any) did they think the members were constructing a biased picture of their movement for the students? How might ideal-typical members of the different cult-watching groups describe the movement?

Teachers might feel it advisable to alert students to ways in which, in some cases, they might feel under pressure to pursue their association with the movement. You might suggest that they not give members of the movement personal contact details, as there are some movements and/or enthusiastic members who could take advantage of an introduction to potential converts. In twenty years of sending university students out on field visits, I have not yet lost one to a movement, but I have always discussed the possible influences to which they might find themselves subjected—which range from "love-bombing" to threats of eternal damnation—but these are usually nonexistent.

Guest Speakers

Inviting guest speakers to talk to the students can be an alternative or a supplement to field visits without some of the potential practical difficulties of the latter. Several NRMs have members who are eager to come and talk about their beliefs. If you invite them, try to ensure that they will also talk about their way of life and leave plenty of time for discussion, which can be helped if the students (1) know something about the movement in advance and (2) have already considered some of the issues they would like to see raised.

There are also a number of cult-watcher groups with members who go around to schools and universities giving talks. Some may expect a fee for doing this, so it is advisable to clarify such details in advance. Your availability of speakers will vary according to location, but initial inquiries for the United States might be addressed to the International Cultic Studies Association, telephone (239) 514-3081, or e-mail at mail@icsamail.com. It is also possible that someone from a local church, synagogue, or mosque would be willing to talk about his or her religion and its attitude toward NRMs. Following each talk students can discuss ways in which the speaker does and does not fit a particular type.

Developing Verstehen

Verstehen (German for "empathic understanding") can be developed through role playing and lecturing. You may allocate roles to students and ask them to act out a scenario that you have outlined for them, the aim being to encourage them to imagine themselves in different circumstances and to recognize how they might develop a particular perspective of the situation according to their interests and "where they are coming from." The following are just some suggestions, but the teacher and, indeed, the students can think up other situations, drawing on materials they have studied.

- Pat is approached by Jean and Guy, who ask him/her to attend a meeting at the house where they live with some friends. S/he is not very keen on doing so, but the other two are insistent and suggest that they have some important Truth and this is a wonderful opportunity to learn about it.
- Jean, a member of an NRM, approaches a group of students and tries to persuade them to come to a meeting her movement is giving. Is Jean more or less successful than she was when she was with Guy and speaking only to Pat? Why?
- Pat arrives at the house and is greeted by a group of young people who encourage him/her to go away for the weekend with them to a special camp in the country.
- Pat's parents become worried about her/his increasing interest in the group and go to a special meeting arranged by a cult-awareness group. Several other parents of cult members are present, and some former members of the group. How does the picture that emerges from

the cult-awareness group differ from that painted by the movement itself?
- Pat's parents confront Pat about what they have learned about the movement. Pat has already been warned about anti-cult organizations by the movement.
- In a court of law, lawyers for the prosecution and the defense question a number of witnesses, including members of different CWGs, in a case where The Church of God the Savior is accused of brainwashing its members.

Another way of encouraging students to present a perspective that they themselves may not share is to ask them to give two-minute lectures. The subject and the perspective can be picked out of a hat and could relate to their previous study. Possible examples might include:

- The leader of a group announcing the imminent end of the world
- An enthusiastic member of a religion explaining why people should join
- A former member describing why s/he left the movement
- The strong believer in one religion denouncing another religion
- A politician introducing a new law to control the activities of cults
- A sociologist lecturing on a particular religious movement

Evaluating Truth Claims through Content Analysis

To help sharpen the students' analytical skills, ask them to discuss how they would assess the truth or validity of a number of statements, and what further information they might want to resolve ambiguities. Here are some examples, most of which could give rise to more than one response, but it might be preferable to use examples from the literature or Web sites that students have been studying—and the students can be asked to produce their own examples for discussion.

- The children are made to take part in Satanic rituals.
- John is a cultist so he must be brainwashed.
- The guru is so rich he cannot be really religious.
- I know the religion exploits people because Mary's cousin had to sell flowers all day.
- The Master receives messages directly from God.
- The poor shouldn't eat the food devotees hand out because it has been offered to a false god.
- The movement gets its money by selling drugs.
- Our leader is friends with the president, so that shows he is a good man.
- The Temple of Thor was on a list of dangerous cults in the government report, so we shouldn't let them hire the church hall for their meetings.
- You keep seeing stories about people in these new religions committing suicide; they must be really dangerous places.

A more challenging exercise would be to present the students with a report or Web site that has a number of truth claims and ask them to evaluate the status of each claim. They could be asked to find examples of (1) logical statements (including fallacious arguments), (2) definitional assumptions, (3) both true and false factual claims, (4) moral evaluations, and (5) theological assertions.

Further questions for consideration could include:

- What is the underlying question (explicit or implicit) being addressed?
- What is the answer that is given?
- Does the language that is being used carry assumptions and/or try to influence us in any way? (Are the concepts value-laden or emotionally evocative? Is the writer implying anything by using the passive or active voice? Is there a rhetoric implying that anyone who is sensible or normal would "know" such and such is true?)
- If an evaluation is being made, what is this?
- Is there a factual basis for generalizations? Are generalizations made on the grounds of random samples and/or control groups?
- Are any double standards being employed?
- What of relevance has been omitted?
- What have you learned? Are you learning more about the writer/speaker or the subject s/he is speaking about? In what ways?

Concluding Remarks

There have been periods in history when battles to determine the "right way" of seeing things have been fought with torture, swords, or guns (consider the Inquisition, the Crusades, or the sixteenth-century Wars of Religion in France). Today we have witnessed the use of terrorist techniques, with suicide bombings by fanatics who see themselves as martyrs for the Truth. More frequently, however, contemporary campaigns are fought with words or with the law, sometimes crudely, but sometimes with considerable subtlety and sophistication.

The aim of this chapter has not, however, been to describe the "cult wars" so much as to consider the diversity of NRM images that are constructed by those with different interests in the movements. The challenge for the student of NRMs is to become sensitized to this diversity, to recognize where the different images are coming from, and to learn how these might be critically analyzed and assessed. It has been suggested that while some accounts would seem to be diametrically opposed to each other, others can be seen as complementary insofar as they concentrate on different aspects and address different questions. There are, undoubtedly, some accounts that are unequivocally wrong, but far more are partially wrong because they contain only partial truths.

If we wish to understand the "cult scene" and the dynamics of the relationships among the different participants within and without the movements, it is imperative that we be able to recognize the conscious and unconscious motives and methods by which images of NRMs are constructed, for these constitute part of our data. Confronted by the variety of images presented by cult-watching groups, students of NRMs can be led astray; but with informed and careful guidance, they can develop insights, sensitivities, and analytical skills that can be applied not only to the cult scene but also to countless other situations that they confront every day in contemporary society.

ACKNOWLEDGMENT

The author gratefully acknowledges support from the Nuffield Foundation for the research upon which this chapter is based.

REFERENCES

Barker, Eileen. 1989. *New Religious Movements: A Practical Introduction*. London: Her Majesty's Stationery Office.

———. 1995. "The Scientific Study of Religion? You Must Be Joking!" *Journal for the Scientific Study of Religion* 34, 287–310.

———. 2001. "INFORM: Bringing the Sociology of Religion to the Public Space." In *Frontier Religions in Public Space*, ed. Pauline Côté, 21–34. Ottawa: University of Ottawa Press.

———. 2002. "Watching for Violence: A Comparative Analysis of the Roles of Five Cult-Watching Groups." In *Cults, Religion, and Violence*, ed. David G. Bromley and J. Gordon Melton, 123–48. Cambridge, UK: Cambridge University Press.

Bromley, David G., ed. 1988. *Falling from the Faith: Causes and Consequences of Religious Apostasy*. Newbury Park, CA: Sage.

Fitzgerald, Frances. 1986. *Cities on a Hill*. New York: Simon & Schuster.

Langone, Michael D. 2005. "Cult Awareness Groups and NRM Scholars: Toward Depolarization of Key Issues." *Cultic Studies Review* 4, 146–68.

Lewis, James R. 1986. "Restructuring the 'Cult' Experience: Post-Involvement Attitudes as a Function of Mode of Exit and Post-Involvement Socialization." *Sociological Analysis* 47, 151–59.

Popper, Karl R. 1963. *Conjectures and Refutations: The Growth of Scientific Knowledge*. London: Routledge and Kegan Paul.

Weber, Max. 1949. *The Methodology of the Social Sciences*. New York: Free Press.

Zablocki, Benjamin, and Thomas Robbins, eds. 2002. *Misunderstanding Cults: Searching for Objectivity in a Controversial Field*. Toronto: University of Toronto Press.

New Religious Movements: A Bibliographic Essay

William Sims Bainbridge

This annotated bibliography is chiefly intended to offer good material for class lectures and for guiding discussions, although it may also be the basis of a class bibliography provided to students.

As I define the term, the *new* in new religious movements (NRMs) identifies a group as novel when it appeared, not necessarily recent in time, and much of the best theory-relevant information concerns historical groups. The new religious movements of today will become historical movements over time, and movements of the past illustrate enduring tendencies that will be recapitulated by movements of the future. That is, movements change over time, and a relatively small number of processes shape the fates of many movements, regardless of the particular decade in which they are born. At the same time, particular historical circumstances can raise challenges to all the movements active in the period.

Many of the most useful publications are books, but a large number of good articles are strewn across a variety of specialty and general journals, in social science, history, and religious studies. Many of the most influential articles were published in *Journal for the Scientific Study of Religion*, but others can be found in the pages of *Journal of Contemporary Religion*, *Review of Religious Research*, *Sociology of Religion*, and a journal devoted to new religions, *Nova Religio*. Depending on the focus and departmental discipline of the course, the vast anthropological literature on "primitive religions" may also be useful because it describes phenomena found in new religions, including shamanism, magic, ritual, secret societies, and how religious innovation fits into the surrounding culture and the way of life of believers.

The aim here is to identify a few publications that can be valuable for preparing lectures or for writing term papers, including classic works and reliable descriptive studies of particular religious movements. Some of the books described below would be suitable for use as the central textbook for a course on new religious movements. Others are collections that could contribute readings if the instructor prefers to organize an NRM course around a number of shorter works, rather than using a textbook, or if the goal is to create a section on NRMs for a more general course in the social science of religion. Many of the works cited are written in a style accessible for undergraduates, but graduate students will also find these publications appropriate for more advanced study.

Major Issues in the Study of New Religious Movements

This section covers the chief themes addressed by research in the field. Previous chapters in this book described some excellent sources in detail, so this bibliography does not duplicate all those references, instead suggesting a wide range of useful materials.

What Is a New Religious Movement? Defining the Area of Study

Bainbridge, William Sims. 1997. *The Sociology of Religious Movements*. New York: Routledge.
    A comprehensive textbook on religious movements, with sections on schism, innovation, and transformation. Groups: Holiness Movement, Adventists, Asian imports to the United States, The Family, the Process, and New Age.
Chryssides, George D. 1999. *Exploring New Religions*. London: Cassell.
    A survey of contemporary religious movements (NRMs of past generations plus recent movements that can be described as New Christian, Hindu, Buddhist, Human Potential, New Age, Wicca, and pagan), taking a phenomenological approach and addressing also methodological issues, the issue of suicide, and the counter-cult movement.
Clark, Elmer T. 1937. *The Small Sects in America*. Nashville, TN: Cokesbury.
    Descriptions and histories of many groups classified as pessimistic, perfectionist, charismatic, communistic, and legalistic (in distinction to the personalistic quality of the other categories), from the perspective of early twentieth-century scholarship.
Dawson, Lorne L. 1998. *Comprehending Cults: The Sociology of New Religious Movements*. New York: Oxford University Press.
    An introduction that asks what new religious movements are, why they emerged, who joins, whether members are brainwashed, why a small minority of such groups become violent, and how significant new religious movements are in modern culture.
Gallagher, Eugene V. 2004. *The New Religious Movements Experience in America*. Westport, CT: Greenwood.
    A descriptive introduction to the topic, dividing groups into several traditions (biblical, New Age, Eastern, Middle Eastern and African, neo-pagan, and miscellaneous "New Foundations"), with themes including leadership, recruitment, defection, violence, women, and children.

Hunt, Stephen. 2003. *Alternative Religions: A Sociological Introduction.* Burlington, VT: Ashgate.
A broad survey of the social origins and impacts of movements including Christian Fundamentalists and Pentecostals along with new religious movements such as those in the New Age and neo-pagan traditions.

Disciplinary Perspectives on New Religious Movements: Views from the Humanities and Social Sciences

Barker, Eileen. 1986. "Religious Movements: Cult and Anticult Since Jonestown." *Annual Review of Sociology* 12, 329–46.
An overview of theoretical and empirical work carried out by sociologists of religion in the study of new religious movements and the anti-cult movement over the previous decade.

Robbins, Thomas, and Dick Anthony. 1979. "The Sociology of Contemporary Religious Movements." *Annual Review of Sociology* 5, 75–89.
This literature review organizes research under these categories: sources of heterodox religiosity (secularization, value crisis, crisis of community, individualism), social consequences, classification of groups, and processes of conversion and indoctrination.

Saliba, John A. 2003. *Understanding New Religious Movements.* Walnut Creek, CA: Altamira.
A survey of the scholarly literature, from psychological, sociological, legal, and Christian theological perspectives, with an historical overview and consideration of the challenges new religious movement pose for counseling members and their families.

Methodological and Ethical Issues in Studying New Religious Movements

Cosgel, Metin M. 2001. "The Commitment Process in a Religious Commune: The Shakers." *Journal for the Scientific Study of Religion* 40, 27–38.
This study shows that historical census records for a communal religious movement can be exploited to test theories about the factors that strengthen commitment.

Côté, Pauline, and James T. Richardson. 2001. "Disciplined Litigation, Vigilant Litigation, and Deformation: Dramatic Organization Change in Jehovah's Witnesses." *Journal for the Scientific Study of Religion* 40, 11–25.
This study of organizational change in Jehovah's Witnesses illustrates the use of qualitative historical data to clarify, explore, and to some extent support an abstract theory that may apply widely across new religious movements.

Festinger, Leon, Henry W. Riecken, and Stanley Schachter. 1956. *When Prophecy Fails.* New York: Harper & Row.
An ethnographic study of a 1950s UFO millenarian group led by Dorothy Martin (disguised by the pseudonym Marian Keech in the book), illustrating predictions of Festinger's theory of cognitive dissonance that when people's beliefs lead to disappointment they will tend to proselytize even more strongly for these beliefs. This book is a prime example of the ethical issue of studying a group covertly by joining, and of the methodological issue of whether one can validly approach an NRM from the perspective of a single, well-defined theory.

Hood, Ralph W., W. Paul Williamson, and Ronald J. Morris. 2000. "Changing Views of Serpent Handling: A Quasi-Experimental Study." *Journal for the Scientific Study of Religion* 39, 287–96.
> A rare example of a study about religion that follows the paradigm of laboratory social-psychology experimentation, showing that learning about what serpent handlers actually believe can increase tolerance of them.

Wuthnow, Robert. 1976. *The Consciousness Reformation*. Berkeley: University of California Press.

———. 1978. *Experimentation in American Religion*. Berkeley: University of California Press.
> These books show how a major questionnaire study of religion, administered in the San Francisco area of California, can be used to discover facts and test theories about how beliefs and practices like those of new religious movements relate to changing currents in modern culture.

New Religious Movements, Countermovements, Moral Panics, and the Media

Bromley, David G., and Anson D. Shupe Jr. 1981. *Strange Gods: The Great American Cult Scare*. Boston: Beacon Press.
> An early overview, including defining cults, their challenge to conventional society, recruitment, leadership, fund-raising, brainwashing, and the beginnings of the anti-cult movement.

Bromley, David G., and James T. Richardson, eds. 1983. *The Brainwashing/ Deprogramming Controversy*. New York: Edwin Mellen Press.
> Twenty-one essays from historical, sociological, psychological, legal, and multi-disciplinary perspectives.

Bromley, David G., ed. 1998. *The Politics of Religious Apostasy*. Westport, CT: Praeger.
> Essays by many of the most prominent sociologists of the field, looking at the role of apostates in arousing hostility toward new religious movements.

Davis, Derek H., and Barry Hankins, eds. 2002. *New Religious Movements and Religious Liberty in America*. Waco, TX: Baylor University Press.
> A collection of essays about church-state issues. Groups: Scientology, Cult Awareness Network, Satanism, Witchcraft, Branch Davidians.

Horowitz, Irving Louis, ed. 1978. *Science, Sin, and Scholarship*. Cambridge, MA: MIT Press.
> A collection of critical essays focused on the Unification Church and its practice of inviting scientists (including experts on new religious movements) to participate in scholarly conferences.

Richardson, James T., Joel Best, and David G. Bromley, eds. 1991. *The Satanism Scare*. New York: Aldine de Gruyter.
> Collection of eighteen essays by social scientists examining the social construction of Satanism as a presumed social problem, chiefly treating Satanism as a popular myth but including some information about self-proclaimed Satanists.

Wilson, Bryan, and Jamie Cresswell, eds. 1999. *New Religious Movements: Challenge and Response*. London: Routledge.
> An international perspective featuring Britain, Italy, Brazil, Germany, and the United States, especially emphasizing interaction and tension with institutions of the surrounding society. Themes: economics, the legal dimension, mass

media, mental health, women and feminism, relations with conventional churches, anti-cult movements. Groups: Damanhur, Asian religion in the West, Japanese new religions in Latin America.

Zablocki, Benjamin, and Thomas Robbins, eds. 2001. *Misunderstanding Cults: Searching for Objectivity in a Controversial Field.* Toronto: University of Toronto Press.
This book is a debate among twelve authors in thirteen chapters over whether cults are harmful and often brainwash members.

The Meaning and Significance of New Religious Movements: Movements as Indicators of Social Continuity, Conflict, and Change

Beckford, James A., ed. 1986. *New Religious Movements and Rapid Social Change.* Beverly Hills, CA: Sage.
An international survey covering North America, Western Europe, Japan, Korea, Nigeria, Sri Lanka, India, and some Islamic nations.

Eck, Diana. 2001. *A New Religious America: How a "Christian Country" Has Become the World's Most Religiously Diverse Nation.* New York: HarperCollins.
An ethnographic or observational survey of Hinduism, Buddhism and Islam that emphasizes how non-Christian immigrants have established their traditions in the United States, thus helping to create a pluralistic religious context.

Eister, Allan W. 1972. "A Theory of Cults." *Journal for the Scientific Study of Religion* 11, 319–33.
A classic statement of the theory that culture crises promote the growth of cult movements.

Jenkins, Philip. 2000. *Mystics and Messiahs: Cults and New Religions in American History.* New York: Oxford University Press.
A historical survey of new religious movements in the United States in the nineteenth and twentieth centuries, suggesting a cyclic theory of four stages: emergence, reaction, speculation, and second peak.

Stark, Rodney, and William Sims Bainbridge. 1985. *The Future of Religion.* Berkeley: University of California Press.
A comprehensive analysis of secularization, sectarian revival, and cult formation based on historical, ethnographic, ecological, and survey data. Groups: Scientology, Transcendental Meditation, statistical data on several early twentieth-century NRMs.

Tipton, Steven M. 1982. *Getting Saved from the Sixties.* Berkeley: University of California Press.
The view that NRMs are a response to rapid social change or social disorganization is illustrated by the apparent increase of such movements as a response to the social and cultural upheavals of the 1960s.

Wallace, Anthony F. C. 1956. "Revitalization Movements." *American Anthropologist* 58, 264–81.
Threats to a society can produce greatly increased stress on members, leading some individuals to achieve valuable cultural reformulations, often in the form of new religious movements that can be used as the basis of social action to revitalize their society.

Cultural Building Blocks of Religious Movements:
Myth and Ritual

Campbell, Colin. 1972. "The Cult, the Cultic Milieu and Secularization." *A Sociological Yearbook of Religion in Britain* 5, 119–36.
>A theory that cults emerge from a wider cultic milieu that exists in opposition to the dominant culture, serves as a channel for diffusion of alien ideas, and nourishes mystical innovations.

Cohn, Norman. 1961. *The Pursuit of the Millennium.* New York: Harper.
>An influential historical study of how enduring myths and social tensions prepare the way for rapid organization of millenarian movements.

Kanter, Rosabeth Moss. 1972. *Commitment and Community.* Cambridge, MA: Harvard University Press.
>Although Kanter downplays the fact, this theoretical and empirical analysis of commitment to nineteenth-century communes chiefly identifies six factors tied to religious commitment in NRMs: sacrifice, investment, renunciation, communion, mortification, and transcendence.

Saler, Benson, Charles A. Ziegler, and Charles B. Moore. 1997. *UFO Crash at Roswell.* Washington, DC: Smithsonian Institution Press.
>The emergence of beliefs about extraterrestrials in American culture, conceptualized as folk narratives that are comparable to the historically influential myths of the great world religions.

Stark, Rodney. 1996. "Why Religious Movements Succeed or Fail." *Journal of Contemporary Religion* 11, 133–46.
>Ten characteristics of new religious movements, many of which can be described as aspects of culture, that strengthen the groups.

Social Building Blocks of Religious Movements: Organization and Leadership

Cantril, Hadley, and Muzafer Sherif. 1941. "The Kingdom of Father Divine." In *The Psychology of Social Movements,* ed. Hadley Cantril, 123–41. New York: John Wiley.
>An early social-psychological study of racism and charisma, focusing on the African-American new religious movement, the Peace Mission.

Friedland, William H. 1964. "For a Sociological Concept of Charisma." *Social Forces* 43, 18–26.
>A classic argument that charisma is not a special property of a leader, but arises in the needs of a group of people to find a voice for their dissatisfactions where it is hazardous to express them in society.

Lalich, Janja. 1998. *Bounded Choice: True Believers and Charismatic Cults.* Berkeley: University of California Press.
>A study of the processes by which highly cohesive groups possessing charismatic leaders and having transcendent ideologies can demand compliance from committed members, comparing two distinctive cases, Heaven's Gate and the Democratic Workers Party.

Melton, J. Gordon. 1986. *Biographical Dictionary of American Cult and Sect Leaders.* New York: Garland.
>Brief biographies of leaders of many groups and diffuse movements.

The Dynamics of Movement Membership: Joining and Leaving
New Religious Movements

Bainbridge, William Sims. 2006. *God from the Machine: Artificial Intelligence Models of Religious Cognition*. Lanham, MD: Altamira.
This study employs a variety of computer simulation methods to model religious innovation, conversion, and competition between religious movements; illustrating the new computational methodologies now available for exploring the implications of theories.

Balch, Robert W., and David Taylor. 1977. "Seekers and Saucers." *American Behavioral Scientist* 20, 839–59.
The important role of the cultic milieu in joining a UFO cult, raising the broader issue of what cultural preparation facilitates conversion to a new religious movement.

Catton, William R. 1957. "What Kind of People Does a Religious Cult Attract?" *American Sociological Review* 22, 561–66.
A pioneering questionnaire and field study of public appearances by Krishna Venta, empirically and theoretically distinguishing mere observers in the audience from seekers who were potential recruits to a movement.

Galanter, Marc, Richard Rabkin, Judith Rabkin, and Alexander Deutsch. 1979. "The 'Moonies.'" *American Journal of Psychiatry* 136, 165–70.
A psychological study of conversion and membership in the Unification Church.

Lofland, John, and Rodney Stark. 1965. "Becoming a World-Saver: A Theory of Conversion to a Deviant Perspective." *American Sociological Review* 30, 862–75.
Drawing on the collective behavior literature of its day, as well as ethnographic observation of one group, this influential theory article offers a seven-step model of conversion: (1) a person experiences enduring tension (frustration), (2) within a religious problem-solving perspective, (3) becoming a religious seeker, (4) encountering the group at a turning point in life, (5) developing social bonds with members, (6) as bonds with nonmembers weaken, and (7) experiencing intensive interaction with the group.

Stephan, Karen H., and G. Edward Stephan. 1973. "Religion and the Survival of Utopian Communities." *Journal for the Scientific Study of Religion* 12, 89–100.
This quantitative study compares religious communes with nonreligious ones, finding that the religious communes tend to last much longer, thus that faith deters defection.

Zablocki, Benjamin. 1980. *Alienation and Charisma*. New York: Free Press.
Although this study does not emphasize the religious character of some of the communes studied, it does provide valuable theoretical ideas and facts concerning the dynamics of commitment to contemporary American communes, based on an extensive questionnaire survey.

Men and Women in New Religious Movements: Constructing
Alternative Gender Roles

Andelson, Jonathan G. 1985. "The Gift to Be Single." *Communal Societies* 5, 1–32.
A study of celibacy and religious enthusiasm in the Amana community, based on detailed analysis of the group's own records.

Foster, Lawrence. 1981. *Religion and Sexuality*. New York: Oxford University Press.
Studies of alternatives to marriage and sexual equality among Shakers, Oneida,

and Mormons in the nineteenth century; celibacy, episodic group marriage, and polygamy.

Kern, Louis J. 1981. *An Ordered Love.* Chapel Hill: University of North Carolina Press.
Sex roles and erotic behavior among the Shakers, Mormons, and Oneida.

Lewis, Ian M. 1971. *Ecstatic Religion.* Baltimore: Penguin.
Anthropological study of how power conflicts, notably those between the sexes, can energize emotional religious movements such as the women's compensatory Sar or Zar movements of Ethiopia and Somalia, where women are excluded from conventional (Islamic) religious organizations.

Palmer, Susan J. 1993. "Women's 'Cocoon Work' in New Religious Movements: Sexual Experimentation and Feminine Rites of Passage." *Journal for the Scientific Study of Religion* 32, 343–56.
Analysis of how temporary membership in a new religious movement can enable women to experiment with alternative adult roles and serve as a rite of passage.

———. 1994. *Moon Sisters, Krishna Mothers, Rajneesh Lovers: Women's Roles in New Religions.* Syracuse, NY: Syracuse University Press.
A comparative study with integrative interpretations of Hare Krishna, the Rajneesh Movement, the Unification Church, the Institute for Applied Metaphysics, the Messianic Community, the Raelian Movement, the Institute for the Development of the Harmonious Human Being.

Puttick, Elizabeth. 1997. *Women in New Religions: In Search of Community, Sexuality, and Spiritual Power.* New York: St. Martin's.
Themes: New religions and the counterculture, the master-disciple relationship, abuse of power, devotion and female spirituality, sexuality, motherhood, gender roles, female spiritual leadership, goddess spirituality, and a new model of spiritual needs and values.

Spiro, Melford E. 1979. *Gender and Culture: Kibbutz Women Revisited.* Durham, NC: Duke University Press.
A study of how definitions of sexual equality in the communes shifted from "identity" (the same roles for both sexes) to "equivalence" (different but equally valued roles).

The Dark Side of Utopia: Exploitation and Abuse in New Religious Movements

Dohrman, H. T. 1958. *California Cult.* Boston: Beacon Press.
A description of Mankind United, documenting some of the ways that Arthur Bell deceived members into believing they were part of a worldwide movement.

Kiev, Ari, and John L. Francis. 1964. "Subud and Mental Illness." *American Journal of Psychotherapy* 18, 66–78.
An early but still interesting study of the conditions under which involvement in a new religious movement can be psychologically harmful, suggesting that harm is limited if the group offers ways of relieving tensions such as guilt feelings.

Langone, Michael D., ed. 1993. *Recovery from Cults.* New York: Norton.
The perspective of the original Cult Awareness Network and American Family Foundation that new religious movements are often emotionally abusive, suggesting that counseling can be helpful in freeing former members from psychological coercion.

Palmer, Susan J., and Charlotte E. Hardman, eds. 1999. *Children in New Religions.*
New Brunswick, NJ: Rutgers University Press.
How children change movements, how movements mold their children, how
society responds. Groups include: witches, Hare Krishna, the Rajneesh movement, Sahaja Yoga, Damanhur, Messianic Communities.

New Religious Movements and Violence

Bromley, David G., and J. Gordon Melton, eds. 2002. *Cults, Religion, and Violence.*
Cambridge, UK: Cambridge University Press.
Themes (factors that may be associated with violent incidents): dramatic de-
nouements, volatility, charismatic legitimacy, government-movement confron-
tations, and cult-watching groups. Groups: Branch Davidians, Order of the Solar
Temple, Aum Shinrikyo, and Heaven's Gate.
Wessinger, Catherine. 2000a. *How the Millennium Comes Violently.* New York: Seven
Bridges Press.
A comparative study of the Peoples Temple, Branch Davidians, Aum Shinrikyo,
the Montana Freemen, Solar Temple, Heaven's Gate, and Chen Tao.
————, ed. 2000b. *Millennialism, Persecution, and Violence.* Syracuse, NY: Syracuse
University Press.
Sixteen historical essays including essays about the Mormons, Branch Davidians,
the Peoples Temple, the Solar Temple, and Aum Shinrikyo.

Issues in Classroom Teaching of New Religious Movements

Gibran, Kahlil. 1923. *The Prophet.* New York: Knopf.
Comparable to Nietzsche's *Zarathustra*, but much milder and optimistic, this
poetic narrative gives the reader a sense of what it can be like to be in the
presence of a beloved spiritual master.
Heinlein, Robert A. 1961. *Stranger in a Strange Land.* New York: Putnam.
An influential science fiction novel that illustrates the creativity of a culturally
radical new religious movement, and the hostility with which society may respond.
Herbert, Frank. 1965. *Dune.* Philadelphia: Chilton Books.
The widely read and twice-filmed science fiction novel about a messiah who
fulfills ancient prophecy in a corrupt world, where his cult may be a vast im-
provement over secular society.
Nietzsche, Friedrich Wilhelm. 1966. *Thus Spoke Zarathustra.* New York: Viking.
A mysterious philosophical exploration, comparable to a third testament of the
Bible, that casts all conventional beliefs into doubt through the story of an en-
lightened recluse who cannot find anyone spiritually advanced enough to become
his follower.
Redfield, James. 1993. *The Celestine Prophecy.* New York: Time Warner.
A novel depicting a spiritual quest, from which many readers have gained a new
sense of spiritual possibilities in life, without the need to join a group or accept an
esoteric doctrine.
Redfield, James, and Carol Adrienne. 1994. *The Celestine Prophecy: An Experiential
Guide.* New York: Warner.
An instructional manual for applying the Celestine perspective to aspects of one's
daily life; an example or two might help students understand what mystical
feelings are all about, without the need for any alien practice.

Reps, Paul, ed. 1989. *Zen Flesh, Zen Bones*. New York: Anchor.
   This anthology is an accessible introduction to a very alien way of thought,
   from the Western perspective, and even brief quotations can stimulate
   insights.

Schiffer, Herbert. 1979. *Shaker Architecture*. Exton, PA: Schiffer.
   A picture book of Shaker buildings, especially useful if the instructor includes a
   few picture shows (with slide projector, overhead projector, or PowerPoint
   computer projector) in a lecture class; it communicates the simple beauty of
   Shaker architecture and furniture, showing that Shakerism is a valuable part of
   our historical heritage and thus suggesting that other groups may have made
   valuable cultural contributions as well.

New Religious Movements on the Web: Internet Resources for Teaching

BOOKS AND ARTICLES

Cowan, Douglas E. 2005. "Online U-Topia: Cyberspace and the Mythology of Place-
   lessness." *Journal for the Scientific Study of Religion* 44, 257–63.
   This article compares online religious spaces (such as Web sites) with "real"
   places as ways of organizing experiences, frameworks for action, and platforms
   for community.

Dawson, Lorne L., and Douglas E. Cowan, eds. 2004. *Religion Online: Finding Faith on
   the Internet*. New York: Routledge.
   This extensive collection of essays, written at a time by which religion has established itself solidly on the Internet, covers a wide range of topics relevant to new
   religious movement, including recruitment, innovation, and opposition to cults.

Hadden, Jeffrey K., and Douglas Cowan, eds. 2000. *Religion and the Internet*.
   Greenwich, CT: JAI Press.
   The essay covers a wide range of ways in which religion (in general) is using
   Internet and the Web, plus insights about how researchers may use it to
   study religion, thus providing useful background for understanding the Web
   sites of new religious movements and other Web-based resources that may be
   valuable for students and instructors.

Krogh, Marilyn C., and Brooke Ashley Pillifant. 2004. "Kemetic Orthodoxy: Ancient
   Egyptian Religion on the Internet." *Sociology of Religion* 65, 167–75.
   This is a study of a small new religious movement devoted to reviving An-
   cient Egyptian religion that has employed online outreach, comparing it with
   Wicca.

Scheitle, Christopher P. 2005. "The Social and Symbolic Boundaries of Congregations: An Analysis of Website Links." *Interdisciplinary Journal of Research on Religion* 1. Available at www.religjournal.com. Accessed October 11, 2006.
   A pioneering study that shows how analysis of the links of congregational Web
   pages can be used to chart their location in cultural space.

INTERNET SITES

Ontario Consultants on Religious Tolerance: http://www.religioustolerance.org.
   A long-established resource including information about many particular groups
   and conflicts, with statements about spirituality and ethics.

Religious Movements Homepage Project: http://religiousmovements.lib.virginia.edu.
An extensive encyclopedic resource originally created by the late Professor Jeffrey
K. Hadden and his students, now edited by Professor Douglas E. Cowan, including not only essays on many particular movements, but also cult group
controversies, course materials, a religious freedom page, and a religious
broadcasting page.

The Watchman Fellowship: http://www.watchman.org.
This site describes itself thus: "Watchman Fellowship is an independent
Christian research and apologetics ministry focusing on new religious movements, cults, the occult and the New Age. We serve the Christian and secular
community as a resource for cult education, counseling, and non-coercive
intervention." Of all the sites opposed to new religious movements, this one
is notable for the magnitude and relative objectivity of the information
provided.

Studies of Specific Movements

For the lecturer, it is practically essential to include descriptive information
about specific new religious movements, both to illustrate theoretical concepts
and to convey the human experience of participating in one of these movements. Depending on the course, it may be wise to select three to five different
movements and continually return to them for examples, thereby allowing
students to develop coherent mental pictures of movements and integrate the
ideas into conceptual wholes. If the instructor has studied or has access to a
suitable movement, then it should be among the examples, while the other
examples are taken from the literature. On the other hand, it also can be valuable to refer very briefly to a large number of movements, so long as they can
be described sufficiently and the lectures do not degenerate into incoherent
movement name-dropping.

Instructors should consider including an historical example among their
case studies because the literature is often extremely rich and the movement is
old enough that much of its full life cycle has been studied. Among the best-
documented cases are the communal intentional communities, such as the
Shakers and Oneida, or diffuse popular movements, such as spiritualism and
Millerism. The historical context matters, so brand-new movements of the
twenty-first century will differ significantly from the movements of the nineteenth century. However, to the extent that our theories really concern fundamental social processes they should apply equally well across time.

For many courses, it will be educationally valid to assign students to write
papers about particular movements. In a seminar, for example, the entire
second half of the course may be devoted to student discussion of term-paper
projects as they develop. Alternately, students may be asked to write brief
papers on one particular aspect of a movement (recruitment practices of the
Unification Church, for example), in a course that also includes exams and
other assignments. Discussions in class will be more productive to the extent
that students have read about and can report on different movements. For example, a student who is not academically inclined may still contribute success-

fully if he or she has read about a different movement and can inform the rest of the class about its interesting facts.

Amana

A classic German Anabaptist group that moved to the United States, notable for combining a traditional family kinship structure with communal ownership of property, more culturally innovative than most other Anabaptist groups, and therefore a true NRM.

Barthel, Diane. 1984. *Amana: From Pietist Sect to American Community*. Lincoln: University of Nebraska Press.
A sociological study by a descendent of the Amana community, explaining the process by which it opened to the surrounding world and eventually dissolved.

Aum Shinrikyo

The Japanese group infamous for staging a lethal nerve gas attack on the Tokyo subways in 1995, also notable for drawing on so many different religious traditions, including Hinduism, Buddhism, Christianity, and New Age.

Lifton, Robert Jay. 1999. *Destroying the World to Save It: Aum Shinrikyo, Apocalyptic Violence, and the New Global Terrorism*. New York: Metropolitan.
A psychoanalytic study of leader Shoko Asahara and individual followers, based on an analysis of contemporary Japanese society and with comparisons to the Peoples Temple, Heaven's Gate, Charles Manson, and Timothy McVeigh.

Branch Davidians

A splinter group in the Adventist tradition that became the target of the controversial and tragic siege at Waco, which led to the deaths of four federal agents and more than seventy movement members.

Lewis, James R., ed. 1994. *From the Ashes: Making Sense of Waco*. Lanham, MD: Rowman and Littlefield.
Wright, Stuart A., ed. 1995. *Armageddon in Waco*. Chicago: University of Chicago Press.
These two collections show how the authorities' failure to understand or communicate effectively with the Branch Davidians led to the catastrophe, underscoring the widespread misunderstanding and hostility toward new religious movements.

Bruderhof

A religious communal movement, somewhat similar to the Hutterites and other German Anabaptist groups of the nineteenth century, that began in Germany in the twentieth century, with members who emigrated to Latin America, then relocated in the United States.

Zablocki, Benjamin. 1971. *The Joyful Community*. Baltimore: Penguin.
> An observational study of the Bruderhof way of life and its meaning for members, based on the author's full year of living within the group as a sociological ethnographer.

Church Universal and Triumphant

Led by Elizabeth Clare Prophet, this metaphysical group possesses esoteric beliefs in the "I Am" tradition and was newsworthy around 1990 for its concern about the danger of nuclear war.

Lewis, James. R., and J. Gordon Melton, eds. 1994. *Church Universal and Triumphant in Scholarly Perspective*. Stanford, CA: Center for Academic Publication.
> Eleven authors offer nine chapters covering the group's history, beliefs, membership, treatment of children, hostility from outsiders, and legal controversies.

Whitsel, Bradley C. 2003. *The Church Universal and Triumphant: Elizabeth Clare Prophet's Apocalyptic Movement*. Syracuse, NY: Syracuse University Press.
> Written from the perspective of political science, this study is chiefly based on published sources, but also on some interviews and observation; it focuses on the political ideology of the group and responses to the disconfirmation of prophecy.

Falun Gong

This Chinese religious movement with millenarian undertones is a recent variant of the Qigong approach, which seeks to achieve advancement through five exercises that combine slow bodily movements with mental discipline; despite its peaceful demeanor it has been repressed by the People's Republic of China.

Wessinger, Catherine, ed. 2003. "Falun Gong Symposium." *Nova Religio* 6, 215–364.
> A special issue of the journal, containing eight articles that cover a range of topics, including the historical and international background, a theoretical paradigm of sectarianism, the group's resistance or challenge to government control, and the role of the Internet in spreading the group's message.

The Family International (Children of God)

An international communal, millenarian movement that for a time practiced a sexual ministry and became one of the prime targets of the anti-cult movement.

Bainbridge, William Sims. 2002. *The Endtime Family*. Albany: State University of New York Press.
> The heart of this research study is an analysis of how over a thousand members responded to a long questionnaire based on the General Social Survey, comparing members with a cross-section of Americans, also supported by observational, interview, and documentary evidence.

Chancellor, James D. 2000. *Life in The Family*. Syracuse, NY: Syracuse University Press.
An oral history, based largely on extensive interviews and visits to many of this group's far-flung communes, describing its unusual authority and erotic relations, but also including much information about the culture and way of life of this remarkable missionary movement.

Lewis, James R., and J. Gordon Melton, eds. 1994. *Sex, Slander, and Salvation*. Stanford, CA: Center for Academic Publications.
A somewhat irregular but informative collection of essays by more than a dozen scholars who are familiar with The Family International.

Krishna Movement

The International Society for Krishna Consciousness was founded in the United States in 1965 by a remarkable seventy-year-old visitor from India, A. C. Bhaktivedanta Swami; it emphasized an austere communal life style combined with ecstatic chanting.

Bromley, David G., and Larry D. Shinn, eds. 1989. *Krishna Consciousness in the West*. Lewisburg, PA: Bucknell University Press.
Scholarly and social scientific papers presented at a conference sponsored by the International Society for Krishna Consciousness.

Judah, J. Stillson. 1974. *Hare Krishna and the Counterculture*. New York: John Wiley.
Suggests that six factors gave ISKCON strength to endure as a movement: unity of purpose, common discipline, similarity in age and background of members, common ritual, successful business enterprises, and a variety of alternative lifestyles.

Nineteenth-Century Communes

These books compare and contrast multiple groups from the wealth of well-documented American religious communes of the period.

Nordhoff, Charles. 1875. *The Communistic Societies of the United States*. London: John Murray.
The classic eye-witness and historical description of American communal new religious movements by a journalist who visited them himself. Groups: Amana, Aurora, Bethel, Harmony, Icaria, Oneida, Shakers, and Zoar.

Noyes, John Humphrey. 1870. *History of American Socialisms*. Philadelphia: Lippincott.
A pioneer empirical and theoretical study comparing religious and nonreligious nineteenth-century American communal movements, written by the founder of the Oneida commune and presenting a theory that both religious ideology and prior acquaintance of the members strengthen commitment to a utopian community.

Whitworth, John McKelvie. 1975. *God's Blueprints*. London: Routledge and Kegan Paul.
An historical study of the nineteenth-century Shakers and Oneida perfectionists, and of the twentieth-century Bruderhof movement.

Oneida

The most striking example of a "free love" religious movement in nineteenth-century America, based on an ideology of religious perfectionism, communal relations rather than individual social bonds, and the conscious breeding of human beings to advance their spiritual level.

Carden, Maren Lockwood. 1969. *Oneida: Utopian Community to Modern Corporation.* Baltimore: Johns Hopkins University Press.
  A study of how members of Oneida managed to keep alive an unusual set of ideals over a long period of time, in the context of tension between the interests of individuals and of the group, despite evolution of the radical culture from utopian to ideological to more pragmatic.

Pagan, Wicca, and Ritual Magic Groups

Groups that seek to revive one or another of the pre-Christian religions of Europe, or that practice supposedly ancient techniques for spiritual development, often though a graded series of learning experiences and rituals.

Adler, Margot. 1979. *Drawing Down the Moon.* Boston: Beacon Press.
  A study of diverse groups in the witchcraft and pagan traditions, including Druids and Goddess worshipers.
Berger, Helen A., Evan A. Leach, and Leigh S. Shaffer. 2003. *Voices from the Pagan Census: A National Survey of Witches and Neo-Pagans in the United States.* Columbia: University of South Carolina Press.
  Simply presented results of a questionnaire study of 2,089 Wiccans, neo-pagans, Goddess worshipers, Odenists, and others of similar orientation.
Jorgensen, Danny L., and Scott E. Russell. 1999. "American Neopaganism: The Participants' Social Identities." *Journal for the Scientific Study of Religion* 38, 325–38.
  Social characteristics of neo-pagans, based on a questionnaire administered to 643 members.
Luhrmann, Tanya M. 1989. *Persuasion of the Witch's Craft: Ritual Magic in Contemporary England.* Cambridge, MA: Harvard University Press.
  An anthropological observation study of ritual magic groups in the London area.

Peoples Temple

Officially merely a congregation of the respectable Disciples of Christ, this was an apocalyptic, semi-Marxist religious movement that moved from California to Guyana where, on November 18, 1978, members murdered U.S. Congressman Leo Ryan along with some of his investigative group, after which murder and suicide led to the deaths of 914 members, including 276 children and charismatic leader Jim Jones.

Chidester, David. 1988. *Salvation and Suicide.* Bloomington: Indiana University Press.
  A wide-ranging analysis by a scholar who is especially noted for his writings on how different religious traditions deal with death.

Hall, John R. 1987. *Gone from the Promised Land*. New Brunswick, NJ: Transaction.
  An analysis of Jonestown in the context of American cultural history, following a
  standard sociological perspective in the Weberian tradition.

Process

A nominally Satanic communal movement that employed a variety of spiritual
training practices, some of them drawn from Scientology, to transform members based on a personality theory involving four god-patterns: Luciferian, Je-
hovian, Christian, and Satanic.

Bainbridge, William Sims. 1978. *Satan's Power*. Berkeley: University of California
  Press.
  Ethnographic study, based on two full years of field observation, plus interviews
  and documents; the analysis of member recruitment stresses cultural and social-
  bond factors rather than personal deprivations of recruits, and the analysis of the
  ideology employs principles from structural anthropology.

Rosicrucianism

A system of movements and organizations dating back at least three centuries
and claiming ancient heritage, stressing initiatory levels of spiritual enlightenment and reflected in modern groups like the Rosicrucian Fellowship
(Oceanside, California), and AMORC: Ancient and Mystical Order Rosae Crucis
(San José, California).

McIntosh, Christopher. 1980. *The Rosy Cross Unveiled: The History, Mythology, and
  Rituals of an Occult Order*. Wellingborough, Northamptonshire, UK: Aquarian
  Press.
  An overview of the Rosicrucian movement, from the publication of the *Fama
  Fraternitatis* in 1614 through the establishment of twentieth-century Rosicrucian
  organizations in Europe and America.
  ———. 1992. *The Rose Cross and the Age of Reason: Eighteenth-Century Rosicrucianism
  in Central Europe and Its Relationship to the Enlightenment*. New York: Brill.
  An historical study of the emergence of the Rosicrucian movement, conceptualized as an important "Gnostic undercurrent" of Western civilization and analyzed in the context of the cultural movements and counter movements of its era.

Scientology

Despite some affinities to Buddhism and to early-twentieth-century ritual magick groups, the Church of Scientology is among the most innovative movements, claiming to offer powerful spiritual technologies developed by L. Ron
Hubbard, who had been a prolific writer of adventure stories and science fiction.

Wallis, Roy. 1976. *The Road to Total Freedom*. New York: Columbia University Press.
  A study of the first quarter-century of the Church of Scientology, informative yet
  based almost entirely on publicly available information rather than research inside the group.

Shakers

The most famous nineteenth-century communal millenarian movement, revered for the aesthetic style of its furniture, founded by an English immigrant named Ann Lee whose disciples established an austere, celibate lifestyle and were recruited from various religious revivals and from orphanages before population decline led to demographic extinction.

Andrews, Edward Deming. 1953. *The People Called Shakers*. New York: Oxford University Press.
  An early scholarly study that established the romantic image of the Shakers held by scholars for many years.
Bainbridge, William Sims. 1982. "Shaker Demographics, 1840–1900." *Journal for the Scientific Study of Religion* 21, 352–65.
  The first publication, based on research that located the historical U.S. census records of the Shaker communities, to examine the group's demographic characteristics and shifts over the decades.
Stein, Stephen J. 1992. *The Shaker Experience in America*. New Haven, CT: Yale University Press.
  Detailed "revisionist" study of the Shakers, tempering traditional accounts of their history with the more modern critiques including information about variations across the geographically distributed communities and the evolution of the Shaker myth.

Shiloh

A Christian group with a millenarian vision; at its peak this group had about 1,000 members living communally in several locations in the United States, following principles of sobriety, service, predictability, sacredness, and male supremacy.

Richardson, James T., Mary White Stewart, and Robert B. Simmonds. 1979. *Organized Miracles*. New Brunswick, NJ: Transaction.
  Using the pseudonym "Christ Communal Organization" for Shiloh, this book employs many theories to analyze organizational development, lifestyle, and commitment of this group, based on interviews, observations, documents, and personality tests.
Taslimi, Cheryl Rowe, Ralph W. Hood, Jr., and P. J. Watson. 1991. "Assessment of Former Members of Shiloh." *Journal for the Scientific Study of Religion* 30, 306–11.
  Study of 128 former members, using adjective check list method, finding the ex-members more normal than might have been expected.

Spiritualism

A nineteenth-century religious movement, still active today, that defied church authority, taught that spiritually adept individuals can communicate with the dead, and was especially hospitable to feminist principles.

Braude, Ann. 1989. *Radical Spirits*. Boston: Beacon Press.
    The author argues that the Spiritualist movement was, in great measure, a
    branch of feminism that endeavored to harness energies from another world to
    promote women's rights here on earth.

UFO Groups

This tradition of new religious movements postulates that extraterrestrials have
evolved to a higher level of spiritual development and have made contact with
selecting earthlings.

Lewis, James R., ed. 1995. *The Gods Have Landed: New Religions from Other Worlds*.
    Albany: State University of New York Press.
    Several authors describe the general UFO-oriented movement, with special at-
    tention to Aetherius, Unarius, and the "Bo and Peep" group later called Heaven's
    Gate.
Palmer, Susan J. 1995. "The Raelian Movement International." In *New Religions in the
    New Europe*, ed. Robert Towler, 194–210. Aarhus, Denmark: Aarhus University
    Press.
    Initially founded in France, this relatively large UFO group relocated to Canada,
    where it practices a new form of sensual meditation and advocates human
    cloning and space travel, based on the belief that our species was implanted on
    Earth by extraterrestrial Elohim beings.
Partridge, Christopher, ed. 2003. *UFO Religions*. London: Routledge.
    Chapters describe specific movements (including Aetherius, Ashtar Command,
    Heaven's Gate, the Nuwaubian Nation of Moors, the Raelian Movement, Un-
    arius, and Urantia) and analyze the mythologies (notably contact and abduction
    claims), social processes, and relationships to science of extraterrestrial-oriented
    groups.

Unification Church

The church founded by reverend Sun Myung Moon and often called "Moonies," which combines Christianity (Presbyterian and Adventist influences) with
Korean traditions of spiritualism; it went through a millenarian phase and
became somewhat influential in Japan and the United States.

Barker, Eileen. 1984. *The Making of a Moonie*. New York: Basil Blackwell.
    A systematic study of the processes by which a fraction of the people who en-
    countered the Unification Church became members, refuting the brainwashing
    conception of recruitment to new religious movements.
Bromley, David G., and Anson D. Shupe, Jr. 1979. *"Moonies" in America*. Beverly
    Hills, CA: Sage.
    Based largely on documents but also on interviews and observations, this book
    analyzes the early history of the Unification Church in the United States and
    identifies many hypotheses for further study.
Lofland, John. 1966. *Doomsday Cult*. Englewood Cliffs, NJ: Prentice-Hall.
    An observational field research study of the first branch of the Unification
    Church to reach the United States, at a time when the group was markedly
    millenarian, focusing on recruitment and other social dynamics.

Lowney, Kathleen S. 1992. *Passport to Heaven: Gender Roles in the Unification Church.* New York: Garland.
    A study based on interviews and literature analysis, from a feminist standpoint but seeking to understand what Unificationism means to women members themselves.

Zen

A Japanese Buddhist tradition that has been influential for decades in European and American intellectual circles, perhaps because its strong emphasis on detachment from the world harmonizes with the despair quality in the existentialist movement or because it offers a therapeutic escape from unwanted psychological states.

Tworkov, Helen. 1994. *Zen in America.* New York: Kodansha International.
    A descriptive study that illustrates the fact that Zen outside Japan tends to depend on individual spiritual leaders (both Japanese immigrants and local converts) rather than building large-scale formal organizations.

Primary Source Materials

Historians sometimes distinguish primary source materials—often defined as documents or publications written by people with first-hand knowledge—from secondary materials that summarize or analyze information derived from primary sources. For example, an autobiography would be classified as primary, while a biography is secondary, as are most of the publications listed above. The distinction is not absolutely clear, and either kind of materials may suffer from personal biases, but professional historians generally rely on primary sources whenever possible.

A wealth of primary written sources is available for many new religious movements, and with appropriate care they can be very useful for scientific research studies, preparation of class lectures, and student projects.

First, it is worth noting that primary materials about a movement may originate from the group itself or from individuals or organizations outside the group but with intimate knowledge of it, including disaffected former members and opposition groups. For example, two classic books about the Shakers provide very different first-hand perspectives:

Green, Calvin, and Seth Y. Wells. 1823. *A Summary View of the Millennial Church, or United Society of Believers.* Albany, NY: Packard and Van Benthuysen.
Marshall, Mary (Mary M. Dyer). 1847. *The Rise and Progress of the Serpent from the Garden of Eden.* Concord, NH: Mary Marshall.

These two books cover the same period in the history of the Shakers (Marshall was not able to publish a complete edition of her book until after the passage of years), but from opposite perspectives. Green and Wells were Shaker leaders who sought to present the group favorably to the world, whereas Marshall was a disaffected member who had lost her children to the Shakers and complained of personal mistreatment by them. One might say that the two books have opposite biases, but arguably both are very accurate, merely telling different parts of the Shaker story. Thus, these books illustrate two important principles: (1) the information in a written work must be evaluated carefully in terms of the known or probable biases of the author; (2) the fact that an author may have powerful biases does not necessarily invalidate the factual claims in the writing.

The standard way journalists check important facts is to get them from at least two independent primary sources. Secondary sources may merely repeat a claim made by one biased source without sufficient corroboration. Unfortunately, in the case of religious movements, multiple primary sources may merely repeat the group's official version of the facts and thus not really be independent. Therefore, it can sometimes be essential to invest considerable energy looking for a completely independent source of information; the difficulty in finding this source of information does not necessarily invalidate a factual claim.

A category of primary sources that can be especially valuable in verifying facts is contemporary documents—written documents that were not intended for publication and that played a role in the event they described. These can include personal letters or e-mail messages, incorporation documents or other papers filed in a court or government agency, and many kinds of internal records generated by new religious movements themselves. Like conventional churches, new religious movements often advertise upcoming events, print programs of religious services, and generate newsletters that may include many kinds of objective facts, such as the addresses and leadership names for local chapters.

Most religious movements proclaim their message to the world in a variety of tracts, doctrinal books, and now Web sites. These are a good source of the official doctrines of a group, and thus valid sources for theological analysis or for incorporation in sociological analysis that locates the ideology in its social context. However, many new religious movements have two or more levels of initiation to membership, so there may be hidden doctrines and practices not mentioned in freely available publications.

Many groups publish member testimonials, often in the form of little stories written in the first person telling how the group has helped the author. These can be analyzed for their rhetorical content, but sometimes they may be valid sources for other kinds of information, such as the geographic and social-class origins of recruits. Testimonials may mention the particular kinds of life problems that motivated recruits to join, or at least represent the kinds of problem the group believes it can solve—such as medical problems, emotional problems, economic poverty, or dissatisfaction about the state of society. On the other hand, if a group claims it can solve human problems, testimonials may exaggerate the problems over doctrinally neutral factors such as development of friendship ties with members as causes of religious conversion, so caution must be taken in analyzing testimonials. If the content of testimonials changes over the years, then some kind of change must be going on the group, and other sources must be sought to define it.

It is very important to date each primary source and understand it in the context of its time. One of the chief challenges for new religious movements, seldom studied adequately, is the transformation of doctrines over time and the associated changing social structure of the group, both of which may be reflected in publications as well as internal documents. New religious movements tend to emerge from earlier ones, forming family lineages, so publications from one group can be informative about another or useful in analyzing relations between two or more.

Groups vary in terms of how much internal publication takes place and how closely the group protects internal publications from outsiders. Many new religious movements are sufficiently well organized to keep reliable statistics, just as ordinary denominations do, and they represent a largely untapped research and teaching resource. Given the challenges they face in an unbelieving society, new religious movements are naturally reluctant to share internal data with outsiders, but trustworthy scholars who invest the time to become well known to a group are sometimes rewarded with remarkable access to information. Many internal publications instruct members and local organizations in how to observe various practices of the group, and these can be extremely valuable for researchers, teachers, and students.

Faculty members, graduate students, or especially industrious undergraduates may amass significant collections of literature from a new religious movement, and some thought should be given to the responsibility for preserving these ephemera. Often even major publications do not find their way into the Library of Congress or the largest university libraries, and it would be a shame if publications of all kinds were lost to future scholars who might find them invaluable.

If a particular collection is relatively complete, a university or municipal library may be willing to accept it as a unit. It is essential to discuss this with the library staff because often a particular library cannot take on such a responsibility but may be able to suggest another archive that will. Other suggestions may come from scholars who have published on a particular group, and in some cases they may be able to band together to convince an archive to take their combined collection. One of these organizations devoted to studying new religions may be willing to take good representative material into its own archive, or to suggest other options:

The Institute for the Study of American Religion: www.americanreligion
    .org
Center for Studies on New Religions: www.cesnur.org
Information Network on Religious Movements: www.inform.ac/infmain
    .html

The Wider Cultural Context

Many writers have noted a close connection between many new religious movements and a broader phenomenon, variously called the New Age, the occult milieu, or the subculture of paranormal beliefs. Although the boundaries of this phenomenon are unclear, it includes quasi-religious beliefs such as telepathy or ESP, pseudosciences such as astrology, and mythologies such as stories about UFOs or lost civilizations of the past. Theoretically, one can argue that the New Age subculture is either cause or effect of new religious movements, or that both represent aspects of a widespread cultural shift currently taking place in Western societies. In any case, they harmonize with each other and may implicitly support each other in recruiting believers.

In addition to lecturing about these phenomena, an instructor might consider carrying out a brief class project involving a questionnaire about New Age beliefs to assess their prevalence on campuses today. A number of studies, including those listed below, have employed questionnaires, and their items can be selected for the class questionnaire. If the class is very large, the respondents could simply be the members of the class. If the class is smaller, students can be asked to distribute questionnaires among their friends. If the questionnaire is well designed, it can be used over several semesters, thus assembling a large number of respondents; faculty members at several schools may cooperate and combine their data. The questionnaire should be anonymous, and the instructor should verify with his or her institution that it meets all the requirements for research with human subjects. It may be presented legitimately both as a pilot study and as an educational exercise.

One design principle might be to combine measures from different published studies to see how they correlate with each other. Another might be to replicate findings of published studies about the social, demographic, or psychological correlates of paranormal beliefs. New questionnaire items may also be included—for example, assessing the students' reactions to the beliefs and practices of particular new religious movements that will be discussed during the lectures.

There are several practical approaches to how the data can be entered into a computer and analyzed. One approach is to have respondents answer the questions using optical-scan or mark-sense forms, following whatever system is used on campus for grading multiple-choice tests. Another approach is to give graduate students the responsibility for entering and analyzing the data as part of their training. A third possibility is to administer the questionnaire via computer, either online or in a computer lab. It is even possible to provide the students in the class with a preformatted spreadsheet on which to enter data from paper questionnaires, thereby gaining brief practice with this essential step in social research; then, the instructor can merge the spreadsheets and port the data into a statistical analysis program. Here are five recent journal articles that should be helpful:

Bainbridge, William Sims. 2004. "After the New Age." *Journal for the Scientific Study of Religion* 43, 379–92.
    This study uses data from a large online survey and finds a curvilinear relationship between religiousness and belief in the New Age (or paranormal beliefs): people who are moderately religious are much more accepting of ideas like

astrology and ESP than are either irreligious people or those who consider themselves strongly religious.

Granqvist, Pehr, and Berit Hagekull. 2001. "Seeking Security in the New Age: On Attachment and Emotional Compensation." *Journal for the Scientific Study of Religion* 40, 527–45.

A Swedish study that aimed to develop a multi-item New Age scale, and used it to assess theories postulating that New Age beliefs might compensate people for low emotional attachments to other people.

McKinnon, Andrew M. 2003. "The Religious, the Paranormal, and Church Attendance." *Journal for the Scientific Study of Religion* 42, 299–303.

This brief article reanalyzes Orenstein's data and comes to a somewhat different conclusion, suggesting that paranormal beliefs substitute for religious involvement for people who hold conventional religious beliefs but who only infrequently attend church.

Orenstein, Alan. 2002. "Religion and Paranormal Belief." *Journal for the Scientific Study of Religion* 41, 301–11.

Using Canadian survey data, this study examines the complex relationship among religious beliefs, church attendance, and paranormal beliefs, finding there is a positive correlation between the two kinds of belief, and that there is a negative correlation between church attendance and paranormal belief when statistically controlling for religious belief.

Rice, Tom W. 2003. "Believe It or Not: Religious and Other Paranormal Beliefs in the United States." *Journal for the Scientific Study of Religion* 42, 95–106.

This questionnaire study reports that social background factors do not consistently explain belief in paranormal phenomena, and that these beliefs do not correlate significantly with religious beliefs.

Miscellaneous Edited Collections

The typical volume in the group below includes a mixture of essays about theoretical themes or specific groups.

Bromley, David G., and Jeffrey K. Hadden, eds. 1993. *The Handbook on Cults and Sects in America*. 2 vols. Greenwich, CT: Association for the Sociology of Religion and JAI Press.

Themes: leadership, conversion, defection, healing, families, quasi-religious phenomena, opposition to NRMs, and numerous emerging issues for the social science of new religious movements.

Bromley, David G., and Phillip E. Hammond. 1987. *The Future of New Religious Movements*. Macon, GA: Mercer University Press.

Themes: how new religions succeed or fail; historical, sociological, and cultural perspectives. Groups: the Unification Church, Scientology, Hare Krishna, Nichiren Shoshu, and the anti-cult movement.

Dawson, Lorne, ed. 2003. *Cults and New Religious Movements: A Reader*. Oxford: Blackwell.

A collection of reprinted classical articles and more recent overviews on the general field and study of NRMs, the historical and social context, joining, the brainwashing controversy, violence, sex and gender, and the future.

Glock, Charles Y., and Robert N. Bellah, eds. 1976. *The New Religious Consciousness*. Berkeley: University of California Press.

A varied collection covering groups in the Asian and Western traditions, new

quasi-religious movements, the responses from established religions, and the
social and historical contexts.

Lewis, James R., ed. 2004. *The Oxford Handbook of New Religious Movements*. New
York: Oxford University Press.
   Twenty-two essays by specialists on new religions and modernization, social
   conflict, social and psychological dimensions, and esotericism—with examples
   of many specific movements.

Lewis, James R., and J. Gordon Melton, eds. 1992. *Perspectives on the New Age*. Albany:
State University of New York Press.
   Defining New Age as a subculture concerned with spiritual transformation, this
   collection surveys its history, the range of phenomena within it, comparison
   with other movements, and international impact.

Meldgaard, Helle, and Johannes Aagaard, eds. 1997. *New Religious Movements in
Europe*. Aarhus, Denmark: Aarhus University Press.
   A survey emphasizing Greece, Italy, Switzerland, Ireland, Britain, Netherlands,
   Germany, Austria, and Denmark.

Richardson, James T., ed. 2004. *Regulating Religion: Case Studies from around the
Globe*. New York: Kluwer/Plenum.
   One of a series concerning "critical issues in social justice," this thirty-three-
   chapter volume surveys the legal controls placed on religion in a wide range of
   societies around the world, highlighting the situations faced by new religious
   movements.

Stark, Rodney, ed. 1985. *Religious Movements: Genesis, Exodus, and Numbers*. New York:
Paragon House.
   Themes: cultural genetics, personal morality, fundamentalism and politics,
   Europe's receptivity. Groups: Heaven's Gate, Unification Church, ISKCON (Hare
   Krishna), Rajneesh, Human Potential movement, astrology.

Wilson, Bryan, ed. 1981. *The Social Impact of New Religious Movements*. New York: Rose
of Sharon Press.
   Themes: modernity, youth, supernatural character of religion, apostates, and atrocity stories. Groups: Unification Church, The Family (Children of God),
   Transcendental Meditation.

General Reference Works

These publications not only provide overviews of many groups and topics but
also offer a wealth of bibliographic citations.

Landes, Richard, ed. 2000. *Encyclopedia of Millennialism and Millennial Movements*.
New York: Routledge.
   A reference work on new religious or spiritual movements that can be described
   as "crisis cults, nativistic movements, messianic cults, cargo cults, chiliastic
   movements, revitalization movements, utopian movements, apocalyptic movements, and millennial movements."

Lewis, James R. 1998. *The Encyclopedia of Cults, Sects, and New Religions*. Amherst, NY:
Prometheus.
   Many brief descriptions of groups with an extensive bibliography.

Melton, J. Gordon. 1992. *Encyclopedic Handbook of Cults in America*. New York:
Garland.
   Descriptive and historical material on many new religious movements, organized

by families and by "established cults," the New Age movement, "newer cults," and counter-cult groups.

Saliba, John. 1990. *Social Science and the Cults: An Annotated Bibliography*. New York: Garland.
One-paragraph summaries of fully 2,219 publications on the topic.

ACKNOWLEDGMENT

The views expressed in this chapter do not necessarily represent the views of the National Science Foundation or of the United States.

Index